Isabellae

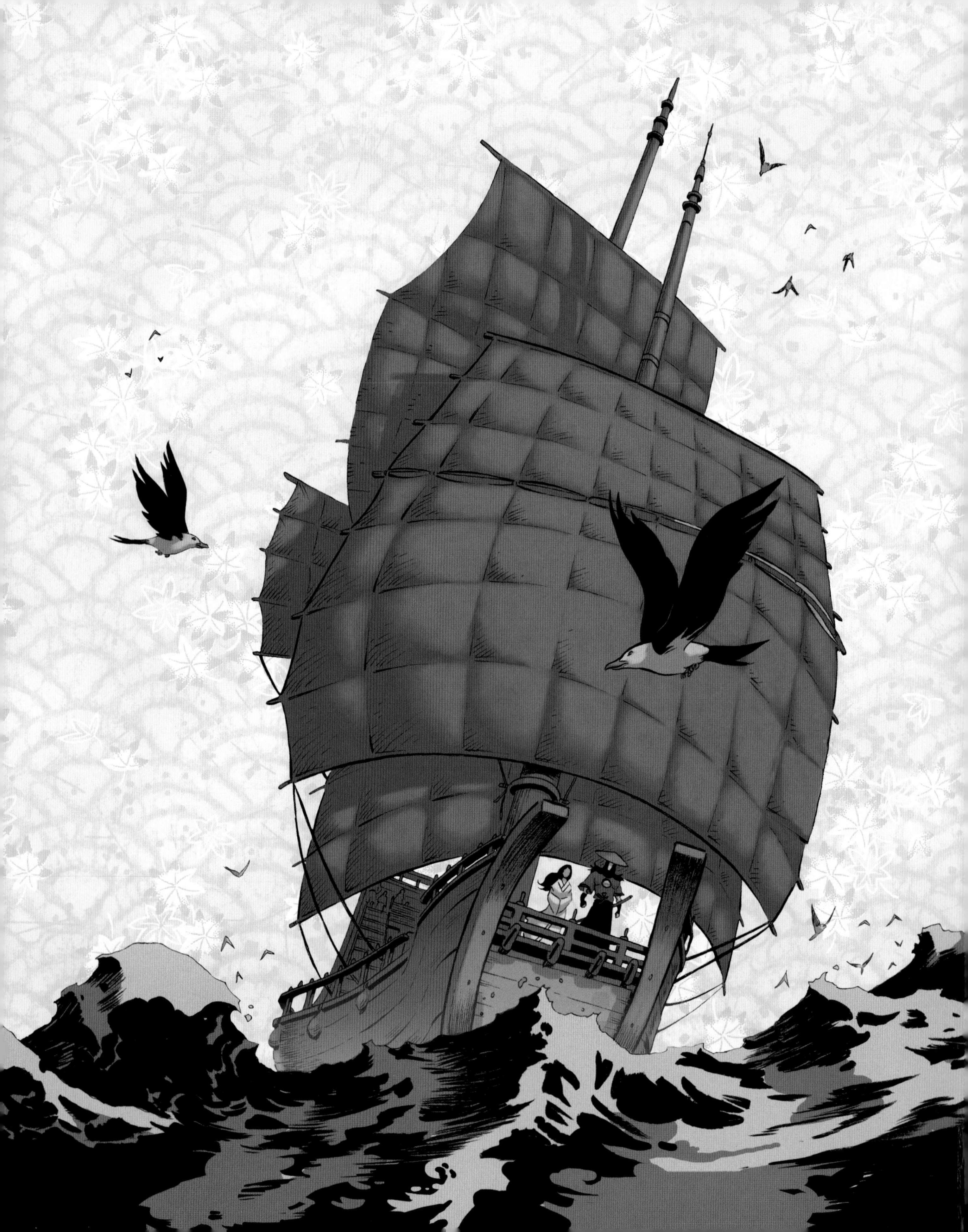

Isabellae

VOLUME ONE

written by **RAULE**

illustrated by **GABOR**

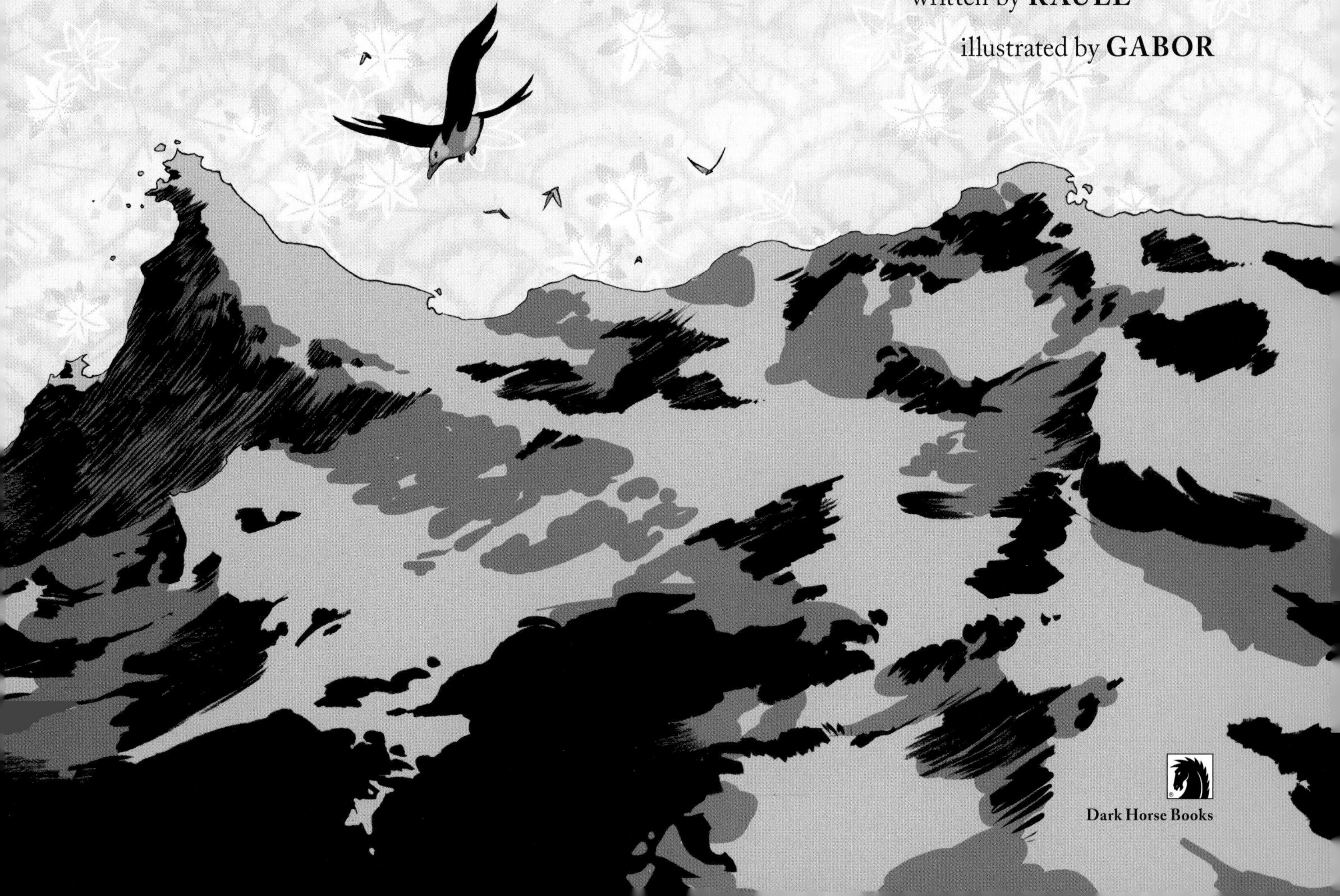

Dark Horse Books

Publisher **MIKE RICHARDSON**
Editor **MEGAN WALKER**
Assistant Editor **JOSHUA ENGLEDOW**
Designer **LIN HUANG**
Digital Art Technician **SAMANTHA HUMMER**

Special thanks to **KARI TORSON** for editorial assistance and advice.

This omnibus volume collects *Isabellae* volumes 1–3, originally published in France.

Isabellae 1—L'homme-nuit
Isabellae 2—Une mer de cadavres
Isabellae 3—Filles de Ériu

Published by Dark Horse Books
A division of Dark Horse Comics LLC
10956 SE Main Street
Milwaukie, OR 97222

DarkHorse.com
Facebook.com/DarkHorseComics
Twitter.com/DarkHorseComics

To find a comics shop in your area, visit comicshoplocator.com

First edition: August 2019
ISBN 978-1-50671-274-1
10 9 8 7 6 5 4 3 2 1
Printed in China

Library of Congress Cataloging-in-Publication Data

Names: Raule, 1971- writer. | Gabor, 1946- illustrator.
Title: Isabellae / written by Raule ; illustrated by Gabor.
Other titles: Isabellae. English
Description: First edition. | Milwaukie, OR : Dark Horse Books, 2019- | "This
  volume collects the following translated French Isabellae volumes: Vol. 1:
  The Night-Man, Vol. 2: A Sea of Corpses, and Vol. 3: Daughters of Eriu."
Identifiers: LCCN 2019007210 | ISBN 9781506712741 (v. 1 : hardback)
Subjects: LCSH: Graphic novels. | BISAC: COMICS & GRAPHIC NOVELS / Fantasy. |
  COMICS & GRAPHIC NOVELS / Horror.
Classification: LCC PN6777.R38 I8313 2019 | DDC 741.5/946--dc23
LC record available at https://lccn.loc.gov/2019007210

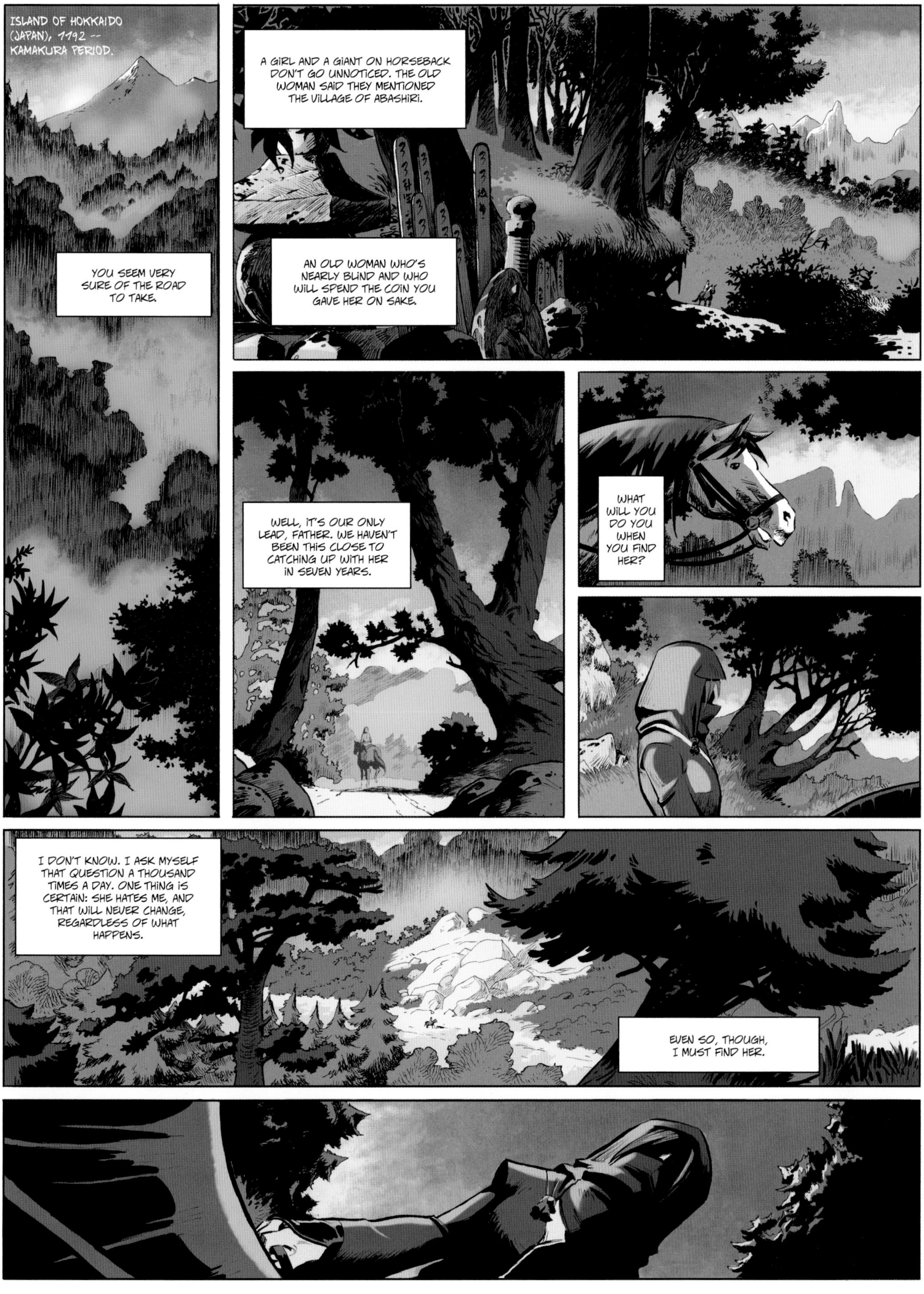
ISLAND OF HOKKAIDO (JAPAN), 1192 -- KAMAKURA PERIOD.
YOU SEEM VERY SURE OF THE ROAD TO TAKE.
A GIRL AND A GIANT ON HORSEBACK DON'T GO UNNOTICED. THE OLD WOMAN SAID THEY MENTIONED THE VILLAGE OF ABASHIRI.
AN OLD WOMAN WHO'S NEARLY BLIND AND WHO WILL SPEND THE COIN YOU GAVE HER ON SAKE.
WELL, IT'S OUR ONLY LEAD, FATHER. WE HAVEN'T BEEN THIS CLOSE TO CATCHING UP WITH HER IN SEVEN YEARS.
WHAT WILL YOU DO YOU WHEN YOU FIND HER?
I DON'T KNOW. I ASK MYSELF THAT QUESTION A THOUSAND TIMES A DAY. ONE THING IS CERTAIN: SHE HATES ME, AND THAT WILL NEVER CHANGE, REGARDLESS OF WHAT HAPPENS.
EVEN SO, THOUGH, I MUST FIND HER.

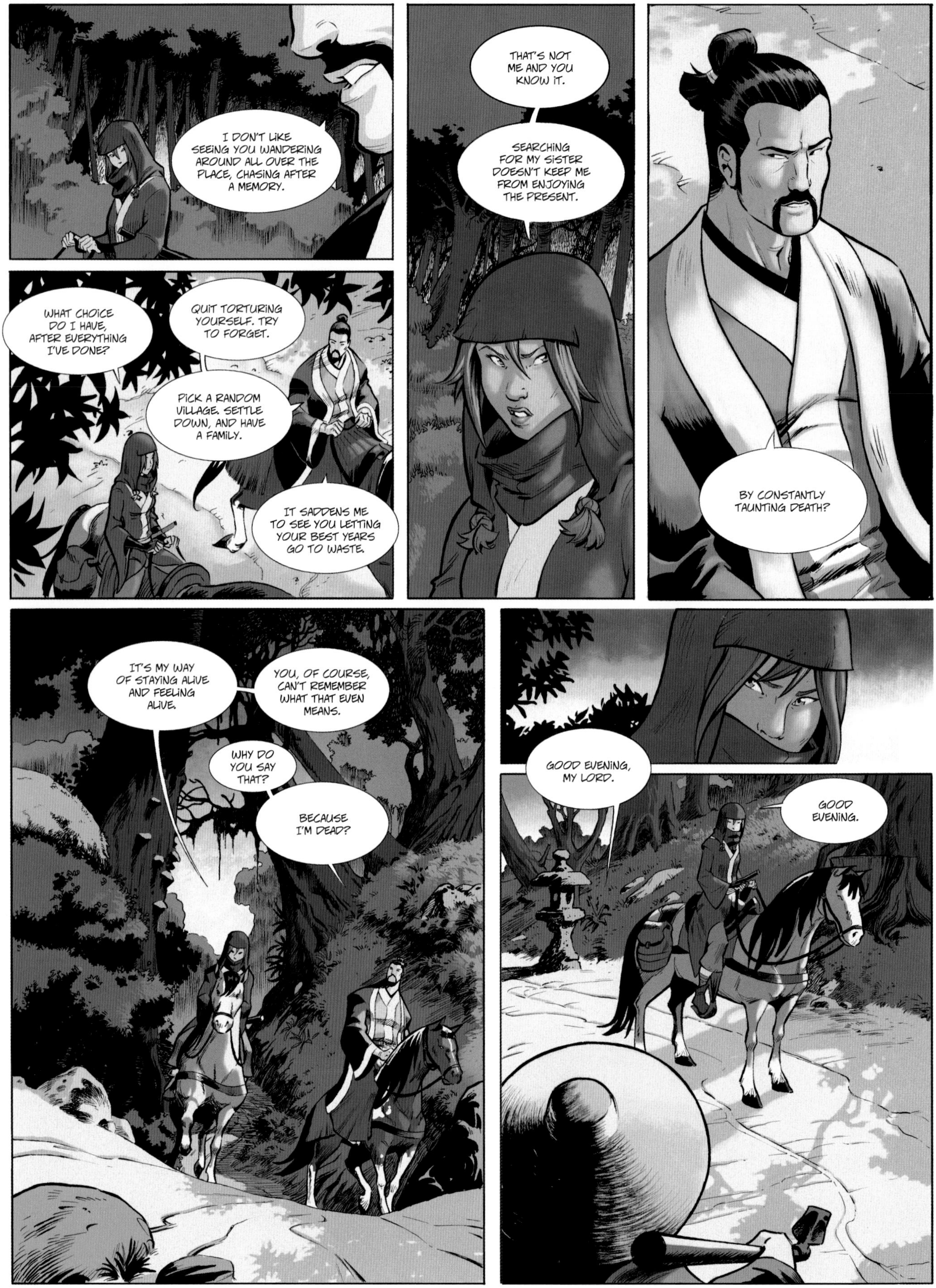
I DON'T LIKE SEEING YOU WANDERING AROUND ALL OVER THE PLACE, CHASING AFTER A MEMORY.
THAT'S NOT ME AND YOU KNOW IT.
SEARCHING FOR MY SISTER DOESN'T KEEP ME FROM ENJOYING THE PRESENT.
BY CONSTANTLY TAUNTING DEATH?
WHAT CHOICE DO I HAVE, AFTER EVERYTHING I'VE DONE?
QUIT TORTURING YOURSELF. TRY TO FORGET.
PICK A RANDOM VILLAGE. SETTLE DOWN, AND HAVE A FAMILY.
IT SADDENS ME TO SEE YOU LETTING YOUR BEST YEARS GO TO WASTE.
IT'S MY WAY OF STAYING ALIVE AND FEELING ALIVE.
YOU, OF COURSE, CAN'T REMEMBER WHAT THAT EVEN MEANS.
WHY DO YOU SAY THAT?
BECAUSE I'M DEAD?
GOOD EVENING, MY LORD.
GOOD EVENING.

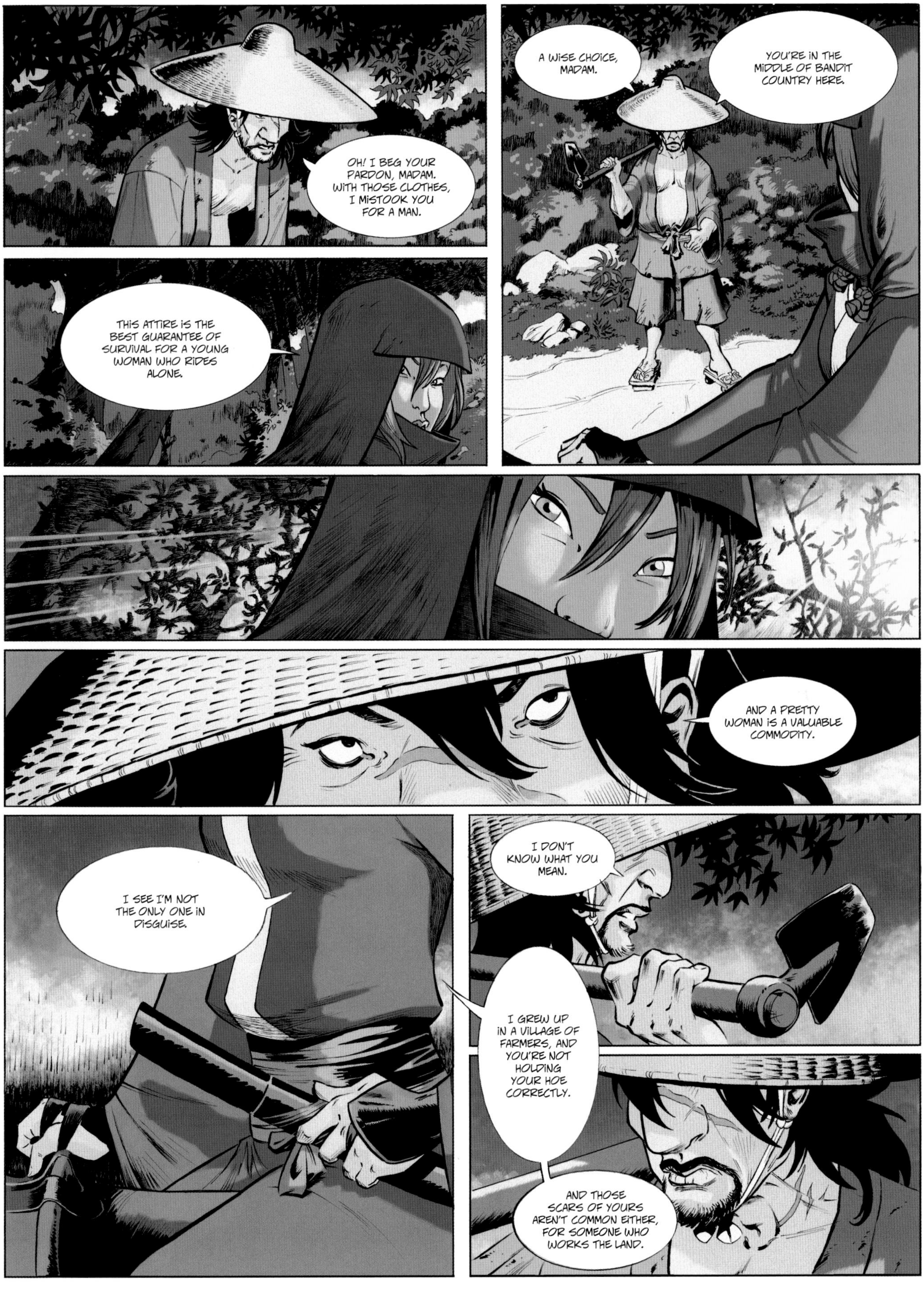
OH! I BEG YOUR PARDON, MADAM. WITH THOSE CLOTHES, I MISTOOK YOU FOR A MAN.
THIS ATTIRE IS THE BEST GUARANTEE OF SURVIVAL FOR A YOUNG WOMAN WHO RIDES ALONE.
A WISE CHOICE, MADAM.
YOU'RE IN THE MIDDLE OF BANDIT COUNTRY HERE.
AND A PRETTY WOMAN IS A VALUABLE COMMODITY.
I SEE I'M NOT THE ONLY ONE IN DISGUISE.
I DON'T KNOW WHAT YOU MEAN.
I GREW UP IN A VILLAGE OF FARMERS, AND YOU'RE NOT HOLDING YOUR HOE CORRECTLY.
AND THOSE SCARS OF YOURS AREN'T COMMON EITHER, FOR SOMEONE WHO WORKS THE LAND.

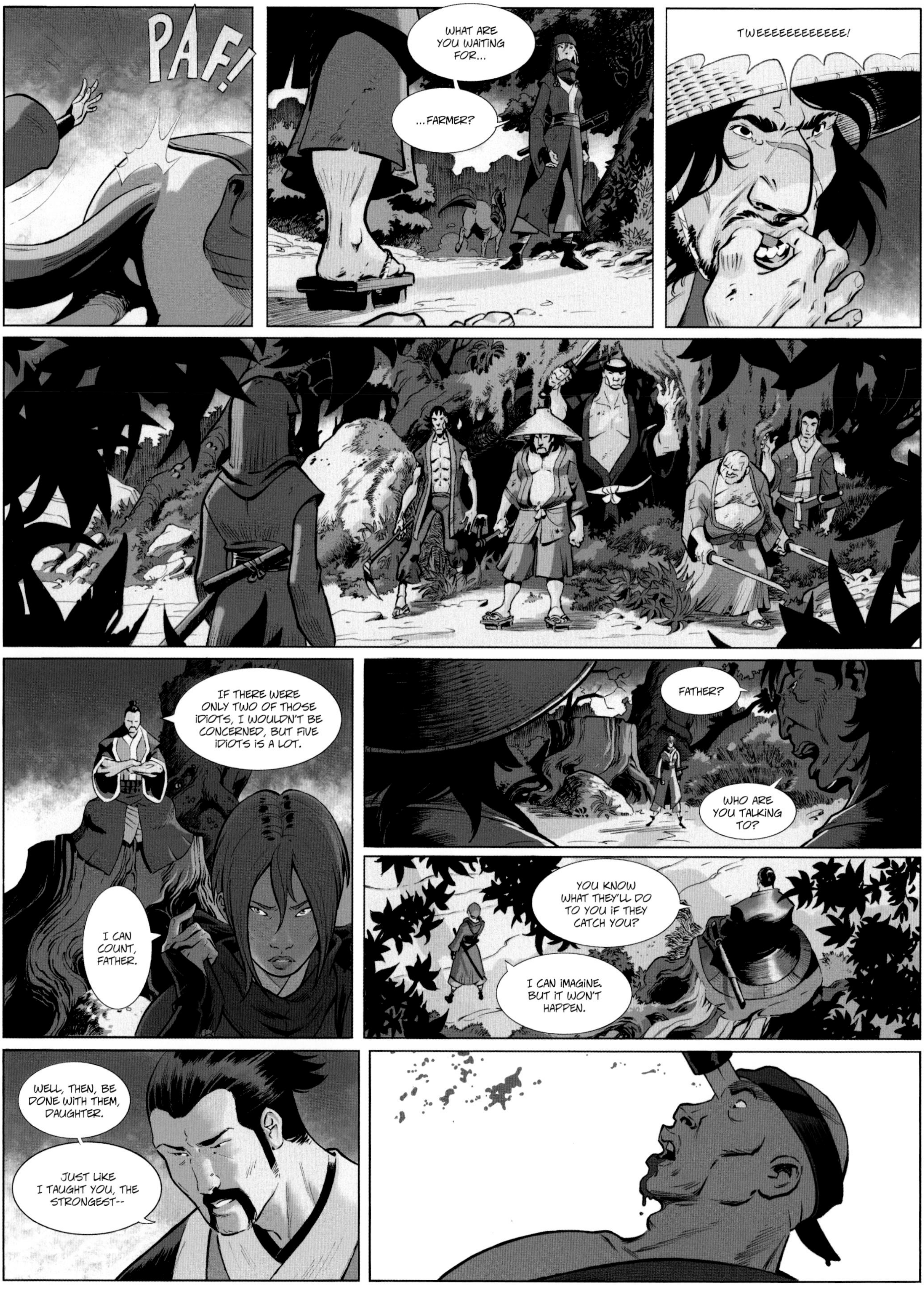
PAF!
WHAT ARE YOU WAITING FOR...
...FARMER?
TWEEEEEEEEEEEE!
IF THERE WERE ONLY TWO OF THOSE IDIOTS, I WOULDN'T BE CONCERNED, BUT FIVE IDIOTS IS A LOT.
I CAN COUNT, FATHER.
FATHER?
WHO ARE YOU TALKING TO?
YOU KNOW WHAT THEY'LL DO TO YOU IF THEY CATCH YOU?
I CAN IMAGINE. BUT IT WON'T HAPPEN.
WELL, THEN, BE DONE WITH THEM, DAUGHTER.
JUST LIKE I TAUGHT YOU, THE STRONGEST--

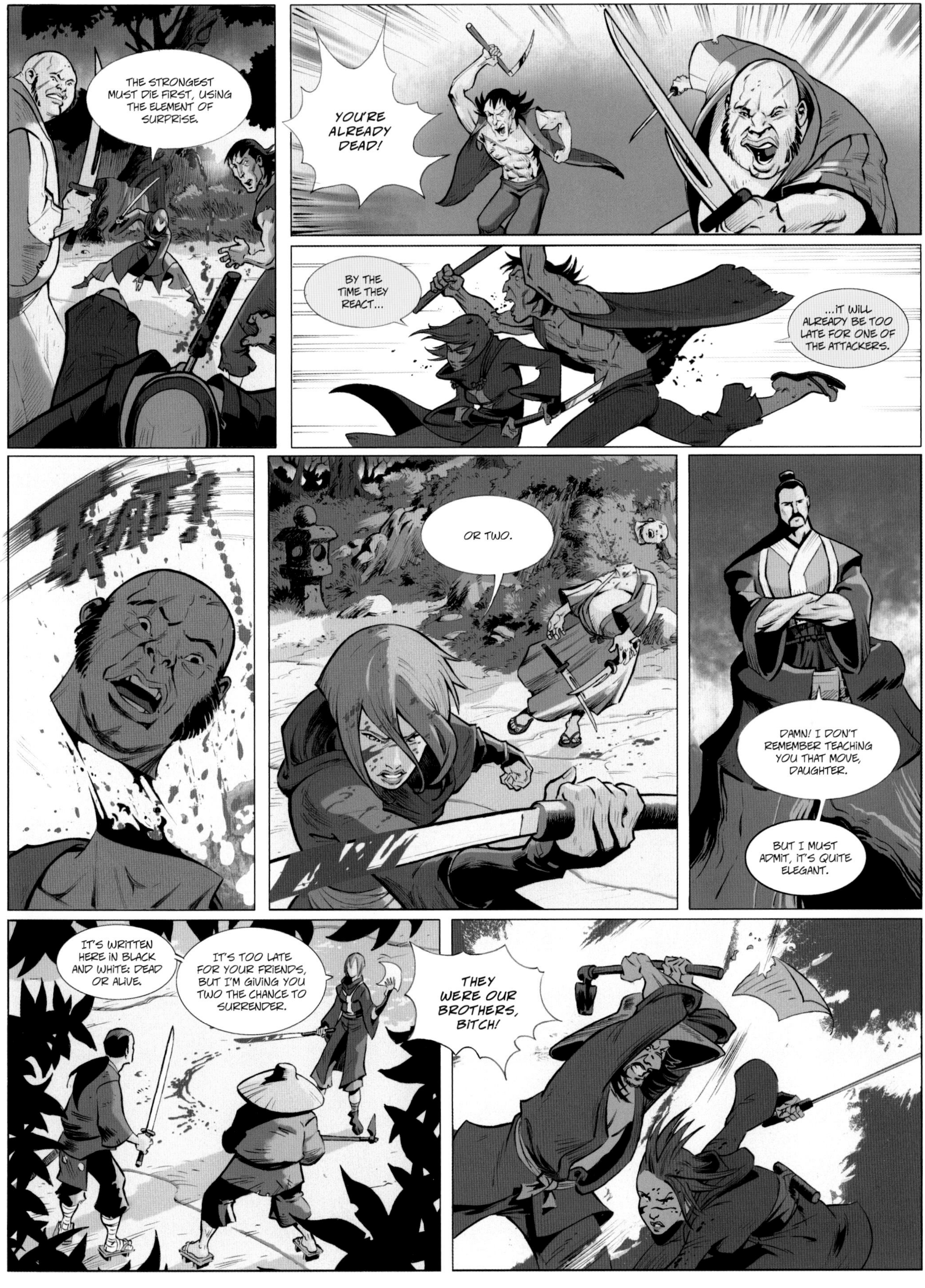
THE STRONGEST MUST DIE FIRST, USING THE ELEMENT OF SURPRISE.
YOU'RE ALREADY DEAD!
BY THE TIME THEY REACT...
...IT WILL ALREADY BE TOO LATE FOR ONE OF THE ATTACKERS.
OR TWO.
DAMN! I DON'T REMEMBER TEACHING YOU THAT MOVE, DAUGHTER.
BUT I MUST ADMIT, IT'S QUITE ELEGANT.
IT'S WRITTEN HERE IN BLACK AND WHITE: DEAD OR ALIVE.
IT'S TOO LATE FOR YOUR FRIENDS, BUT I'M GIVING YOU TWO THE CHANCE TO SURRENDER.
THEY WERE OUR BROTHERS, BITCH!

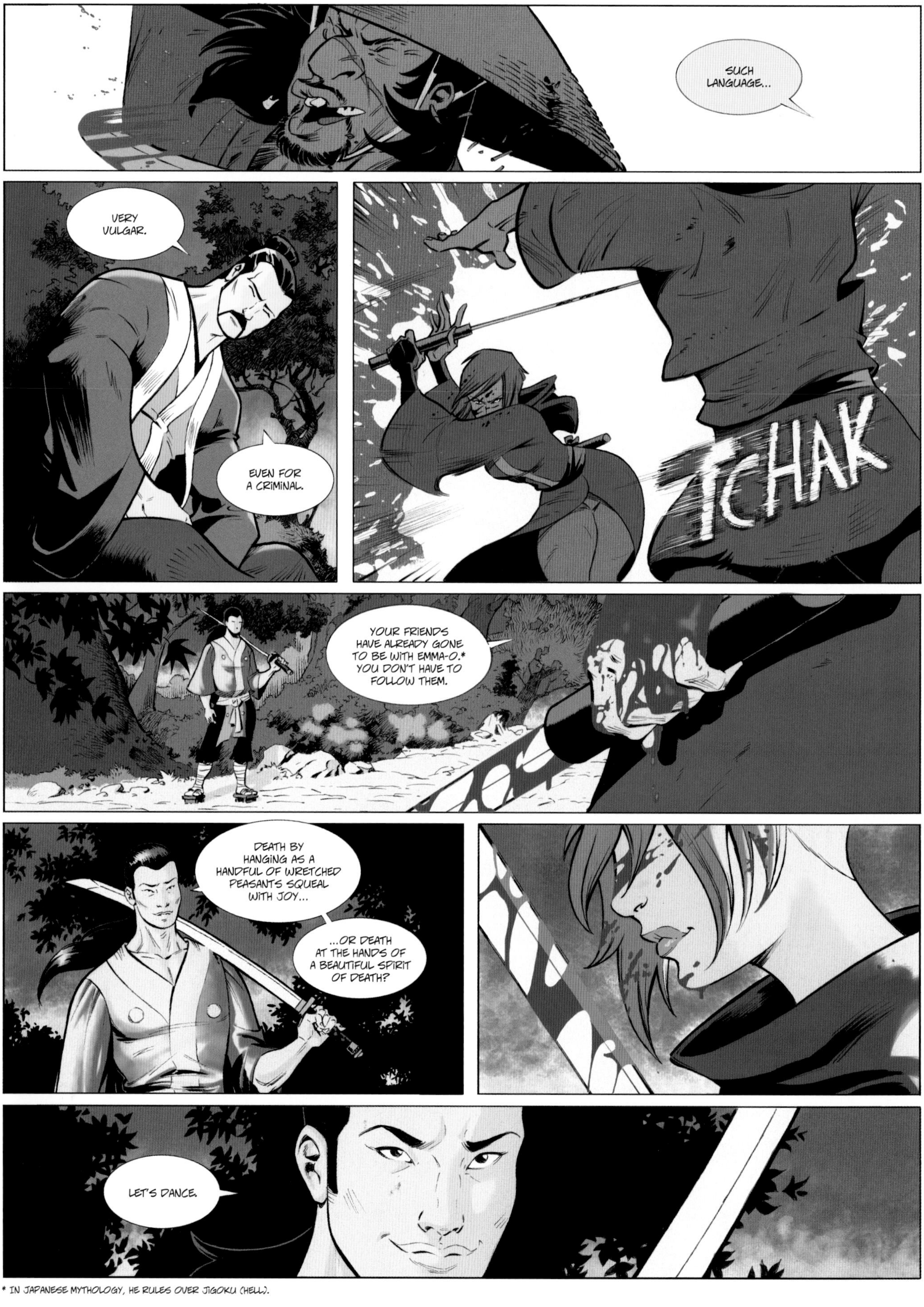
SUCH LANGUAGE...
VERY VULGAR.
EVEN FOR A CRIMINAL.
TCHAK
YOUR FRIENDS HAVE ALREADY GONE TO BE WITH EMMA-O.* YOU DON'T HAVE TO FOLLOW THEM.
DEATH BY HANGING AS A HANDFUL OF WRETCHED PEASANTS SQUEAL WITH JOY...
...OR DEATH AT THE HANDS OF A BEAUTIFUL SPIRIT OF DEATH?
LET'S DANCE.

* IN JAPANESE MYTHOLOGY, HE RULES OVER JIGOKU (HELL).

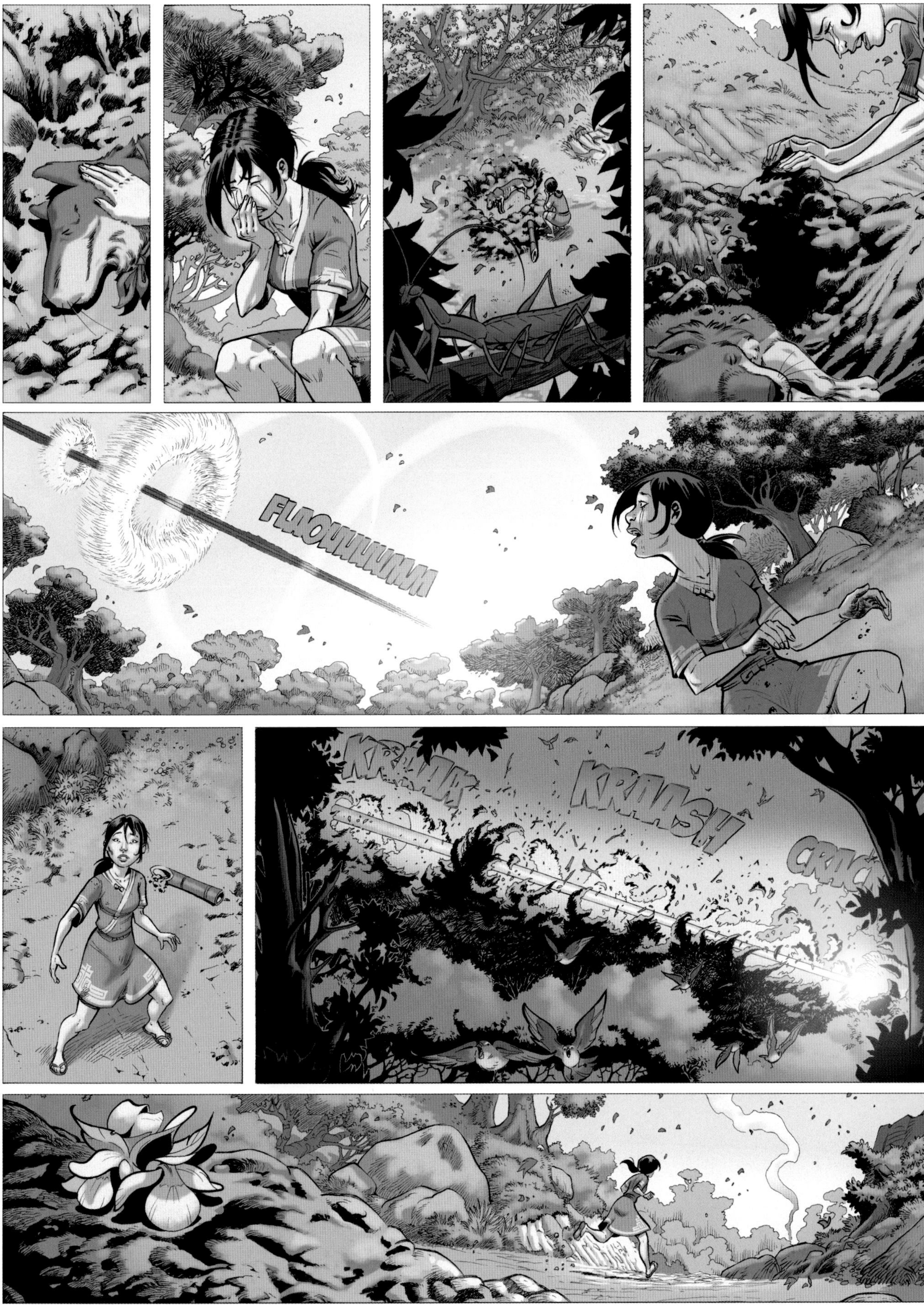
FLAOUUUUUM
KRAAAK
KRAASH
CRAC

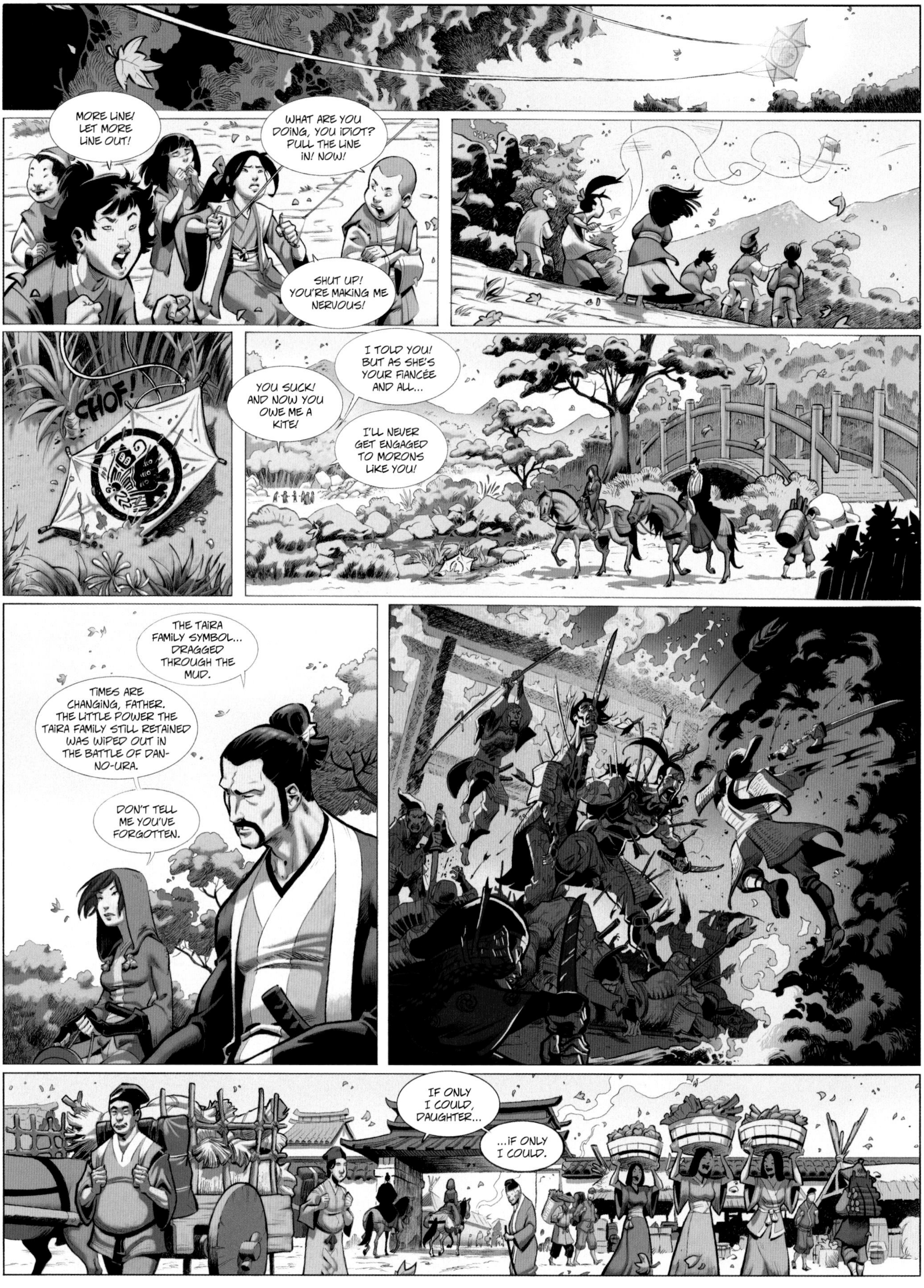
MORE LINE! LET MORE LINE OUT!
WHAT ARE YOU DOING, YOU IDIOT? PULL THE LINE IN! NOW!
SHUT UP! YOU'RE MAKING ME NERVOUS!
CHOF!
YOU SUCK! AND NOW YOU OWE ME A KITE!
I TOLD YOU! BUT AS SHE'S YOUR FIANCÉE AND ALL...
I'LL NEVER GET ENGAGED TO MORONS LIKE YOU!
THE TAIRA FAMILY SYMBOL... DRAGGED THROUGH THE MUD.
TIMES ARE CHANGING, FATHER. THE LITTLE POWER THE TAIRA FAMILY STILL RETAINED WAS WIPED OUT IN THE BATTLE OF DAN-NO-URA.
DON'T TELL ME YOU'VE FORGOTTEN.
IF ONLY I COULD, DAUGHTER...
...IF ONLY I COULD.

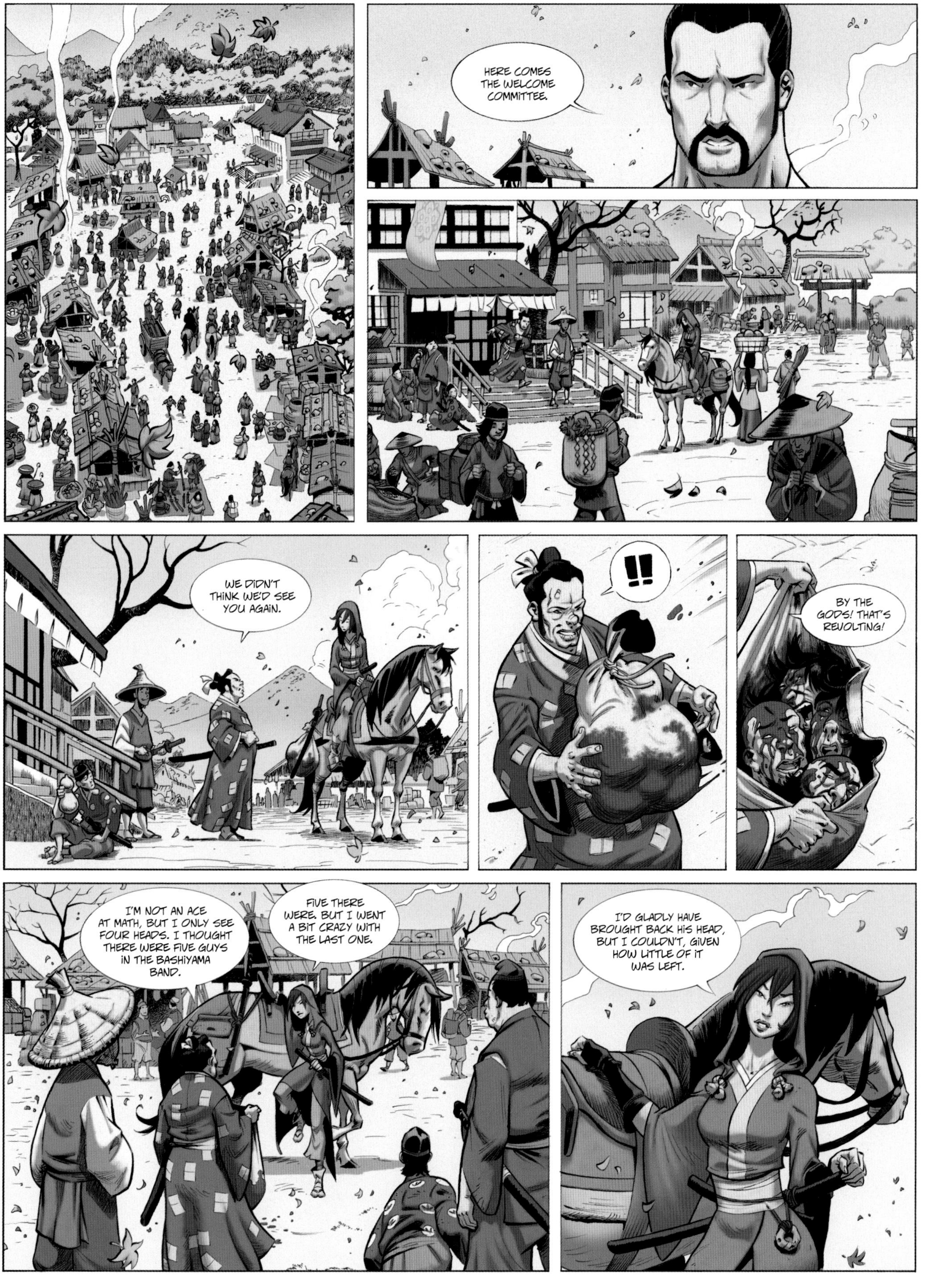
HERE COMES THE WELCOME COMMITTEE.
WE DIDN'T THINK WE'D SEE YOU AGAIN.
!!
BY THE GODS! THAT'S REVOLTING!
I'M NOT AN ACE AT MATH, BUT I ONLY SEE FOUR HEADS. I THOUGHT THERE WERE FIVE GUYS IN THE BASHIYAMA BAND.
FIVE THERE WERE. BUT I WENT A BIT CRAZY WITH THE LAST ONE.
I'D GLADLY HAVE BROUGHT BACK HIS HEAD, BUT I COULDN'T, GIVEN HOW LITTLE OF IT WAS LEFT.

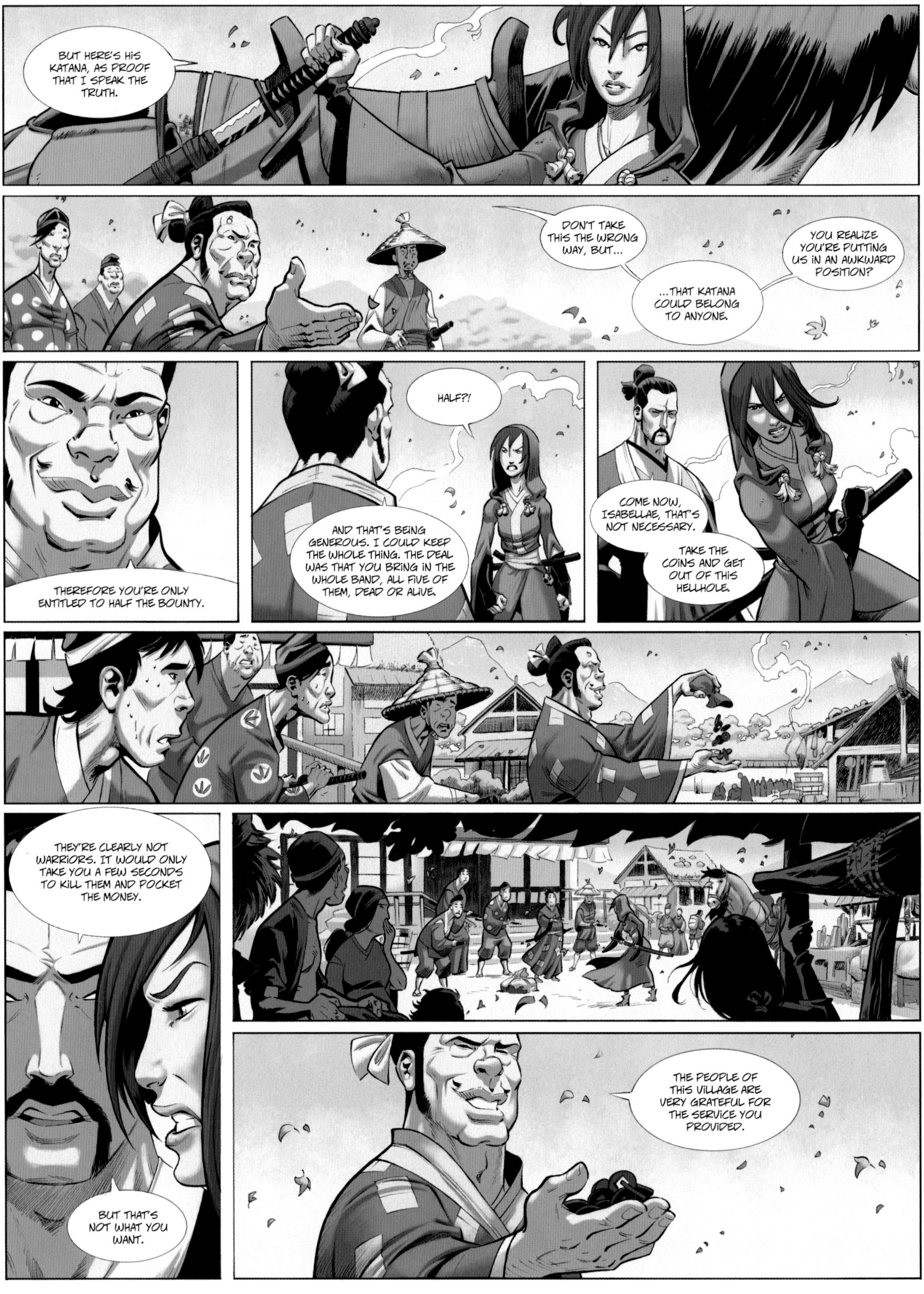
BUT HERE'S HIS KATANA, AS PROOF THAT I SPEAK THE TRUTH.
DON'T TAKE THIS THE WRONG WAY, BUT...
...THAT KATANA COULD BELONG TO ANYONE.
YOU REALIZE YOU'RE PUTTING US IN AN AWKWARD POSITION?
THEREFORE YOU'RE ONLY ENTITLED TO HALF THE BOUNTY.
HALF?!
AND THAT'S BEING GENEROUS. I COULD KEEP THE WHOLE THING. THE DEAL WAS THAT YOU BRING IN THE WHOLE BAND, ALL FIVE OF THEM, DEAD OR ALIVE.
COME NOW, ISABELLAE, THAT'S NOT NECESSARY.
TAKE THE COINS AND GET OUT OF THIS HELLHOLE.
THEY'RE CLEARLY NOT WARRIORS. IT WOULD ONLY TAKE YOU A FEW SECONDS TO KILL THEM AND POCKET THE MONEY.
BUT THAT'S NOT WHAT YOU WANT.
THE PEOPLE OF THIS VILLAGE ARE VERY GRATEFUL FOR THE SERVICE YOU PROVIDED.

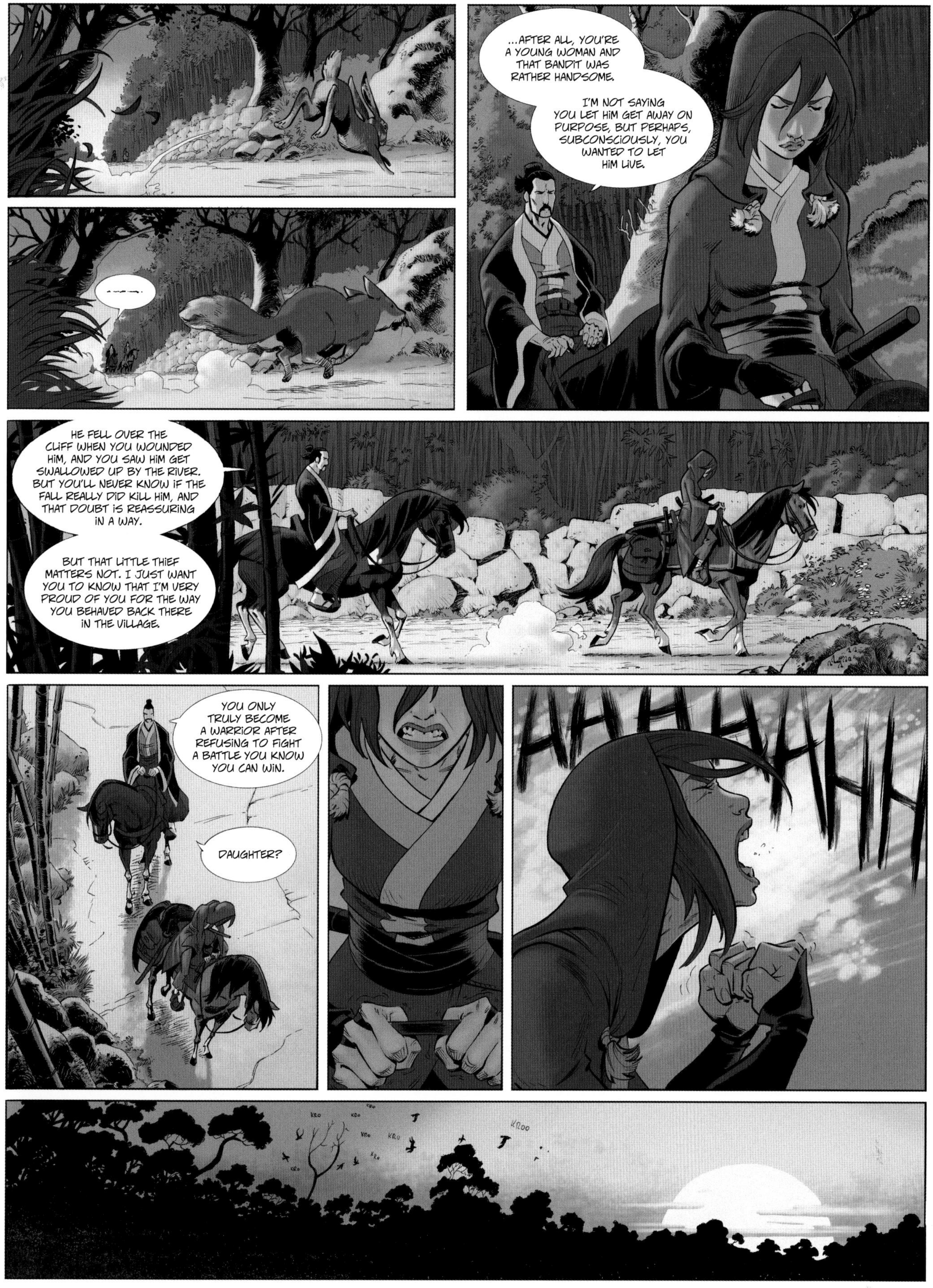
...AFTER ALL, YOU'RE A YOUNG WOMAN AND THAT BANDIT WAS RATHER HANDSOME.
I'M NOT SAYING YOU LET HIM GET AWAY ON PURPOSE, BUT PERHAPS, SUBCONSCIOUSLY, YOU WANTED TO LET HIM LIVE.
HE FELL OVER THE CLIFF WHEN YOU WOUNDED HIM, AND YOU SAW HIM GET SWALLOWED UP BY THE RIVER. BUT YOU'LL NEVER KNOW IF THE FALL REALLY DID KILL HIM, AND THAT DOUBT IS REASSURING IN A WAY.
BUT THAT LITTLE THIEF MATTERS NOT. I JUST WANT YOU TO KNOW THAT I'M VERY PROUD OF YOU FOR THE WAY YOU BEHAVED BACK THERE IN THE VILLAGE.
YOU ONLY TRULY BECOME A WARRIOR AFTER REFUSING TO FIGHT A BATTLE YOU KNOW YOU CAN WIN.
DAUGHTER?

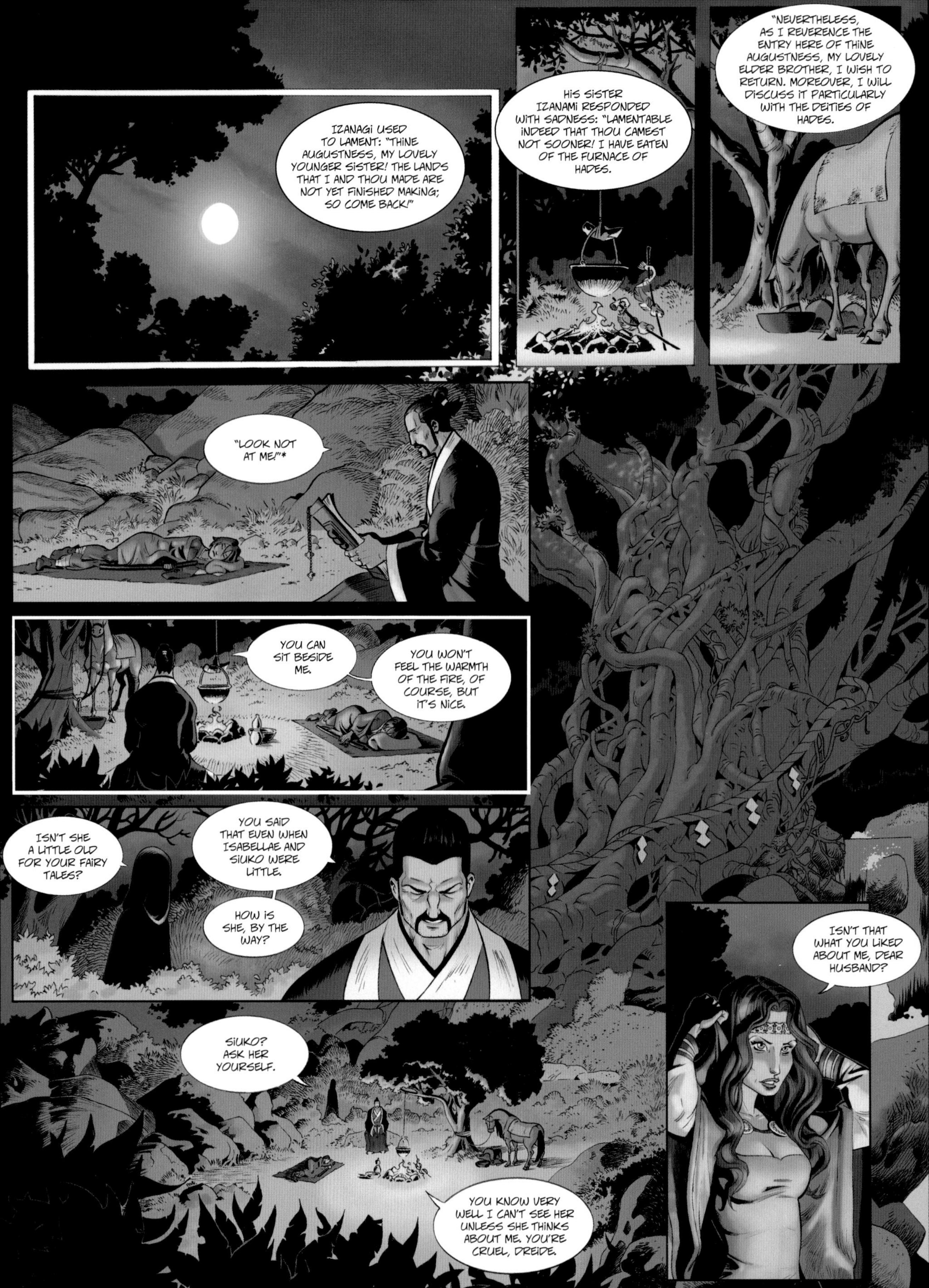
IZANAGI USED TO LAMENT: "THINE AUGUSTNESS, MY LOVELY YOUNGER SISTER! THE LANDS THAT I AND THOU MADE ARE NOT YET FINISHED MAKING; SO COME BACK!"
HIS SISTER IZANAMI RESPONDED WITH SADNESS: "LAMENTABLE INDEED THAT THOU CAMEST NOT SOONER! I HAVE EATEN OF THE FURNACE OF HADES.
"NEVERTHELESS, AS I REVERENCE THE ENTRY HERE OF THINE AUGUSTNESS, MY LOVELY ELDER BROTHER, I WISH TO RETURN. MOREOVER, I WILL DISCUSS IT PARTICULARLY WITH THE DEITIES OF HADES.
"LOOK NOT AT ME!"*
YOU CAN SIT BESIDE ME.
YOU WON'T FEEL THE WARMTH OF THE FIRE, OF COURSE, BUT IT'S NICE.
ISN'T SHE A LITTLE OLD FOR YOUR FAIRY TALES?
YOU SAID THAT EVEN WHEN ISABELLAE AND SIUKO WERE LITTLE.
HOW IS SHE, BY THE WAY?
SIUKO? ASK HER YOURSELF.
YOU KNOW VERY WELL I CAN'T SEE HER UNLESS SHE THINKS ABOUT ME. YOU'RE CRUEL, DREIDE.
ISN'T THAT WHAT YOU LIKED ABOUT ME, DEAR HUSBAND?

* AN EXCERPT FROM THE FIRST PART OF THE KOJIKI, A COLLECTION OF TEXTS DATING BACK TO THE YEAR 712. IT IS THE OLDEST BOOK AVAILABLE ON THE HISTORY OF JAPAN.

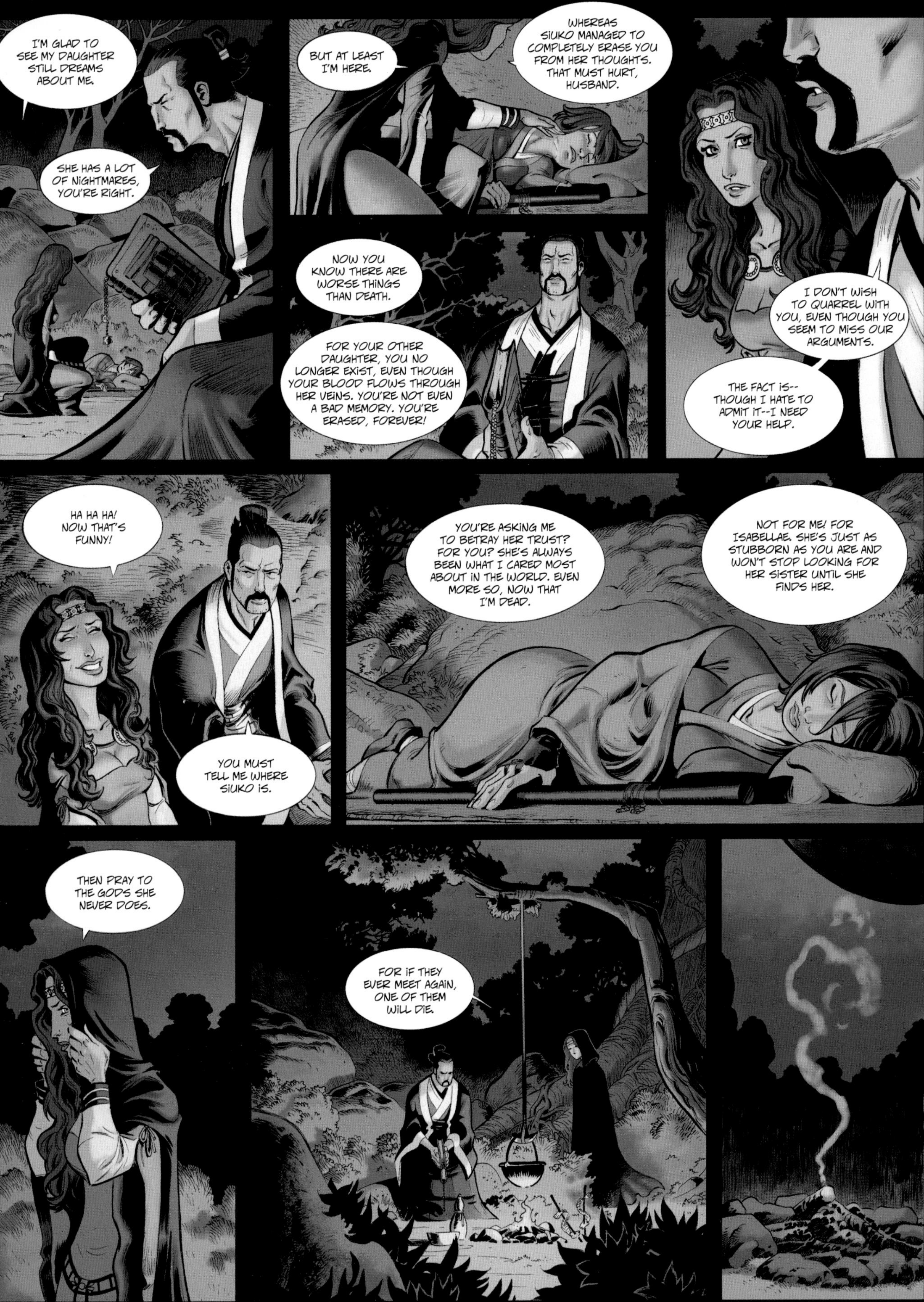
I'M GLAD TO SEE MY DAUGHTER STILL DREAMS ABOUT ME.
SHE HAS A LOT OF NIGHTMARES, YOU'RE RIGHT.
BUT AT LEAST I'M HERE.
WHEREAS SIUKO MANAGED TO COMPLETELY ERASE YOU FROM HER THOUGHTS. THAT MUST HURT, HUSBAND.
NOW YOU KNOW THERE ARE WORSE THINGS THAN DEATH.
FOR YOUR OTHER DAUGHTER, YOU NO LONGER EXIST, EVEN THOUGH YOUR BLOOD FLOWS THROUGH HER VEINS. YOU'RE NOT EVEN A BAD MEMORY. YOU'RE ERASED, FOREVER!
I DON'T WISH TO QUARREL WITH YOU, EVEN THOUGH YOU SEEM TO MISS OUR ARGUMENTS.
THE FACT IS--THOUGH I HATE TO ADMIT IT--I NEED YOUR HELP.
HA HA HA! NOW THAT'S FUNNY!
YOU MUST TELL ME WHERE SIUKO IS.
YOU'RE ASKING ME TO BETRAY HER TRUST? FOR YOU? SHE'S ALWAYS BEEN WHAT I CARED MOST ABOUT IN THE WORLD. EVEN MORE SO, NOW THAT I'M DEAD.
NOT FOR ME! FOR ISABELLAE. SHE'S JUST AS STUBBORN AS YOU ARE AND WON'T STOP LOOKING FOR HER SISTER UNTIL SHE FINDS HER.
THEN PRAY TO THE GODS SHE NEVER DOES.
FOR IF THEY EVER MEET AGAIN, ONE OF THEM WILL DIE.

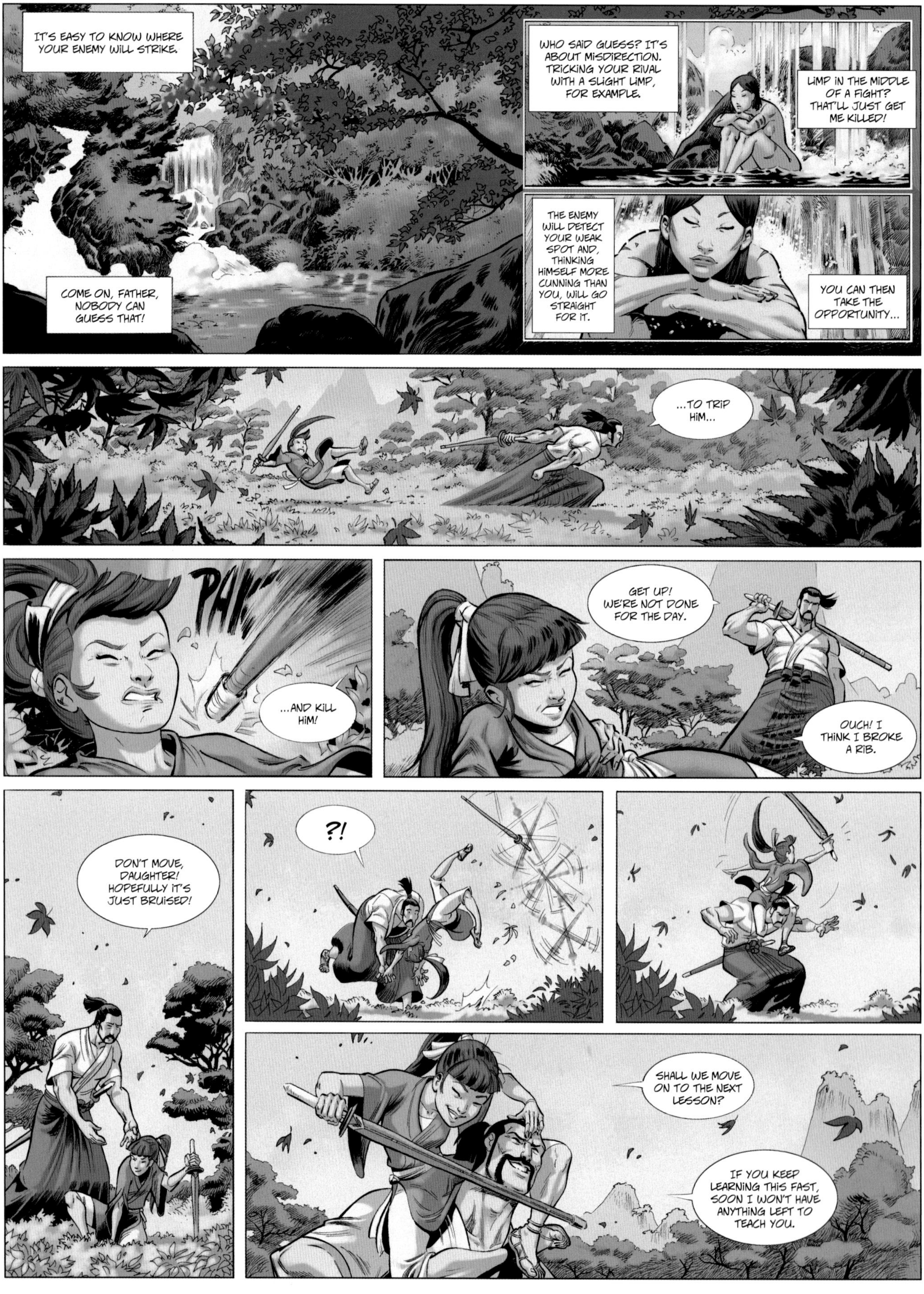
IT'S EASY TO KNOW WHERE YOUR ENEMY WILL STRIKE.
COME ON, FATHER, NOBODY CAN GUESS THAT!
WHO SAID GUESS? IT'S ABOUT MISDIRECTION. TRICKING YOUR RIVAL WITH A SLIGHT LIMP, FOR EXAMPLE.
LIMP IN THE MIDDLE OF A FIGHT? THAT'LL JUST GET ME KILLED!
THE ENEMY WILL DETECT YOUR WEAK SPOT AND, THINKING HIMSELF MORE CUNNING THAN YOU, WILL GO STRAIGHT FOR IT.
YOU CAN THEN TAKE THE OPPORTUNITY...
...TO TRIP HIM...
PA
...AND KILL HIM!
GET UP! WE'RE NOT DONE FOR THE DAY.
OUCH! I THINK I BROKE A RIB.
DON'T MOVE, DAUGHTER! HOPEFULLY IT'S JUST BRUISED!
?!
SHALL WE MOVE ON TO THE NEXT LESSON?
IF YOU KEEP LEARNING THIS FAST, SOON I WON'T HAVE ANYTHING LEFT TO TEACH YOU.

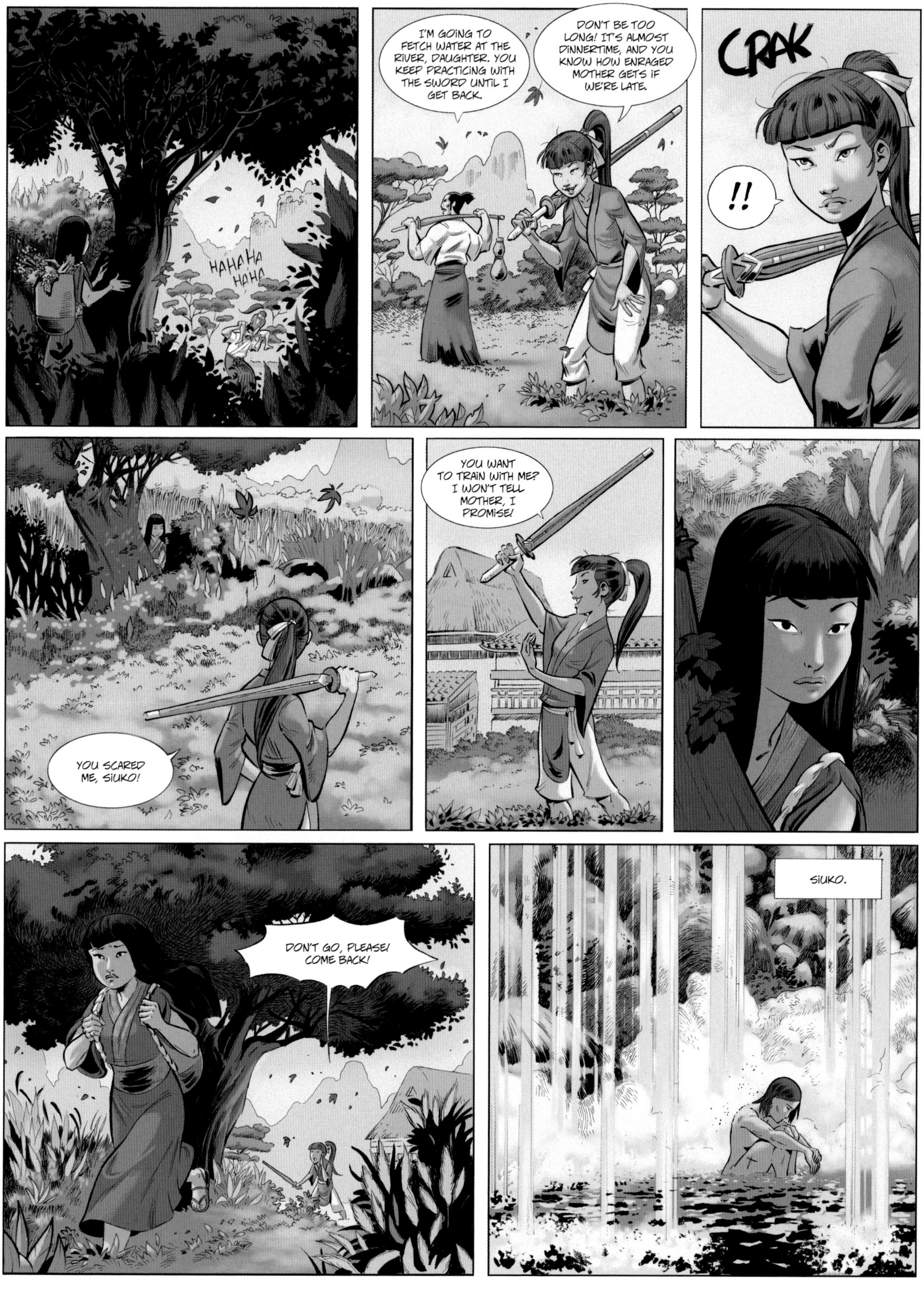
HAHAHA
HAHA
I'M GOING TO FETCH WATER AT THE RIVER, DAUGHTER. YOU KEEP PRACTICING WITH THE SWORD UNTIL I GET BACK.
DON'T BE TOO LONG! IT'S ALMOST DINNERTIME, AND YOU KNOW HOW ENRAGED MOTHER GETS IF WE'RE LATE.
CRAK
!!
YOU SCARED ME, SIUKO!
YOU WANT TO TRAIN WITH ME? I WON'T TELL MOTHER, I PROMISE!
DON'T GO, PLEASE! COME BACK!
SIUKO.

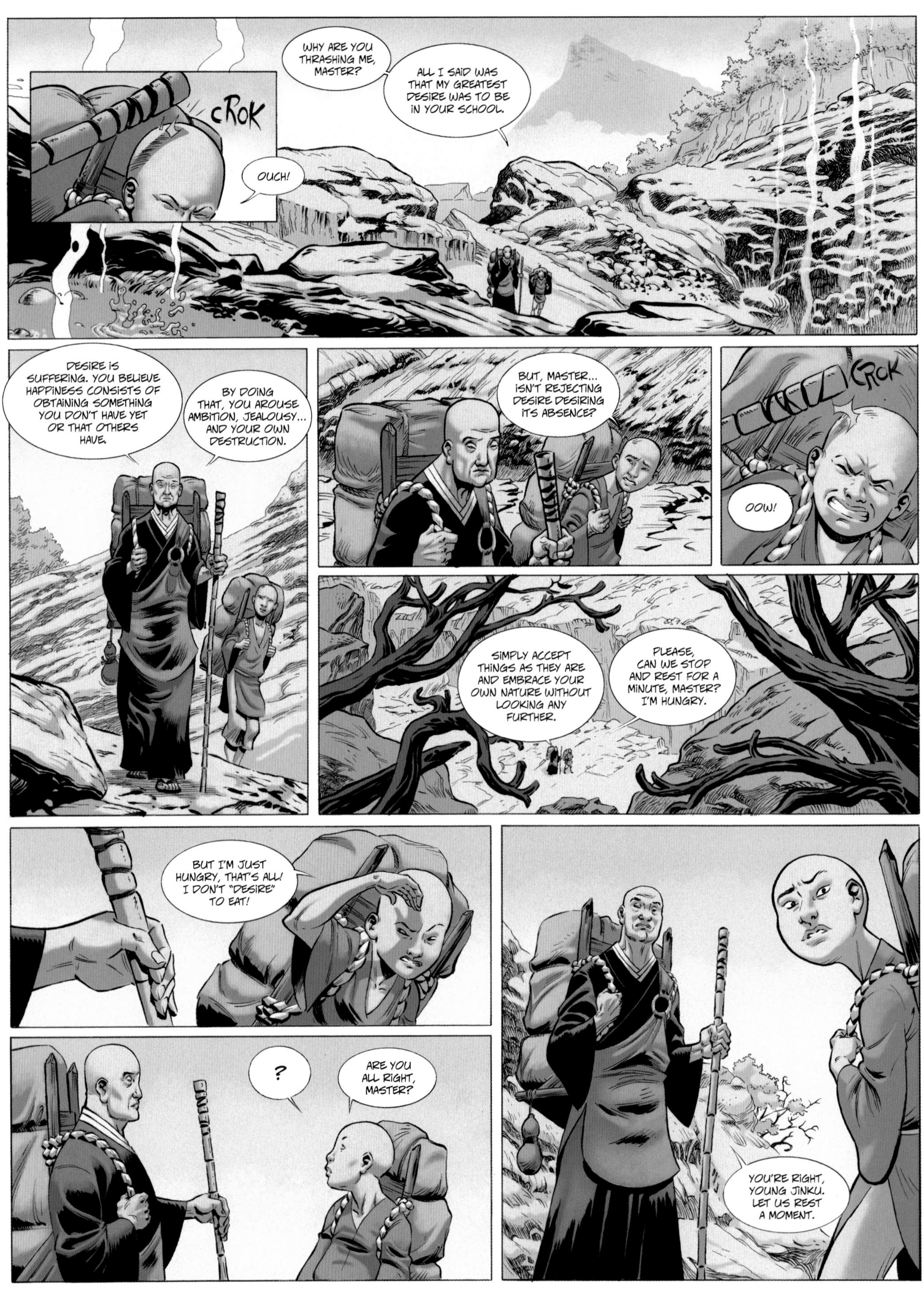
CROK
OUCH!
WHY ARE YOU THRASHING ME, MASTER?
ALL I SAID WAS THAT MY GREATEST DESIRE WAS TO BE IN YOUR SCHOOL.
DESIRE IS SUFFERING. YOU BELIEVE HAPPINESS CONSISTS OF OBTAINING SOMETHING YOU DON'T HAVE YET OR THAT OTHERS HAVE.
BY DOING THAT, YOU AROUSE AMBITION, JEALOUSY... AND YOUR OWN DESTRUCTION.
BUT, MASTER... ISN'T REJECTING DESIRE DESIRING ITS ABSENCE?
CROK
OOW!
SIMPLY ACCEPT THINGS AS THEY ARE AND EMBRACE YOUR OWN NATURE WITHOUT LOOKING ANY FURTHER.
PLEASE, CAN WE STOP AND REST FOR A MINUTE, MASTER? I'M HUNGRY.
BUT I'M JUST HUNGRY, THAT'S ALL! I DON'T "DESIRE" TO EAT!
?
ARE YOU ALL RIGHT, MASTER?
YOU'RE RIGHT, YOUNG JINKU. LET US REST A MOMENT.

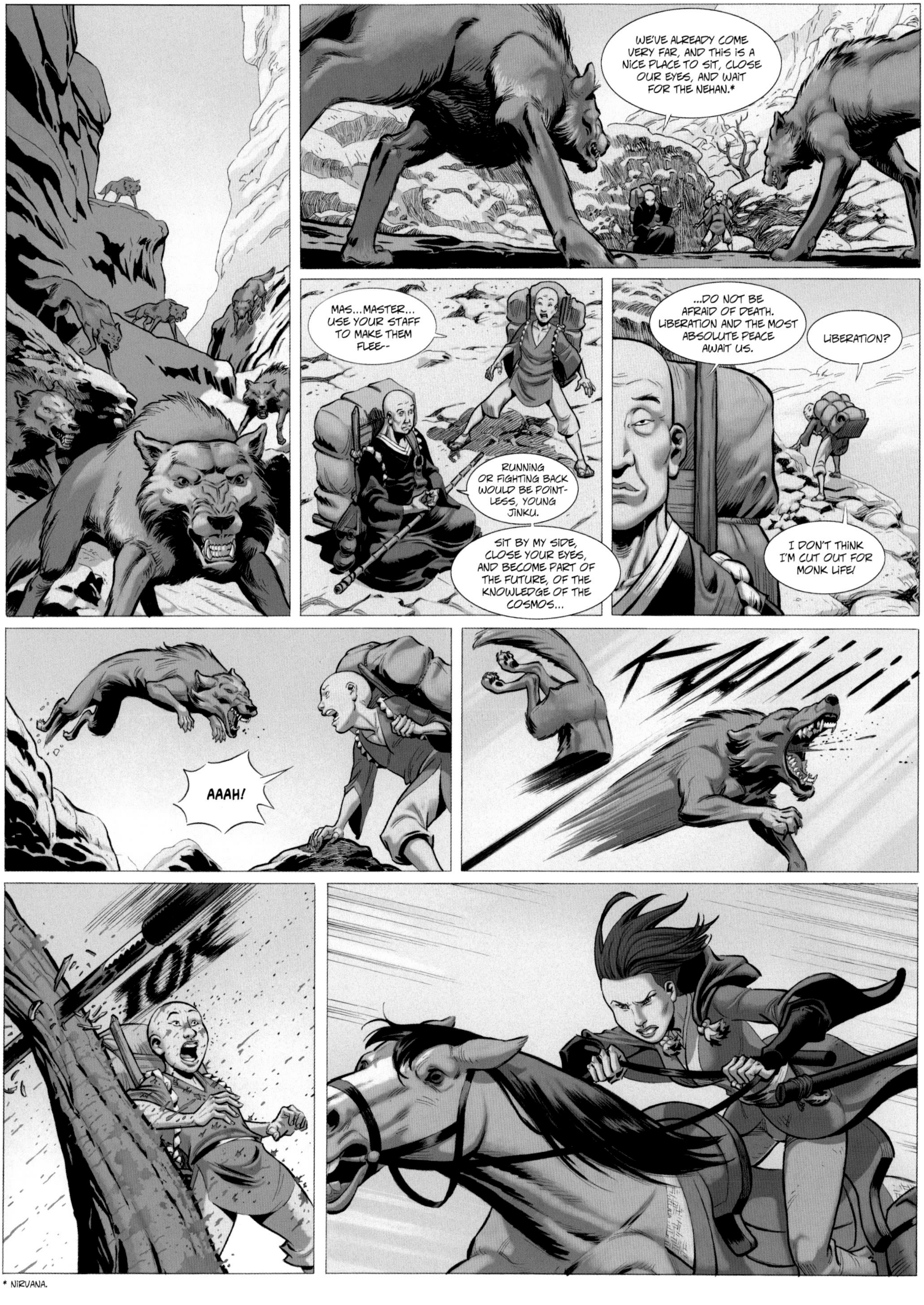
WE'VE ALREADY COME VERY FAR, AND THIS IS A NICE PLACE TO SIT, CLOSE OUR EYES, AND WAIT FOR THE NEHAN.*
MAS...MASTER... USE YOUR STAFF TO MAKE THEM FLEE--
RUNNING OR FIGHTING BACK WOULD BE POINTLESS, YOUNG JINKU.
SIT BY MY SIDE, CLOSE YOUR EYES, AND BECOME PART OF THE FUTURE, OF THE KNOWLEDGE OF THE COSMOS...
...DO NOT BE AFRAID OF DEATH. LIBERATION AND THE MOST ABSOLUTE PEACE AWAIT US.
LIBERATION?
I DON'T THINK I'M CUT OUT FOR MONK LIFE!
AAAH!
KAAAI!!!
TOK

* NIRVANA.

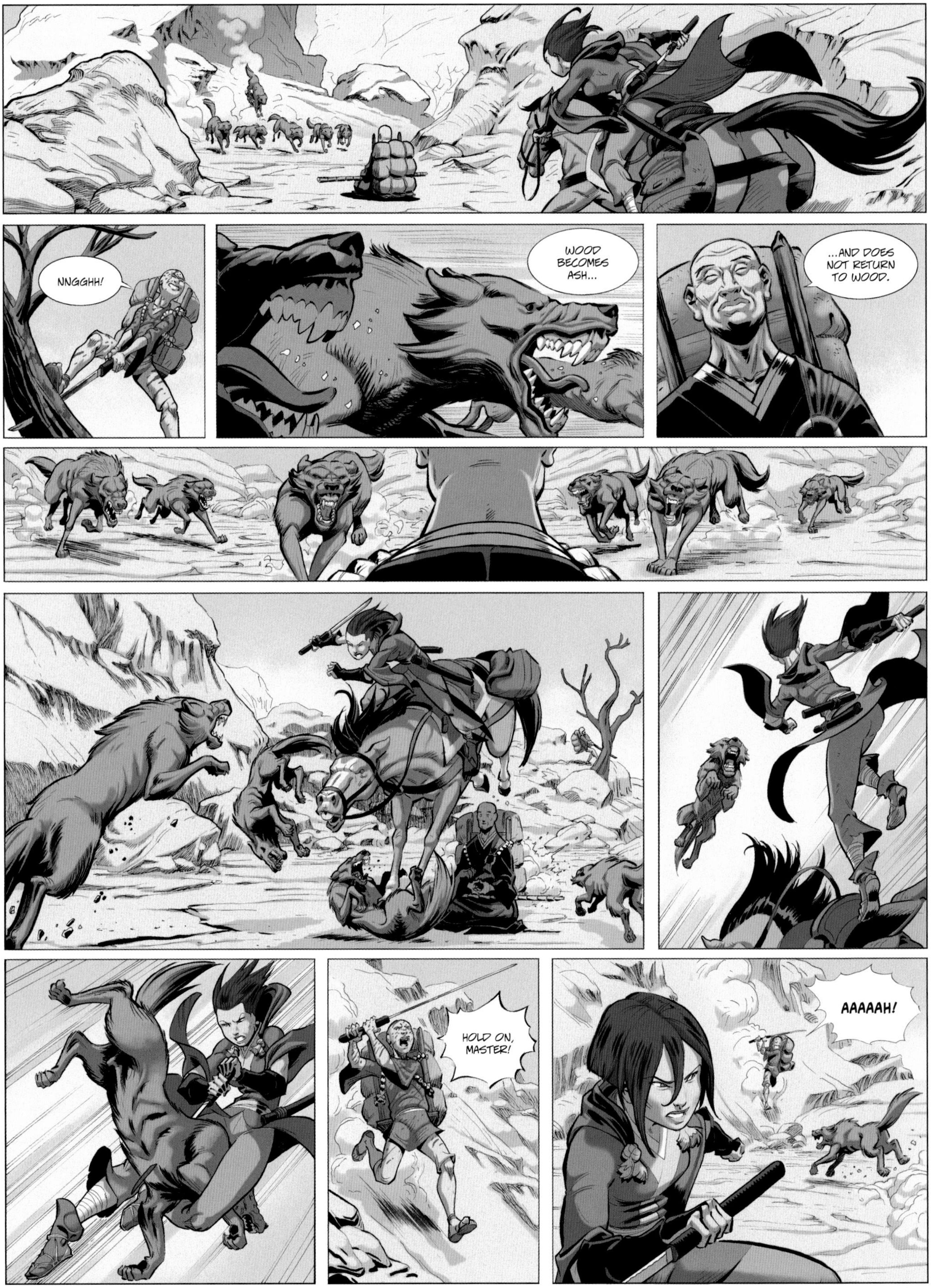
NNGGHH!
WOOD BECOMES ASH...
...AND DOES NOT RETURN TO WOOD.
HOLD ON, MASTER!
AAAAAH!

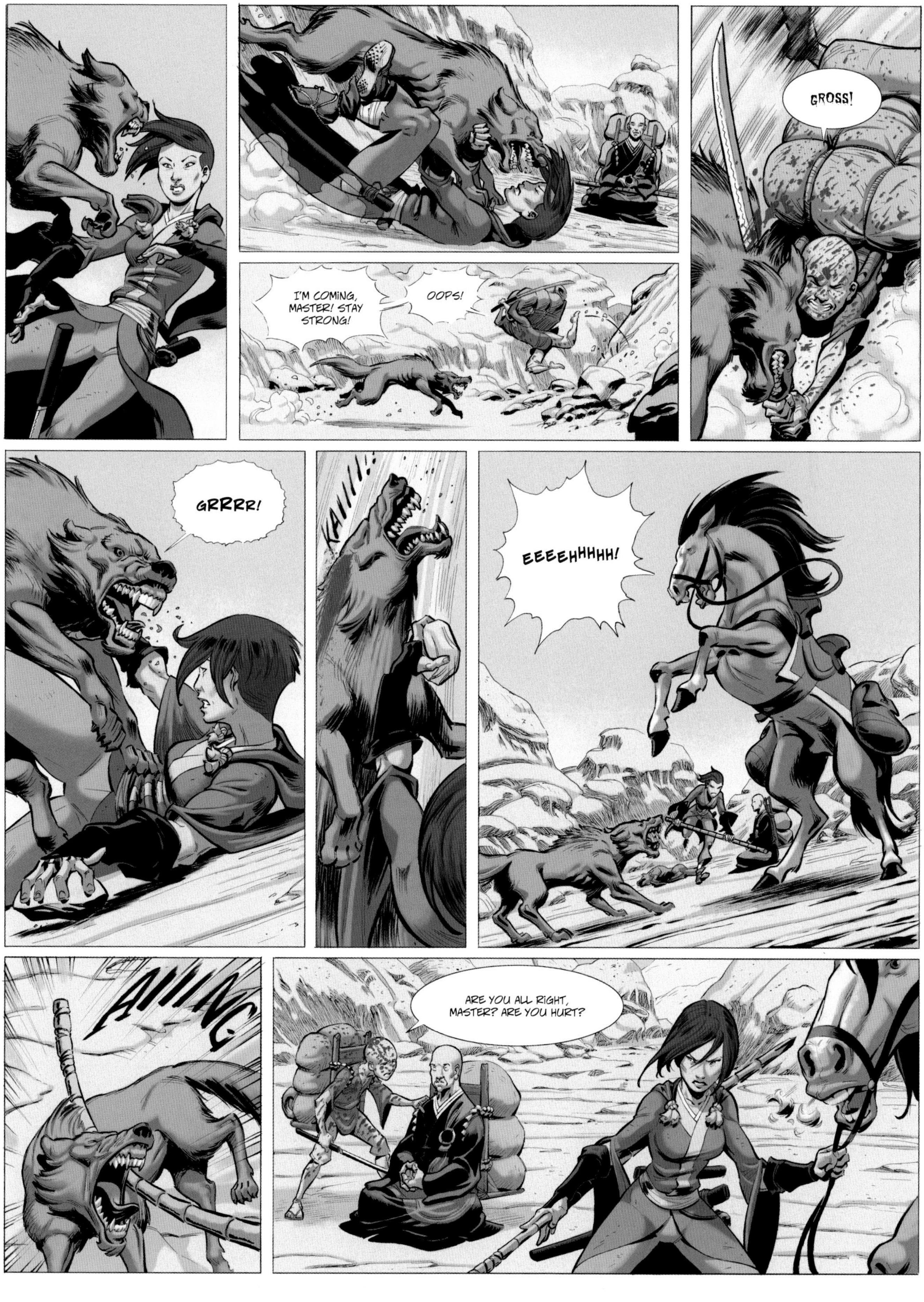
GROSS!
I'M COMING, MASTER! STAY STRONG!
OOPS!
GRRRR!
KAI!!!!
EEEEHHHHH!
AIIING
ARE YOU ALL RIGHT, MASTER? ARE YOU HURT?

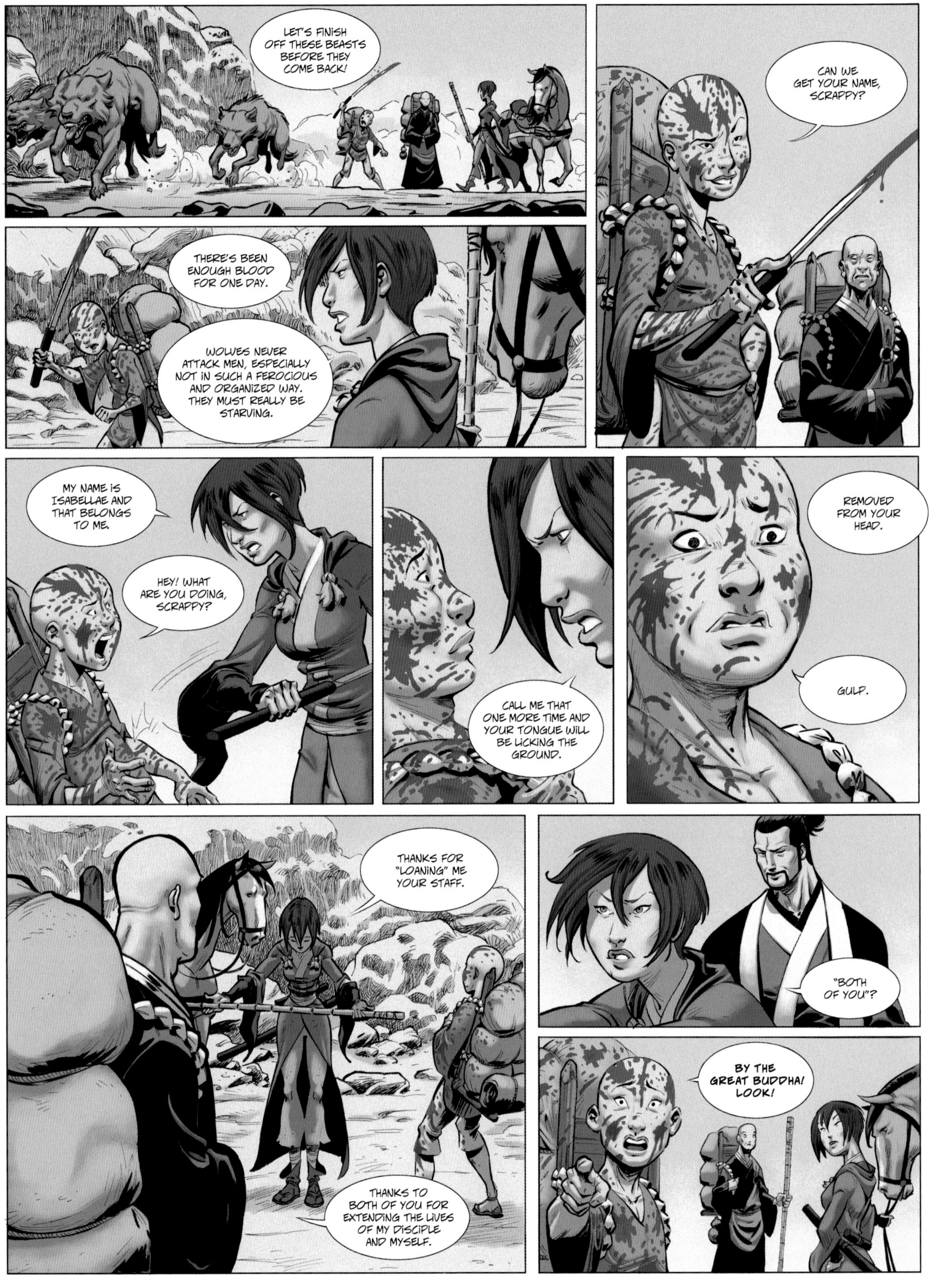
LET'S FINISH OFF THESE BEASTS BEFORE THEY COME BACK!
CAN WE GET YOUR NAME, SCRAPPY?
THERE'S BEEN ENOUGH BLOOD FOR ONE DAY.
WOLVES NEVER ATTACK MEN, ESPECIALLY NOT IN SUCH A FEROCIOUS AND ORGANIZED WAY. THEY MUST REALLY BE STARVING.
MY NAME IS ISABELLAE AND THAT BELONGS TO ME.
HEY! WHAT ARE YOU DOING, SCRAPPY?
CALL ME THAT ONE MORE TIME AND YOUR TONGUE WILL BE LICKING THE GROUND.
REMOVED FROM YOUR HEAD.
GULP.
THANKS FOR "LOANING" ME YOUR STAFF.
THANKS TO BOTH OF YOU FOR EXTENDING THE LIVES OF MY DISCIPLE AND MYSELF.
"BOTH OF YOU"?
BY THE GREAT BUDDHA! LOOK!

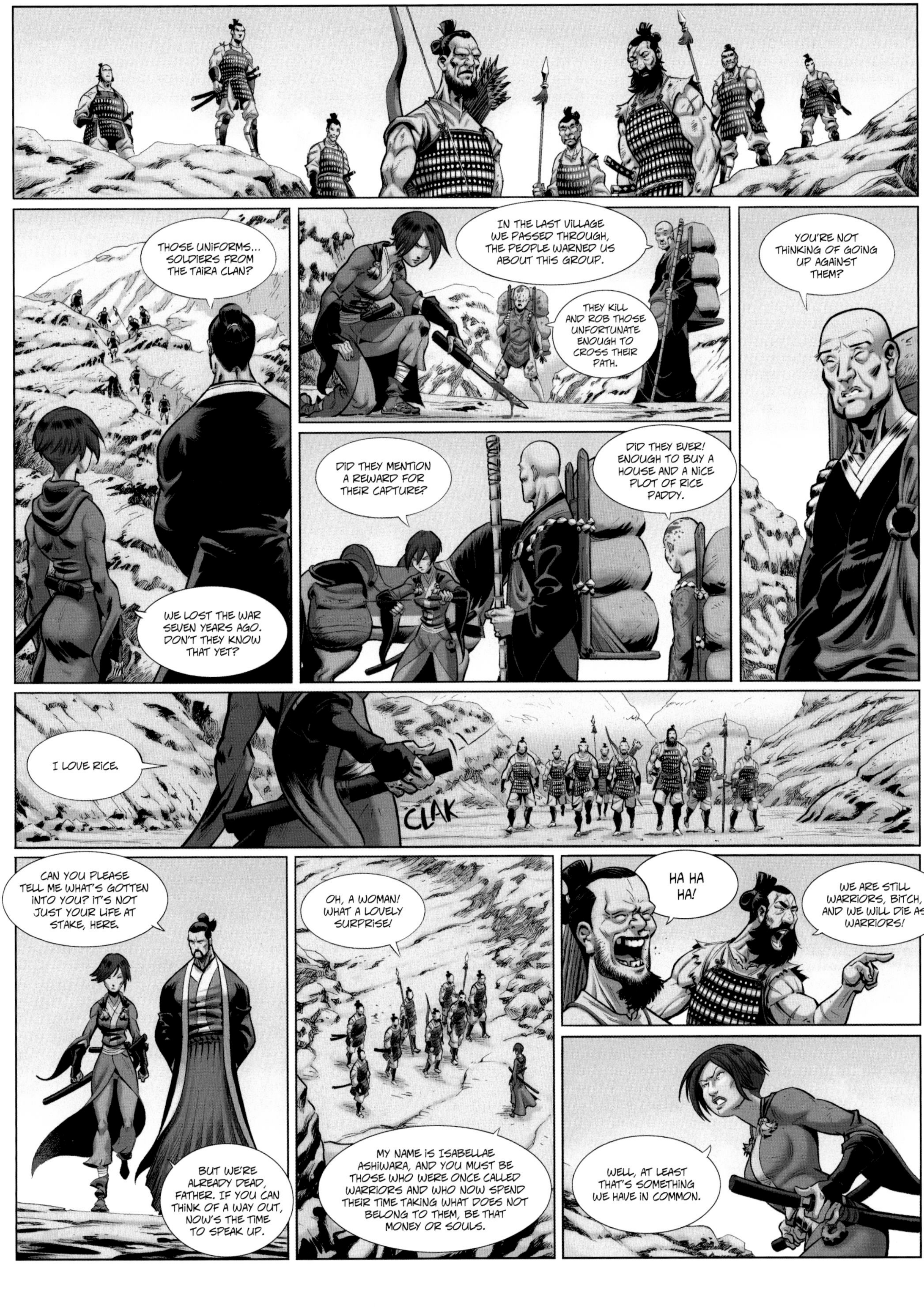
THOSE UNIFORMS... SOLDIERS FROM THE TAIRA CLAN?
WE LOST THE WAR SEVEN YEARS AGO. DON'T THEY KNOW THAT YET?
IN THE LAST VILLAGE WE PASSED THROUGH, THE PEOPLE WARNED US ABOUT THIS GROUP.
THEY KILL AND ROB THOSE UNFORTUNATE ENOUGH TO CROSS THEIR PATH.
DID THEY MENTION A REWARD FOR THEIR CAPTURE?
DID THEY EVER! ENOUGH TO BUY A HOUSE AND A NICE PLOT OF RICE PADDY.
YOU'RE NOT THINKING OF GOING UP AGAINST THEM?
I LOVE RICE.
CLAK
CAN YOU PLEASE TELL ME WHAT'S GOTTEN INTO YOU? IT'S NOT JUST YOUR LIFE AT STAKE, HERE.
BUT WE'RE ALREADY DEAD, FATHER. IF YOU CAN THINK OF A WAY OUT, NOW'S THE TIME TO SPEAK UP.
OH, A WOMAN! WHAT A LOVELY SURPRISE!
MY NAME IS ISABELLAE ASHIWARA, AND YOU MUST BE THOSE WHO WERE ONCE CALLED WARRIORS AND WHO NOW SPEND THEIR TIME TAKING WHAT DOES NOT BELONG TO THEM, BE THAT MONEY OR SOULS.
HA HA HA!
WE ARE STILL WARRIORS, BITCH, AND WE WILL DIE AS WARRIORS!
WELL, AT LEAST THAT'S SOMETHING WE HAVE IN COMMON.

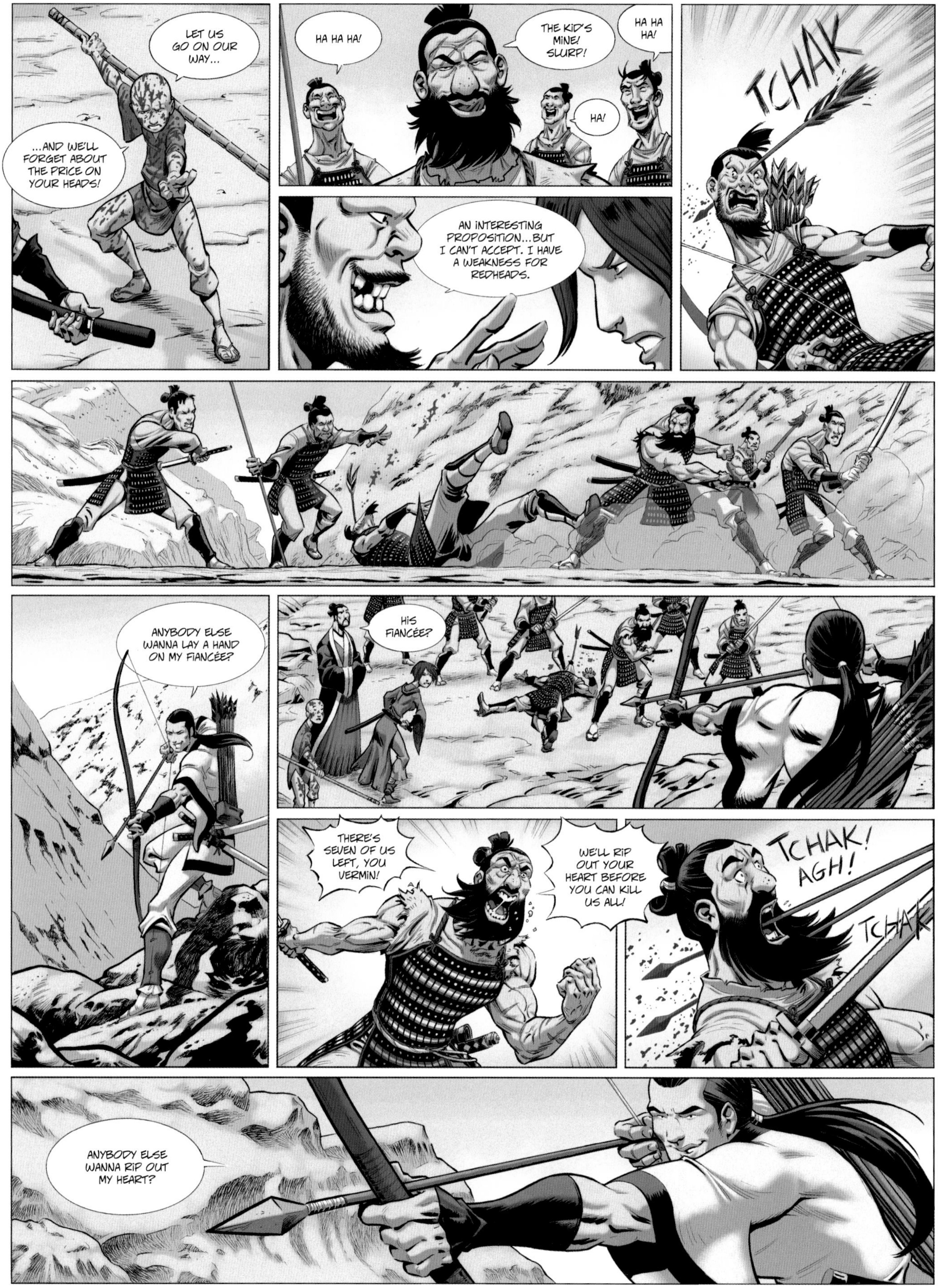
LET US GO ON OUR WAY...
...AND WE'LL FORGET ABOUT THE PRICE ON YOUR HEADS!
HA HA HA!
THE KID'S MINE! SLURP!
HA HA HA!
HA!
AN INTERESTING PROPOSITION... BUT I CAN'T ACCEPT. I HAVE A WEAKNESS FOR REDHEADS.
TCHAK
ANYBODY ELSE WANNA LAY A HAND ON MY FIANCÉE?
HIS FIANCÉE?
THERE'S SEVEN OF US LEFT, YOU VERMIN!
WE'LL RIP OUT YOUR HEART BEFORE YOU CAN KILL US ALL!
TCHAK! AGH!
TCHAK
ANYBODY ELSE WANNA RIP OUT MY HEART?

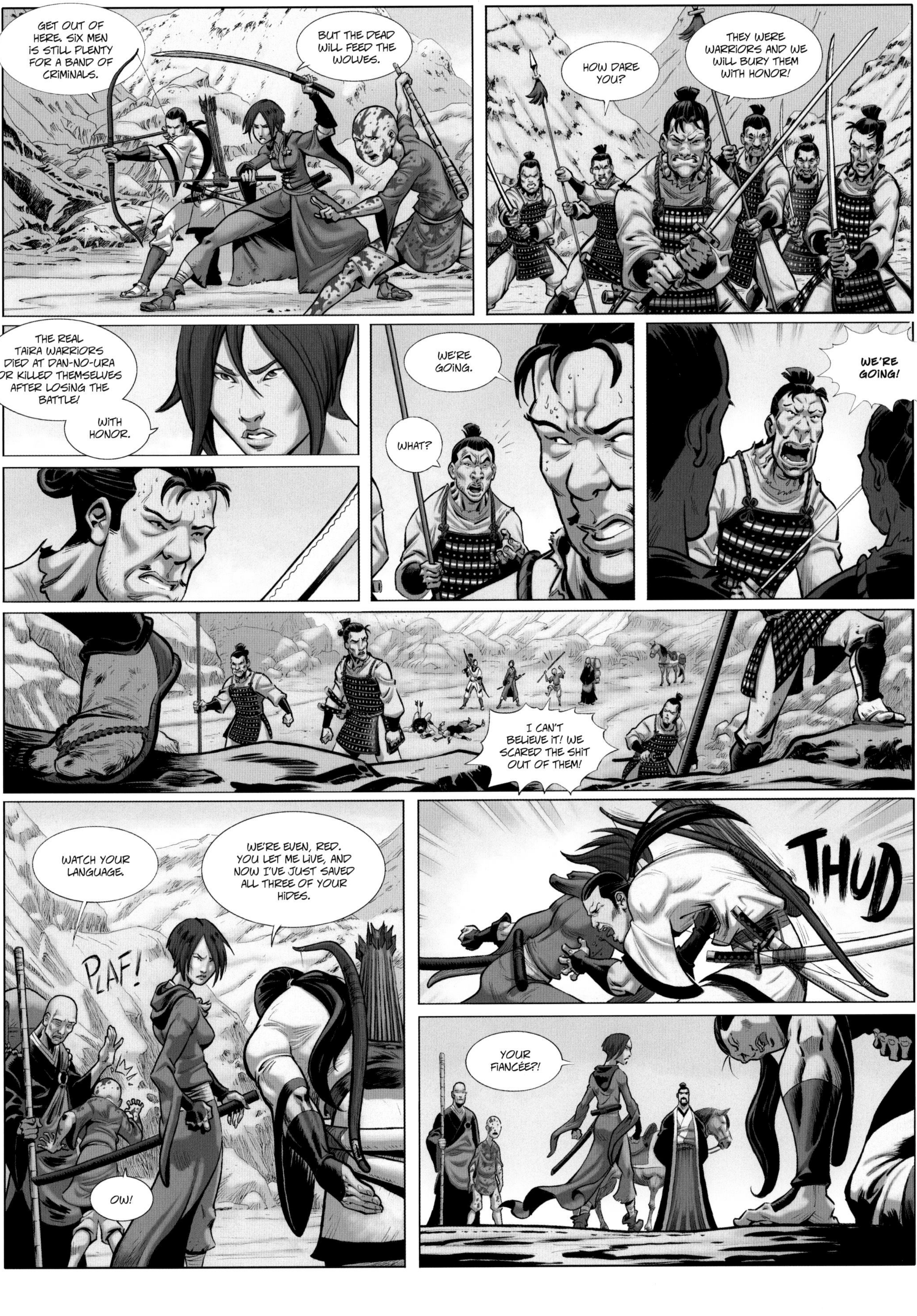
GET OUT OF HERE. SIX MEN IS STILL PLENTY FOR A BAND OF CRIMINALS.
BUT THE DEAD WILL FEED THE WOLVES.
HOW DARE YOU?
THEY WERE WARRIORS AND WE WILL BURY THEM WITH HONOR!
THE REAL TAIRA WARRIORS DIED AT DAN-NO-URA OR KILLED THEMSELVES AFTER LOSING THE BATTLE!
WITH HONOR.
WE'RE GOING.
WHAT?
WE'RE GOING!
I CAN'T BELIEVE IT! WE SCARED THE SHIT OUT OF THEM!
WATCH YOUR LANGUAGE.
WE'RE EVEN, RED. YOU LET ME LIVE, AND NOW I'VE JUST SAVED ALL THREE OF YOUR HIDES.
PLAF!
OW!
THUD
YOUR FIANCÉE?!

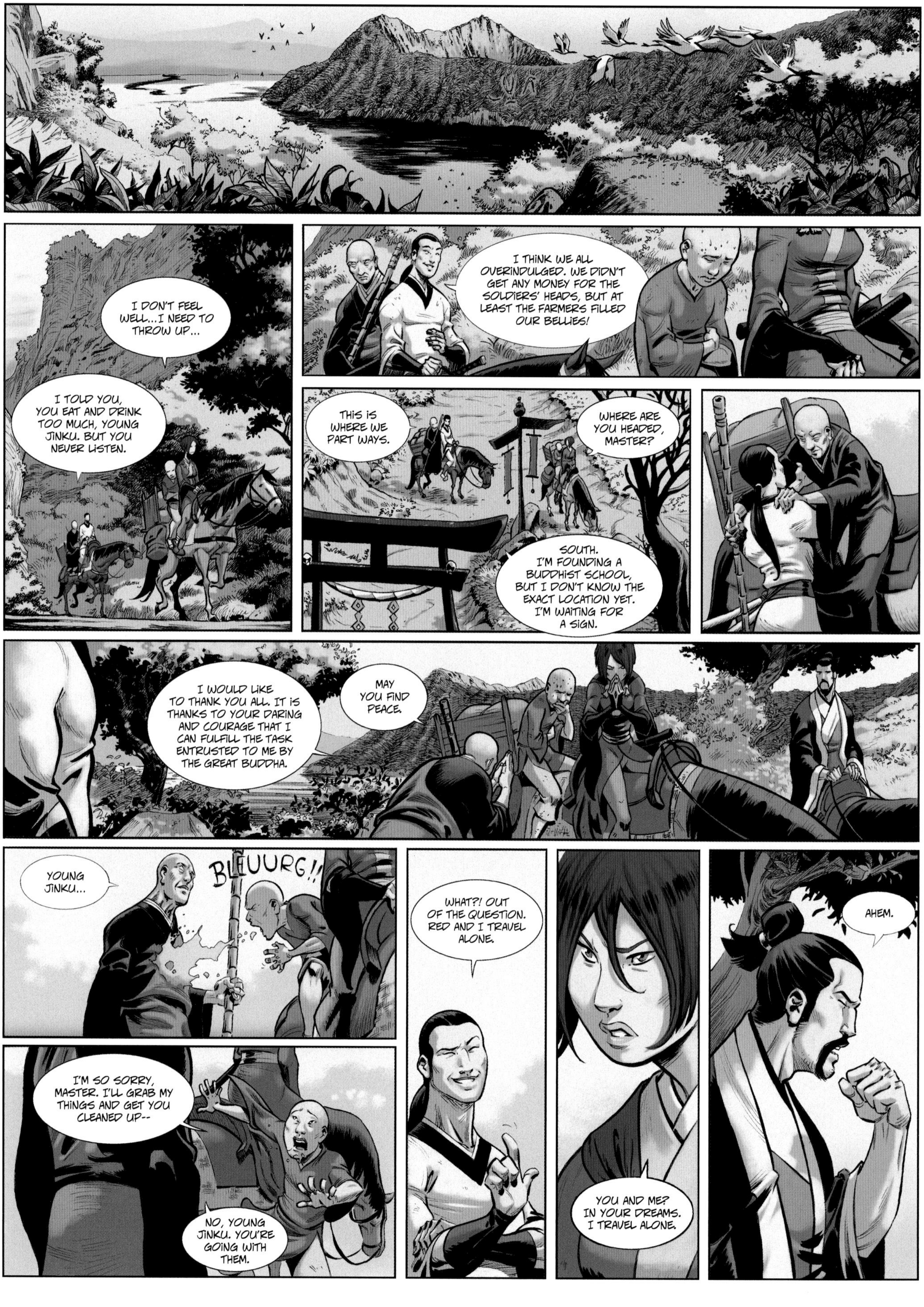
I DON'T FEEL WELL...I NEED TO THROW UP...
I TOLD YOU, YOU EAT AND DRINK TOO MUCH, YOUNG JINKU. BUT YOU NEVER LISTEN.
I THINK WE ALL OVERINDULGED. WE DIDN'T GET ANY MONEY FOR THE SOLDIERS' HEADS, BUT AT LEAST THE FARMERS FILLED OUR BELLIES!
THIS IS WHERE WE PART WAYS.
WHERE ARE YOU HEADED, MASTER?
SOUTH. I'M FOUNDING A BUDDHIST SCHOOL, BUT I DON'T KNOW THE EXACT LOCATION YET. I'M WAITING FOR A SIGN.
I WOULD LIKE TO THANK YOU ALL. IT IS THANKS TO YOUR DARING AND COURAGE THAT I CAN FULFILL THE TASK ENTRUSTED TO ME BY THE GREAT BUDDHA.
MAY YOU FIND PEACE.
YOUNG JINKU...
BLEUURG!!
I'M SO SORRY, MASTER. I'LL GRAB MY THINGS AND GET YOU CLEANED UP--
NO, YOUNG JINKU. YOU'RE GOING WITH THEM.
WHAT?! OUT OF THE QUESTION. RED AND I TRAVEL ALONE.
YOU AND ME? IN YOUR DREAMS. I TRAVEL ALONE.
AHEM.

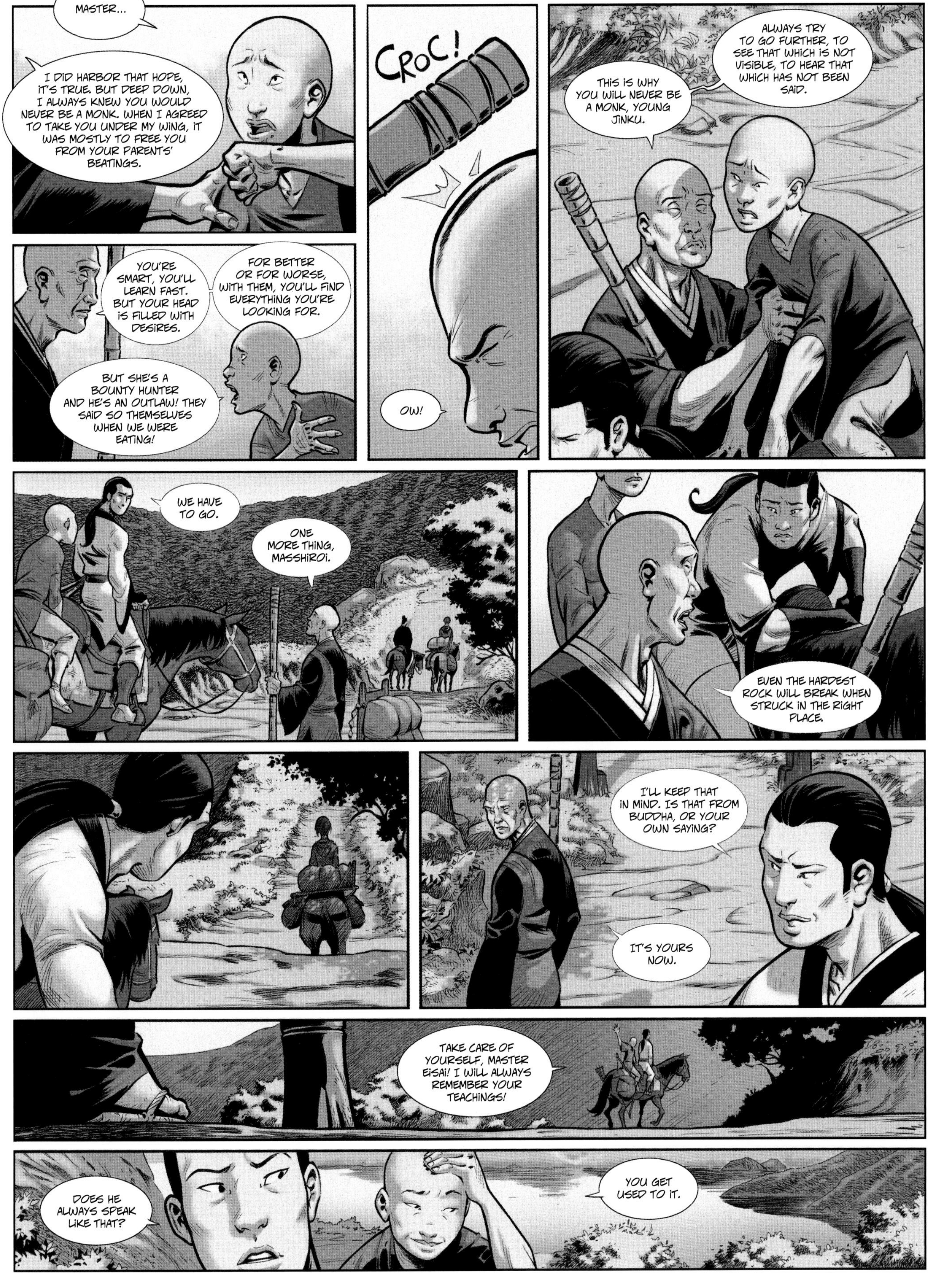
MASTER...
I DID HARBOR THAT HOPE, IT'S TRUE. BUT DEEP DOWN, I ALWAYS KNEW YOU WOULD NEVER BE A MONK. WHEN I AGREED TO TAKE YOU UNDER MY WING, IT WAS MOSTLY TO FREE YOU FROM YOUR PARENTS' BEATINGS.
CROC!
OW!
ALWAYS TRY TO GO FURTHER, TO SEE THAT WHICH IS NOT VISIBLE, TO HEAR THAT WHICH HAS NOT BEEN SAID.
THIS IS WHY YOU WILL NEVER BE A MONK, YOUNG JINKU.
YOU'RE SMART, YOU'LL LEARN FAST. BUT YOUR HEAD IS FILLED WITH DESIRES.
FOR BETTER OR FOR WORSE, WITH THEM, YOU'LL FIND EVERYTHING YOU'RE LOOKING FOR.
BUT SHE'S A BOUNTY HUNTER AND HE'S AN OUTLAW! THEY SAID SO THEMSELVES WHEN WE WERE EATING!
WE HAVE TO GO.
ONE MORE THING, MASSHIROI.
EVEN THE HARDEST ROCK WILL BREAK WHEN STRUCK IN THE RIGHT PLACE.
I'LL KEEP THAT IN MIND. IS THAT FROM BUDDHA, OR YOUR OWN SAYING?
IT'S YOURS NOW.
TAKE CARE OF YOURSELF, MASTER EISAI! I WILL ALWAYS REMEMBER YOUR TEACHINGS!
DOES HE ALWAYS SPEAK LIKE THAT?
YOU GET USED TO IT.

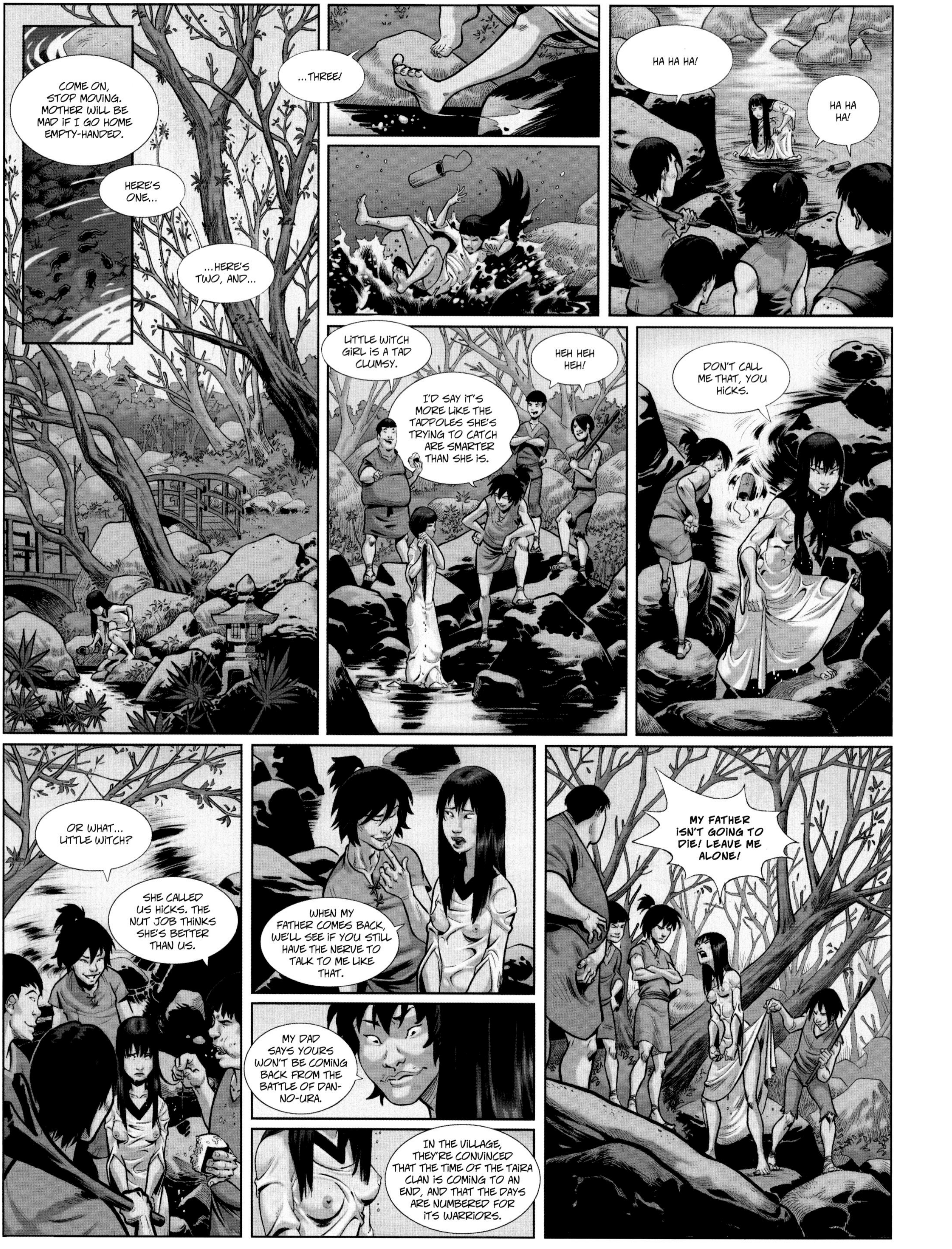
COME ON, STOP MOVING. MOTHER WILL BE MAD IF I GO HOME EMPTY-HANDED.
HERE'S ONE...
...HERE'S TWO, AND...
...THREE!
HA HA HA!
HA HA HA!
LITTLE WITCH GIRL IS A TAD CLUMSY.
HEH HEH HEH!
I'D SAY IT'S MORE LIKE THE TADPOLES SHE'S TRYING TO CATCH ARE SMARTER THAN SHE IS.
DON'T CALL ME THAT, YOU HICKS.
OR WHAT... LITTLE WITCH?
SHE CALLED US HICKS. THE NUT JOB THINKS SHE'S BETTER THAN US.
WHEN MY FATHER COMES BACK, WE'LL SEE IF YOU STILL HAVE THE NERVE TO TALK TO ME LIKE THAT.
MY DAD SAYS YOURS WON'T BE COMING BACK FROM THE BATTLE OF DAN-NO-URA.
IN THE VILLAGE, THEY'RE CONVINCED THAT THE TIME OF THE TAIRA CLAN IS COMING TO AN END, AND THAT THE DAYS ARE NUMBERED FOR ITS WARRIORS.
MY FATHER ISN'T GOING TO DIE! LEAVE ME ALONE!

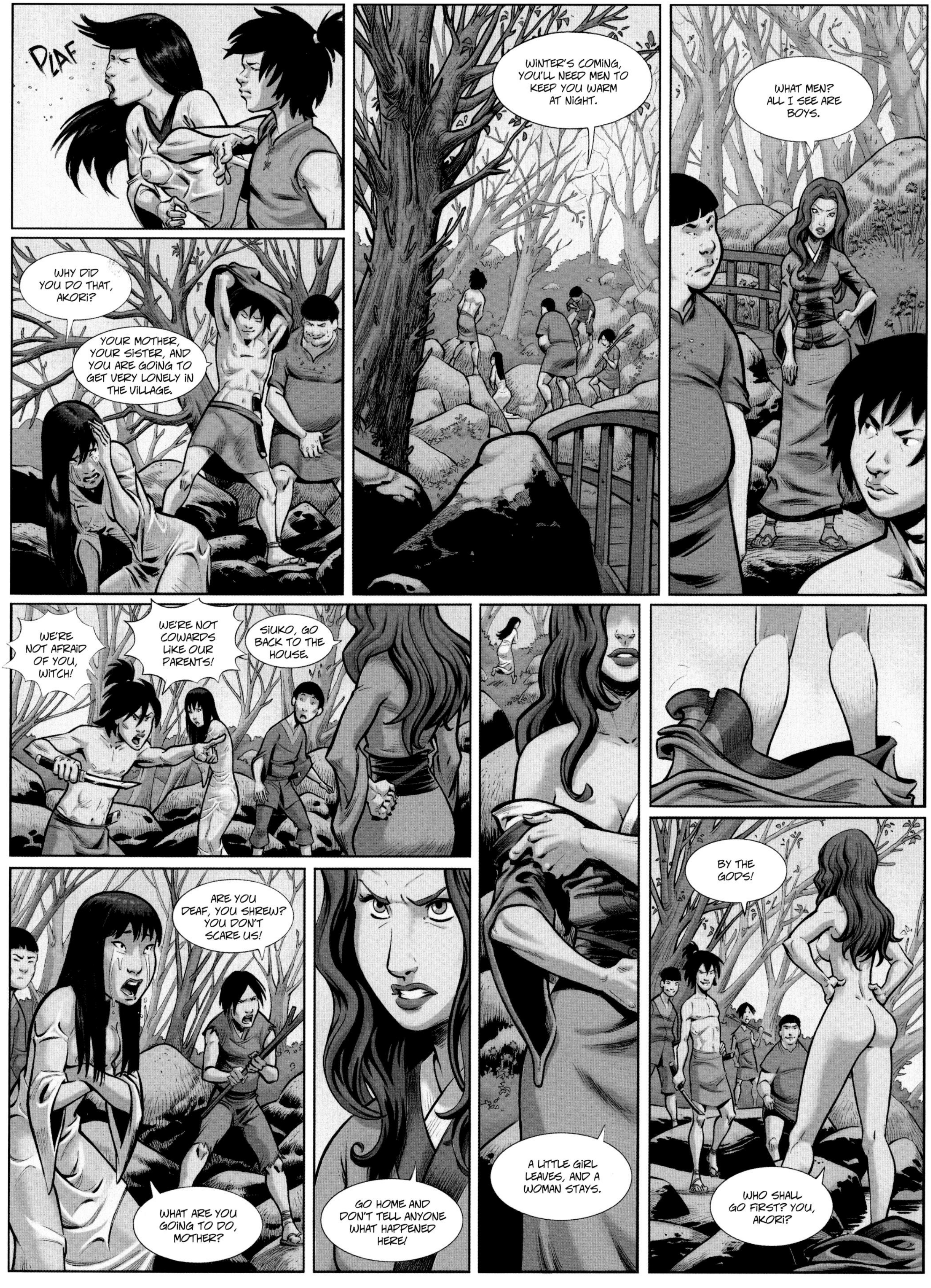
PLAF
WHY DID YOU DO THAT, AKORI?
YOUR MOTHER, YOUR SISTER, AND YOU ARE GOING TO GET VERY LONELY IN THE VILLAGE.
WINTER'S COMING, YOU'LL NEED MEN TO KEEP YOU WARM AT NIGHT.
WHAT MEN? ALL I SEE ARE BOYS.
WE'RE NOT AFRAID OF YOU, WITCH!
WE'RE NOT COWARDS LIKE OUR PARENTS!
SIUKO, GO BACK TO THE HOUSE.
ARE YOU DEAF, YOU SHREW? YOU DON'T SCARE US!
WHAT ARE YOU GOING TO DO, MOTHER?
GO HOME AND DON'T TELL ANYONE WHAT HAPPENED HERE!
A LITTLE GIRL LEAVES, AND A WOMAN STAYS.
BY THE GODS!
WHO SHALL GO FIRST? YOU, AKORI?

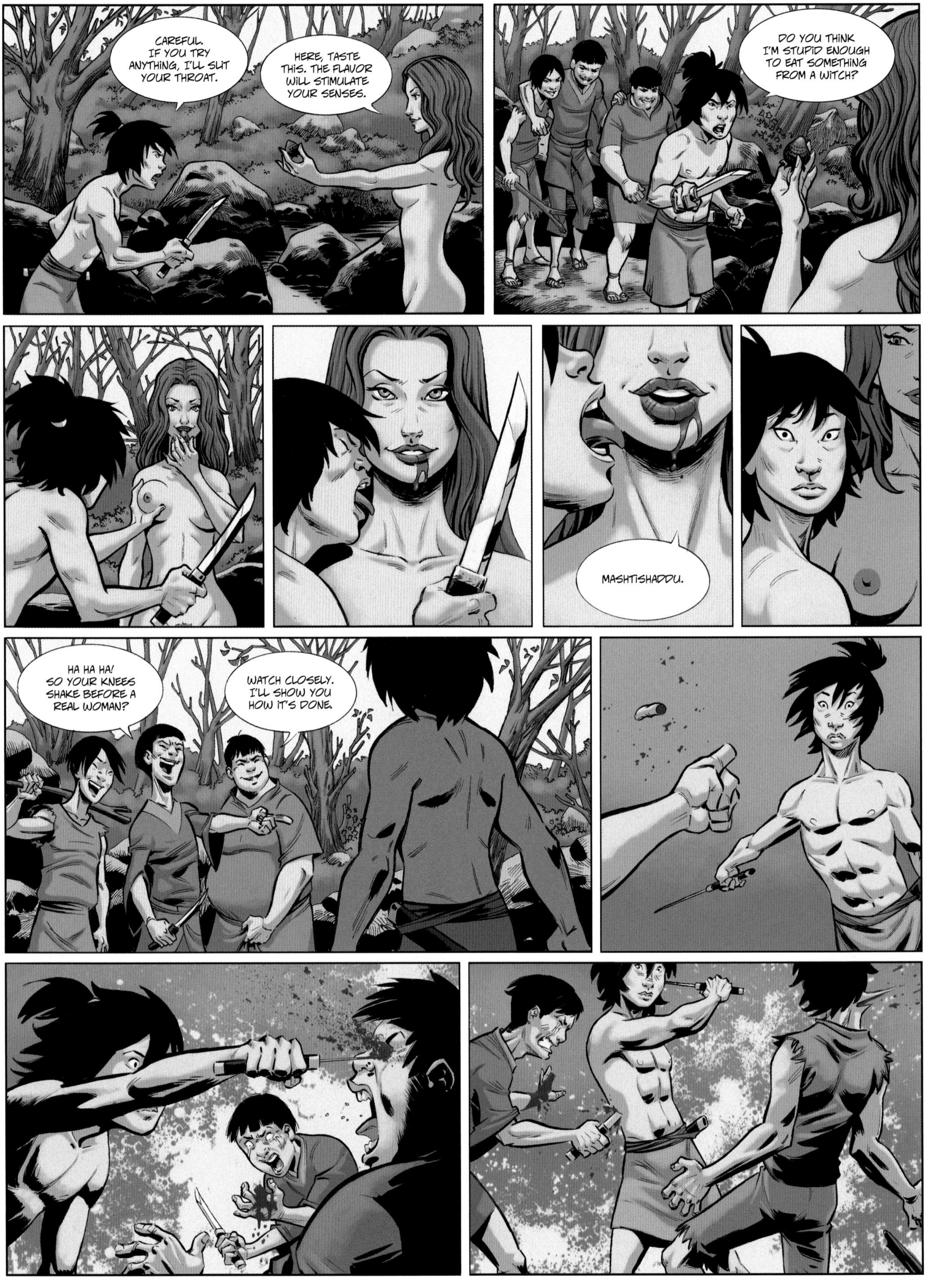
CAREFUL. IF YOU TRY ANYTHING, I'LL SLIT YOUR THROAT.
HERE, TASTE THIS. THE FLAVOR WILL STIMULATE YOUR SENSES.
DO YOU THINK I'M STUPID ENOUGH TO EAT SOMETHING FROM A WITCH?
MASHTISHADDU.
HA HA HA! SO YOUR KNEES SHAKE BEFORE A REAL WOMAN?
WATCH CLOSELY. I'LL SHOW YOU HOW IT'S DONE.

ISA! ISA! HURRY, GRAB YOUR SWORD! MOTHER'S IN DANGER!

ISA...?

ISA!

MOTHER, I WENT LOOKING FOR FATHER. I KNOW IT'S MADNESS, BUT HE TRAINED ME TO BE A WARRIOR AND I BELIEVE MY PLACE IS AT HIS SIDE, IN BATTLE.

BEFORE HE LEFT FOR DAN-NO-URA, FATHER ASKED ME TO WATCH OVER YOU AND TO BE WARY OF OUR NEIGHBORS. AS YOU KNOW, OUR RED HAIR MAKES THEM NERVOUS.

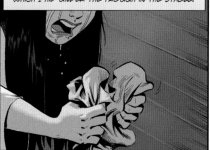

I DON'T THINK THEY WILL DARE HARM YOU, THEY FEAR FATHER'S SWORD TOO MUCH. BUT JUST IN CASE, I'VE LEFT YOU SOME WEAPONS, WHICH I HID UNDER THE TROUGH IN THE STABLE.

WE SHALL SEE EACH OTHER AGAIN IF SUCH IS THE WILL OF THE GODS. I DARE NOT HOPE THAT YOU AND SIUKO WILL UNDERSTAND, BUT I PRAY THAT YOU FORGIVE ME ONE DAY.
ISA

LIOM IS TIM A BHI DOL DACHAIDH.*

"THE TIME HAS COME FOR ME TO GO HOME," IN GAELIC.

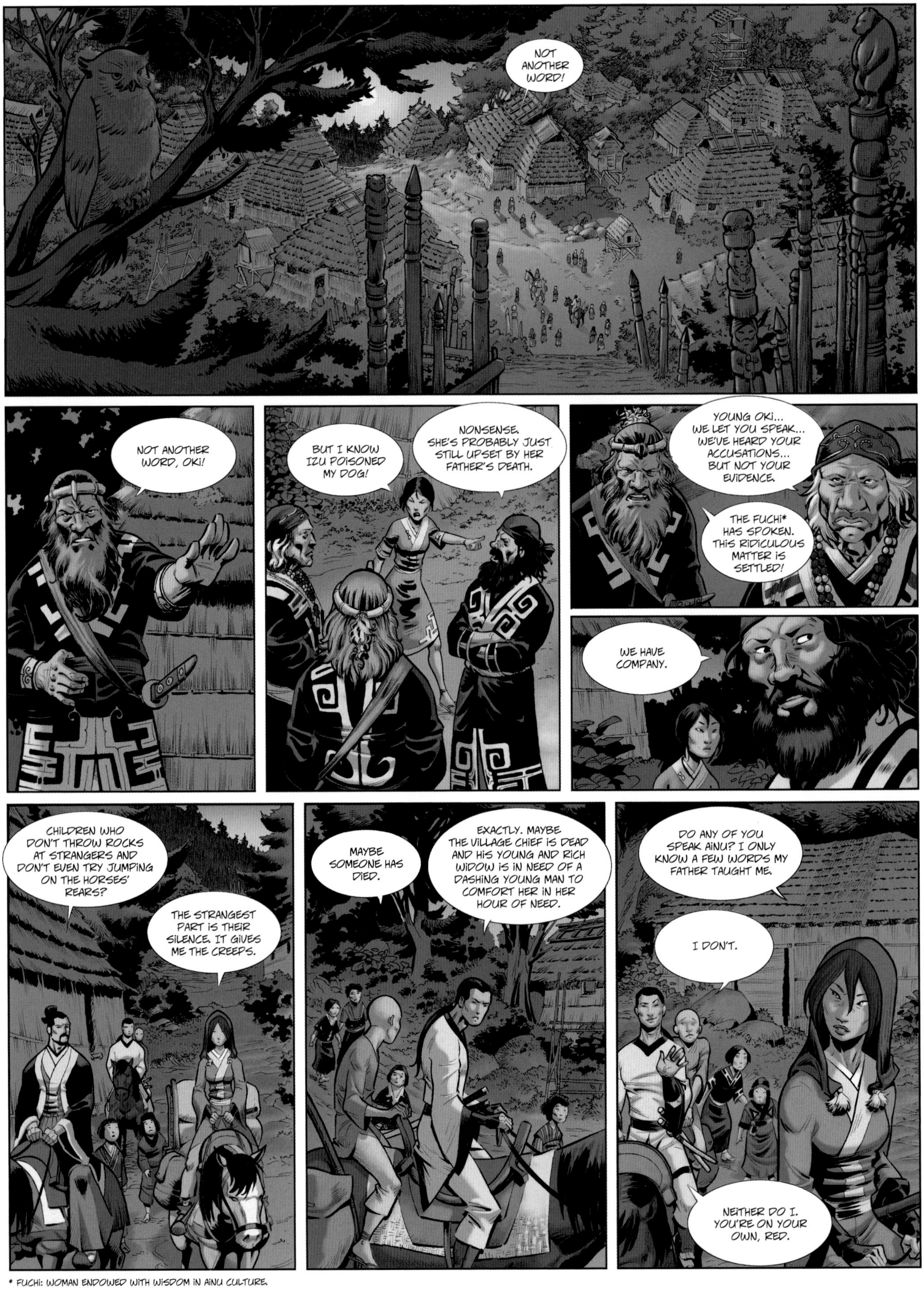
NOT ANOTHER WORD!
NOT ANOTHER WORD, OKI!
BUT I KNOW IZU POISONED MY DOG!
NONSENSE. SHE'S PROBABLY JUST STILL UPSET BY HER FATHER'S DEATH.
YOUNG OKI... WE LET YOU SPEAK... WE'VE HEARD YOUR ACCUSATIONS... BUT NOT YOUR EVIDENCE.
THE FUCHI* HAS SPOKEN. THIS RIDICULOUS MATTER IS SETTLED!
WE HAVE COMPANY.
CHILDREN WHO DON'T THROW ROCKS AT STRANGERS AND DON'T EVEN TRY JUMPING ON THE HORSES' REARS?
THE STRANGEST PART IS THEIR SILENCE. IT GIVES ME THE CREEPS.
MAYBE SOMEONE HAS DIED.
EXACTLY. MAYBE THE VILLAGE CHIEF IS DEAD AND HIS YOUNG AND RICH WIDOW IS IN NEED OF A DASHING YOUNG MAN TO COMFORT HER IN HER HOUR OF NEED.
DO ANY OF YOU SPEAK AINU? I ONLY KNOW A FEW WORDS MY FATHER TAUGHT ME.
I DON'T.
NEITHER DO I. YOU'RE ON YOUR OWN, RED.

* FUCHI: WOMAN ENDOWED WITH WISDOM IN AINU CULTURE.

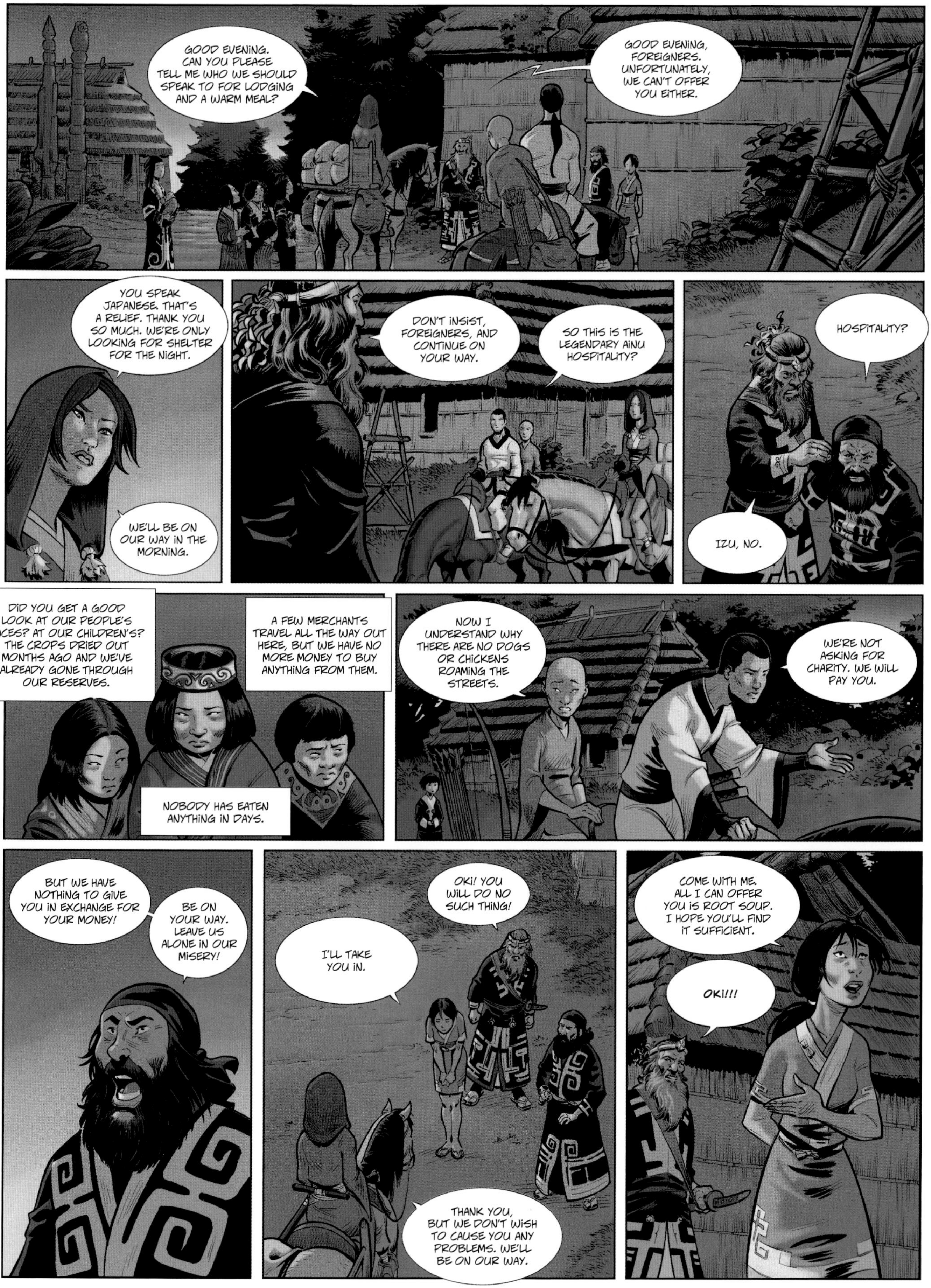
GOOD EVENING. CAN YOU PLEASE TELL ME WHO WE SHOULD SPEAK TO FOR LODGING AND A WARM MEAL?
GOOD EVENING, FOREIGNERS. UNFORTUNATELY, WE CAN'T OFFER YOU EITHER.
YOU SPEAK JAPANESE. THAT'S A RELIEF. THANK YOU SO MUCH. WE'RE ONLY LOOKING FOR SHELTER FOR THE NIGHT.
WE'LL BE ON OUR WAY IN THE MORNING.
DON'T INSIST, FOREIGNERS, AND CONTINUE ON YOUR WAY.
SO THIS IS THE LEGENDARY AINU HOSPITALITY?
HOSPITALITY?
IZU, NO.
DID YOU GET A GOOD LOOK AT OUR PEOPLE'S FACES? AT OUR CHILDREN'S? THE CROPS DRIED OUT MONTHS AGO AND WE'VE ALREADY GONE THROUGH OUR RESERVES.
A FEW MERCHANTS TRAVEL ALL THE WAY OUT HERE, BUT WE HAVE NO MORE MONEY TO BUY ANYTHING FROM THEM.
NOBODY HAS EATEN ANYTHING IN DAYS.
NOW I UNDERSTAND WHY THERE ARE NO DOGS OR CHICKENS ROAMING THE STREETS.
WE'RE NOT ASKING FOR CHARITY. WE WILL PAY YOU.
BUT WE HAVE NOTHING TO GIVE YOU IN EXCHANGE FOR YOUR MONEY!
BE ON YOUR WAY. LEAVE US ALONE IN OUR MISERY!
OKI! YOU WILL DO NO SUCH THING!
I'LL TAKE YOU IN.
THANK YOU, BUT WE DON'T WISH TO CAUSE YOU ANY PROBLEMS. WE'LL BE ON OUR WAY.
COME WITH ME. ALL I CAN OFFER YOU IS ROOT SOUP. I HOPE YOU'LL FIND IT SUFFICIENT.
OKI!!!

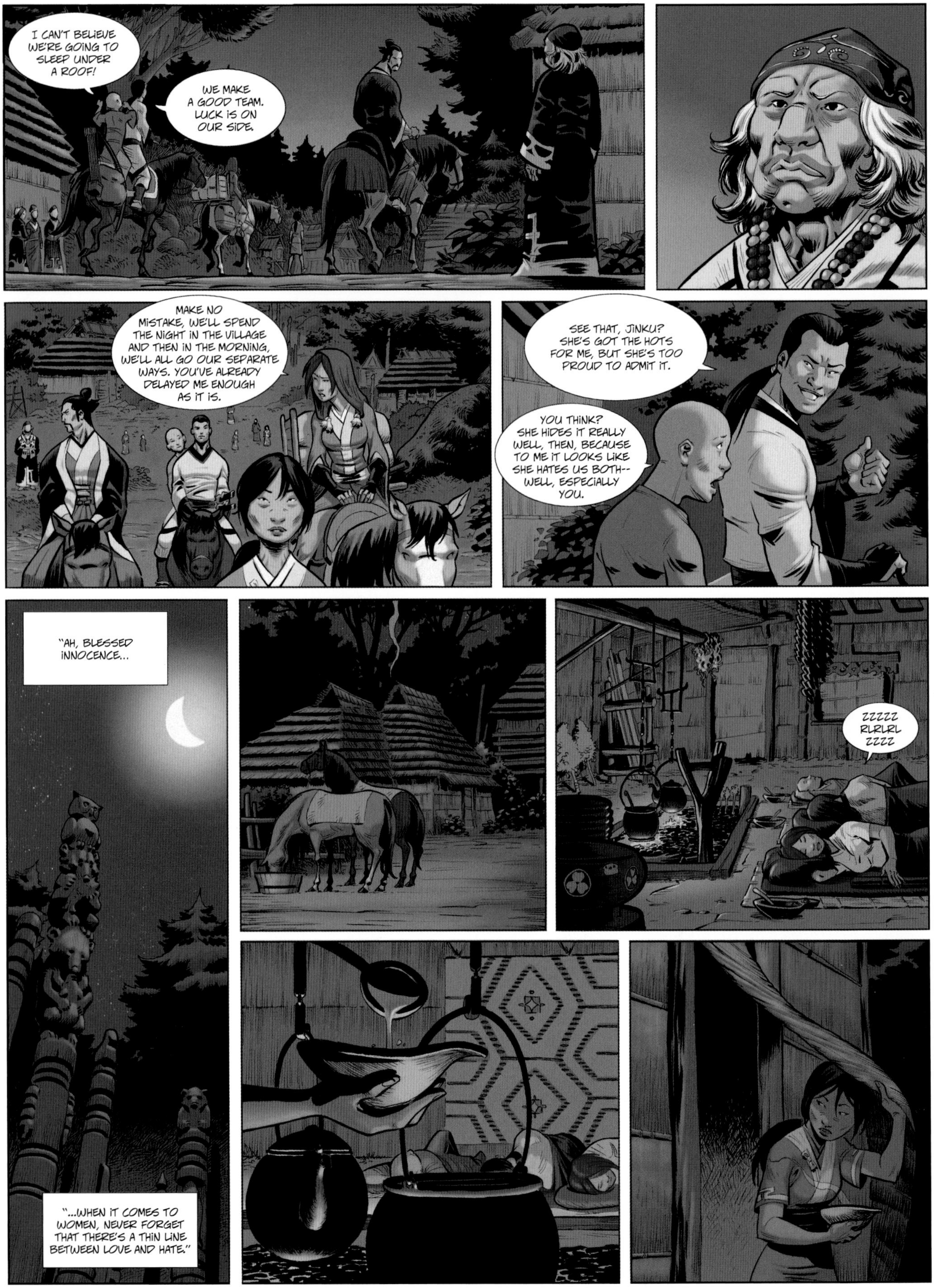
I CAN'T BELIEVE WE'RE GOING TO SLEEP UNDER A ROOF!
WE MAKE A GOOD TEAM. LUCK IS ON OUR SIDE.
MAKE NO MISTAKE, WE'LL SPEND THE NIGHT IN THE VILLAGE AND THEN IN THE MORNING, WE'LL ALL GO OUR SEPARATE WAYS. YOU'VE ALREADY DELAYED ME ENOUGH AS IT IS.
SEE THAT, JINKU? SHE'S GOT THE HOTS FOR ME, BUT SHE'S TOO PROUD TO ADMIT IT.
YOU THINK? SHE HIDES IT REALLY WELL, THEN, BECAUSE TO ME IT LOOKS LIKE SHE HATES US BOTH-- WELL, ESPECIALLY YOU.
"AH, BLESSED INNOCENCE...
"...WHEN IT COMES TO WOMEN, NEVER FORGET THAT THERE'S A THIN LINE BETWEEN LOVE AND HATE."
ZZZZZ RLRLRL ZZZZ

YOU'RE TAKING A BIG RISK THERE, BUDDY. IF UTARI CATCHES YOU SMOKING THAT CRAP, HE'LL BANISH YOU FROM THE VILLAGE.

I NEED SOMETHING TO CHASE THE HUNGER PAINS AWAY, EVEN IF IT'S JUST SMOKE.

HERE, COME ON, I KNOW YOU'RE DYING TO. CAREFUL THOUGH, IT'S STRONG.

COME ON, KU, DON'T GIVE ME THAT. I'M THE ONE WHO TAUGHT YOU HOW TO SMOKE, REMEMBER?

CRAC

WHO'S THERE?

CALM DOWN, GUYS. IT'S JUST ME, OKI.

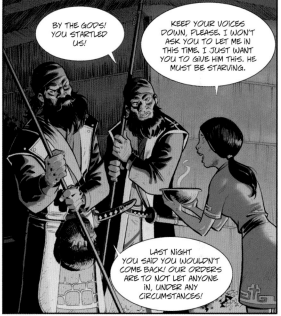

BY THE GODS! YOU STARTLED US!

KEEP YOUR VOICES DOWN, PLEASE. I WON'T ASK YOU TO LET ME IN THIS TIME. I JUST WANT YOU TO GIVE HIM THIS. HE MUST BE STARVING.

LAST NIGHT YOU SAID YOU WOULDN'T COME BACK! OUR ORDERS ARE TO NOT LET ANYONE IN, UNDER ANY CIRCUMSTANCES!

DO YOU TAKE US FOR IDIOTS? YOU TRYING TO GET US IN TROUBLE, IS THAT IT?

YOU KNOW WHAT, WE'RE GOING TO WAKE UP UTARI RIGHT THIS MINUTE, AND YOU CAN EXPLAIN YOURSELF TO HIM!

NO, PLEASE DON'T! I'LL GO HOME. DON'T TELL HIM!

TOO LATE!

KROK

WISH GRANTED.

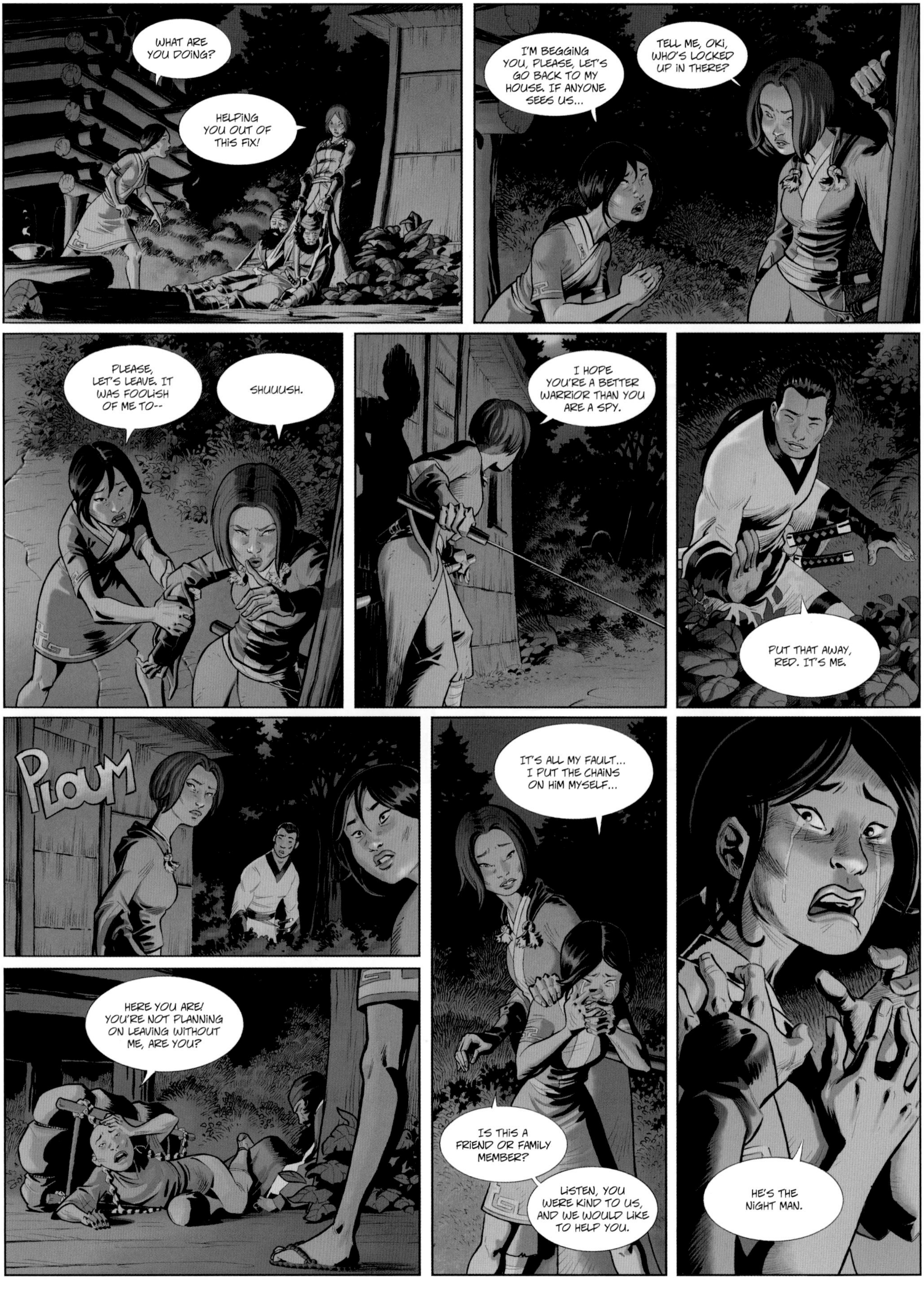
WHAT ARE YOU DOING?
HELPING YOU OUT OF THIS FIX!
I'M BEGGING YOU, PLEASE, LET'S GO BACK TO MY HOUSE. IF ANYONE SEES US...
TELL ME, OKI, WHO'S LOCKED UP IN THERE?
PLEASE, LET'S LEAVE. IT WAS FOOLISH OF ME TO--
SHUUUSH.
I HOPE YOU'RE A BETTER WARRIOR THAN YOU ARE A SPY.
PUT THAT AWAY, RED. IT'S ME.
PLOUM
HERE YOU ARE! YOU'RE NOT PLANNING ON LEAVING WITHOUT ME, ARE YOU?
IT'S ALL MY FAULT... I PUT THE CHAINS ON HIM MYSELF...
IS THIS A FRIEND OR FAMILY MEMBER?
LISTEN, YOU WERE KIND TO US, AND WE WOULD LIKE TO HELP YOU.
HE'S THE NIGHT MAN.

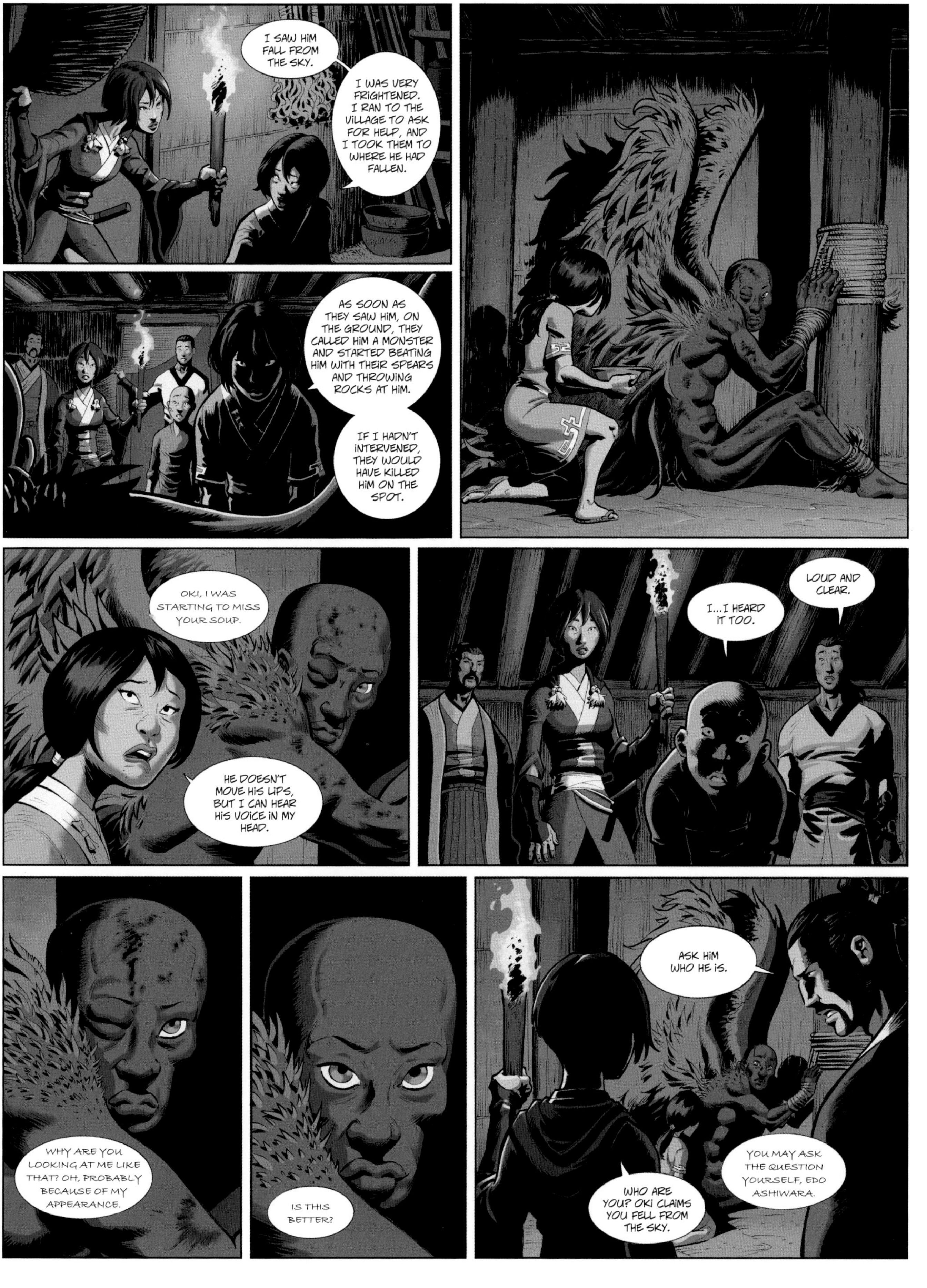

I SAW HIM FALL FROM THE SKY.
I WAS VERY FRIGHTENED. I RAN TO THE VILLAGE TO ASK FOR HELP, AND I TOOK THEM TO WHERE HE HAD FALLEN.
AS SOON AS THEY SAW HIM, ON THE GROUND, THEY CALLED HIM A MONSTER AND STARTED BEATING HIM WITH THEIR SPEARS AND THROWING ROCKS AT HIM.
IF I HADN'T INTERVENED, THEY WOULD HAVE KILLED HIM ON THE SPOT.
OKI, I WAS STARTING TO MISS YOUR SOUP.
HE DOESN'T MOVE HIS LIPS, BUT I CAN HEAR HIS VOICE IN MY HEAD.
I...I HEARD IT TOO.
LOUD AND CLEAR.
WHY ARE YOU LOOKING AT ME LIKE THAT? OH, PROBABLY BECAUSE OF MY APPEARANCE.
IS THIS BETTER?
ASK HIM WHO HE IS.
WHO ARE YOU? OKI CLAIMS YOU FELL FROM THE SKY.
YOU MAY ASK THE QUESTION YOURSELF, EDO ASHIWARA.

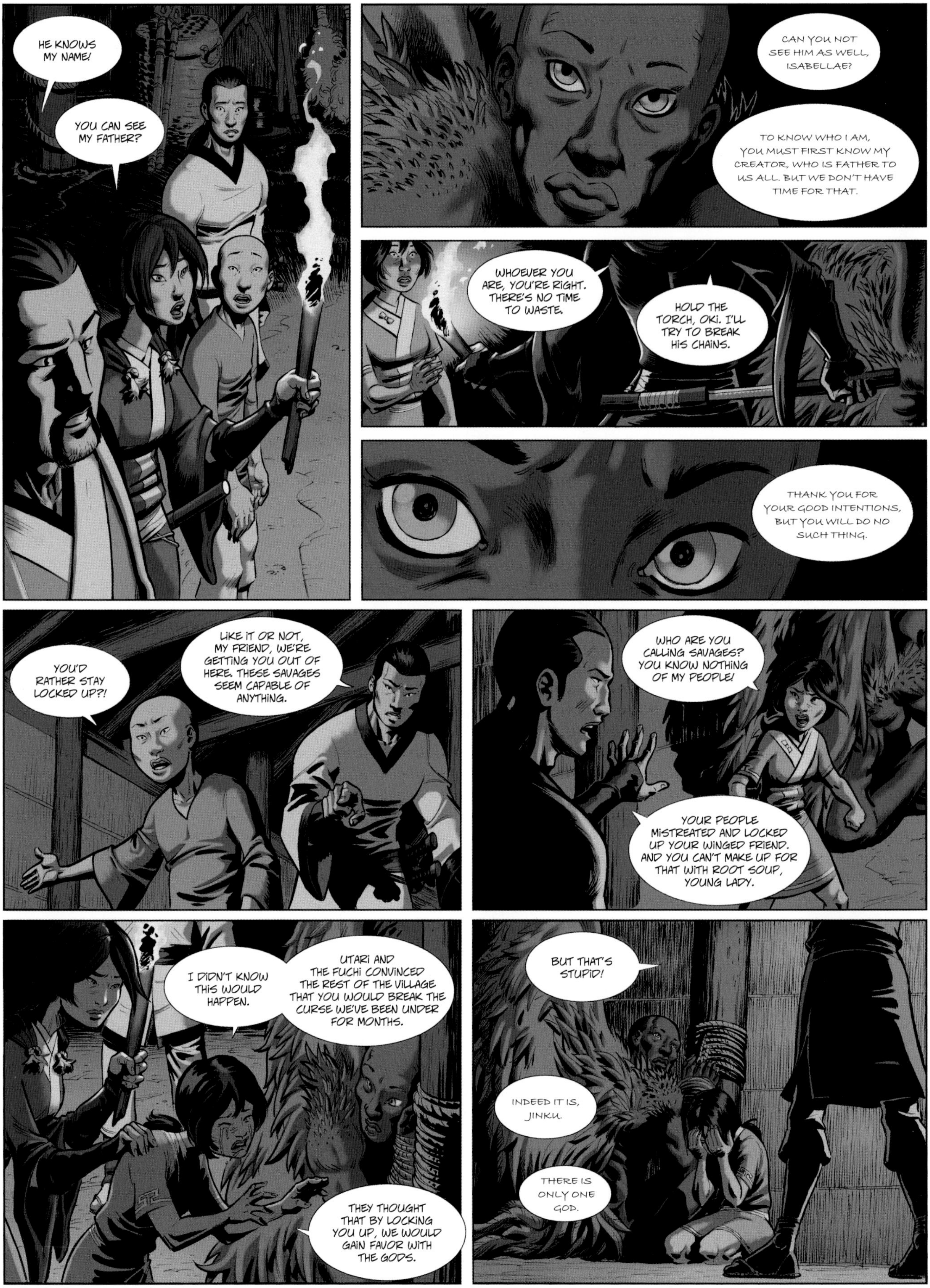
HE KNOWS MY NAME!
YOU CAN SEE MY FATHER?
CAN YOU NOT SEE HIM AS WELL, ISABELLAE?
TO KNOW WHO I AM, YOU MUST FIRST KNOW MY CREATOR, WHO IS FATHER TO US ALL. BUT WE DON'T HAVE TIME FOR THAT.
WHOEVER YOU ARE, YOU'RE RIGHT. THERE'S NO TIME TO WASTE.
HOLD THE TORCH, OKI. I'LL TRY TO BREAK HIS CHAINS.
THANK YOU FOR YOUR GOOD INTENTIONS, BUT YOU WILL DO NO SUCH THING.
YOU'D RATHER STAY LOCKED UP?!
LIKE IT OR NOT, MY FRIEND, WE'RE GETTING YOU OUT OF HERE. THESE SAVAGES SEEM CAPABLE OF ANYTHING.
WHO ARE YOU CALLING SAVAGES? YOU KNOW NOTHING OF MY PEOPLE!
YOUR PEOPLE MISTREATED AND LOCKED UP YOUR WINGED FRIEND. AND YOU CAN'T MAKE UP FOR THAT WITH ROOT SOUP, YOUNG LADY.
I DIDN'T KNOW THIS WOULD HAPPEN.
UTARI AND THE FUCHI CONVINCED THE REST OF THE VILLAGE THAT YOU WOULD BREAK THE CURSE WE'VE BEEN UNDER FOR MONTHS.
THEY THOUGHT THAT BY LOCKING YOU UP, WE WOULD GAIN FAVOR WITH THE GODS.
BUT THAT'S STUPID!
INDEED IT IS, JINKU.
THERE IS ONLY ONE GOD.

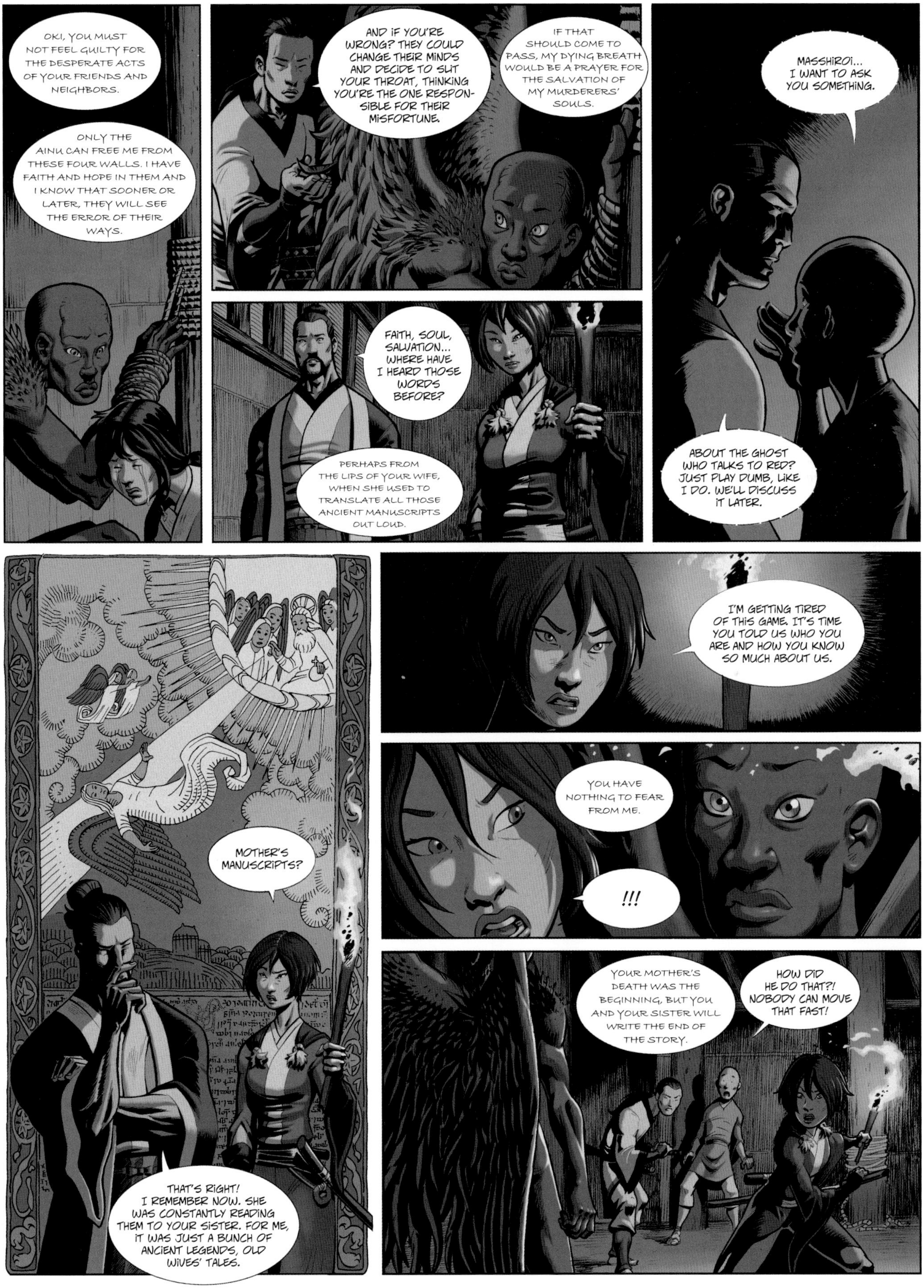
OKI, YOU MUST NOT FEEL GUILTY FOR THE DESPERATE ACTS OF YOUR FRIENDS AND NEIGHBORS.
ONLY THE AINU CAN FREE ME FROM THESE FOUR WALLS. I HAVE FAITH AND HOPE IN THEM AND I KNOW THAT SOONER OR LATER, THEY WILL SEE THE ERROR OF THEIR WAYS.
AND IF YOU'RE WRONG? THEY COULD CHANGE THEIR MINDS AND DECIDE TO SLIT YOUR THROAT, THINKING YOU'RE THE ONE RESPONSIBLE FOR THEIR MISFORTUNE.
IF THAT SHOULD COME TO PASS, MY DYING BREATH WOULD BE A PRAYER FOR THE SALVATION OF MY MURDERERS' SOULS.
FAITH, SOUL, SALVATION... WHERE HAVE I HEARD THOSE WORDS BEFORE?
PERHAPS FROM THE LIPS OF YOUR WIFE, WHEN SHE USED TO TRANSLATE ALL THOSE ANCIENT MANUSCRIPTS OUT LOUD.
MASSHIROI... I WANT TO ASK YOU SOMETHING.
ABOUT THE GHOST WHO TALKS TO RED? JUST PLAY DUMB, LIKE I DO. WE'LL DISCUSS IT LATER.
MOTHER'S MANUSCRIPTS?
THAT'S RIGHT! I REMEMBER NOW. SHE WAS CONSTANTLY READING THEM TO YOUR SISTER. FOR ME, IT WAS JUST A BUNCH OF ANCIENT LEGENDS, OLD WIVES' TALES.
I'M GETTING TIRED OF THIS GAME. IT'S TIME YOU TOLD US WHO YOU ARE AND HOW YOU KNOW SO MUCH ABOUT US.
YOU HAVE NOTHING TO FEAR FROM ME.
!!!
YOUR MOTHER'S DEATH WAS THE BEGINNING, BUT YOU AND YOUR SISTER WILL WRITE THE END OF THE STORY.
HOW DID HE DO THAT?! NOBODY CAN MOVE THAT FAST!

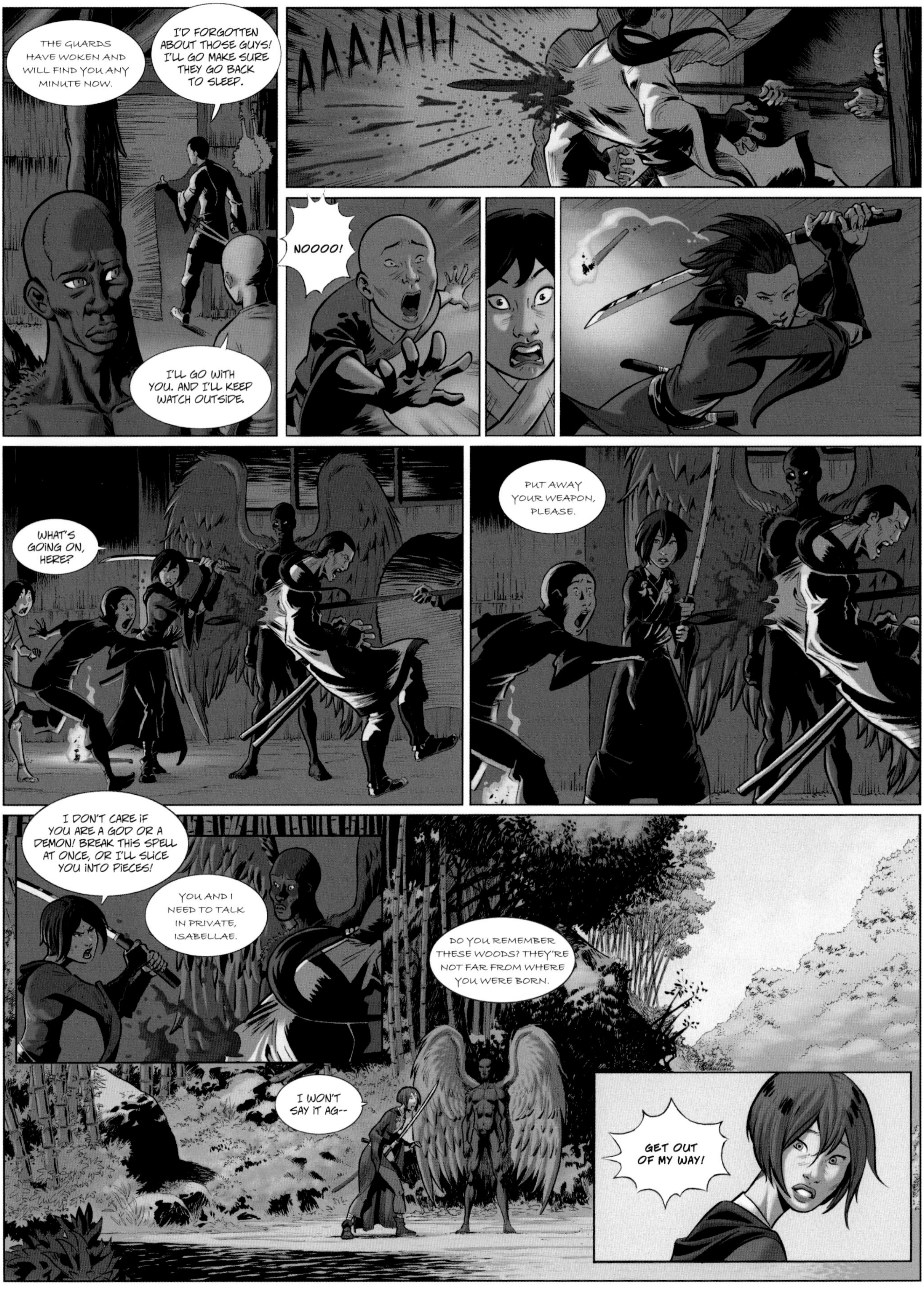
THE GUARDS HAVE WOKEN AND WILL FIND YOU ANY MINUTE NOW.
I'D FORGOTTEN ABOUT THOSE GUYS! I'LL GO MAKE SURE THEY GO BACK TO SLEEP.
I'LL GO WITH YOU. AND I'LL KEEP WATCH OUTSIDE.
AAAAHH
NOOOO!
WHAT'S GOING ON, HERE?
PUT AWAY YOUR WEAPON, PLEASE.
I DON'T CARE IF YOU ARE A GOD OR A DEMON! BREAK THIS SPELL AT ONCE, OR I'LL SLICE YOU INTO PIECES!
YOU AND I NEED TO TALK IN PRIVATE, ISABELLAE.
DO YOU REMEMBER THESE WOODS? THEY'RE NOT FAR FROM WHERE YOU WERE BORN.
I WON'T SAY IT AG--
GET OUT OF MY WAY!

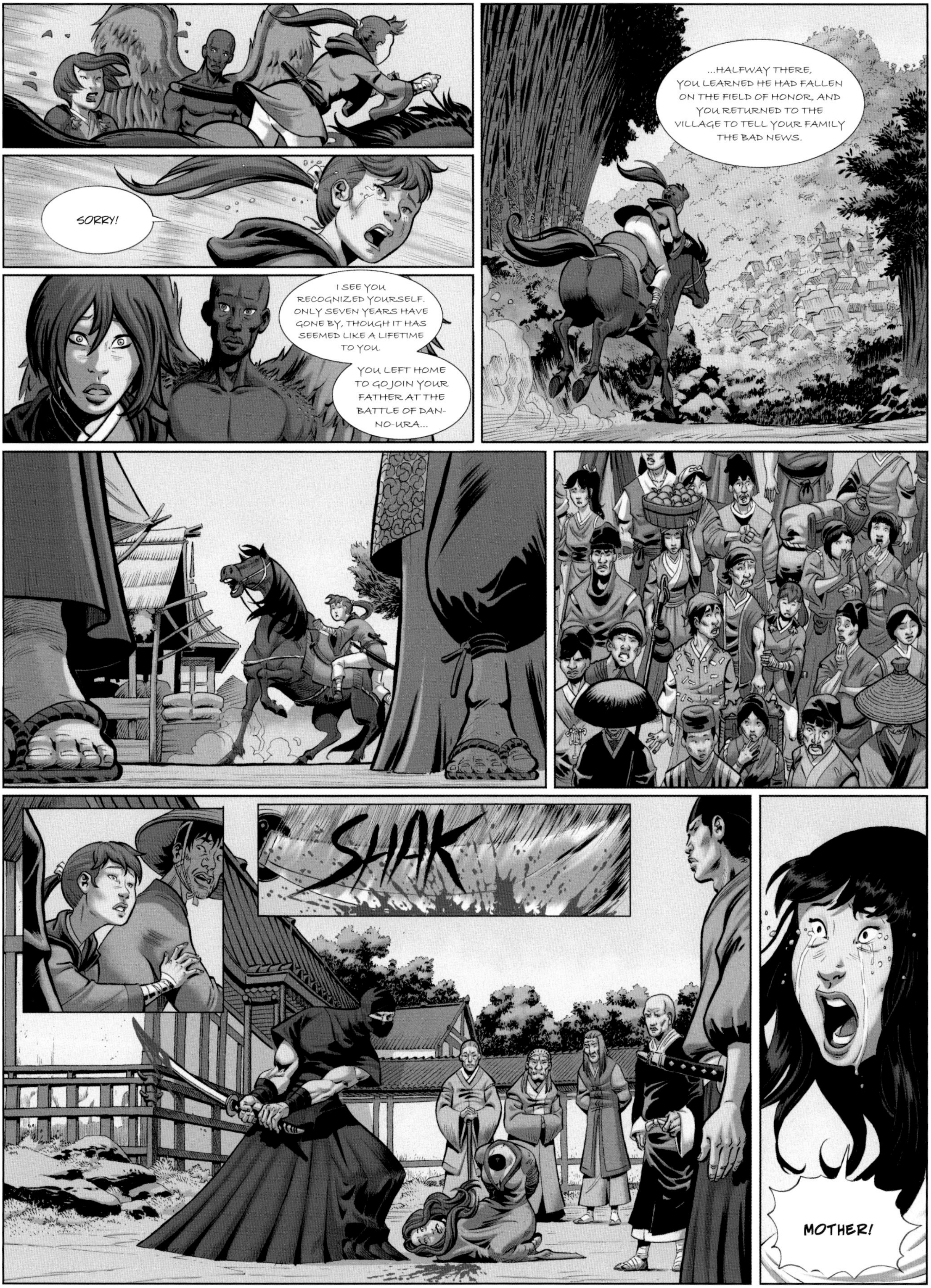
SORRY!
I SEE YOU RECOGNIZED YOURSELF. ONLY SEVEN YEARS HAVE GONE BY, THOUGH IT HAS SEEMED LIKE A LIFETIME TO YOU.
YOU LEFT HOME TO GO JOIN YOUR FATHER AT THE BATTLE OF DAN-NO-URA...
...HALFWAY THERE, YOU LEARNED HE HAD FALLEN ON THE FIELD OF HONOR, AND YOU RETURNED TO THE VILLAGE TO TELL YOUR FAMILY THE BAD NEWS.
SHAK
MOTHER!

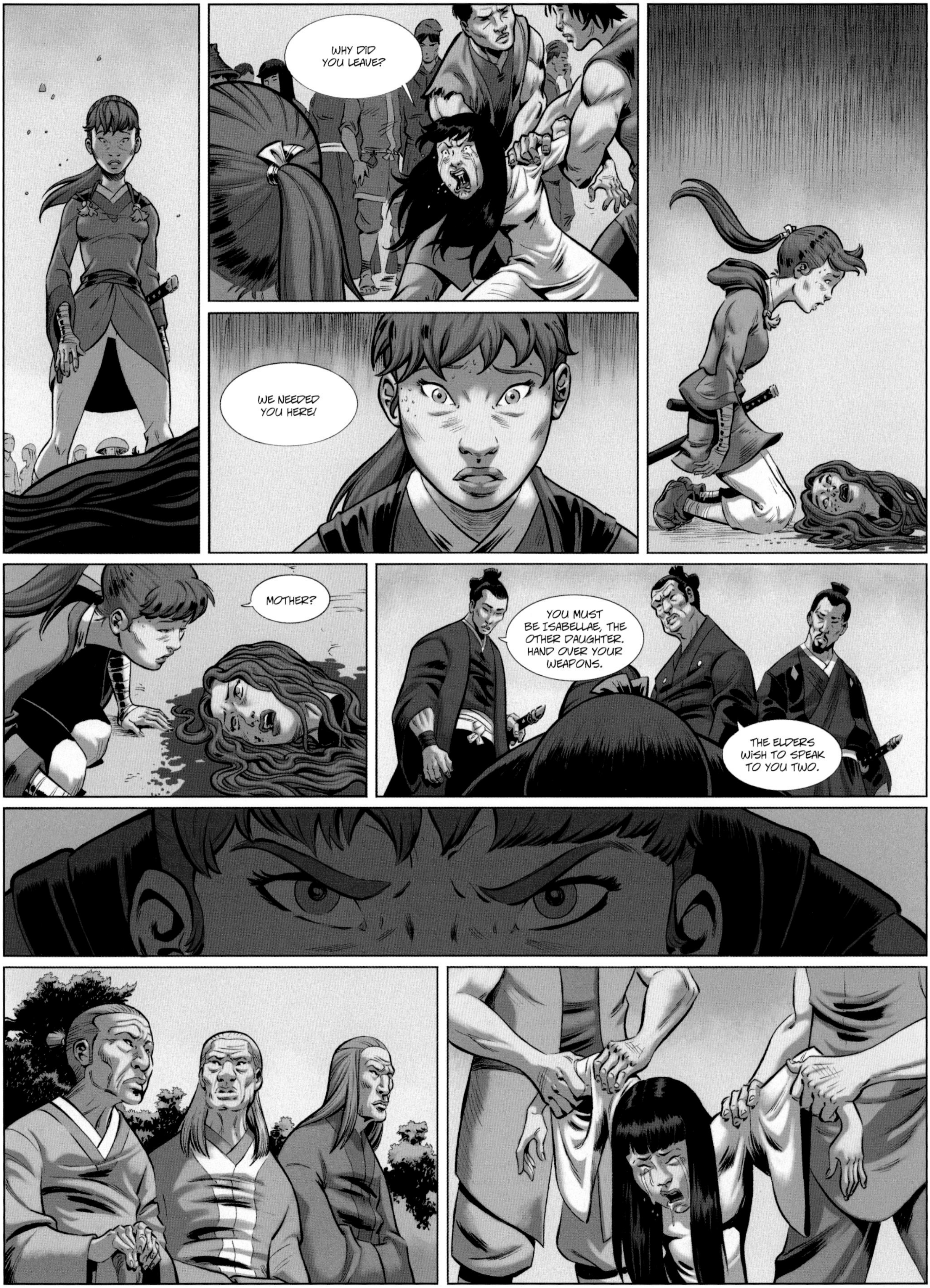
WHY DID YOU LEAVE?
WE NEEDED YOU HERE!
MOTHER?
YOU MUST BE ISABELLAE, THE OTHER DAUGHTER. HAND OVER YOUR WEAPONS.
THE ELDERS WISH TO SPEAK TO YOU TWO.

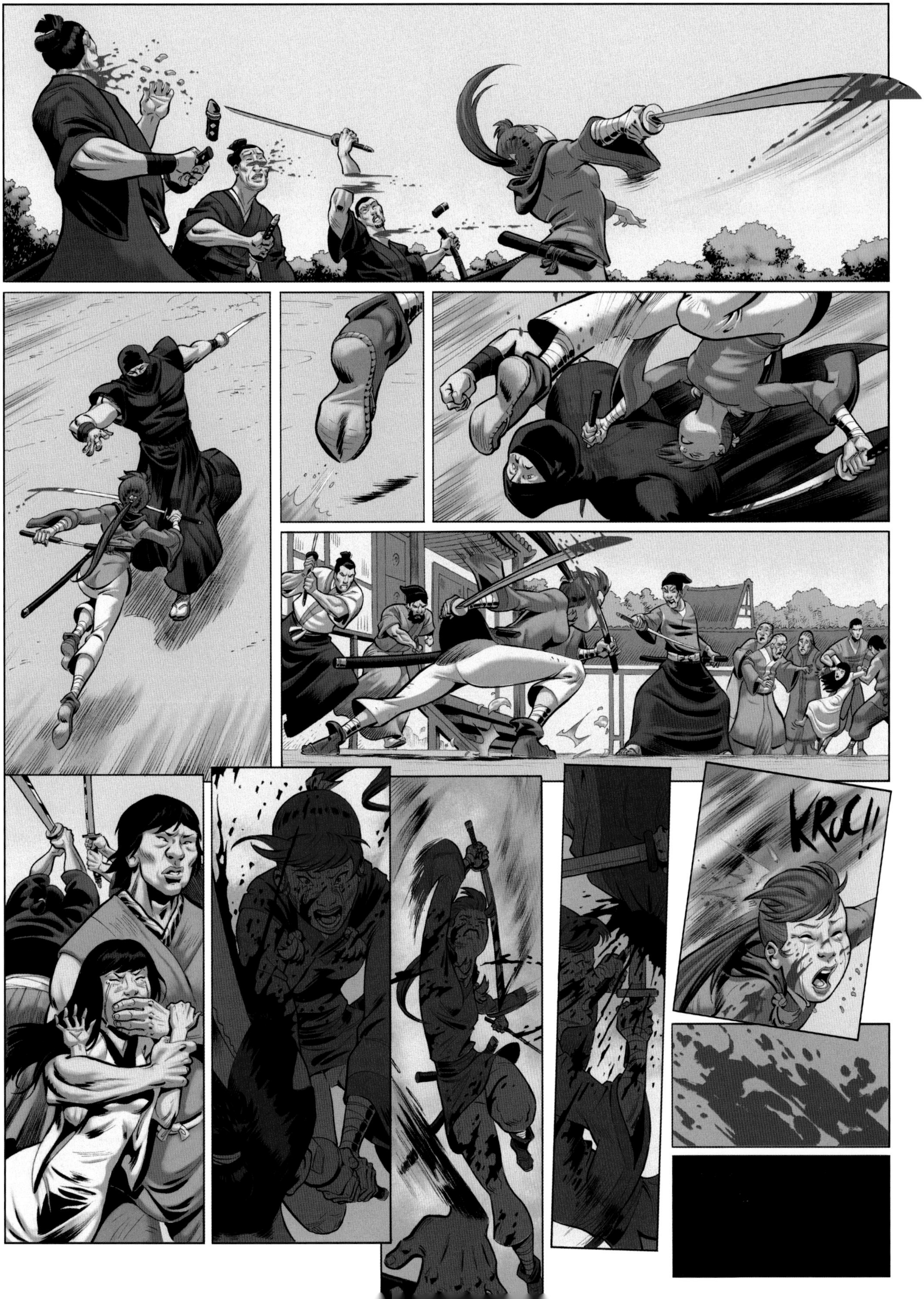
KROC!!

ISABELLAE...

YOU KILLED THIRTEEN PEOPLE THAT DAY, MOST OF THEM NEIGHBORS WHO HAD WATCHED YOU GROW UP. THEY SENTENCED YOU TO DEATH FOR THAT...

...AND AGREED YOU SHOULD DIE THE SAME WAY YOUR MOTHER DID.

THEY BANISHED YOUR SISTER FROM THE VILLAGE AND LOCKED YOU UP FOR A FEW DAYS, AS THEY WAITED FOR A NEW EXECUTIONER TO ARRIVE.

LEAVE ME ALONE!

I COULD HEAR SIUKO SCREAMING... SHE LEFT DISOWNING ME...BLAMING ME FOR MY MOTHER'S DEATH.

THE NIGHT BEFORE THE EXECUTIONER'S ARRIVAL, YOU MANAGED TO LOOSEN YOUR CHAINS AND FLEE THE VILLAGE ON HORSEBACK.

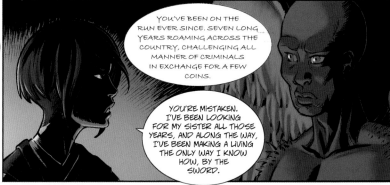

YOU'VE BEEN ON THE RUN EVER SINCE. SEVEN LONG YEARS ROAMING ACROSS THE COUNTRY, CHALLENGING ALL MANNER OF CRIMINALS IN EXCHANGE FOR A FEW COINS.

YOU'RE MISTAKEN. I'VE BEEN LOOKING FOR MY SISTER ALL THOSE YEARS, AND ALONG THE WAY, I'VE BEEN MAKING A LIVING THE ONLY WAY I KNOW HOW, BY THE SWORD.

THE ONLY THING YOU'VE LONGED FOR THIS WHOLE TIME IS FOR ONE OF THOSE BANDITS TO PUT AN END TO YOUR LIFE.

FOR SOMEONE TO PUT AN END TO ALL THAT REGRET ONCE AND FOR ALL. A SWORD THAT MIGHT SLAY YOUR NIGHTMARES IN ONE FELL SWOOP.

UNFORTUNATELY FOR YOU YOUR SKILLS AS A WARRIOR ARE FAR GREATER THAN YOUR DESIRE TO DIE.

THE MORE YOU TALK, THE LESS I UNDERSTAND WHAT YOU WANT FROM ME.

I AM THE SWORD YOU SEEK.

AND I CAN GIVE YOU THAT ABSOLUTE PEACE YOU LONG FOR.

YOU NEED ONLY TO TAKE MY HAND.

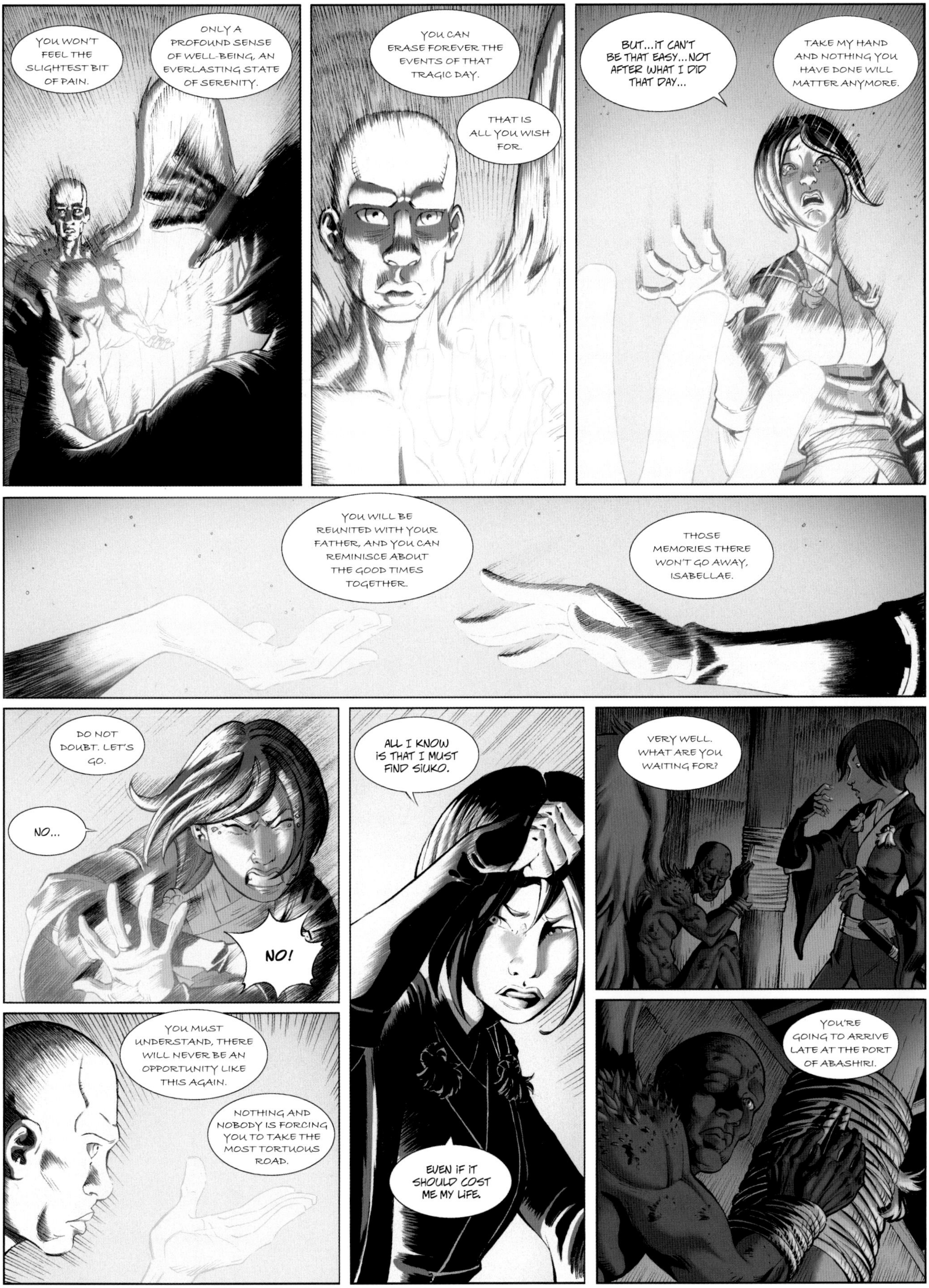
YOU WON'T FEEL THE SLIGHTEST BIT OF PAIN.
ONLY A PROFOUND SENSE OF WELL-BEING, AN EVERLASTING STATE OF SERENITY.
YOU CAN ERASE FOREVER THE EVENTS OF THAT TRAGIC DAY.
THAT IS ALL YOU WISH FOR.
BUT...IT CAN'T BE THAT EASY...NOT AFTER WHAT I DID THAT DAY...
TAKE MY HAND AND NOTHING YOU HAVE DONE WILL MATTER ANYMORE.
YOU WILL BE REUNITED WITH YOUR FATHER, AND YOU CAN REMINISCE ABOUT THE GOOD TIMES TOGETHER.
THOSE MEMORIES THERE WON'T GO AWAY, ISABELLAE.
DO NOT DOUBT. LET'S GO.
NO...
NO!
ALL I KNOW IS THAT I MUST FIND SIUKO.
VERY WELL. WHAT ARE YOU WAITING FOR?
YOU MUST UNDERSTAND, THERE WILL NEVER BE AN OPPORTUNITY LIKE THIS AGAIN.
NOTHING AND NOBODY IS FORCING YOU TO TAKE THE MOST TORTUOUS ROAD.
EVEN IF IT SHOULD COST ME MY LIFE.
YOU'RE GOING TO ARRIVE LATE AT THE PORT OF ABASHIRI.

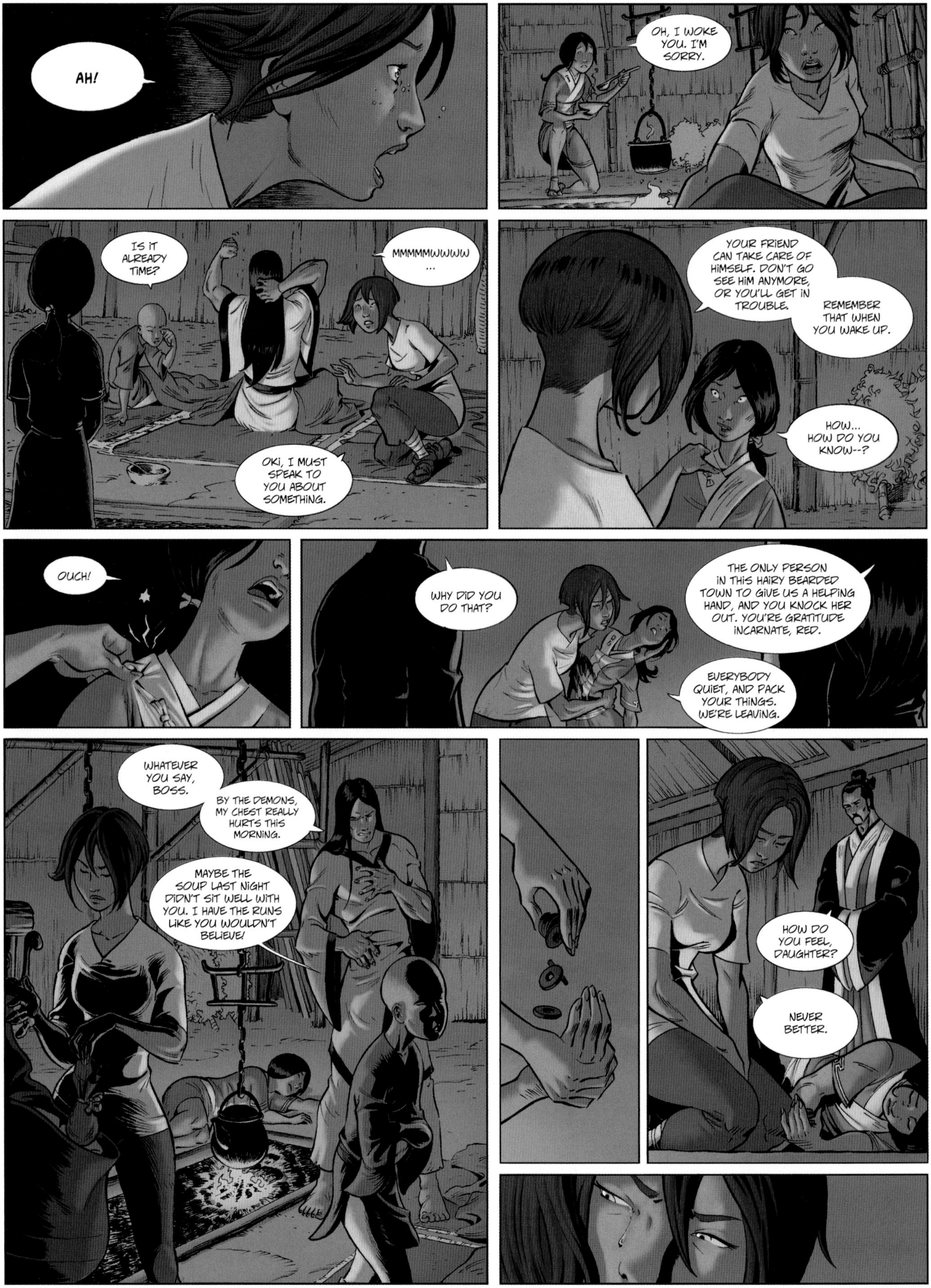
AH!
OH, I WOKE YOU. I'M SORRY.
IS IT ALREADY TIME?
MMMMMWWWW ...
OKI, I MUST SPEAK TO YOU ABOUT SOMETHING.
YOUR FRIEND CAN TAKE CARE OF HIMSELF. DON'T GO SEE HIM ANYMORE, OR YOU'LL GET IN TROUBLE.
REMEMBER THAT WHEN YOU WAKE UP.
HOW... HOW DO YOU KNOW--?
OUCH!
WHY DID YOU DO THAT?
THE ONLY PERSON IN THIS HAIRY BEARDED TOWN TO GIVE US A HELPING HAND, AND YOU KNOCK HER OUT. YOU'RE GRATITUDE INCARNATE, RED.
EVERYBODY QUIET, AND PACK YOUR THINGS. WE'RE LEAVING.
WHATEVER YOU SAY, BOSS.
BY THE DEMONS, MY CHEST REALLY HURTS THIS MORNING.
MAYBE THE SOUP LAST NIGHT DIDN'T SIT WELL WITH YOU. I HAVE THE RUNS LIKE YOU WOULDN'T BELIEVE!
HOW DO YOU FEEL, DAUGHTER?
NEVER BETTER.

I'M BEGGING YOU, I HAVE AN URGENT NEED TO FILL MY BELLY AND SLEEP FOR A WHOLE DAY.

AFTER AN ENTIRE WEEK ON HORSEBACK AND NOT THE SLIGHTEST BIT OF REST, EVERY BONE IN MY BODY ACHES.

GREAT IDEA. GO LOOK FOR LODGING, I'LL MEET UP WITH YOU LATER.

NICE TRY, RED. BUT WE WOULDN'T MISS OUT ON YOUR HEART-WARMING FAMILY REUNION FOR ANYTHING IN THE WORLD.

I DO HOPE, THOUGH, THAT YOU REALIZE YOU'RE LOOKING FOR A NEEDLE IN A HAYSTACK.

YOU DON'T EVEN KNOW IF THEY'VE EVER SET FOOT HERE.

MAY I ASK WHERE YOU'RE GOING?

HELLO, MADAM. I BET YOU SEE A LOT OF PEOPLE GO BY IN A DAY, FROM BEHIND YOUR FRUIT STAND.

HMM...I SURE DO, YOUNG LADY! BUT HARDLY ANYBODY STOPS TO BUY...EITHER IN A RUSH OR NOT ENOUGH MONEY. AND YET I HAVE THE SWEETEST PEARS IN ALL OF ABASHIRI. CARE FOR A TASTE?

WE'RE LOOKING FOR A YOUNG GIRL TRAVELING WITH A GIANT. WE HAVE GOOD REASON TO BELIEVE THEY'VE BEEN THROUGH HERE.

HMM...KIDS, IF I'VE MADE IT THIS FAR IN LIFE, IT'S BECAUSE I AVOID TROUBLE. MY MOTTO IS LOOK, LISTEN, AND KEEP QUIET.

MAY I?

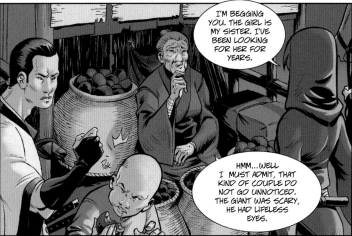

I'M BEGGING YOU. THE GIRL IS MY SISTER. I'VE BEEN LOOKING FOR HER FOR YEARS.

HMM...WELL I MUST ADMIT, THAT KIND OF COUPLE DO NOT GO UNNOTICED. THE GIANT WAS SCARY, HE HAD LIFELESS EYES.

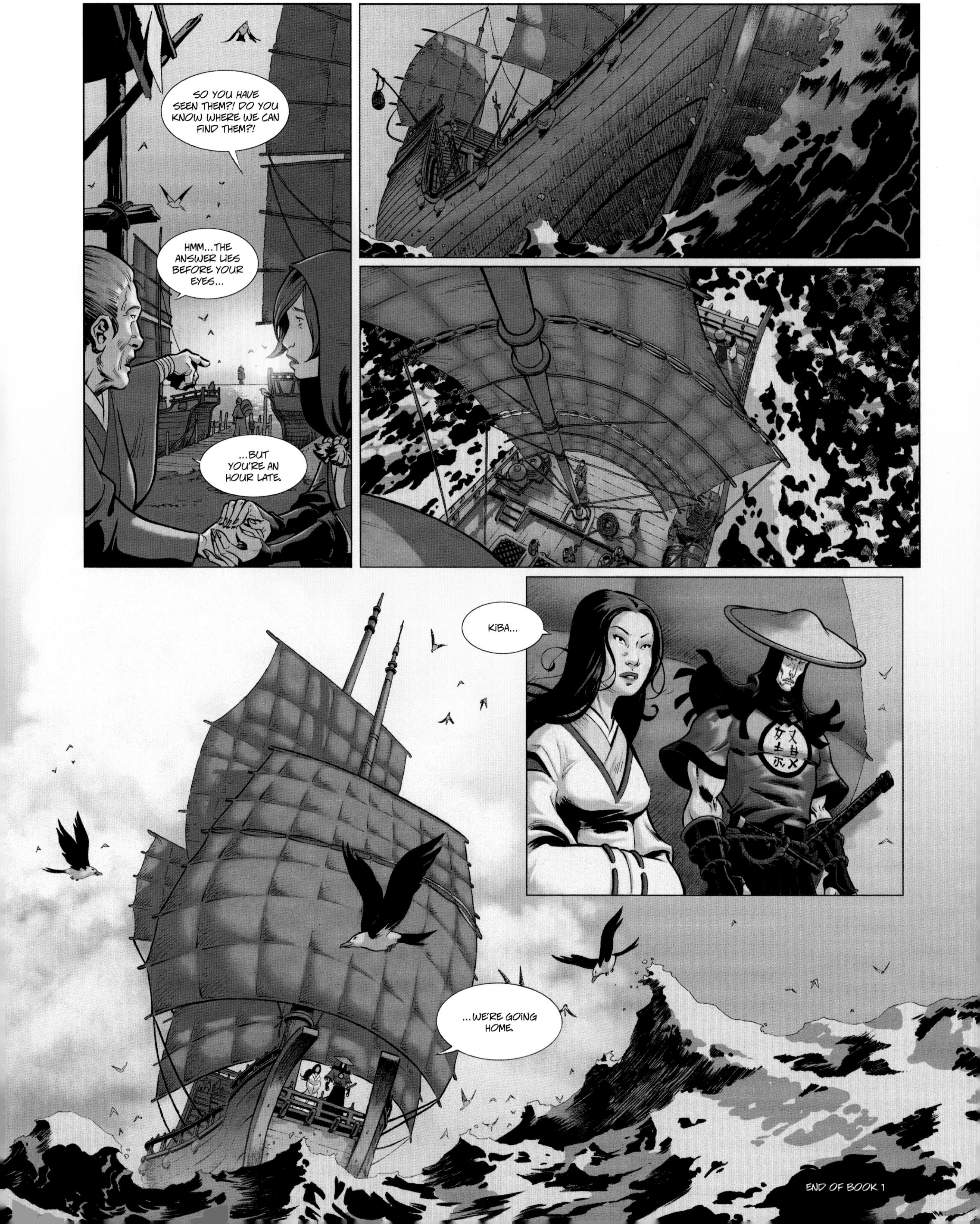
SO YOU HAVE SEEN THEM?! DO YOU KNOW WHERE WE CAN FIND THEM?!
HMM...THE ANSWER LIES BEFORE YOUR EYES...
...BUT YOU'RE AN HOUR LATE.
KIBA...
...WE'RE GOING HOME.
END OF BOOK 1

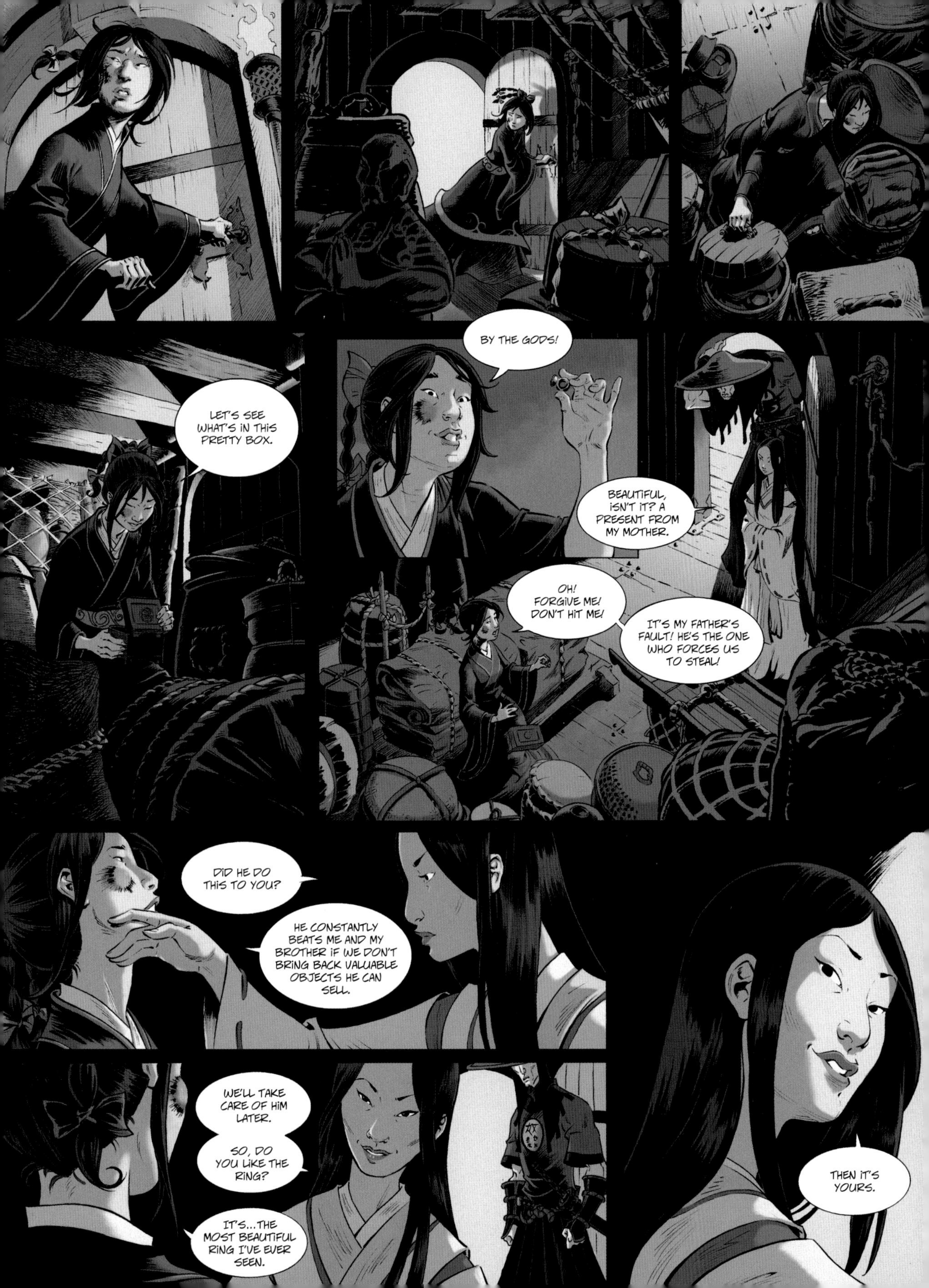
LET'S SEE WHAT'S IN THIS PRETTY BOX.
BY THE GODS!
BEAUTIFUL, ISN'T IT? A PRESENT FROM MY MOTHER.
OH! FORGIVE ME! DON'T HIT ME!
IT'S MY FATHER'S FAULT! HE'S THE ONE WHO FORCES US TO STEAL!
DID HE DO THIS TO YOU?
HE CONSTANTLY BEATS ME AND MY BROTHER IF WE DON'T BRING BACK VALUABLE OBJECTS HE CAN SELL.
WE'LL TAKE CARE OF HIM LATER.
SO, DO YOU LIKE THE RING?
IT'S...THE MOST BEAUTIFUL RING I'VE EVER SEEN.
THEN IT'S YOURS.

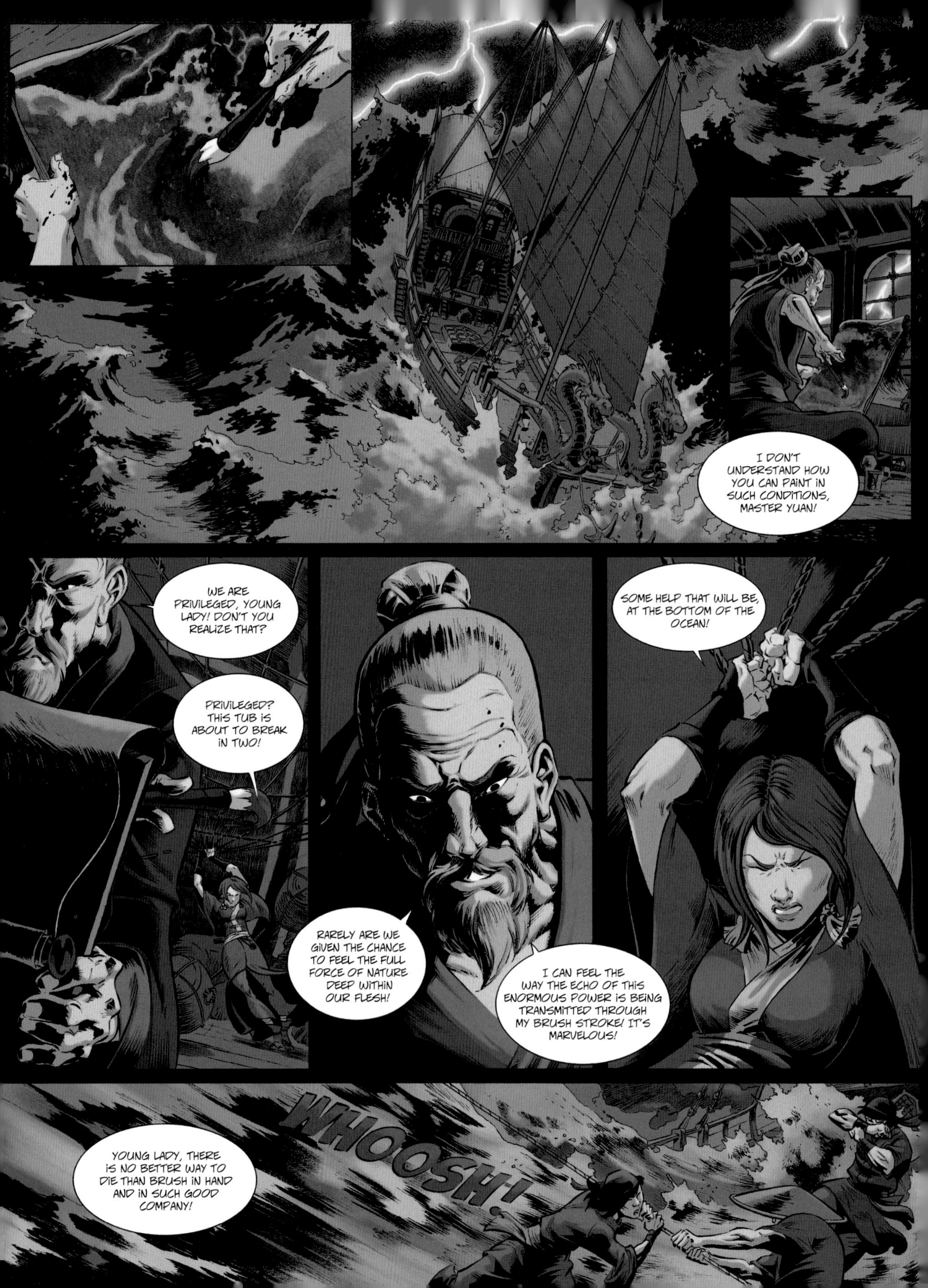
I DON'T UNDERSTAND HOW YOU CAN PAINT IN SUCH CONDITIONS, MASTER YUAN!
WE ARE PRIVILEGED, YOUNG LADY! DON'T YOU REALIZE THAT?
PRIVILEGED? THIS TUB IS ABOUT TO BREAK IN TWO!
RARELY ARE WE GIVEN THE CHANCE TO FEEL THE FULL FORCE OF NATURE DEEP WITHIN OUR FLESH!
I CAN FEEL THE WAY THE ECHO OF THIS ENORMOUS POWER IS BEING TRANSMITTED THROUGH MY BRUSH STROKE! IT'S MARVELOUS!
SOME HELP THAT WILL BE, AT THE BOTTOM OF THE OCEAN!
WHOOSH!
YOUNG LADY, THERE IS NO BETTER WAY TO DIE THAN BRUSH IN HAND AND IN SUCH GOOD COMPANY!

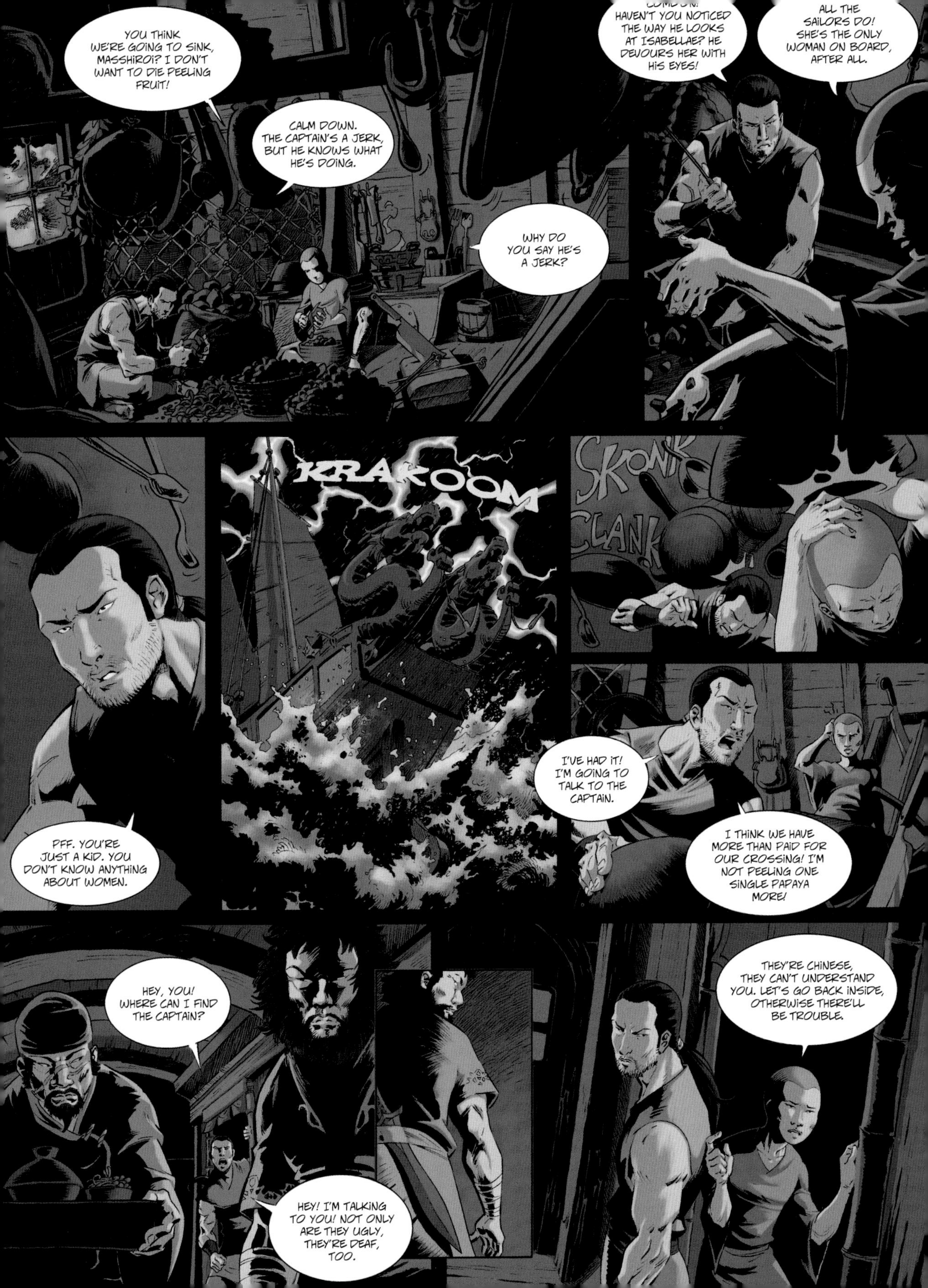

YOU THINK WE'RE GOING TO SINK, MASSHIROI? I DON'T WANT TO DIE PEELING FRUIT!
CALM DOWN. THE CAPTAIN'S A JERK, BUT HE KNOWS WHAT HE'S DOING.
WHY DO YOU SAY HE'S A JERK?
HAVEN'T YOU NOTICED THE WAY HE LOOKS AT ISABELLAE? HE DEVOURS HER WITH HIS EYES!
ALL THE SAILORS DO! SHE'S THE ONLY WOMAN ON BOARD, AFTER ALL.
PFF. YOU'RE JUST A KID. YOU DON'T KNOW ANYTHING ABOUT WOMEN.
KRAKOOM
SKONK
CLANK
I'VE HAD IT! I'M GOING TO TALK TO THE CAPTAIN.
I THINK WE HAVE MORE THAN PAID FOR OUR CROSSING! I'M NOT PEELING ONE SINGLE PAPAYA MORE!
HEY, YOU! WHERE CAN I FIND THE CAPTAIN?
HEY! I'M TALKING TO YOU! NOT ONLY ARE THEY UGLY, THEY'RE DEAF, TOO.
THEY'RE CHINESE, THEY CAN'T UNDERSTAND YOU. LET'S GO BACK INSIDE, OTHERWISE THERE'LL BE TROUBLE.

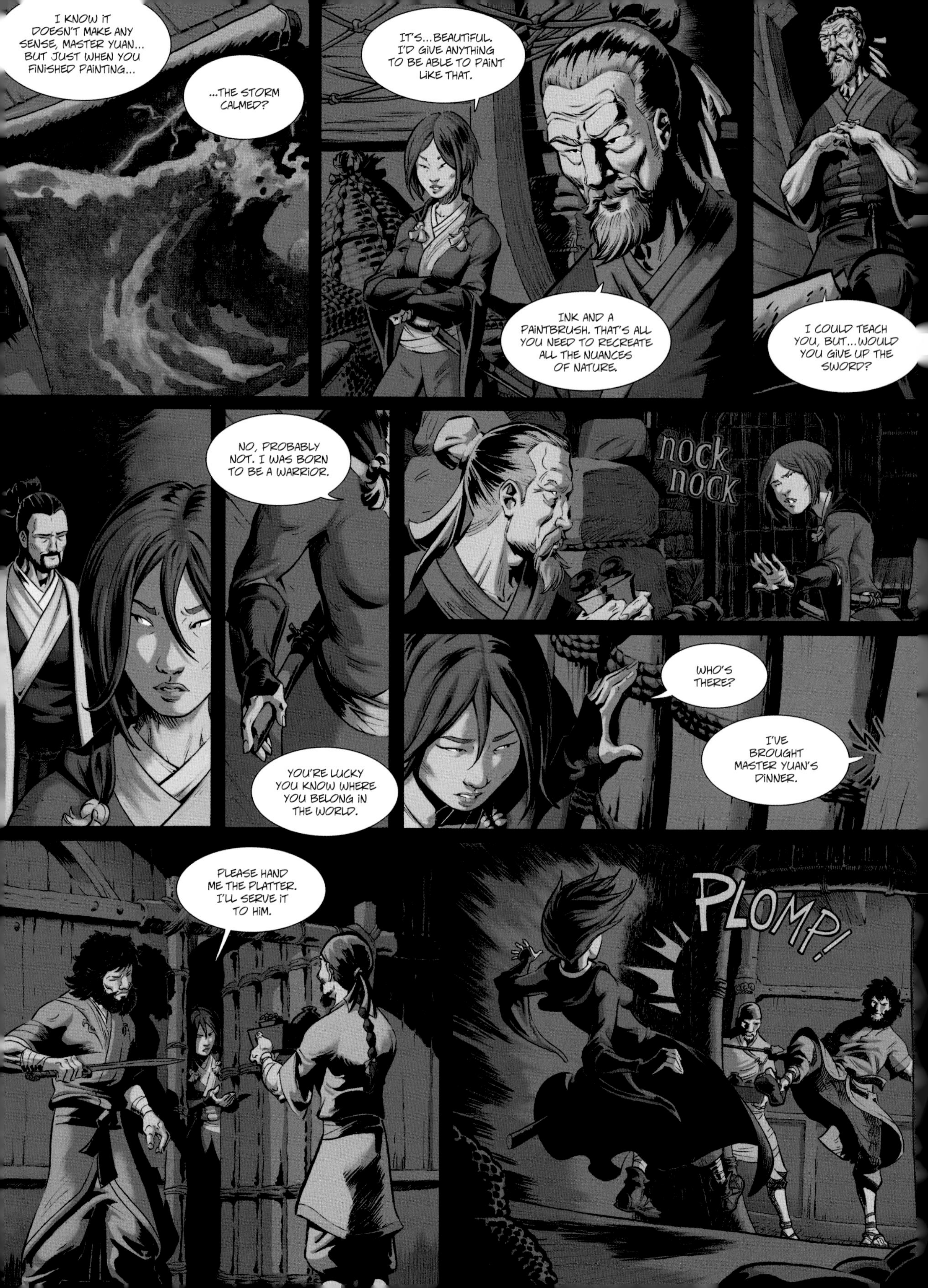
I KNOW IT DOESN'T MAKE ANY SENSE, MASTER YUAN... BUT JUST WHEN YOU FINISHED PAINTING...
...THE STORM CALMED?
IT'S...BEAUTIFUL. I'D GIVE ANYTHING TO BE ABLE TO PAINT LIKE THAT.
INK AND A PAINTBRUSH. THAT'S ALL YOU NEED TO RECREATE ALL THE NUANCES OF NATURE.
I COULD TEACH YOU, BUT...WOULD YOU GIVE UP THE SWORD?
NO, PROBABLY NOT. I WAS BORN TO BE A WARRIOR.
YOU'RE LUCKY YOU KNOW WHERE YOU BELONG IN THE WORLD.
nock nock
WHO'S THERE?
I'VE BROUGHT MASTER YUAN'S DINNER.
PLEASE HAND ME THE PLATTER. I'LL SERVE IT TO HIM.
PLOMP!

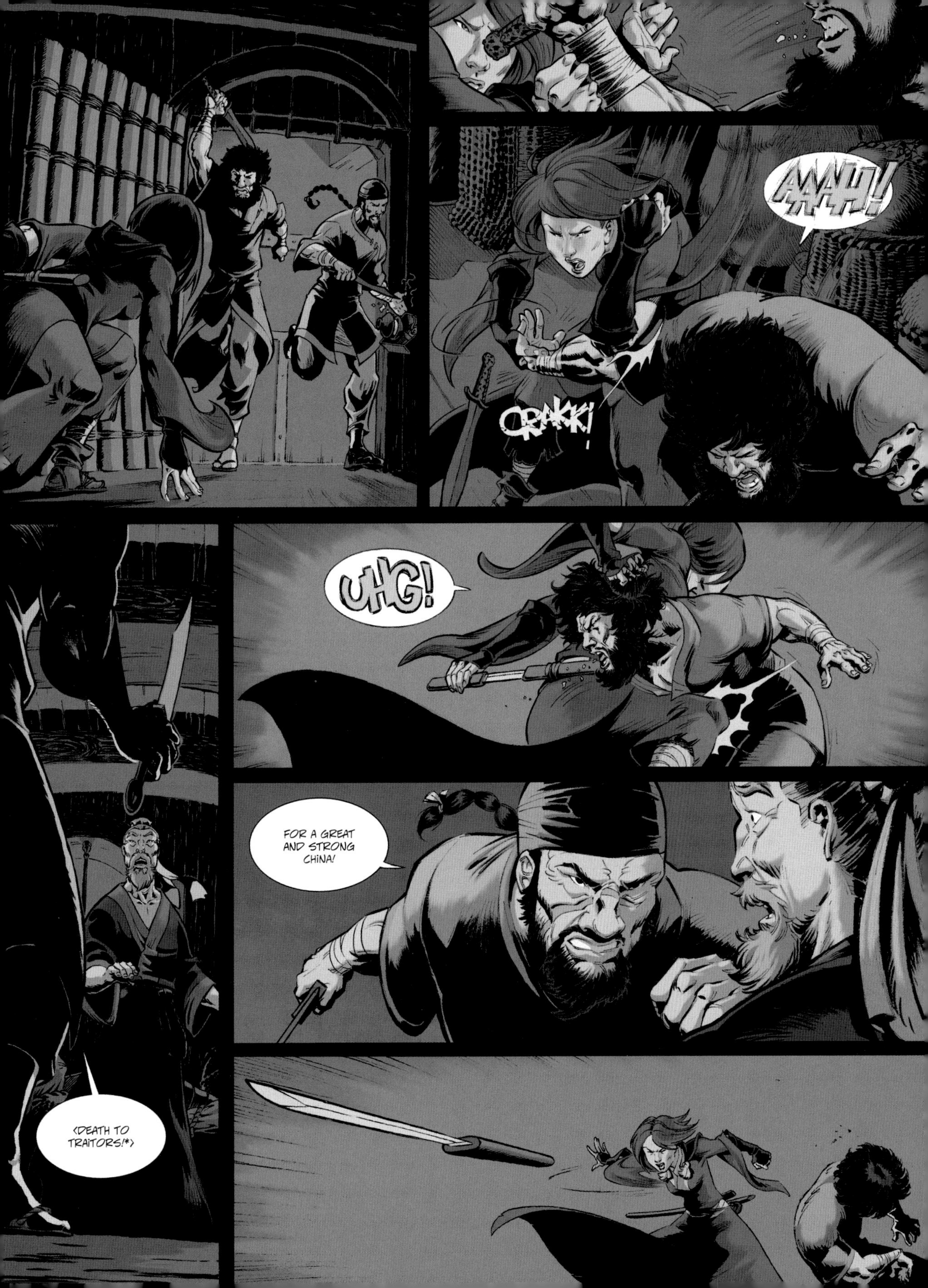
AAAH!
CRAKK!
UHG!
FOR A GREAT AND STRONG CHINA!
‹DEATH TO TRAITORS!*›

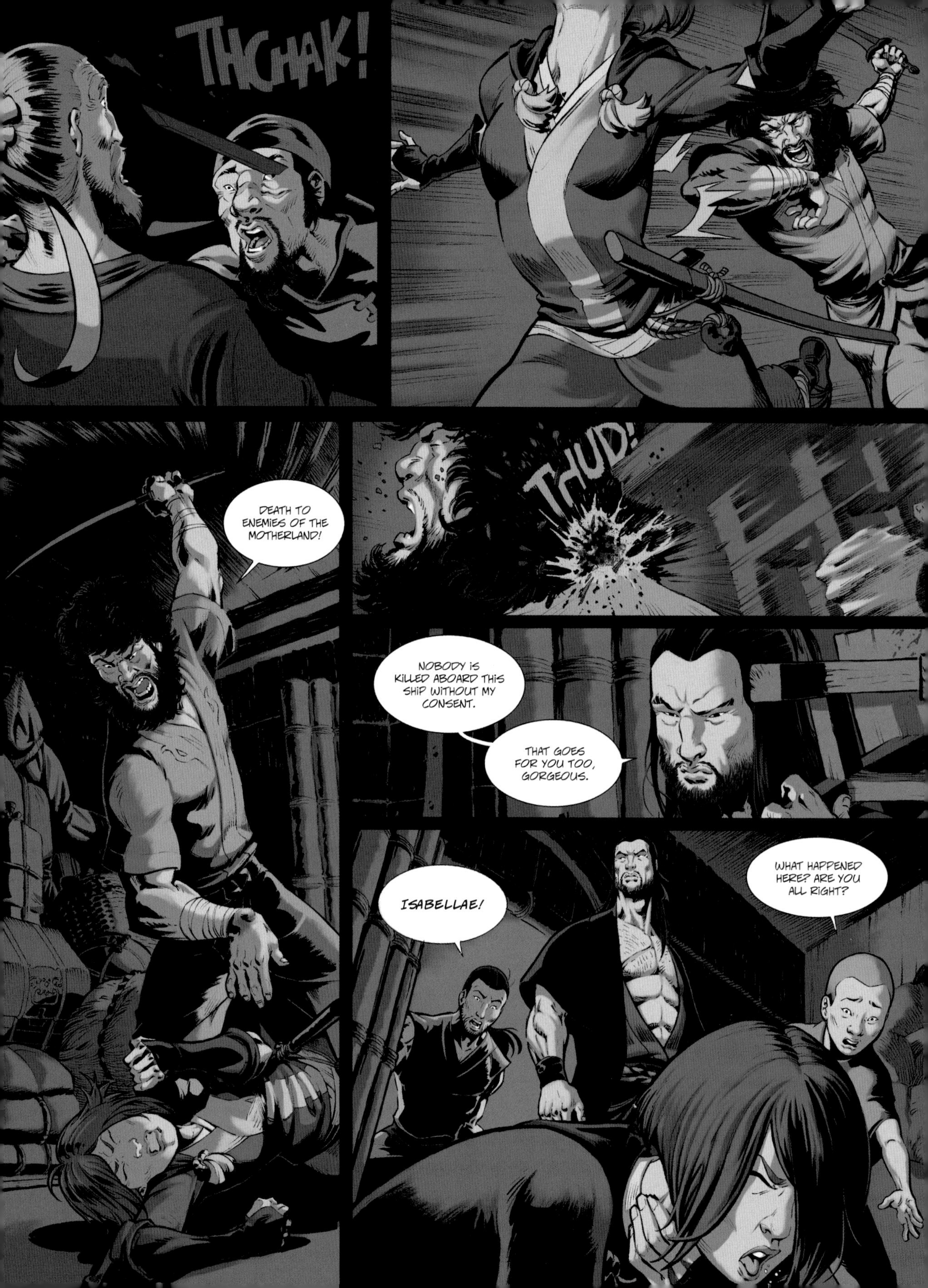
THCHAK!
DEATH TO ENEMIES OF THE MOTHERLAND!
THUD!
NOBODY IS KILLED ABOARD THIS SHIP WITHOUT MY CONSENT.
THAT GOES FOR YOU TOO, GORGEOUS.
ISABELLAE!
WHAT HAPPENED HERE? ARE YOU ALL RIGHT?

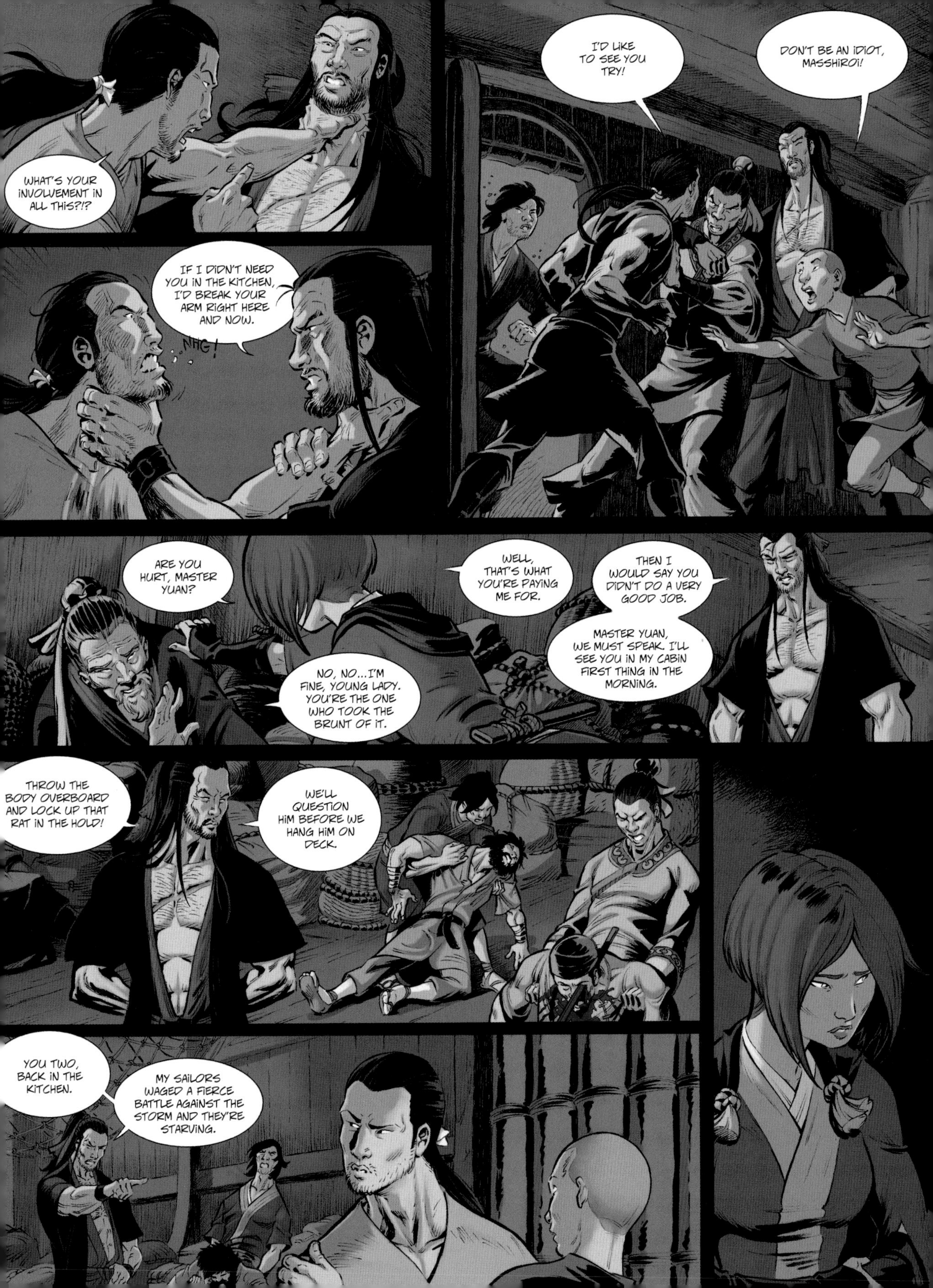

WHAT'S YOUR INVOLVEMENT IN ALL THIS?!?
IF I DIDN'T NEED YOU IN THE KITCHEN, I'D BREAK YOUR ARM RIGHT HERE AND NOW.
NHG!
I'D LIKE TO SEE YOU TRY!
DON'T BE AN IDIOT, MASSHIROI!
ARE YOU HURT, MASTER YUAN?
NO, NO...I'M FINE, YOUNG LADY. YOU'RE THE ONE WHO TOOK THE BRUNT OF IT.
WELL, THAT'S WHAT YOU'RE PAYING ME FOR.
THEN I WOULD SAY YOU DIDN'T DO A VERY GOOD JOB.
MASTER YUAN, WE MUST SPEAK. I'LL SEE YOU IN MY CABIN FIRST THING IN THE MORNING.
THROW THE BODY OVERBOARD AND LOCK UP THAT RAT IN THE HOLD!
WE'LL QUESTION HIM BEFORE WE HANG HIM ON DECK.
YOU TWO, BACK IN THE KITCHEN.
MY SAILORS WAGED A FIERCE BATTLE AGAINST THE STORM AND THEY'RE STARVING.

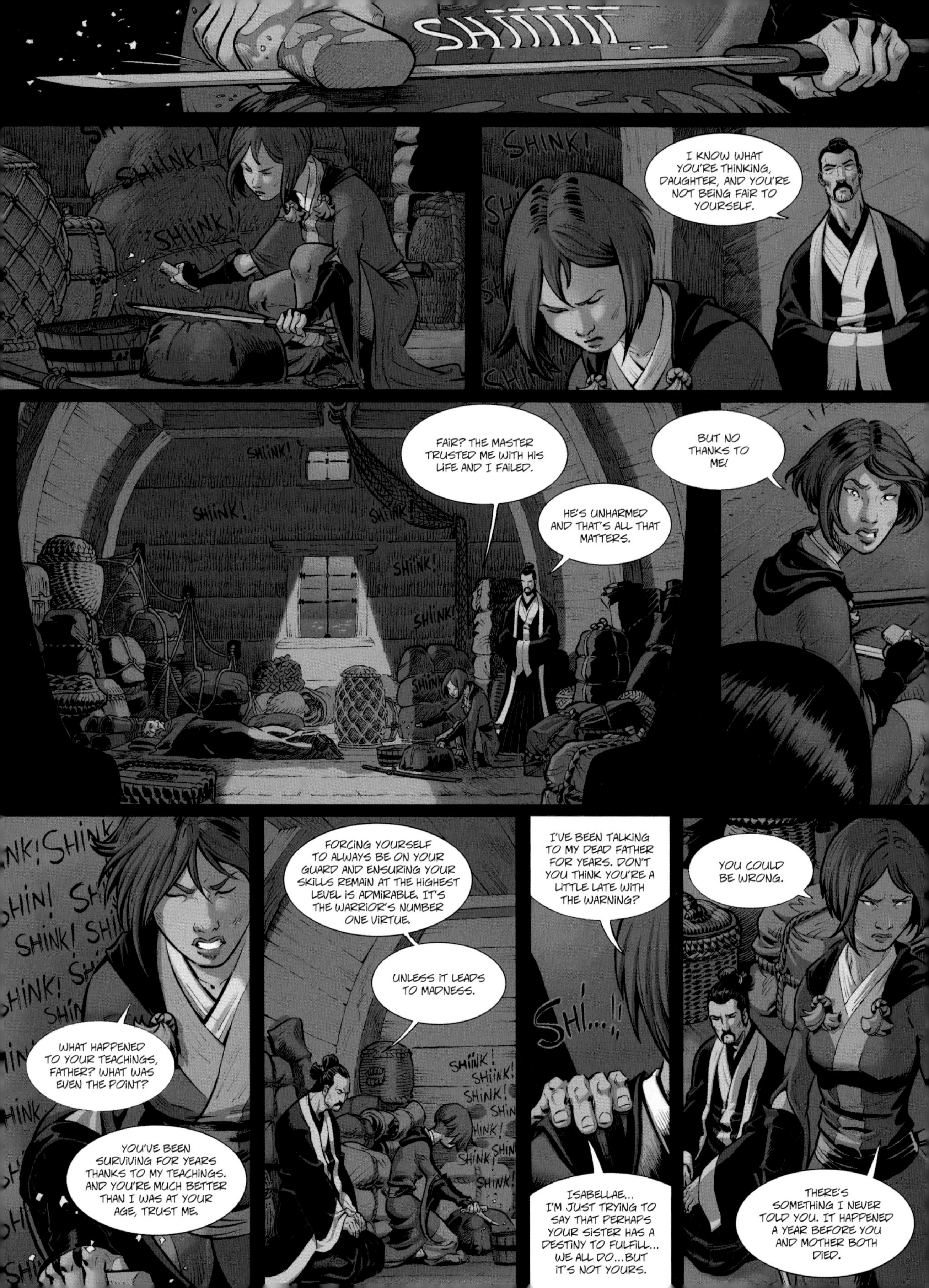
SHIIIIIIII...
SHIINK!
SHIINK!
SHINK!
I KNOW WHAT YOU'RE THINKING, DAUGHTER, AND YOU'RE NOT BEING FAIR TO YOURSELF.
SHIINK!
FAIR? THE MASTER TRUSTED ME WITH HIS LIFE AND I FAILED.
SHIINK!
SHIINK!
HE'S UNHARMED AND THAT'S ALL THAT MATTERS.
SHIINK!
SHIINK!
BUT NO THANKS TO ME!
NK! SHINK
SHIN! SHI
SHINK! SHI
SHINK! SHI
SHIN
WHAT HAPPENED TO YOUR TEACHINGS, FATHER? WHAT WAS EVEN THE POINT?
YOU'VE BEEN SURVIVING FOR YEARS THANKS TO MY TEACHINGS. AND YOU'RE MUCH BETTER THAN I WAS AT YOUR AGE, TRUST ME.
FORCING YOURSELF TO ALWAYS BE ON YOUR GUARD AND ENSURING YOUR SKILLS REMAIN AT THE HIGHEST LEVEL IS ADMIRABLE. IT'S THE WARRIOR'S NUMBER ONE VIRTUE.
UNLESS IT LEADS TO MADNESS.
SHIINK!
SHIINK!
SHINK!
SHINK!
SHINK!
I'VE BEEN TALKING TO MY DEAD FATHER FOR YEARS. DON'T YOU THINK YOU'RE A LITTLE LATE WITH THE WARNING?
SHI...!!
ISABELLAE... I'M JUST TRYING TO SAY THAT PERHAPS YOUR SISTER HAS A DESTINY TO FULFILL... WE ALL DO... BUT IT'S NOT YOURS.
YOU COULD BE WRONG.
THERE'S SOMETHING I NEVER TOLD YOU. IT HAPPENED A YEAR BEFORE YOU AND MOTHER BOTH DIED.

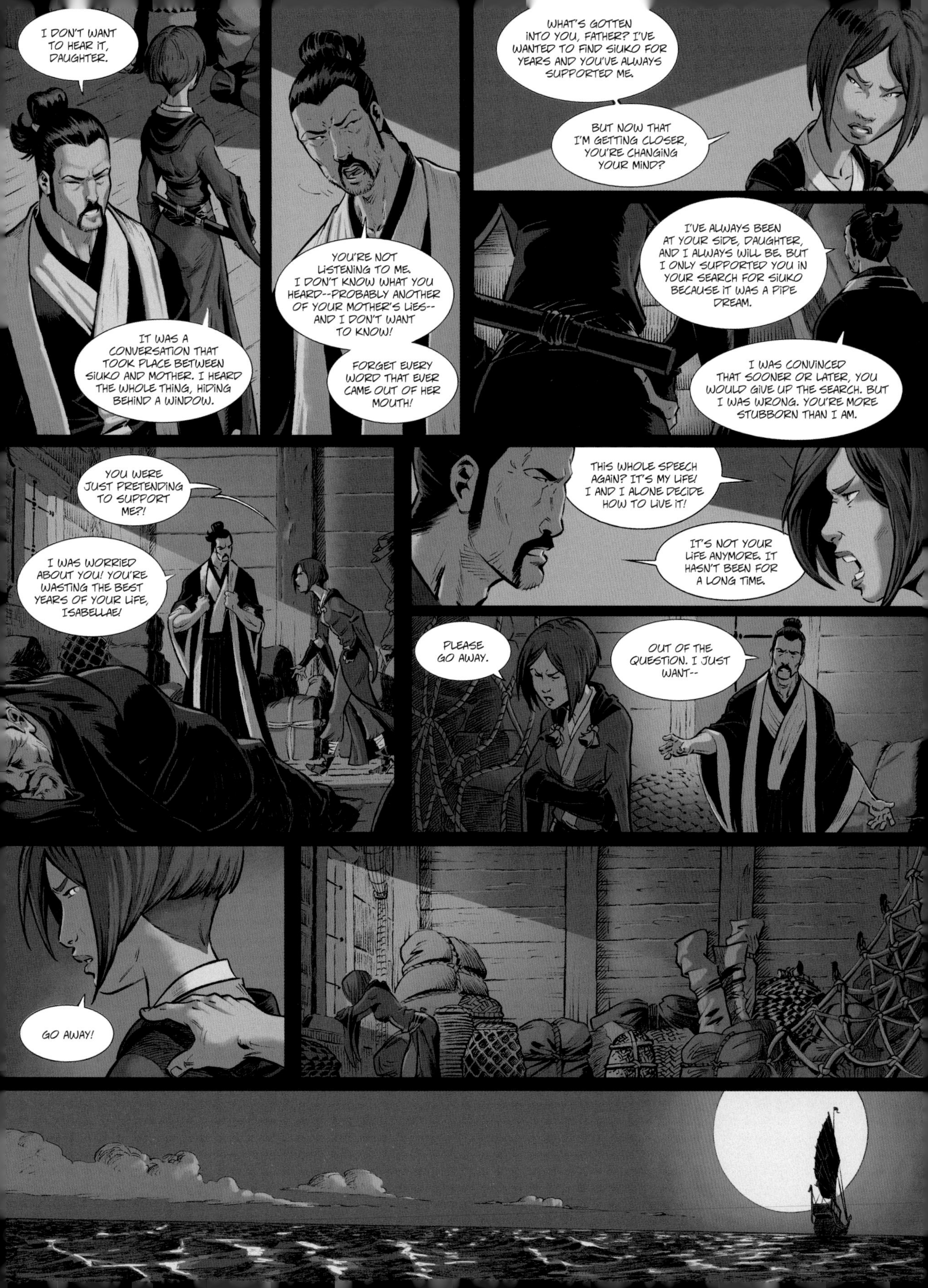

I DON'T WANT TO HEAR IT, DAUGHTER.
IT WAS A CONVERSATION THAT TOOK PLACE BETWEEN SIUKO AND MOTHER. I HEARD THE WHOLE THING, HIDING BEHIND A WINDOW.
YOU'RE NOT LISTENING TO ME. I DON'T KNOW WHAT YOU HEARD--PROBABLY ANOTHER OF YOUR MOTHER'S LIES--AND I DON'T WANT TO KNOW!
FORGET EVERY WORD THAT EVER CAME OUT OF HER MOUTH!
WHAT'S GOTTEN INTO YOU, FATHER? I'VE WANTED TO FIND SIUKO FOR YEARS AND YOU'VE ALWAYS SUPPORTED ME.
BUT NOW THAT I'M GETTING CLOSER, YOU'RE CHANGING YOUR MIND?
I'VE ALWAYS BEEN AT YOUR SIDE, DAUGHTER, AND I ALWAYS WILL BE. BUT I ONLY SUPPORTED YOU IN YOUR SEARCH FOR SIUKO BECAUSE IT WAS A PIPE DREAM.
I WAS CONVINCED THAT SOONER OR LATER, YOU WOULD GIVE UP THE SEARCH. BUT I WAS WRONG. YOU'RE MORE STUBBORN THAN I AM.
YOU WERE JUST PRETENDING TO SUPPORT ME?!
I WAS WORRIED ABOUT YOU! YOU'RE WASTING THE BEST YEARS OF YOUR LIFE, ISABELLAE!
THIS WHOLE SPEECH AGAIN? IT'S MY LIFE! I AND I ALONE DECIDE HOW TO LIVE IT!
IT'S NOT YOUR LIFE ANYMORE. IT HASN'T BEEN FOR A LONG TIME.
PLEASE GO AWAY.
OUT OF THE QUESTION. I JUST WANT--
GO AWAY!

MIAM MIAM

WHY ARE PEOPLE OUT TO KILL YOU, MASTER YUAN? WHO WOULD WISH AN ARTIST DEAD?

THERE IS A TIME AND PLACE FOR EVERYTHING.

HOW LONG HAD THOSE TWO BEEN WORKING FOR YOU?

THEY CAME TO ME THE DAY WE SAILED FROM ABASHIRI.

THEY LOOKED STRONG AND THEY SAID THEY WOULD WORK HARD FOR LITTLE PAY. IT WAS AN OFFER I COULDN'T REFUSE.

ARE YOU IN THE HABIT OF HIRING HELP WITHOUT ANY KNOWLEDGE OF THEIR BACKGROUND OR WORTH?

SOMETIMES. ANY OTHER QUESTIONS?

I'M ONE OF EMPEROR GUANGZONG'S CLOSEST FRIENDS.

OTHER FRIENDS AND ADVISORS OF THE EMPEROR HAVE BEEN MURDERED THESE PAST FEW MONTHS.

WE'RE TRAVELING TO THE COUNTRIES MOST FAVORABLE TO CHINA TO SEEK THE SUPPORT OF THEIR LEADERS. THE SITUATION AT THE PALACE IS VERY TENSE AND ANY HELP WE CAN GET WOULD BE AN ASSET.

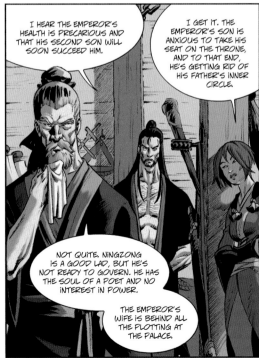

I HEAR THE EMPEROR'S HEALTH IS PRECARIOUS AND THAT HIS SECOND SON WILL SOON SUCCEED HIM.

I GET IT. THE EMPEROR'S SON IS ANXIOUS TO TAKE HIS SEAT ON THE THRONE, AND TO THAT END, HE'S GETTING RID OF HIS FATHER'S INNER CIRCLE.

NOT QUITE. NINGZONG IS A GOOD LAD, BUT HE'S NOT READY TO GOVERN. HE HAS THE SOUL OF A POET AND NO INTEREST IN POWER.

THE EMPEROR'S WIFE IS BEHIND ALL THE PLOTTING AT THE PALACE.

EMPRESS LI? IMPOSSIBLE...

SHE AND MINISTER ZHAO RUYU. WHEN NINGZONG ASCENDS TO THE THRONE, HE'LL BE NOTHING MORE THAN A PUPPET IN THEIR HANDS.

THEY'RE ALL THE SAME. REGARDLESS OF WHO GOVERNS, MASTER YUAN, THE POOR WILL REMAIN POOR. THESE POLITICAL SCHEMES DON'T MATTER MUCH TO THE COMMON PEOPLE.

YOU'RE MISTAKEN, YOUNG LADY. ON THE CONTRARY, THEY MATTER A GREAT DEAL.

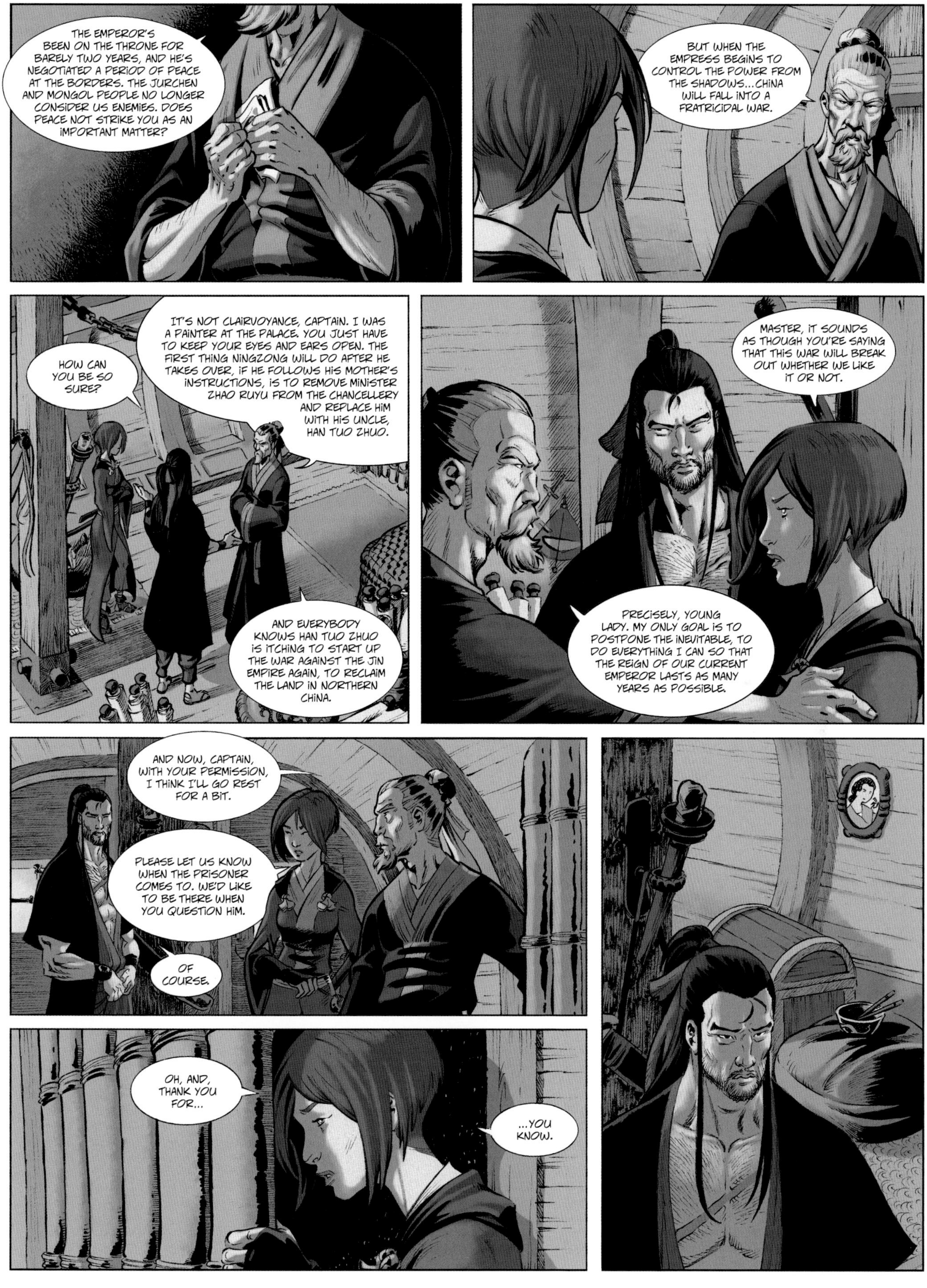
THE EMPEROR'S BEEN ON THE THRONE FOR BARELY TWO YEARS, AND HE'S NEGOTIATED A PERIOD OF PEACE AT THE BORDERS. THE JURCHEN AND MONGOL PEOPLE NO LONGER CONSIDER US ENEMIES. DOES PEACE NOT STRIKE YOU AS AN IMPORTANT MATTER?
BUT WHEN THE EMPRESS BEGINS TO CONTROL THE POWER FROM THE SHADOWS...CHINA WILL FALL INTO A FRATRICIDAL WAR.
HOW CAN YOU BE SO SURE?
IT'S NOT CLAIRVOYANCE, CAPTAIN. I WAS A PAINTER AT THE PALACE. YOU JUST HAVE TO KEEP YOUR EYES AND EARS OPEN. THE FIRST THING NINGZONG WILL DO AFTER HE TAKES OVER, IF HE FOLLOWS HIS MOTHER'S INSTRUCTIONS, IS TO REMOVE MINISTER ZHAO RUYU FROM THE CHANCELLERY AND REPLACE HIM WITH HIS UNCLE, HAN TUO ZHUO.
AND EVERYBODY KNOWS HAN TUO ZHUO IS ITCHING TO START UP THE WAR AGAINST THE JIN EMPIRE AGAIN, TO RECLAIM THE LAND IN NORTHERN CHINA.
MASTER, IT SOUNDS AS THOUGH YOU'RE SAYING THAT THIS WAR WILL BREAK OUT WHETHER WE LIKE IT OR NOT.
PRECISELY, YOUNG LADY. MY ONLY GOAL IS TO POSTPONE THE INEVITABLE, TO DO EVERYTHING I CAN SO THAT THE REIGN OF OUR CURRENT EMPEROR LASTS AS MANY YEARS AS POSSIBLE.
AND NOW, CAPTAIN, WITH YOUR PERMISSION, I THINK I'LL GO REST FOR A BIT.
PLEASE LET US KNOW WHEN THE PRISONER COMES TO. WE'D LIKE TO BE THERE WHEN YOU QUESTION HIM.
OF COURSE.
OH, AND, THANK YOU FOR...
...YOU KNOW.

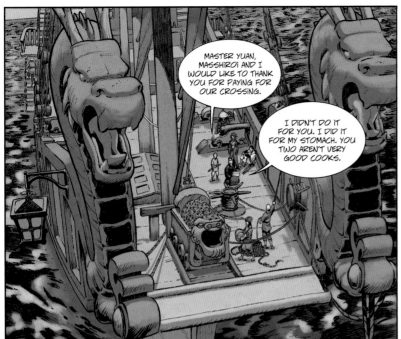

MASTER YUAN, MASSHIROÏ AND I WOULD LIKE TO THANK YOU FOR PAYING FOR OUR CROSSING.

I DIDN'T DO IT FOR YOU. I DID IT FOR MY STOMACH. YOU TWO AREN'T VERY GOOD COOKS.

I SAY THAT IN JEST. YOU SHOULD BE THANKING ISABELLAE. SHE'S THE ONE WHO SUGGESTED I HIRE YOU.

WE DON'T KNOW WHETHER THERE ARE ANY OTHER ASSASSINS ON BOARD, AND YOU'RE THE ONLY ONES WE CAN TRUST.

YOU'RE FORGETTING YOUR DEAR CAPTAIN.

I'M GOING TO QUESTION THE PRISONER. ARE YOU SURE YOU WANT TO BE THERE, MASTER YUAN? IT WON'T BE A PRETTY SIGHT.

YOU'D BE SURPRISED WHAT HORRORS MY EYES HAVE WITNESSED.

IS THERE SOMETHING YOU WANT TO SAY?

FIX YOUR HAIR. HERE COMES YOUR HERO.

WAIT FOR US HERE, PLEASE. THE CAPTAIN IS A DETERMINED MAN, I DOUBT THIS WILL TAKE LONG.

WHAT WOULD YOU LIKE TO ASK THIS BASTARD, MASTER?

OH, I'LL IMPROVISE. HE LOOKS LIKE A SIMPLE MINION. HE PROBABLY DOESN'T KNOW MUCH.

IT IS VITAL THAT WE FIND OUT IF THERE ARE ANY OTHER ASSASSINS ON BOARD.

IF THERE ARE...

...WE'LL FIND OUT VERY SOON.

WHAT THE--?!

HE TOOK A HEAVY BLOW TO THE HEAD, BUT HE'S STILL BREATHING.

Ni...k

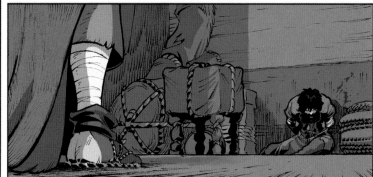

THERE'S THE ANSWER TO YOUR QUERY, YOUNG LADY.

CAPTAIN! CAPTAIN!

YOU NEED TO COME UP ON DECK AT ONCE! BAD OMENS!

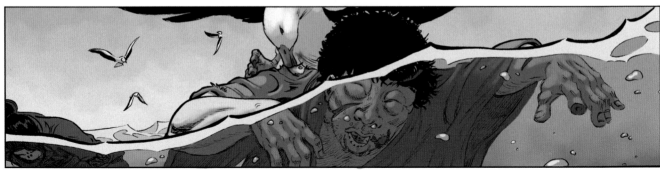

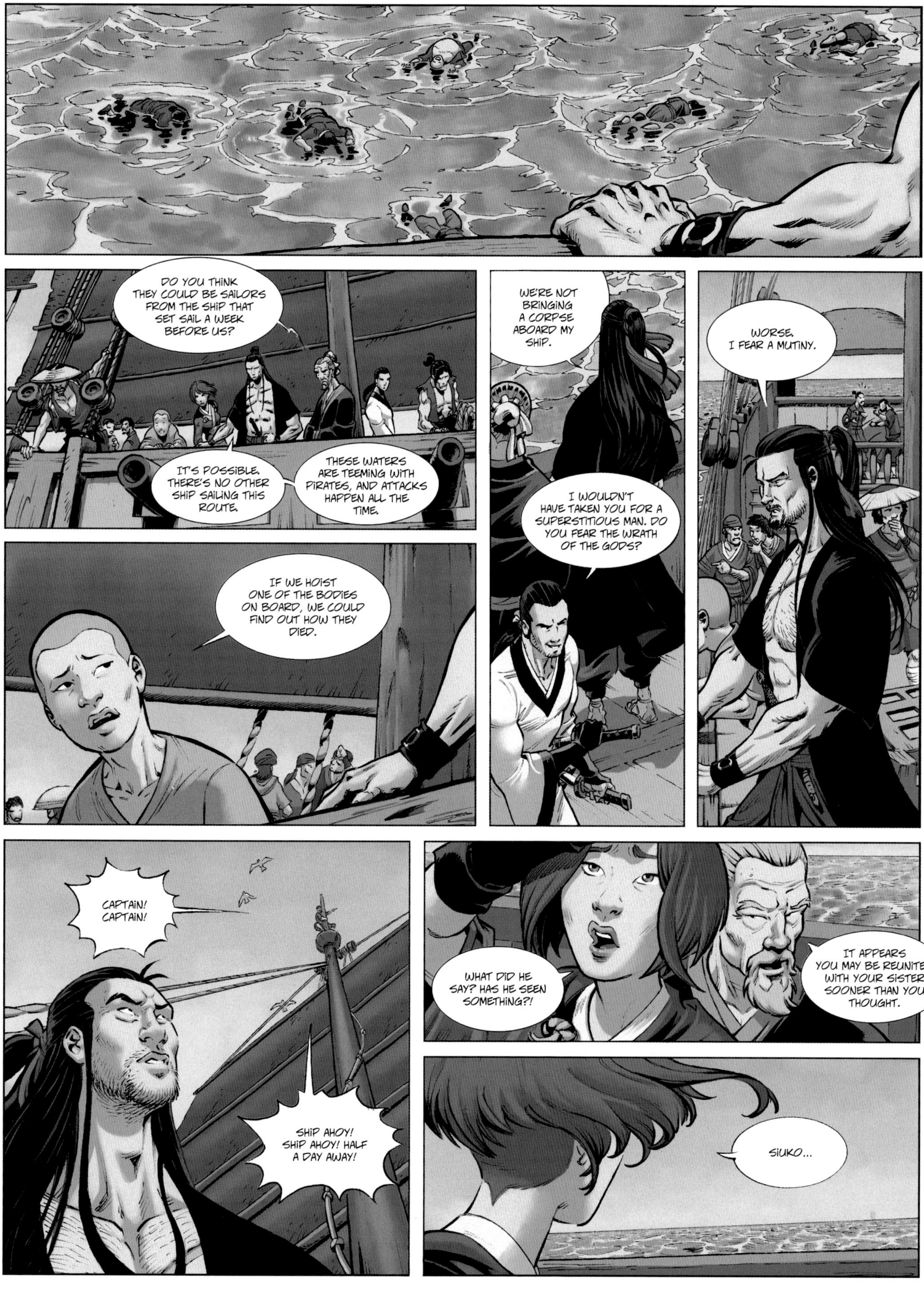
DO YOU THINK THEY COULD BE SAILORS FROM THE SHIP THAT SET SAIL A WEEK BEFORE US?
IT'S POSSIBLE. THERE'S NO OTHER SHIP SAILING THIS ROUTE.
THESE WATERS ARE TEEMING WITH PIRATES, AND ATTACKS HAPPEN ALL THE TIME.
IF WE HOIST ONE OF THE BODIES ON BOARD, WE COULD FIND OUT HOW THEY DIED.
WE'RE NOT BRINGING A CORPSE ABOARD MY SHIP.
I WOULDN'T HAVE TAKEN YOU FOR A SUPERSTITIOUS MAN. DO YOU FEAR THE WRATH OF THE GODS?
WORSE. I FEAR A MUTINY.
CAPTAIN! CAPTAIN!
SHIP AHOY! SHIP AHOY! HALF A DAY AWAY!
WHAT DID HE SAY? HAS HE SEEN SOMETHING?!
IT APPEARS YOU MAY BE REUNITED WITH YOUR SISTER SOONER THAN YOU THOUGHT.
SIUKO...

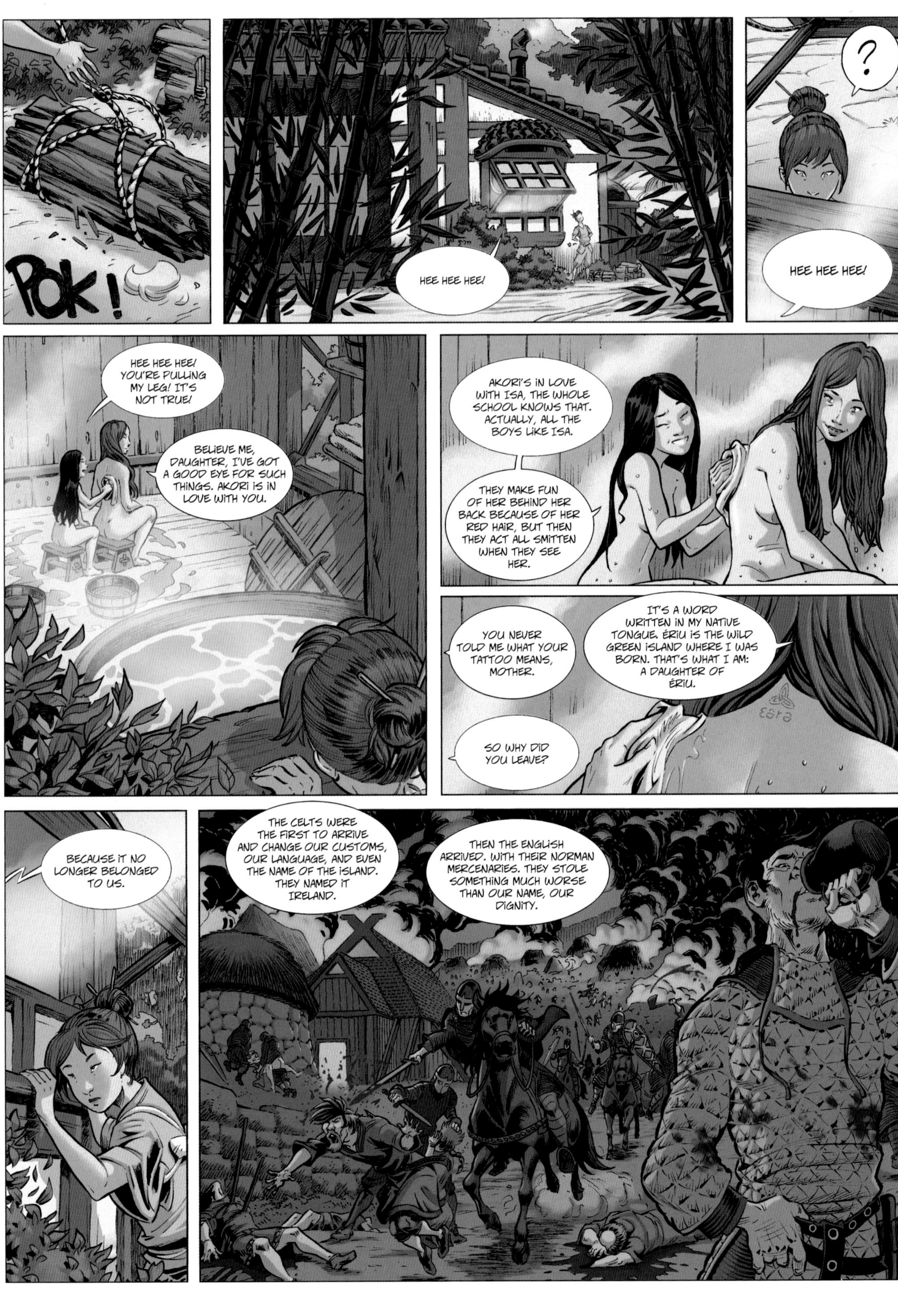
POK!
HEE HEE HEE!
?
HEE HEE HEE!
HEE HEE HEE! YOU'RE PULLING MY LEG! IT'S NOT TRUE!
BELIEVE ME, DAUGHTER, I'VE GOT A GOOD EYE FOR SUCH THINGS. AKORI IS IN LOVE WITH YOU.
AKORI'S IN LOVE WITH ISA, THE WHOLE SCHOOL KNOWS THAT. ACTUALLY, ALL THE BOYS LIKE ISA.
THEY MAKE FUN OF HER BEHIND HER BACK BECAUSE OF HER RED HAIR, BUT THEN THEY ACT ALL SMITTEN WHEN THEY SEE HER.
YOU NEVER TOLD ME WHAT YOUR TATTOO MEANS, MOTHER.
IT'S A WORD WRITTEN IN MY NATIVE TONGUE. ÉRIU IS THE WILD GREEN ISLAND WHERE I WAS BORN. THAT'S WHAT I AM: A DAUGHTER OF ÉRIU.
SO WHY DID YOU LEAVE?
BECAUSE IT NO LONGER BELONGED TO US.
THE CELTS WERE THE FIRST TO ARRIVE AND CHANGE OUR CUSTOMS, OUR LANGUAGE, AND EVEN THE NAME OF THE ISLAND. THEY NAMED IT IRELAND.
THEN THE ENGLISH ARRIVED. WITH THEIR NORMAN MERCENARIES. THEY STOLE SOMETHING MUCH WORSE THAN OUR NAME, OUR DIGNITY.

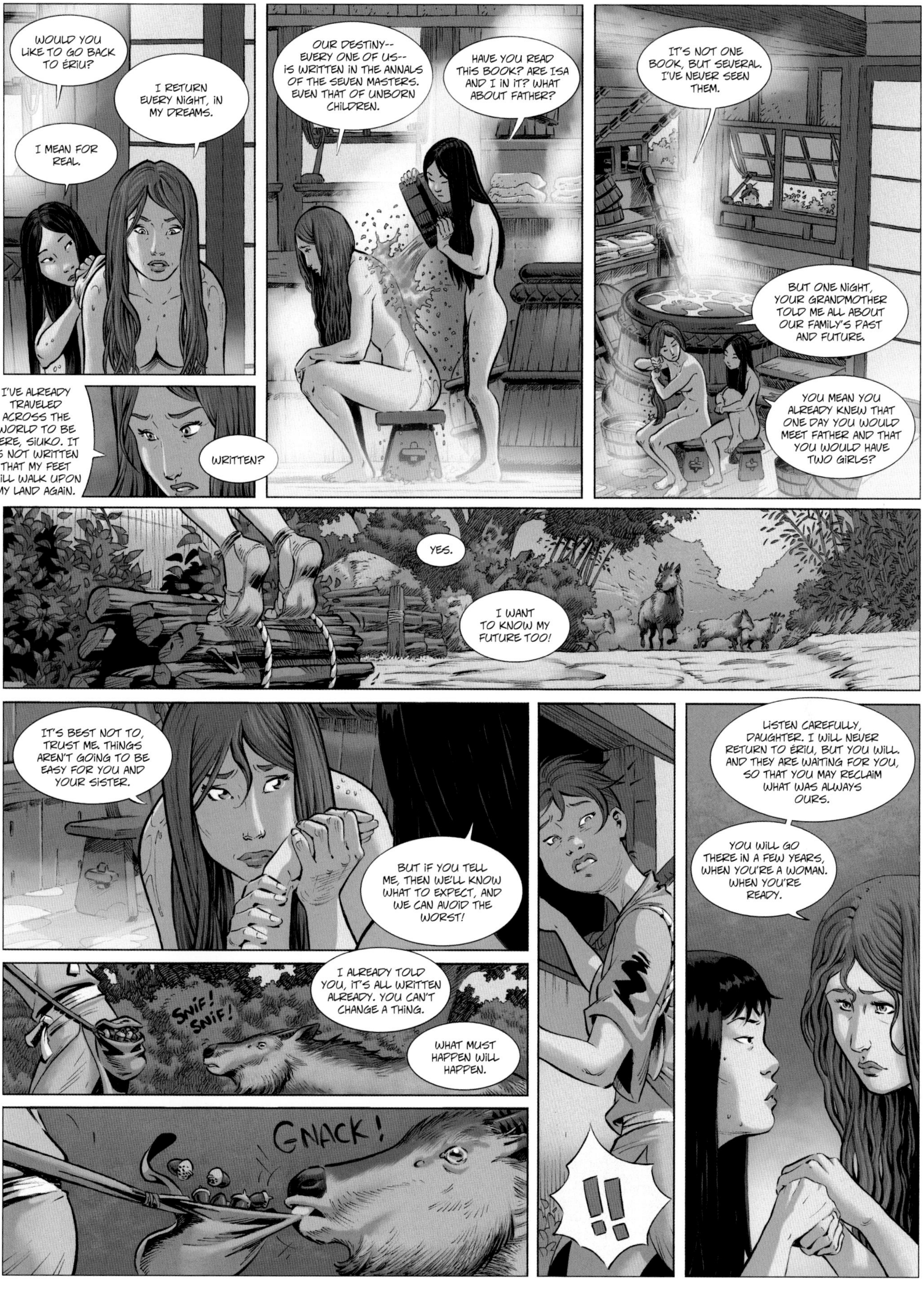
WOULD YOU LIKE TO GO BACK TO ÉRIU?
I RETURN EVERY NIGHT, IN MY DREAMS.
I MEAN FOR REAL.
I'VE ALREADY TRAVELED ACROSS THE WORLD TO BE HERE, SIUKO. IT IS NOT WRITTEN THAT MY FEET WILL WALK UPON MY LAND AGAIN.
WRITTEN?
OUR DESTINY-- EVERY ONE OF US-- IS WRITTEN IN THE ANNALS OF THE SEVEN MASTERS. EVEN THAT OF UNBORN CHILDREN.
HAVE YOU READ THIS BOOK? ARE ISA AND I IN IT? WHAT ABOUT FATHER?
IT'S NOT ONE BOOK, BUT SEVERAL. I'VE NEVER SEEN THEM.
BUT ONE NIGHT, YOUR GRANDMOTHER TOLD ME ALL ABOUT OUR FAMILY'S PAST AND FUTURE.
YOU MEAN YOU ALREADY KNEW THAT ONE DAY YOU WOULD MEET FATHER AND THAT YOU WOULD HAVE TWO GIRLS?
YES.
I WANT TO KNOW MY FUTURE TOO!
IT'S BEST NOT TO, TRUST ME. THINGS AREN'T GOING TO BE EASY FOR YOU AND YOUR SISTER.
BUT IF YOU TELL ME, THEN WE'LL KNOW WHAT TO EXPECT, AND WE CAN AVOID THE WORST!
I ALREADY TOLD YOU, IT'S ALL WRITTEN ALREADY. YOU CAN'T CHANGE A THING.
SNIF! SNIF!
WHAT MUST HAPPEN WILL HAPPEN.
GNACK!
!!
LISTEN CAREFULLY, DAUGHTER. I WILL NEVER RETURN TO ÉRIU, BUT YOU WILL. AND THEY ARE WAITING FOR YOU, SO THAT YOU MAY RECLAIM WHAT WAS ALWAYS OURS.
YOU WILL GO THERE IN A FEW YEARS, WHEN YOU'RE A WOMAN. WHEN YOU'RE READY.

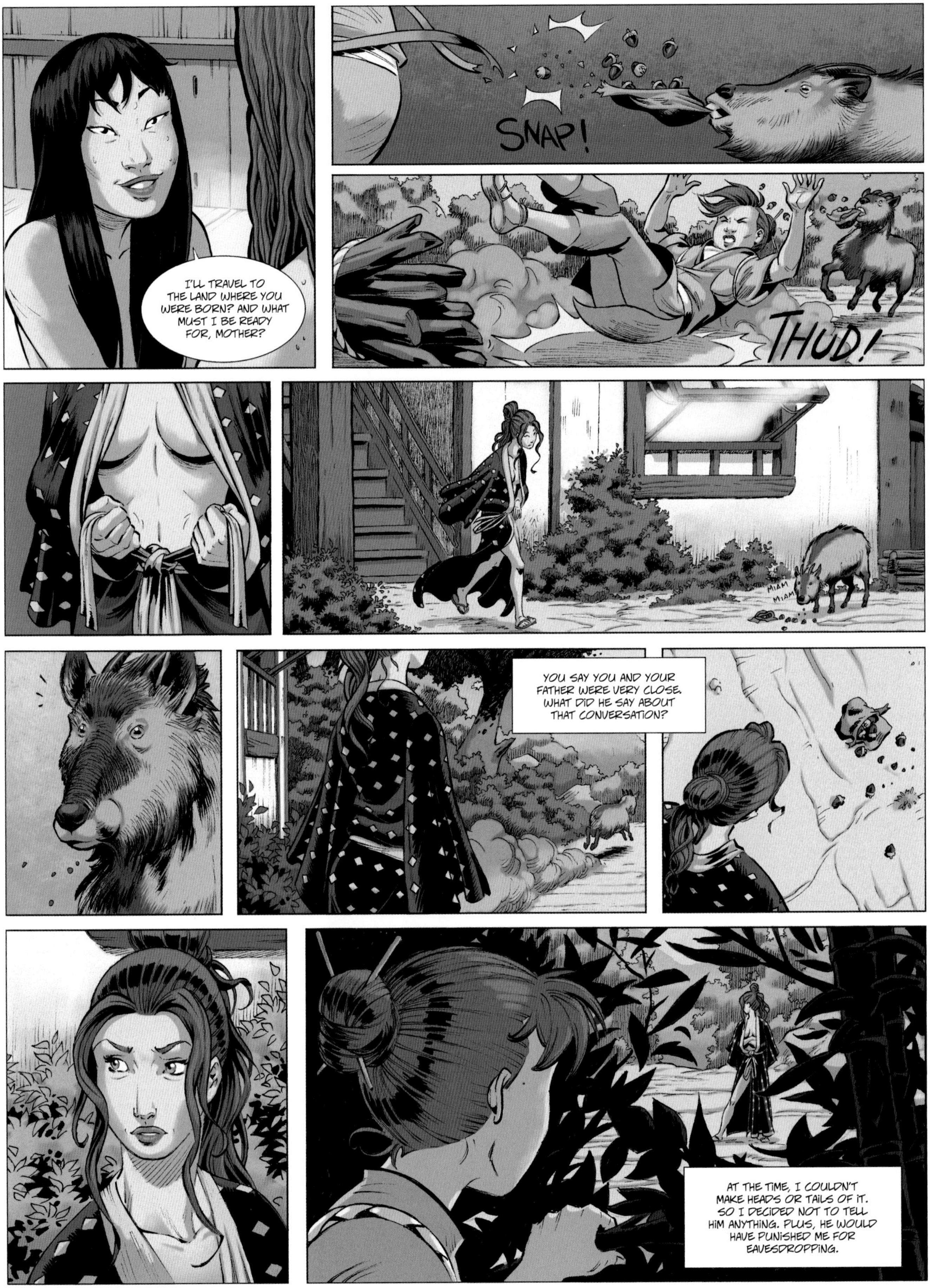
I'LL TRAVEL TO THE LAND WHERE YOU WERE BORN? AND WHAT MUST I BE READY FOR, MOTHER?
SNAP!
THUD!
MIAM MIAM
YOU SAY YOU AND YOUR FATHER WERE VERY CLOSE. WHAT DID HE SAY ABOUT THAT CONVERSATION?
AT THE TIME, I COULDN'T MAKE HEADS OR TAILS OF IT. SO I DECIDED NOT TO TELL HIM ANYTHING. PLUS, HE WOULD HAVE PUNISHED ME FOR EAVESDROPPING.

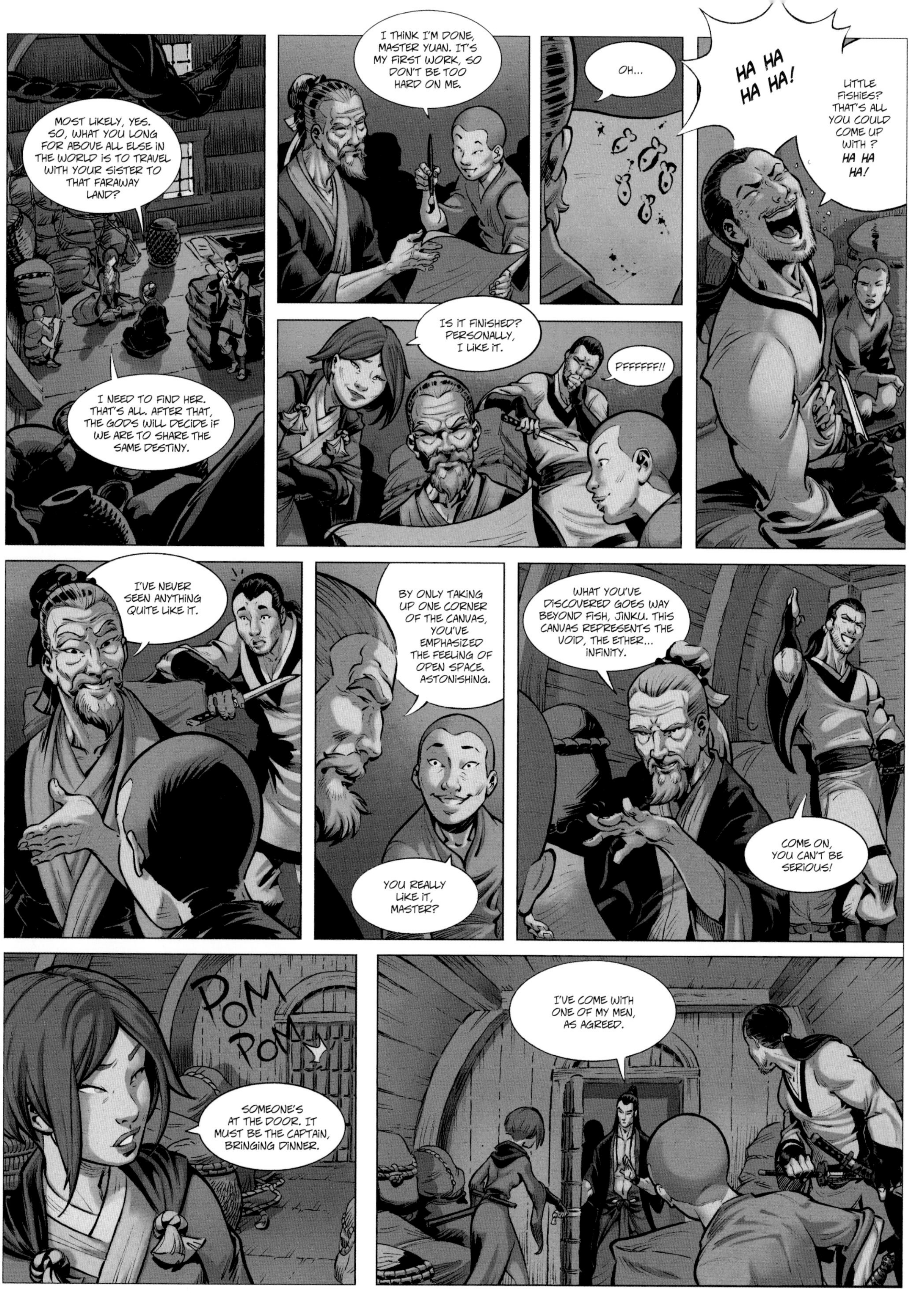
MOST LIKELY, YES. SO, WHAT YOU LONG FOR ABOVE ALL ELSE IN THE WORLD IS TO TRAVEL WITH YOUR SISTER TO THAT FARAWAY LAND?
I NEED TO FIND HER. THAT'S ALL. AFTER THAT, THE GODS WILL DECIDE IF WE ARE TO SHARE THE SAME DESTINY.
I THINK I'M DONE, MASTER YUAN. IT'S MY FIRST WORK, SO DON'T BE TOO HARD ON ME.
OH...
HA HA HA HA!
LITTLE FISHIES? THAT'S ALL YOU COULD COME UP WITH ? HA HA HA!
IS IT FINISHED? PERSONALLY, I LIKE IT.
PFFFFFF!!
I'VE NEVER SEEN ANYTHING QUITE LIKE IT.
BY ONLY TAKING UP ONE CORNER OF THE CANVAS, YOU'VE EMPHASIZED THE FEELING OF OPEN SPACE. ASTONISHING.
YOU REALLY LIKE IT, MASTER?
WHAT YOU'VE DISCOVERED GOES WAY BEYOND FISH, JINKU. THIS CANVAS REPRESENTS THE VOID, THE ETHER... INFINITY.
COME ON, YOU CAN'T BE SERIOUS!
POM POM
SOMEONE'S AT THE DOOR. IT MUST BE THE CAPTAIN, BRINGING DINNER.
I'VE COME WITH ONE OF MY MEN, AS AGREED.

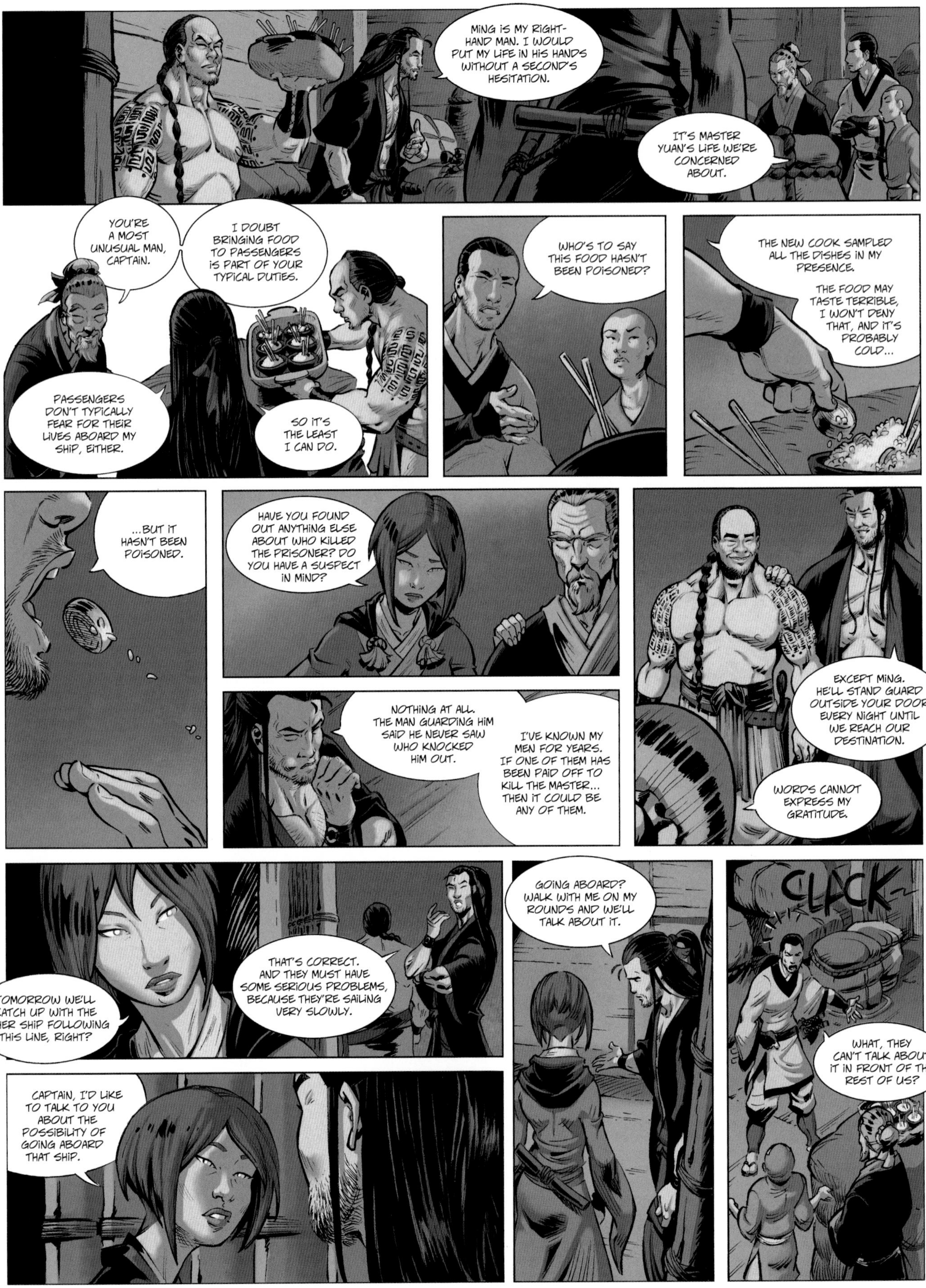
MING IS MY RIGHT-HAND MAN. I WOULD PUT MY LIFE IN HIS HANDS WITHOUT A SECOND'S HESITATION.
IT'S MASTER YUAN'S LIFE WE'RE CONCERNED ABOUT.
YOU'RE A MOST UNUSUAL MAN, CAPTAIN.
I DOUBT BRINGING FOOD TO PASSENGERS IS PART OF YOUR TYPICAL DUTIES.
PASSENGERS DON'T TYPICALLY FEAR FOR THEIR LIVES ABOARD MY SHIP, EITHER.
SO IT'S THE LEAST I CAN DO.
WHO'S TO SAY THIS FOOD HASN'T BEEN POISONED?
THE NEW COOK SAMPLED ALL THE DISHES IN MY PRESENCE.
THE FOOD MAY TASTE TERRIBLE, I WON'T DENY THAT, AND IT'S PROBABLY COLD...
...BUT IT HASN'T BEEN POISONED.
HAVE YOU FOUND OUT ANYTHING ELSE ABOUT WHO KILLED THE PRISONER? DO YOU HAVE A SUSPECT IN MIND?
NOTHING AT ALL. THE MAN GUARDING HIM SAID HE NEVER SAW WHO KNOCKED HIM OUT.
I'VE KNOWN MY MEN FOR YEARS. IF ONE OF THEM HAS BEEN PAID OFF TO KILL THE MASTER... THEN IT COULD BE ANY OF THEM.
EXCEPT MING. HE'LL STAND GUARD OUTSIDE YOUR DOOR EVERY NIGHT UNTIL WE REACH OUR DESTINATION.
WORDS CANNOT EXPRESS MY GRATITUDE.
TOMORROW WE'LL CATCH UP WITH THE OTHER SHIP FOLLOWING THIS LINE, RIGHT?
THAT'S CORRECT. AND THEY MUST HAVE SOME SERIOUS PROBLEMS, BECAUSE THEY'RE SAILING VERY SLOWLY.
CAPTAIN, I'D LIKE TO TALK TO YOU ABOUT THE POSSIBILITY OF GOING ABOARD THAT SHIP.
GOING ABOARD? WALK WITH ME ON MY ROUNDS AND WE'LL TALK ABOUT IT.
CLACK
WHAT, THEY CAN'T TALK ABOUT IT IN FRONT OF THE REST OF US?

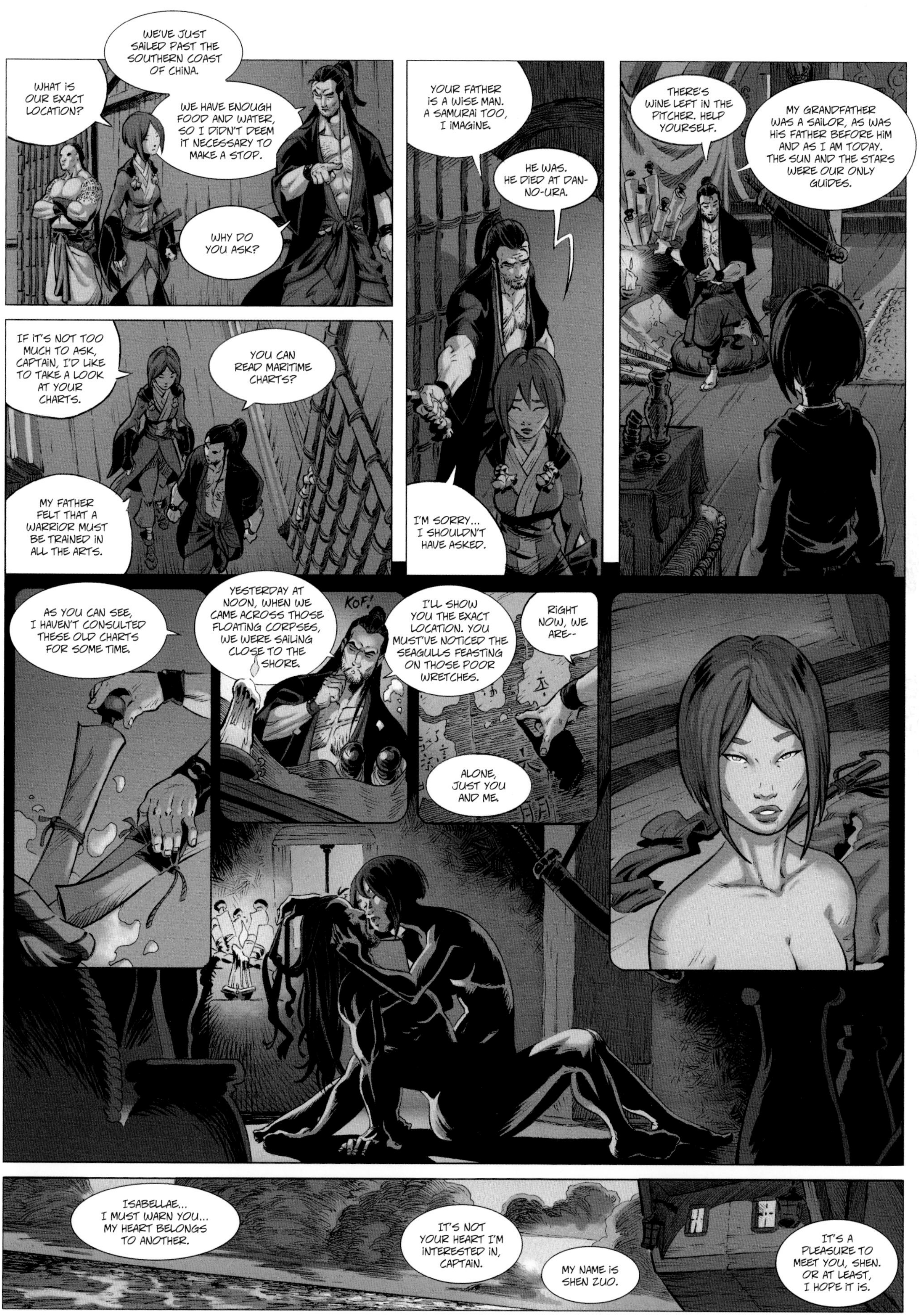
WHAT IS OUR EXACT LOCATION?
WE'VE JUST SAILED PAST THE SOUTHERN COAST OF CHINA.
WE HAVE ENOUGH FOOD AND WATER, SO I DIDN'T DEEM IT NECESSARY TO MAKE A STOP.
WHY DO YOU ASK?
YOUR FATHER IS A WISE MAN. A SAMURAI TOO, I IMAGINE.
HE WAS. HE DIED AT DAN-NO-URA.
THERE'S WINE LEFT IN THE PITCHER. HELP YOURSELF.
MY GRANDFATHER WAS A SAILOR, AS WAS HIS FATHER BEFORE HIM AND AS I AM TODAY. THE SUN AND THE STARS WERE OUR ONLY GUIDES.
IF IT'S NOT TOO MUCH TO ASK, CAPTAIN, I'D LIKE TO TAKE A LOOK AT YOUR CHARTS.
YOU CAN READ MARITIME CHARTS?
MY FATHER FELT THAT A WARRIOR MUST BE TRAINED IN ALL THE ARTS.
I'M SORRY... I SHOULDN'T HAVE ASKED.
AS YOU CAN SEE, I HAVEN'T CONSULTED THESE OLD CHARTS FOR SOME TIME.
YESTERDAY AT NOON, WHEN WE CAME ACROSS THOSE FLOATING CORPSES, WE WERE SAILING CLOSE TO THE SHORE.
KOF!
I'LL SHOW YOU THE EXACT LOCATION. YOU MUST'VE NOTICED THE SEAGULLS FEASTING ON THOSE POOR WRETCHES.
RIGHT NOW, WE ARE--
ALONE, JUST YOU AND ME.
ISABELLAE... I MUST WARN YOU... MY HEART BELONGS TO ANOTHER.
IT'S NOT YOUR HEART I'M INTERESTED IN, CAPTAIN.
MY NAME IS SHEN ZUO.
IT'S A PLEASURE TO MEET YOU, SHEN. OR AT LEAST, I HOPE IT IS.

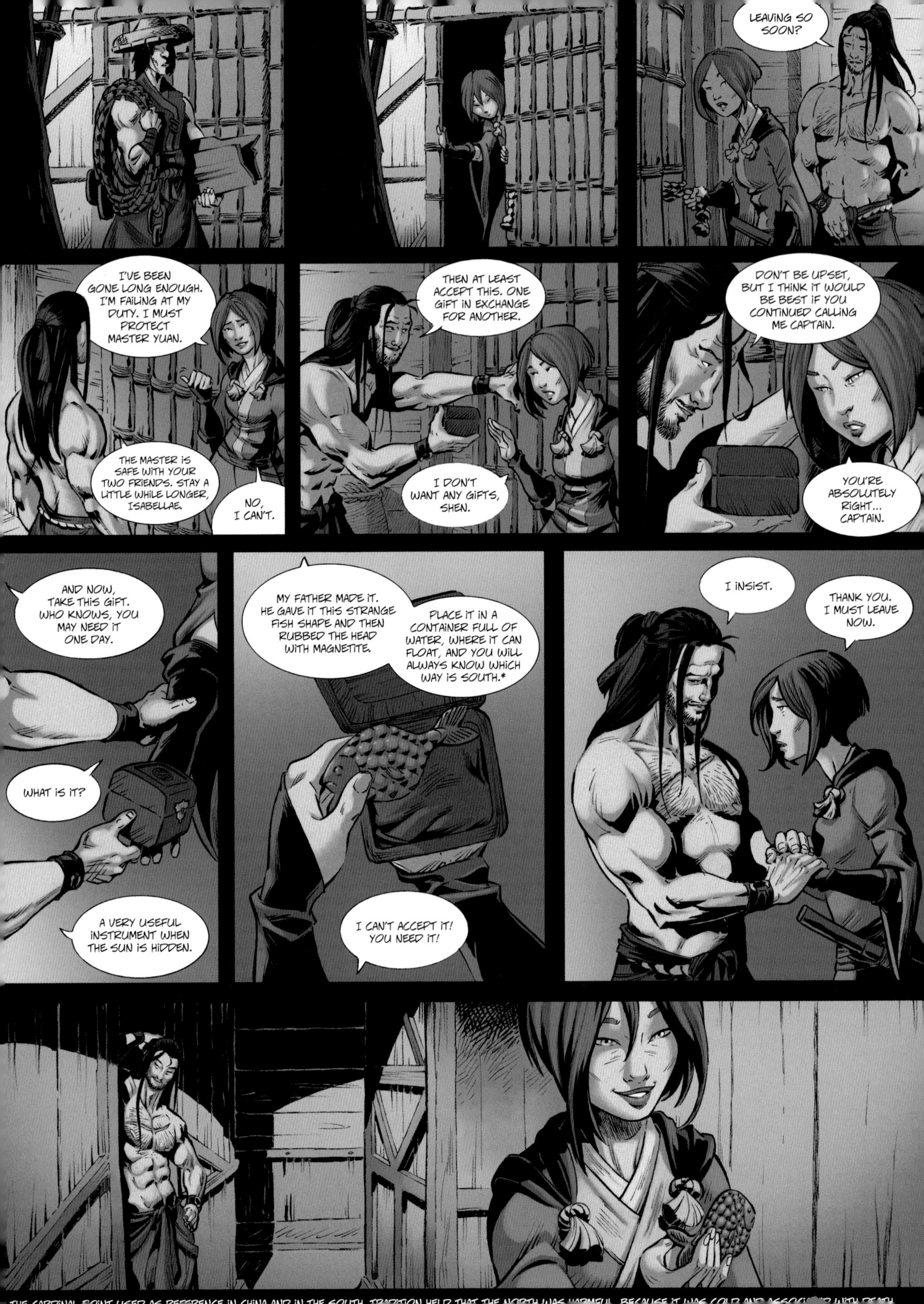
LEAVING SO SOON?
I'VE BEEN GONE LONG ENOUGH. I'M FAILING AT MY DUTY. I MUST PROTECT MASTER YUAN.
THE MASTER IS SAFE WITH YOUR TWO FRIENDS. STAY A LITTLE WHILE LONGER, ISABELLAE.
NO, I CAN'T.
THEN AT LEAST ACCEPT THIS. ONE GIFT IN EXCHANGE FOR ANOTHER.
I DON'T WANT ANY GIFTS, SHEN.
DON'T BE UPSET, BUT I THINK IT WOULD BE BEST IF YOU CONTINUED CALLING ME CAPTAIN.
YOU'RE ABSOLUTELY RIGHT... CAPTAIN.
AND NOW, TAKE THIS GIFT. WHO KNOWS, YOU MAY NEED IT ONE DAY.
WHAT IS IT?
A VERY USEFUL INSTRUMENT WHEN THE SUN IS HIDDEN.
MY FATHER MADE IT. HE GAVE IT THIS STRANGE FISH SHAPE AND THEN RUBBED THE HEAD WITH MAGNETITE.
PLACE IT IN A CONTAINER FULL OF WATER, WHERE IT CAN FLOAT, AND YOU WILL ALWAYS KNOW WHICH WAY IS SOUTH.*
I CAN'T ACCEPT IT! YOU NEED IT!
I INSIST.
THANK YOU. I MUST LEAVE NOW.

*THE CARDINAL POINT USED AS REFERENCE IN CHINA AND IN THE SOUTH. TRADITION HELD THAT THE NORTH WAS HARMFUL, BECAUSE IT WAS COLD AND ASSOCIATED WITH DEATH.

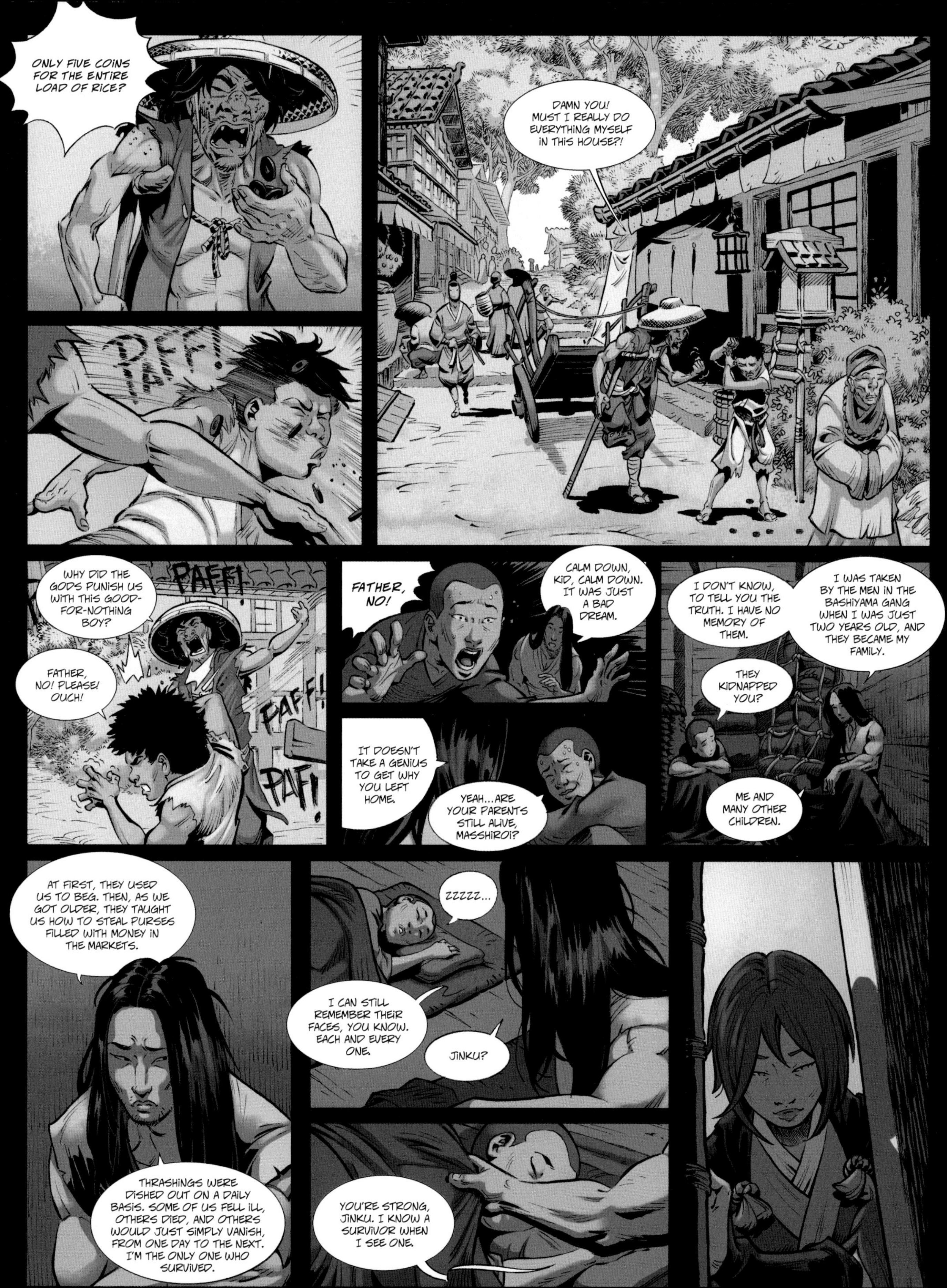
ONLY FIVE COINS FOR THE ENTIRE LOAD OF RICE?
DAMN YOU! MUST I REALLY DO EVERYTHING MYSELF IN THIS HOUSE?!
PAFF!
WHY DID THE GODS PUNISH US WITH THIS GOOD-FOR-NOTHING BOY?
PAFF!
FATHER, NO! PLEASE! OUCH!
PAFF!
PAF!
FATHER, NO!
CALM DOWN, KID, CALM DOWN. IT WAS JUST A BAD DREAM.
IT DOESN'T TAKE A GENIUS TO GET WHY YOU LEFT HOME.
YEAH...ARE YOUR PARENTS STILL ALIVE, MASSHIRO?
I DON'T KNOW, TO TELL YOU THE TRUTH. I HAVE NO MEMORY OF THEM.
I WAS TAKEN BY THE MEN IN THE BASHIYAMA GANG WHEN I WAS JUST TWO YEARS OLD, AND THEY BECAME MY FAMILY.
THEY KIDNAPPED YOU?
ME AND MANY OTHER CHILDREN.
AT FIRST, THEY USED US TO BEG. THEN, AS WE GOT OLDER, THEY TAUGHT US HOW TO STEAL PURSES FILLED WITH MONEY IN THE MARKETS.
THRASHINGS WERE DISHED OUT ON A DAILY BASIS. SOME OF US FELL ILL, OTHERS DIED, AND OTHERS WOULD JUST SIMPLY VANISH, FROM ONE DAY TO THE NEXT. I'M THE ONLY ONE WHO SURVIVED.
ZZZZZ...
I CAN STILL REMEMBER THEIR FACES, YOU KNOW. EACH AND EVERY ONE.
JINKU?
YOU'RE STRONG, JINKU. I KNOW A SURVIVOR WHEN I SEE ONE.

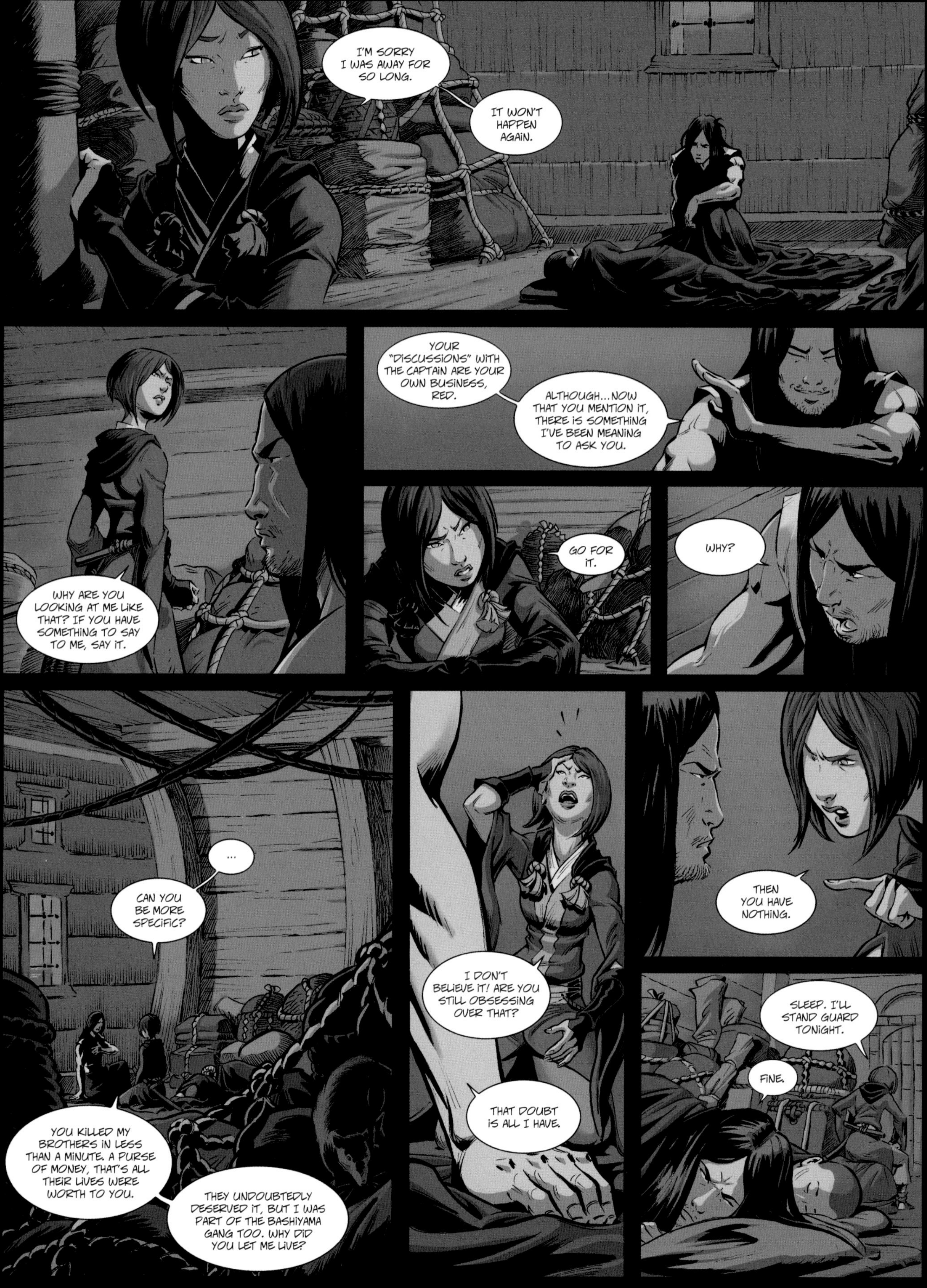
I'M SORRY I WAS AWAY FOR SO LONG.
IT WON'T HAPPEN AGAIN.
WHY ARE YOU LOOKING AT ME LIKE THAT? IF YOU HAVE SOMETHING TO SAY TO ME, SAY IT.
YOUR "DISCUSSIONS" WITH THE CAPTAIN ARE YOUR OWN BUSINESS, RED.
ALTHOUGH...NOW THAT YOU MENTION IT, THERE IS SOMETHING I'VE BEEN MEANING TO ASK YOU.
GO FOR IT.
WHY?
...
CAN YOU BE MORE SPECIFIC?
YOU KILLED MY BROTHERS IN LESS THAN A MINUTE. A PURSE OF MONEY, THAT'S ALL THEIR LIVES WERE WORTH TO YOU.
THEY UNDOUBTEDLY DESERVED IT, BUT I WAS PART OF THE BASHIYAMA GANG TOO. WHY DID YOU LET ME LIVE?
I DON'T BELIEVE IT! ARE YOU STILL OBSESSING OVER THAT?
THAT DOUBT IS ALL I HAVE.
THEN YOU HAVE NOTHING.
SLEEP. I'LL STAND GUARD TONIGHT.
FINE.

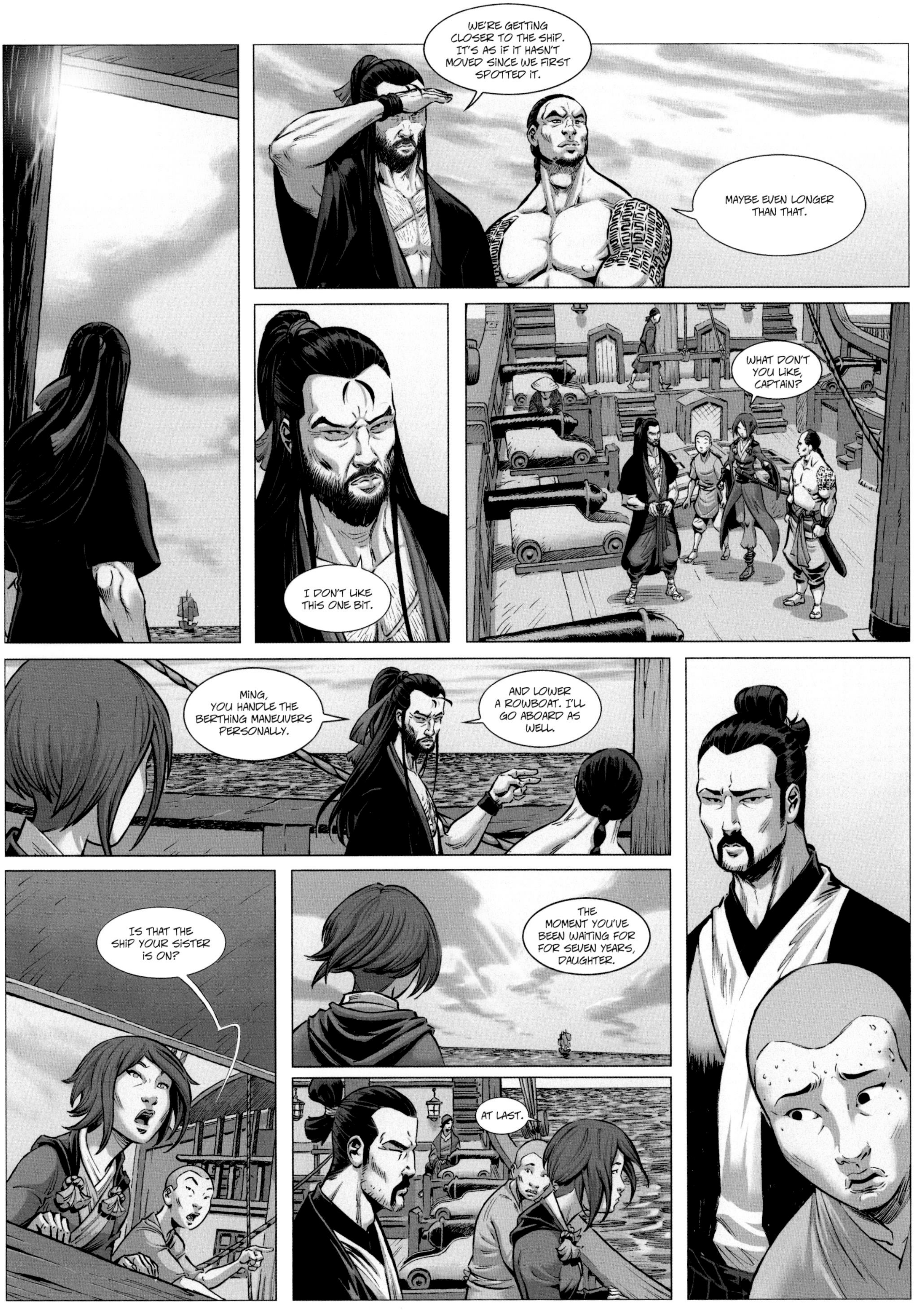
WE'RE GETTING CLOSER TO THE SHIP. IT'S AS IF IT HASN'T MOVED SINCE WE FIRST SPOTTED IT.
MAYBE EVEN LONGER THAN THAT.
I DON'T LIKE THIS ONE BIT.
WHAT DON'T YOU LIKE, CAPTAIN?
MING, YOU HANDLE THE BERTHING MANEUVERS PERSONALLY.
AND LOWER A ROWBOAT. I'LL GO ABOARD AS WELL.
IS THAT THE SHIP YOUR SISTER IS ON?
THE MOMENT YOU'VE BEEN WAITING FOR FOR SEVEN YEARS, DAUGHTER.
AT LAST.

ARE YOU FEELING ALL RIGHT?

HUH?

YOU HAVEN'T SAID A WORD ALL MORNING. IS SOMETHING TROUBLING YOU?

NO...

...NOTHING'S WRONG.

YOU'RE A TERRIBLE LIAR, MASSHIROÏ. I WILL TELL YOU WHAT I THINK.

DEEP DOWN, YOU WOULD HAVE PREFERRED THAT WE NEVER REACH THAT SHIP.

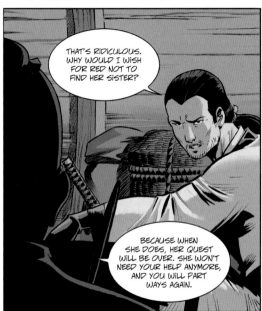

THAT'S RIDICULOUS. WHY WOULD I WISH FOR RED NOT TO FIND HER SISTER?

BECAUSE WHEN SHE DOES, HER QUEST WILL BE OVER. SHE WON'T NEED YOUR HELP ANYMORE, AND YOU WILL PART WAYS AGAIN.

YOU MIGHT BE RIGHT, MASTER. ALL I KNOW IS THAT I WILL NEVER ENCOUNTER A WOMAN LIKE HER AGAIN. AND THE MERE THOUGHT OF LOSING HER IS DRIVING ME INSANE.

WELL, BE PATIENT THEN. SHE WON'T OPEN UP HER HEART UNTIL SHE'S LAID HER PAINFUL PAST TO REST.

SOMEONE ONCE TOLD ME THAT EVEN THE HARDEST ROCK WILL BREAK IF STRUCK AT THE RIGHT PLACE.

WISE WORDS.

WHAT ARE YOU PAINTING, MASTER?

I WAS TRYING TO DEPICT THE MOUNTAINS WHERE I GREW UP. BUT OUR CONVERSATION INSPIRED ME TO ADD THIS SOLITARY MAN, FACING AN INACCESSIBLE DESTINY.

BUT HE HAS NO HEAD!

WE ALL END UP LOSING IT FOR ONE REASON OR ANOTHER, WOULDN'T YOU AGREE?

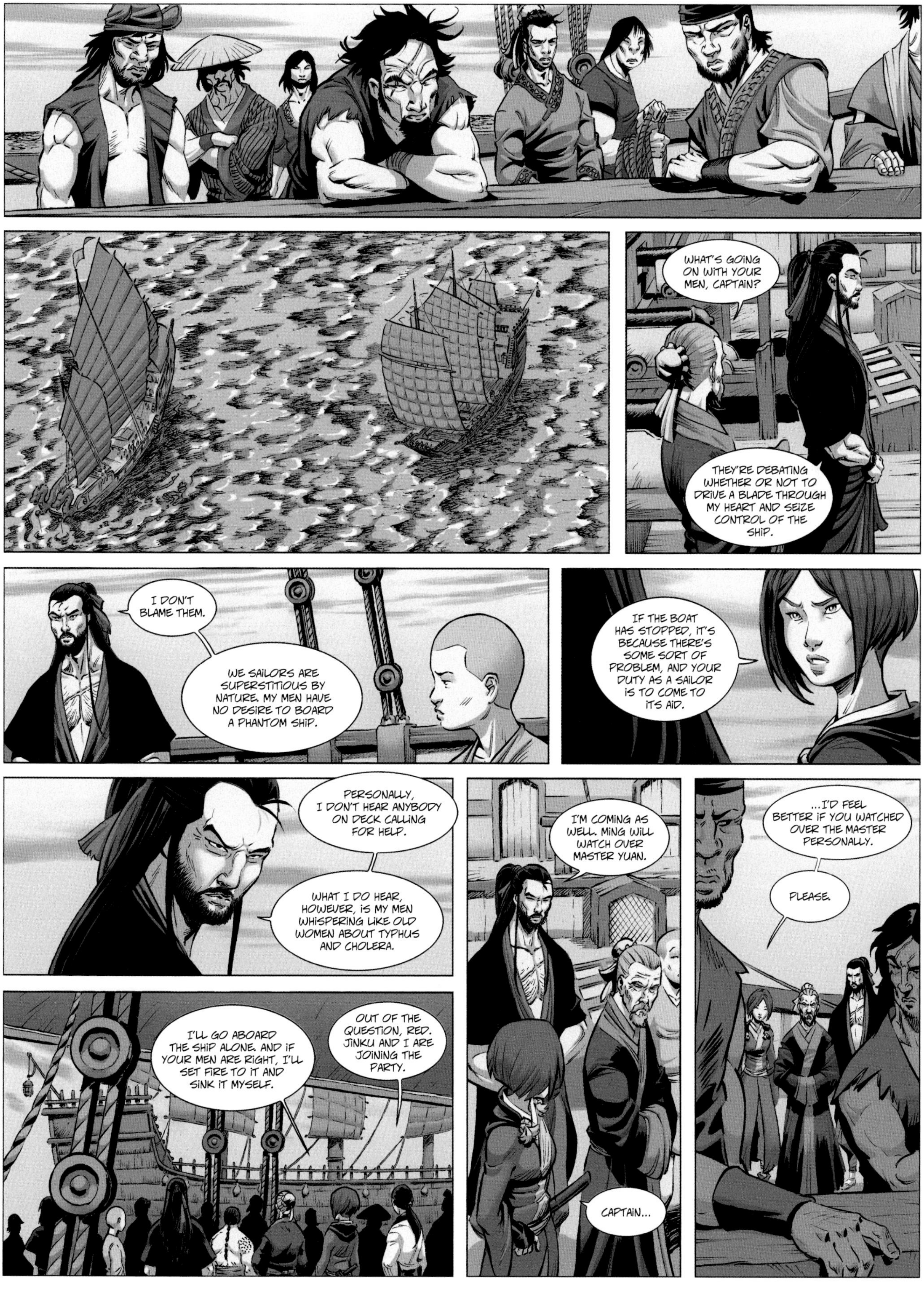
WHAT'S GOING ON WITH YOUR MEN, CAPTAIN?
THEY'RE DEBATING WHETHER OR NOT TO DRIVE A BLADE THROUGH MY HEART AND SEIZE CONTROL OF THE SHIP.
I DON'T BLAME THEM.
WE SAILORS ARE SUPERSTITIOUS BY NATURE. MY MEN HAVE NO DESIRE TO BOARD A PHANTOM SHIP.
IF THE BOAT HAS STOPPED, IT'S BECAUSE THERE'S SOME SORT OF PROBLEM, AND YOUR DUTY AS A SAILOR IS TO COME TO ITS AID.
PERSONALLY, I DON'T HEAR ANYBODY ON DECK CALLING FOR HELP.
WHAT I DO HEAR, HOWEVER, IS MY MEN WHISPERING LIKE OLD WOMEN ABOUT TYPHUS AND CHOLERA.
I'LL GO ABOARD THE SHIP ALONE. AND IF YOUR MEN ARE RIGHT, I'LL SET FIRE TO IT AND SINK IT MYSELF.
OUT OF THE QUESTION, RED. JINKU AND I ARE JOINING THE PARTY.
I'M COMING AS WELL. MING WILL WATCH OVER MASTER YUAN.
CAPTAIN...
...I'D FEEL BETTER IF YOU WATCHED OVER THE MASTER PERSONALLY.
PLEASE.

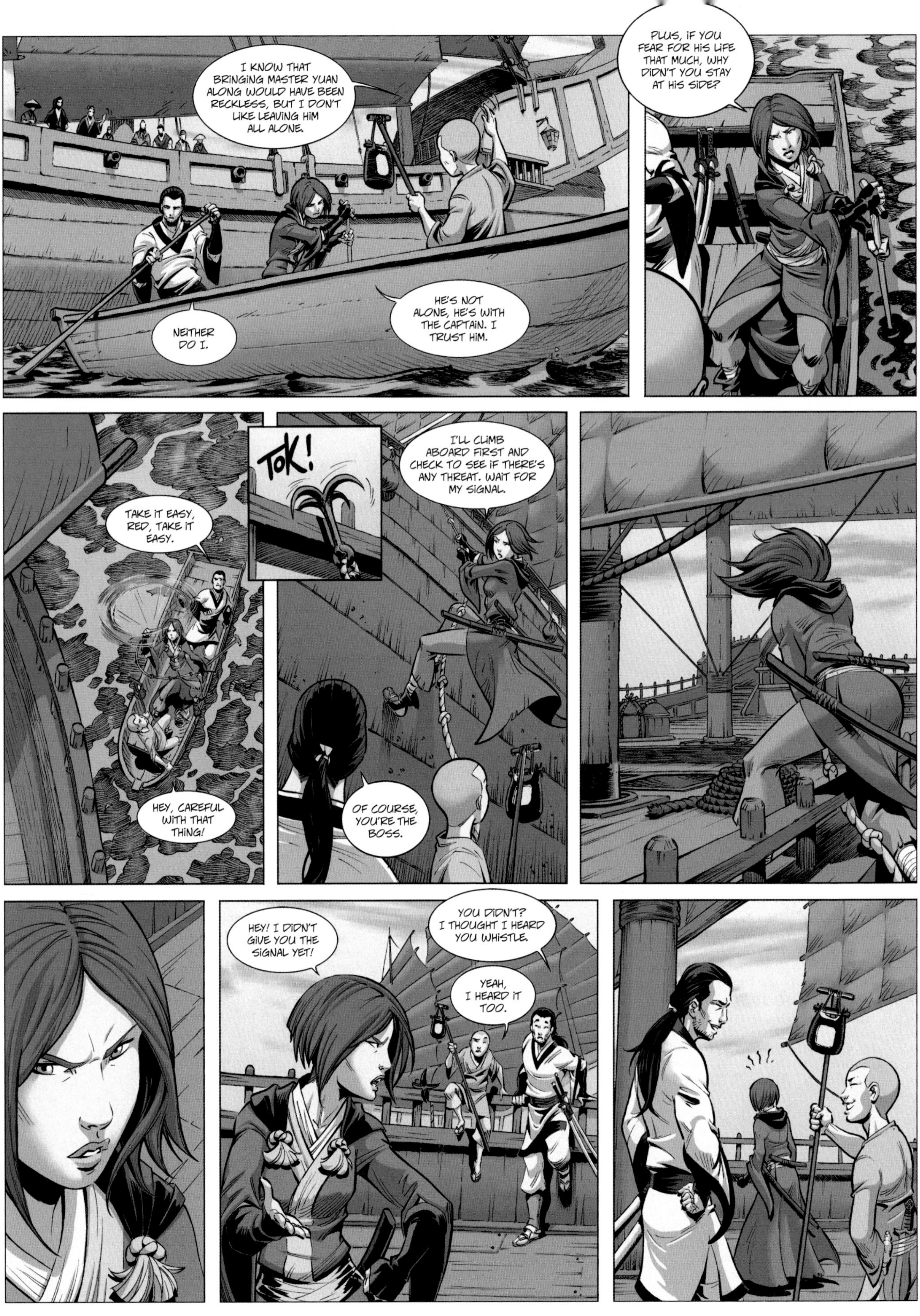
I KNOW THAT BRINGING MASTER YUAN ALONG WOULD HAVE BEEN RECKLESS, BUT I DON'T LIKE LEAVING HIM ALL ALONE.
NEITHER DO I.
HE'S NOT ALONE, HE'S WITH THE CAPTAIN. I TRUST HIM.
PLUS, IF YOU FEAR FOR HIS LIFE THAT MUCH, WHY DIDN'T YOU STAY AT HIS SIDE?
TAKE IT EASY, RED, TAKE IT EASY.
HEY, CAREFUL WITH THAT THING!
TOK!
I'LL CLIMB ABOARD FIRST AND CHECK TO SEE IF THERE'S ANY THREAT. WAIT FOR MY SIGNAL.
OF COURSE, YOU'RE THE BOSS.
HEY! I DIDN'T GIVE YOU THE SIGNAL YET!
YOU DIDN'T? I THOUGHT I HEARD YOU WHISTLE.
YEAH, I HEARD IT TOO.

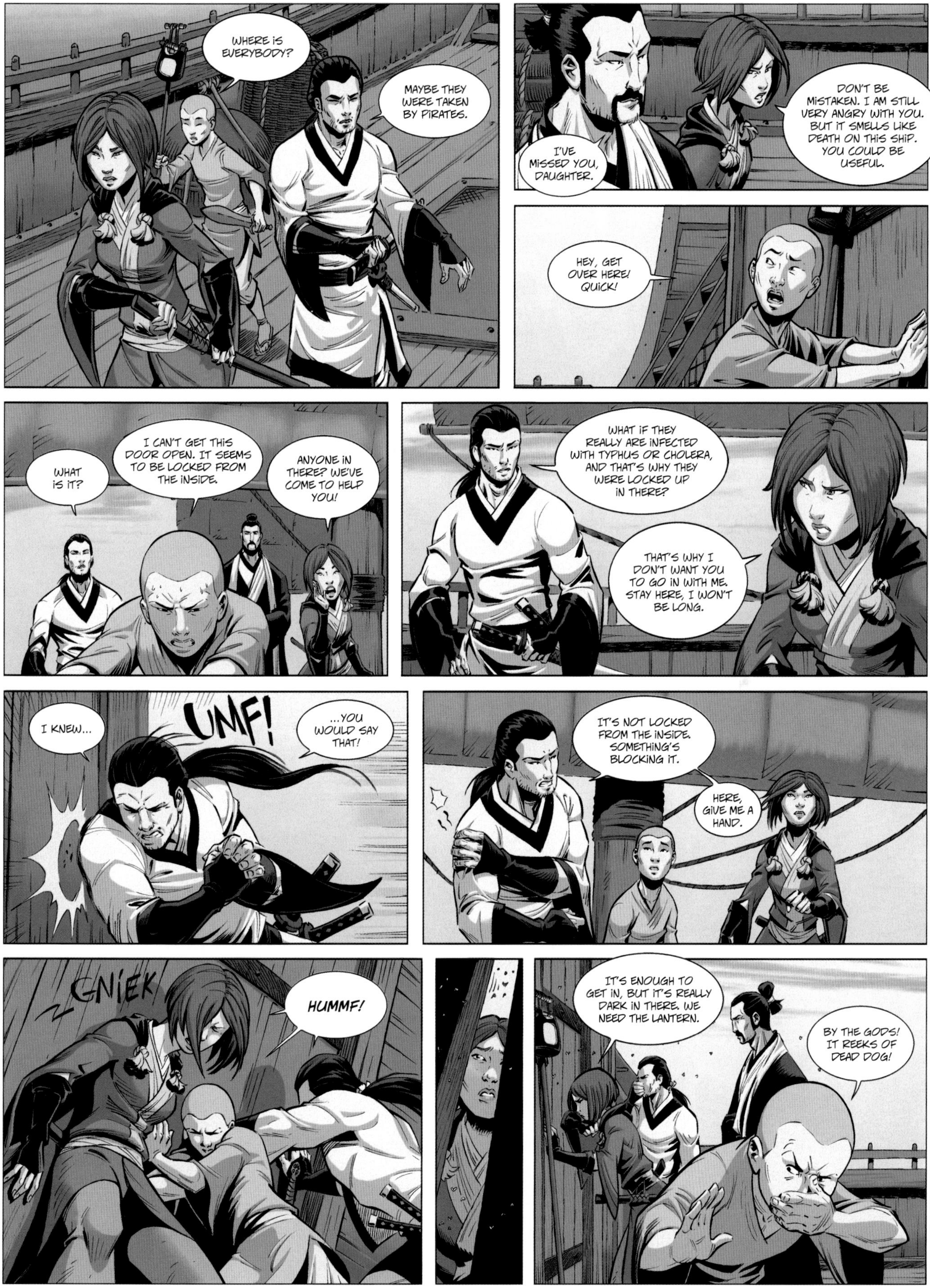

WHERE iS EVERYBODY?
MAYBE THEY WERE TAKEN BY PiRATES.
I'VE MiSSED YOU, DAUGHTER.
DON'T BE MiSTAKEN. I AM STiLL VERY ANGRY WiTH YOU. BUT iT SMELLS LiKE DEATH ON THiS SHiP. YOU COULD BE USEFUL.
HEY, GET OVER HERE! QUiCK!
WHAT iS iT?
I CAN'T GET THiS DOOR OPEN. IT SEEMS TO BE LOCKED FROM THE iNSiDE.
ANYONE iN THERE? WE'VE COME TO HELP YOU!
WHAT iF THEY REALLY ARE iNFECTED WiTH TYPHUS OR CHOLERA, AND THAT'S WHY THEY WERE LOCKED UP iN THERE?
THAT'S WHY I DON'T WANT YOU TO GO iN WiTH ME. STAY HERE, I WON'T BE LONG.
I KNEW...
UMF!
...YOU WOULD SAY THAT!
IT'S NOT LOCKED FROM THE iNSiDE. SOMETHiNG'S BLOCKiNG iT.
HERE, GiVE ME A HAND.
GNiEK
HUMMF!
IT'S ENOUGH TO GET iN, BUT iT'S REALLY DARK iN THERE. WE NEED THE LANTERN.
BY THE GODS! IT REEKS OF DEAD DOG!

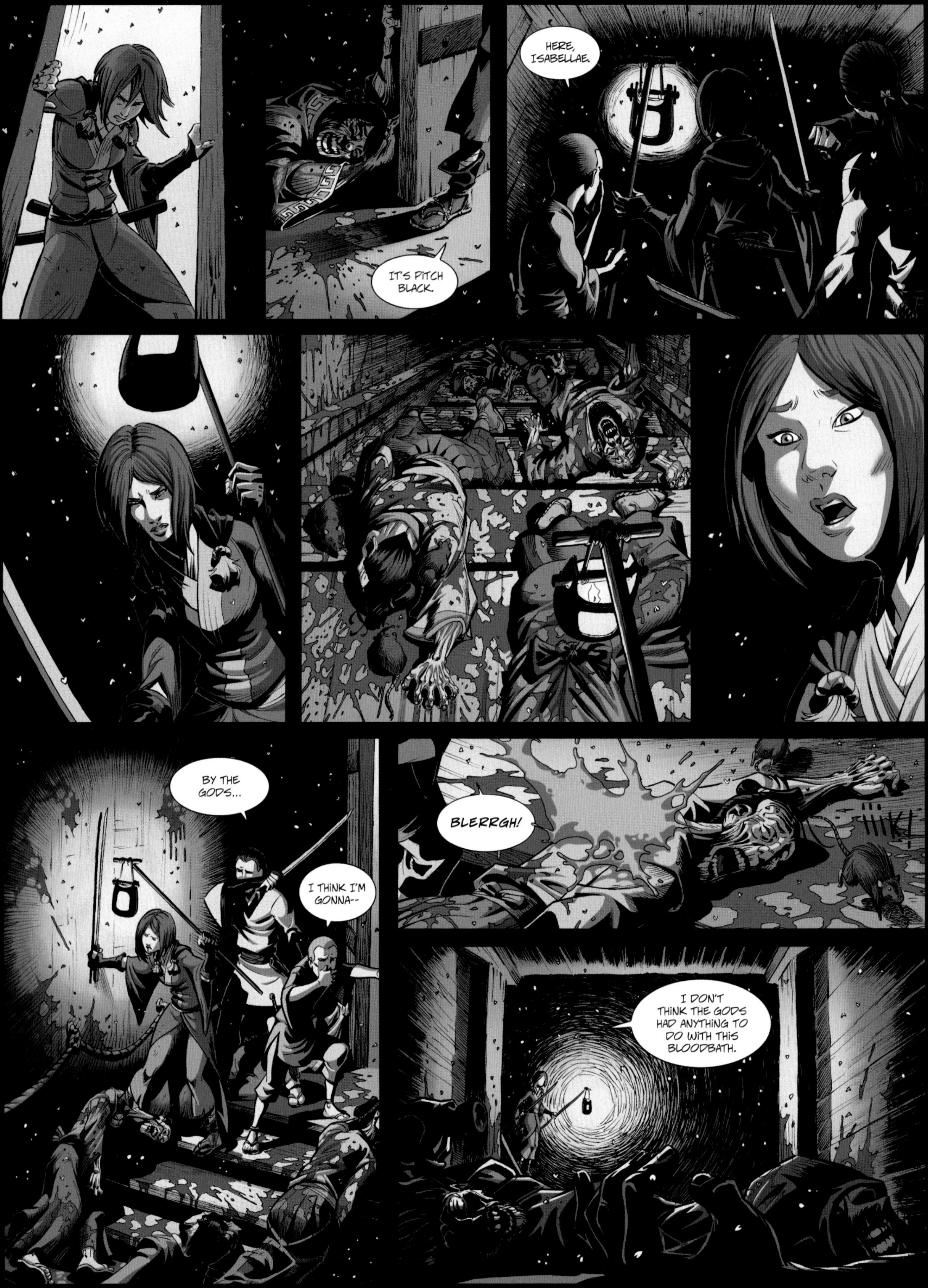
IT'S PITCH BLACK.
HERE, ISABELLAE.
BY THE GODS...
I THINK I'M GONNA--
BLERRGH!
IIIK!
I DON'T THINK THE GODS HAD ANYTHING TO DO WITH THIS BLOODBATH.

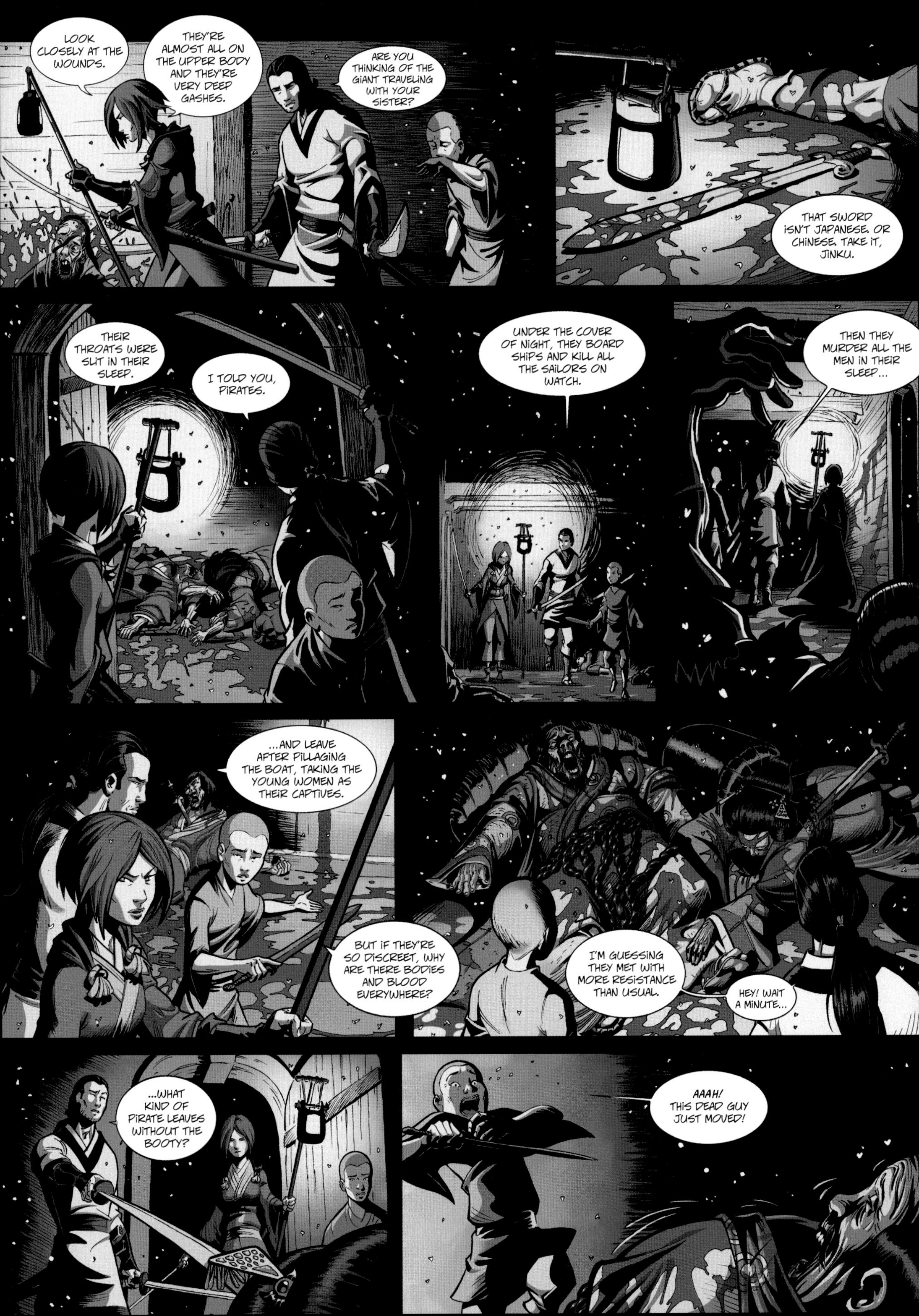
LOOK CLOSELY AT THE WOUNDS.
THEY'RE ALMOST ALL ON THE UPPER BODY AND THEY'RE VERY DEEP GASHES.
ARE YOU THINKING OF THE GIANT TRAVELING WITH YOUR SISTER?
THAT SWORD ISN'T JAPANESE. OR CHINESE. TAKE IT, JINKU.
THEIR THROATS WERE SLIT IN THEIR SLEEP.
I TOLD YOU, PIRATES.
UNDER THE COVER OF NIGHT, THEY BOARD SHIPS AND KILL ALL THE SAILORS ON WATCH.
THEN THEY MURDER ALL THE MEN IN THEIR SLEEP...
...AND LEAVE AFTER PILLAGING THE BOAT, TAKING THE YOUNG WOMEN AS THEIR CAPTIVES.
BUT IF THEY'RE SO DISCREET, WHY ARE THERE BODIES AND BLOOD EVERYWHERE?
I'M GUESSING THEY MET WITH MORE RESISTANCE THAN USUAL.
HEY! WAIT A MINUTE...
...WHAT KIND OF PIRATE LEAVES WITHOUT THE BOOTY?
AAAH! THIS DEAD GUY JUST MOVED!

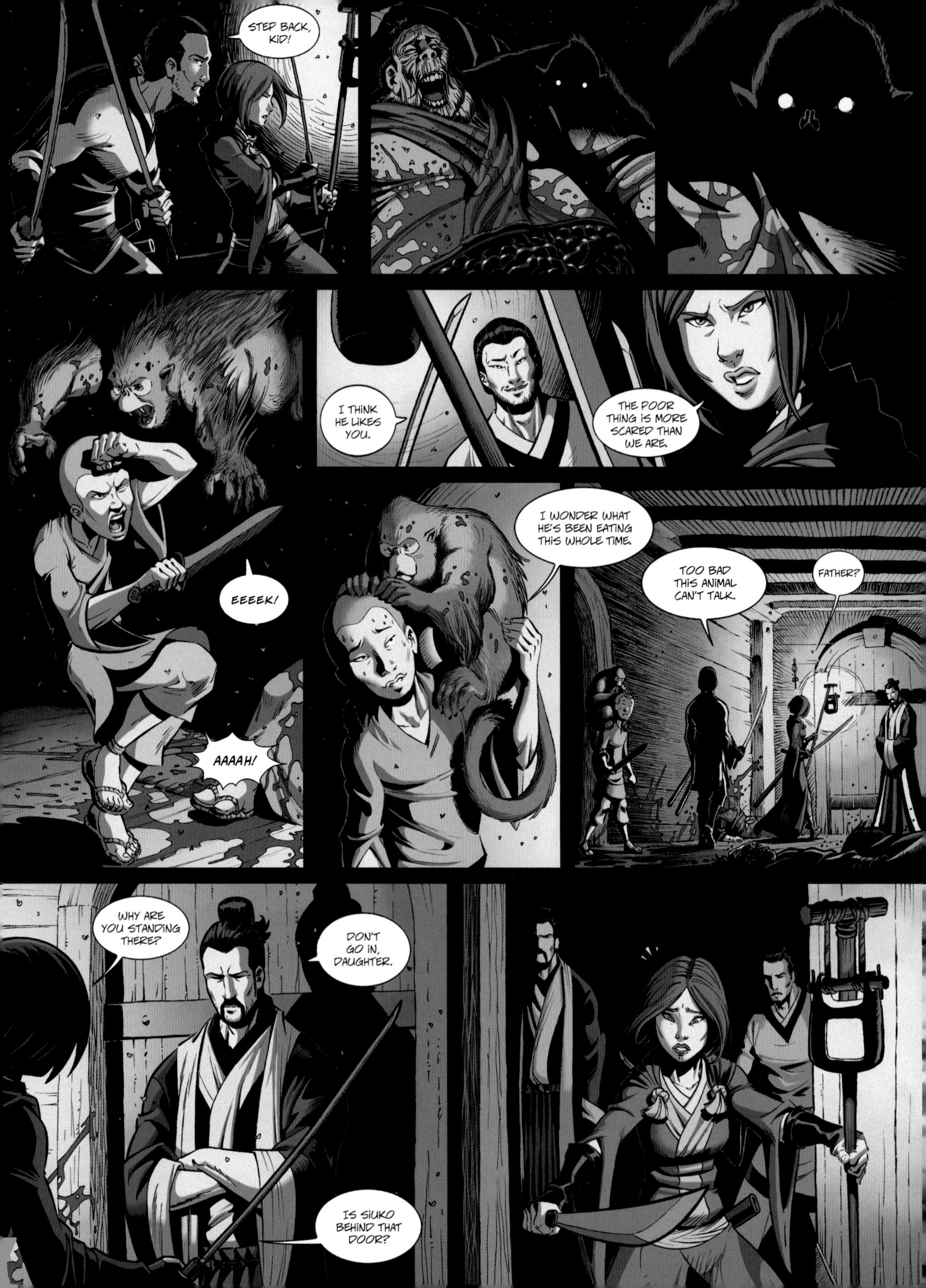
STEP BACK, KID!
EEEEK!
AAAAH!
I THINK HE LIKES YOU.
THE POOR THING IS MORE SCARED THAN WE ARE.
I WONDER WHAT HE'S BEEN EATING THIS WHOLE TIME.
TOO BAD THIS ANIMAL CAN'T TALK.
FATHER?
WHY ARE YOU STANDING THERE?
DON'T GO IN, DAUGHTER.
IS SIUKO BEHIND THAT DOOR?

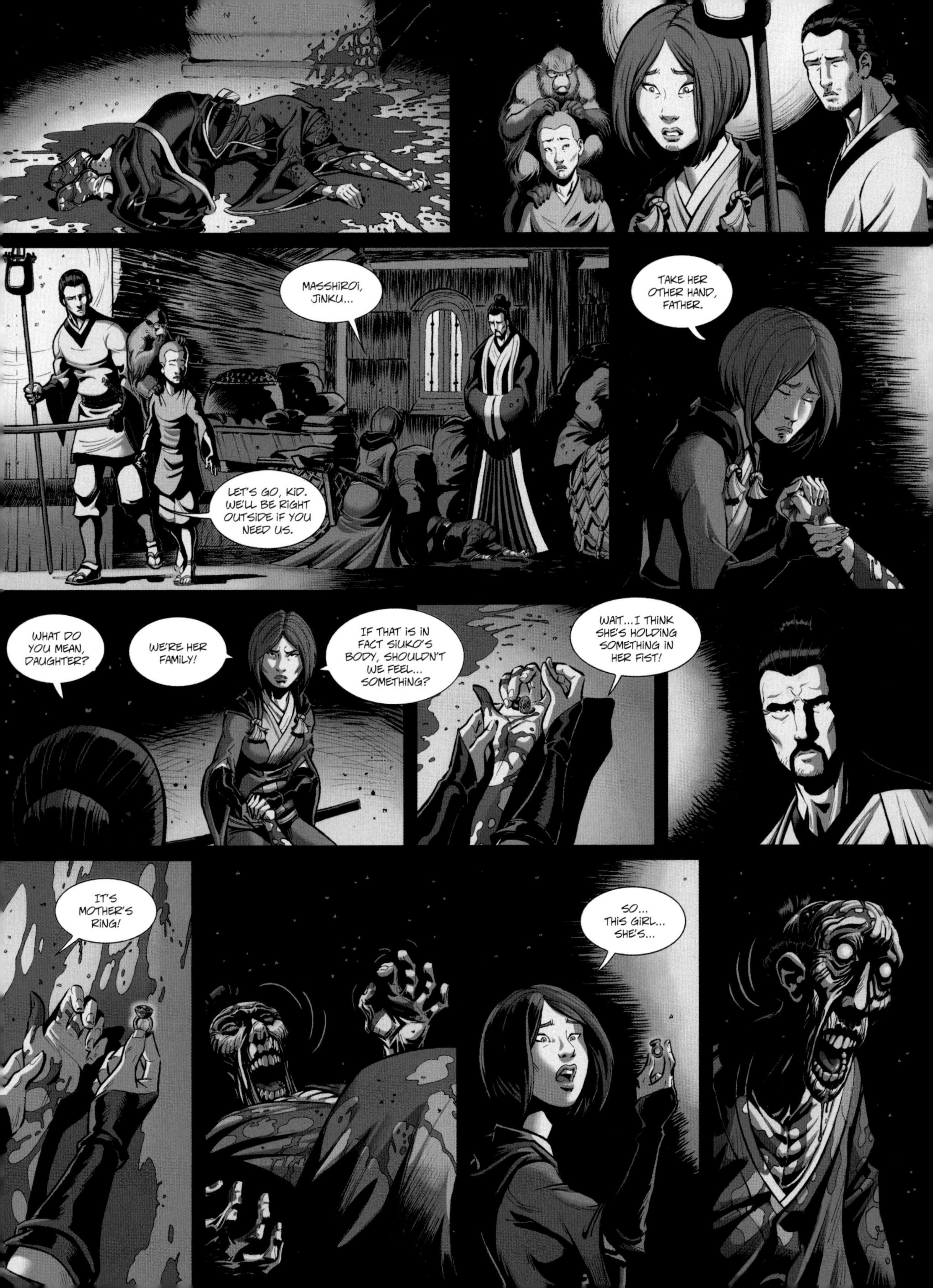
MASSHIROI, JINKU...
LET'S GO, KID. WE'LL BE RIGHT OUTSIDE IF YOU NEED US.
TAKE HER OTHER HAND, FATHER.
WHAT DO YOU MEAN, DAUGHTER?
WE'RE HER FAMILY!
IF THAT IS IN FACT SIUKO'S BODY, SHOULDN'T WE FEEL... SOMETHING?
WAIT... I THINK SHE'S HOLDING SOMETHING IN HER FIST!
IT'S MOTHER'S RING!
SO... THIS GIRL... SHE'S...

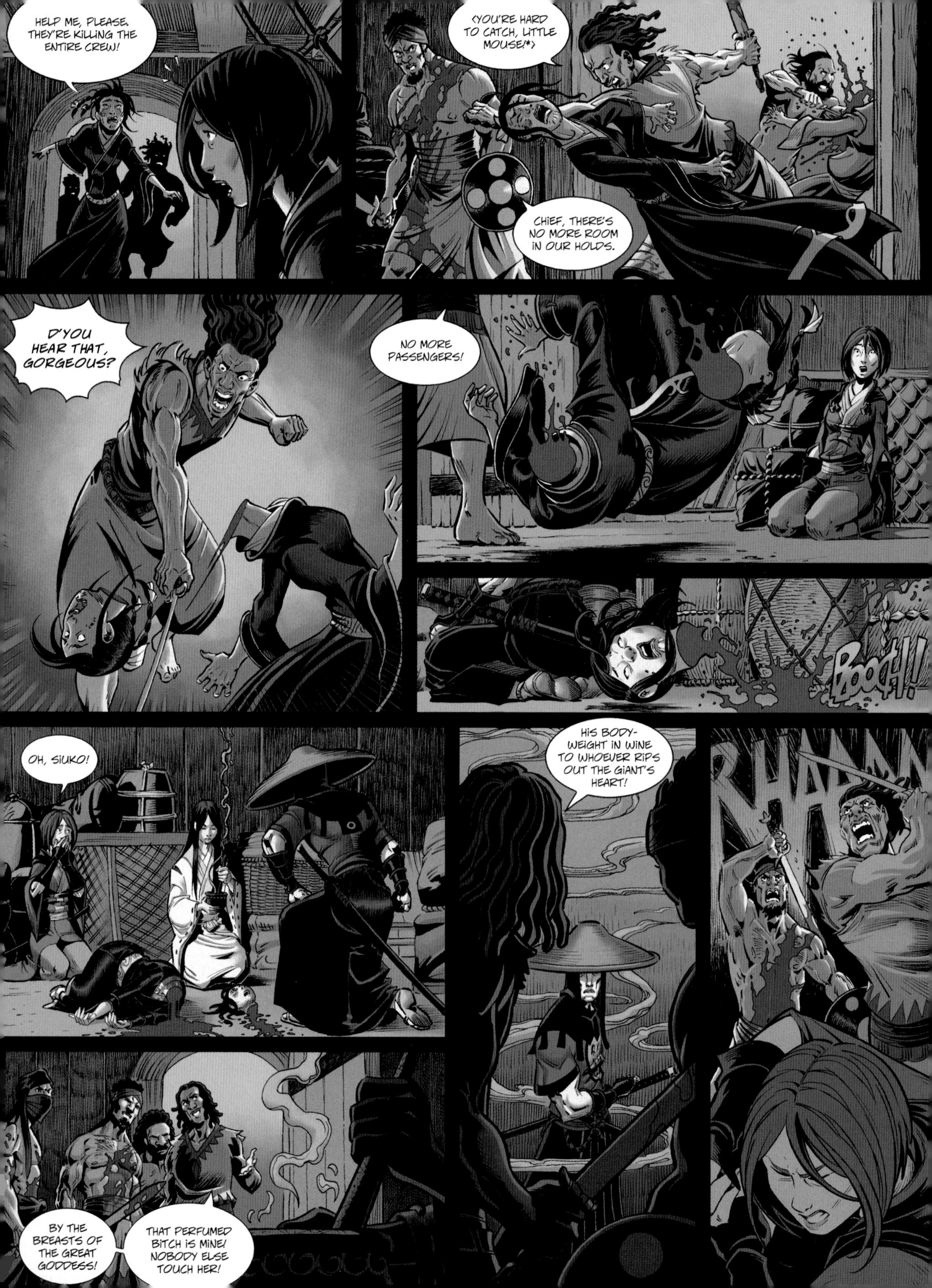
HELP ME, PLEASE. THEY'RE KILLING THE ENTIRE CREW!
‹YOU'RE HARD TO CATCH, LITTLE MOUSE!*›
CHIEF, THERE'S NO MORE ROOM IN OUR HOLDS.
D'YOU HEAR THAT, GORGEOUS?
NO MORE PASSENGERS!
BOOCH!!
OH, SIUKO!
HIS BODY-WEIGHT IN WINE TO WHOEVER RIPS OUT THE GIANT'S HEART!
BY THE BREASTS OF THE GREAT GODDESS!
THAT PERFUMED BITCH IS MINE! NOBODY ELSE TOUCH HER!

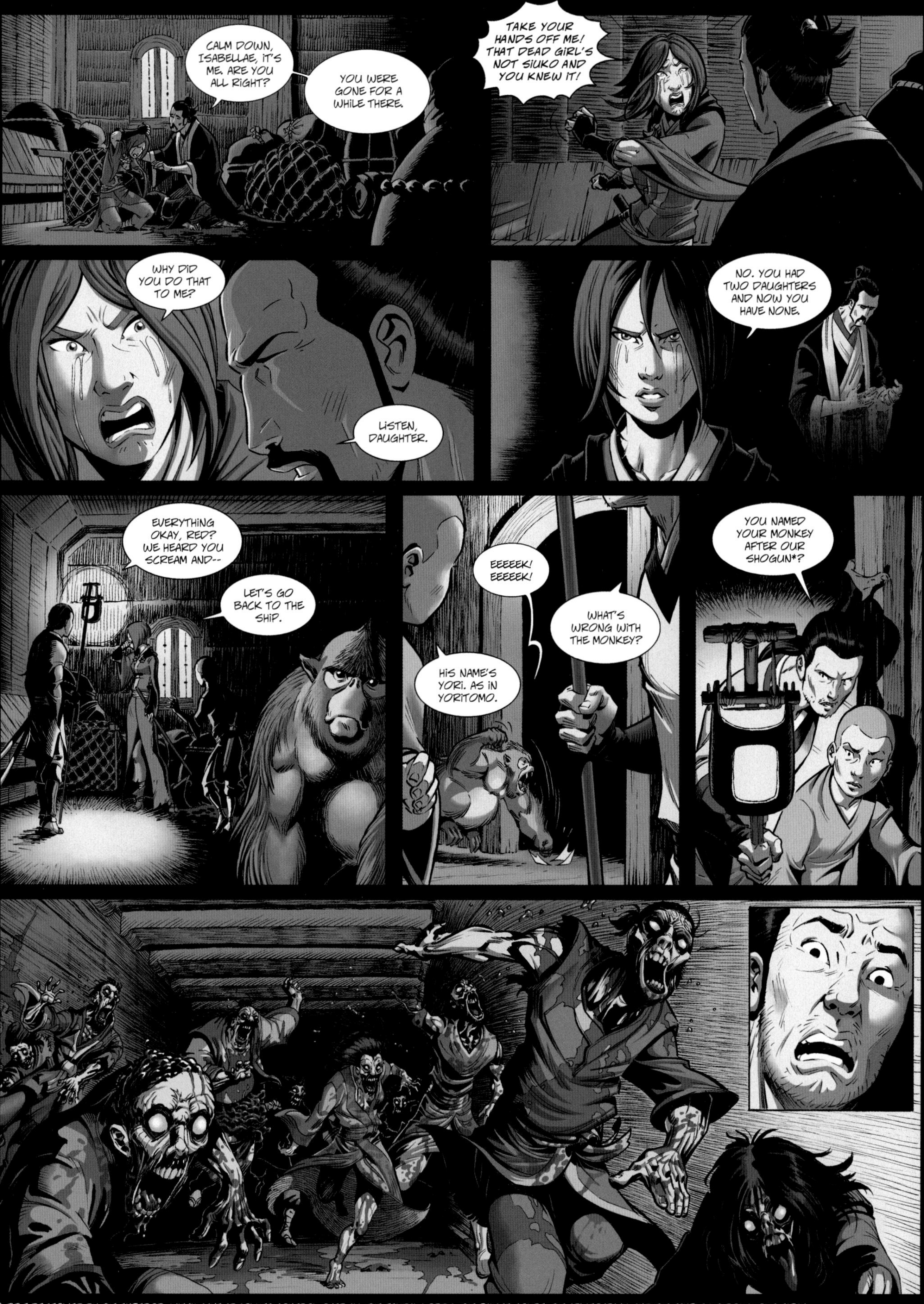
CALM DOWN, ISABELLAE, IT'S ME. ARE YOU ALL RIGHT?
YOU WERE GONE FOR A WHILE THERE.
TAKE YOUR HANDS OFF ME! THAT DEAD GIRL'S NOT SIUKO AND YOU KNEW IT!
WHY DID YOU DO THAT TO ME?
LISTEN, DAUGHTER.
NO. YOU HAD TWO DAUGHTERS AND NOW YOU HAVE NONE.
EVERYTHING OKAY, RED? WE HEARD YOU SCREAM AND--
LET'S GO BACK TO THE SHIP.
EEEEEK! EEEEEK!
WHAT'S WRONG WITH THE MONKEY?
HIS NAME'S YORI. AS IN YORITOMO.
YOU NAMED YOUR MONKEY AFTER OUR SHOGUN*?

* TITLE BESTOWED BY THE EMPEROR, WHICH GAVE ABSOLUTE CONTROL OVER ALL THE FEUDAL LORDS, THE PALACE COURT, THE ARISTOCRACY, AND THE TEMPLES THROUGHOUT JAPAN.

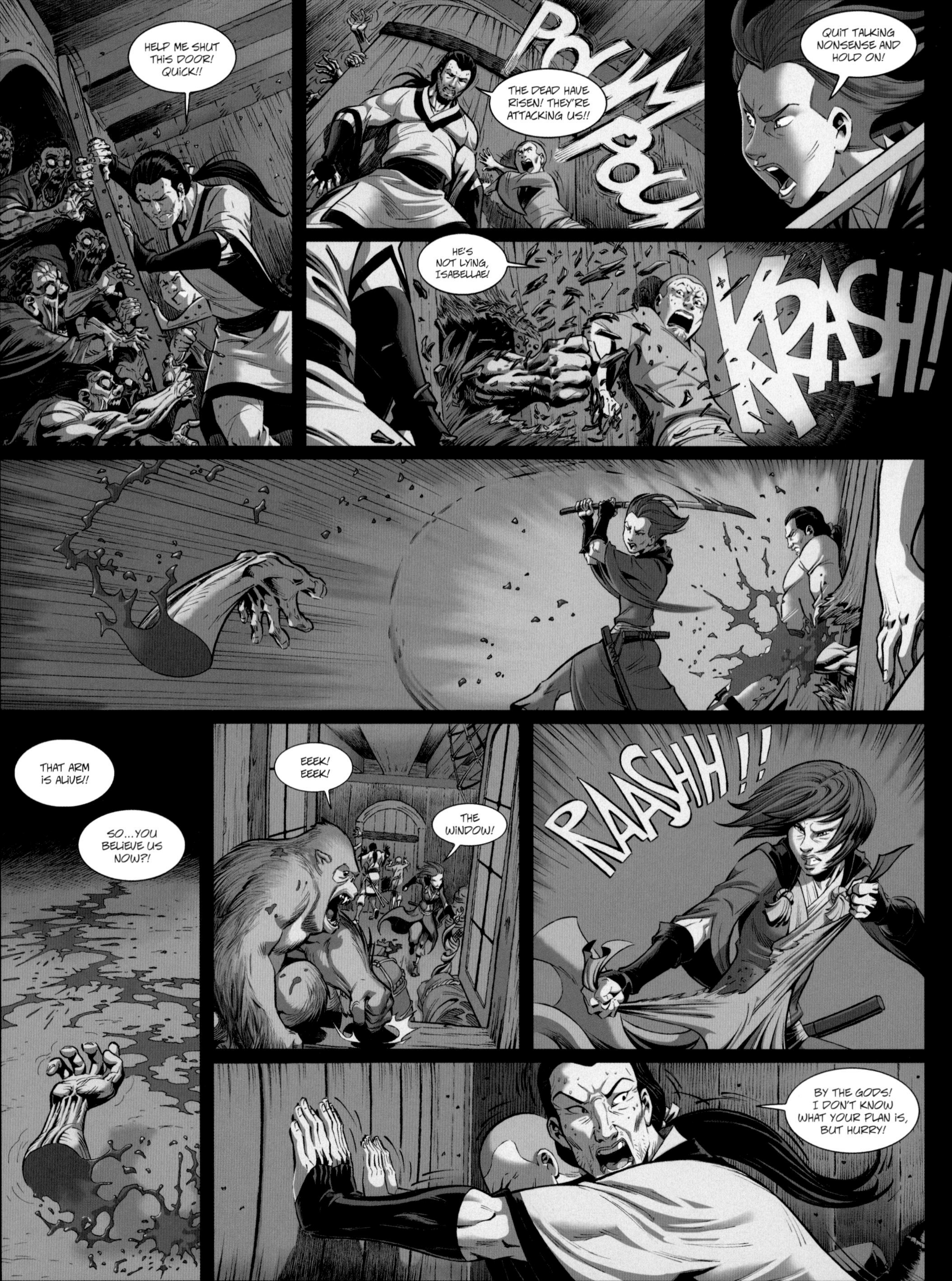
HELP ME SHUT THIS DOOR! QUICK!!
POOM POOM
THE DEAD HAVE RISEN! THEY'RE ATTACKING US!!
QUIT TALKING NONSENSE AND HOLD ON!
HE'S NOT LYING, ISABELLAE!
KRASH!!
THAT ARM IS ALIVE!!
SO...YOU BELIEVE US NOW?!
EEEK! EEEK!
THE WINDOW!
RAASHH!!
BY THE GODS! I DON'T KNOW WHAT YOUR PLAN IS, BUT HURRY!

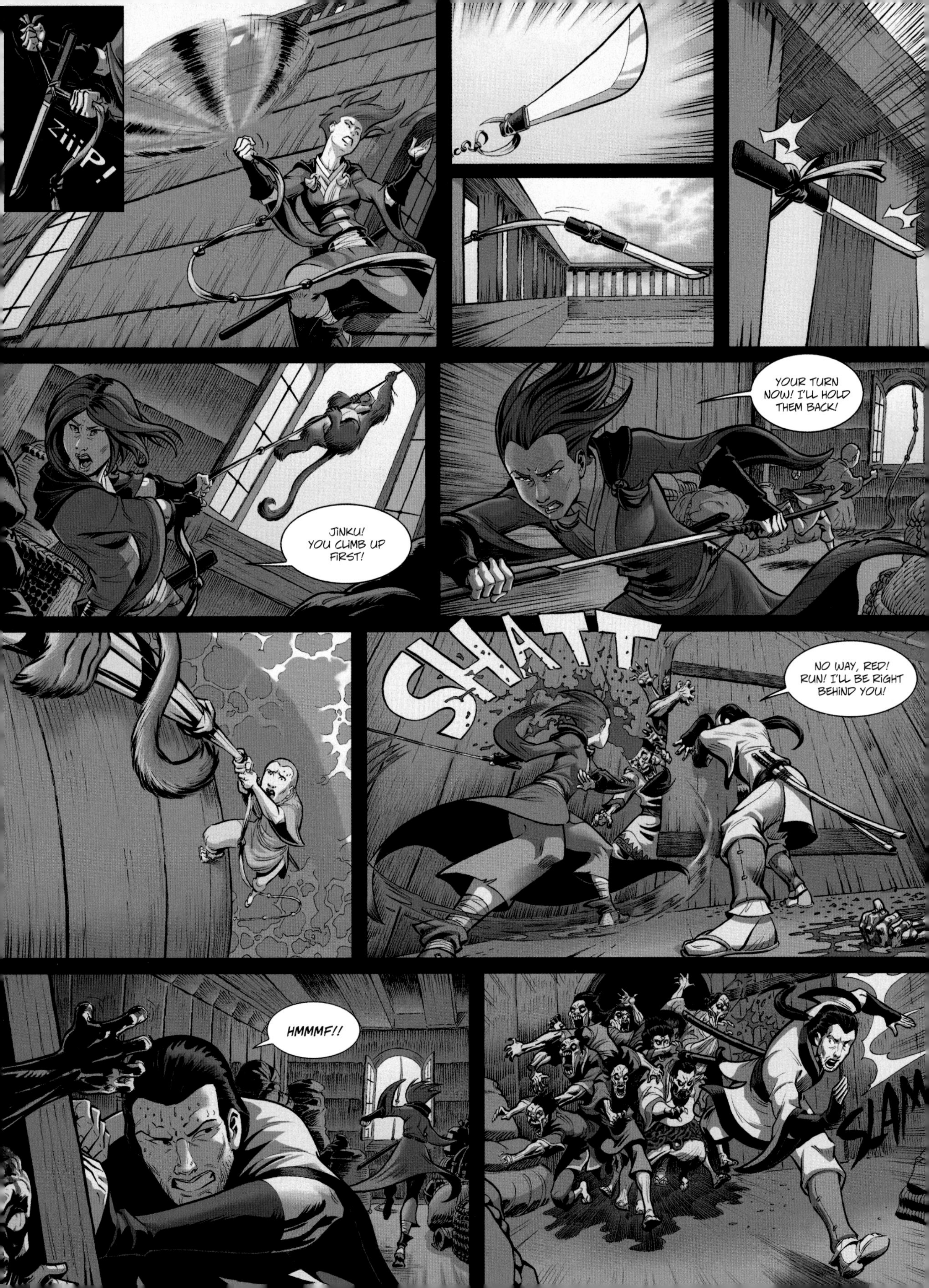
ZiiiP!
JiNKU! YOU CLIMB UP FIRST!
YOUR TURN NOW! I'LL HOLD THEM BACK!
SHATT
NO WAY, RED! RUN! I'LL BE RIGHT BEHiND YOU!
HMMMF!!
SLAM

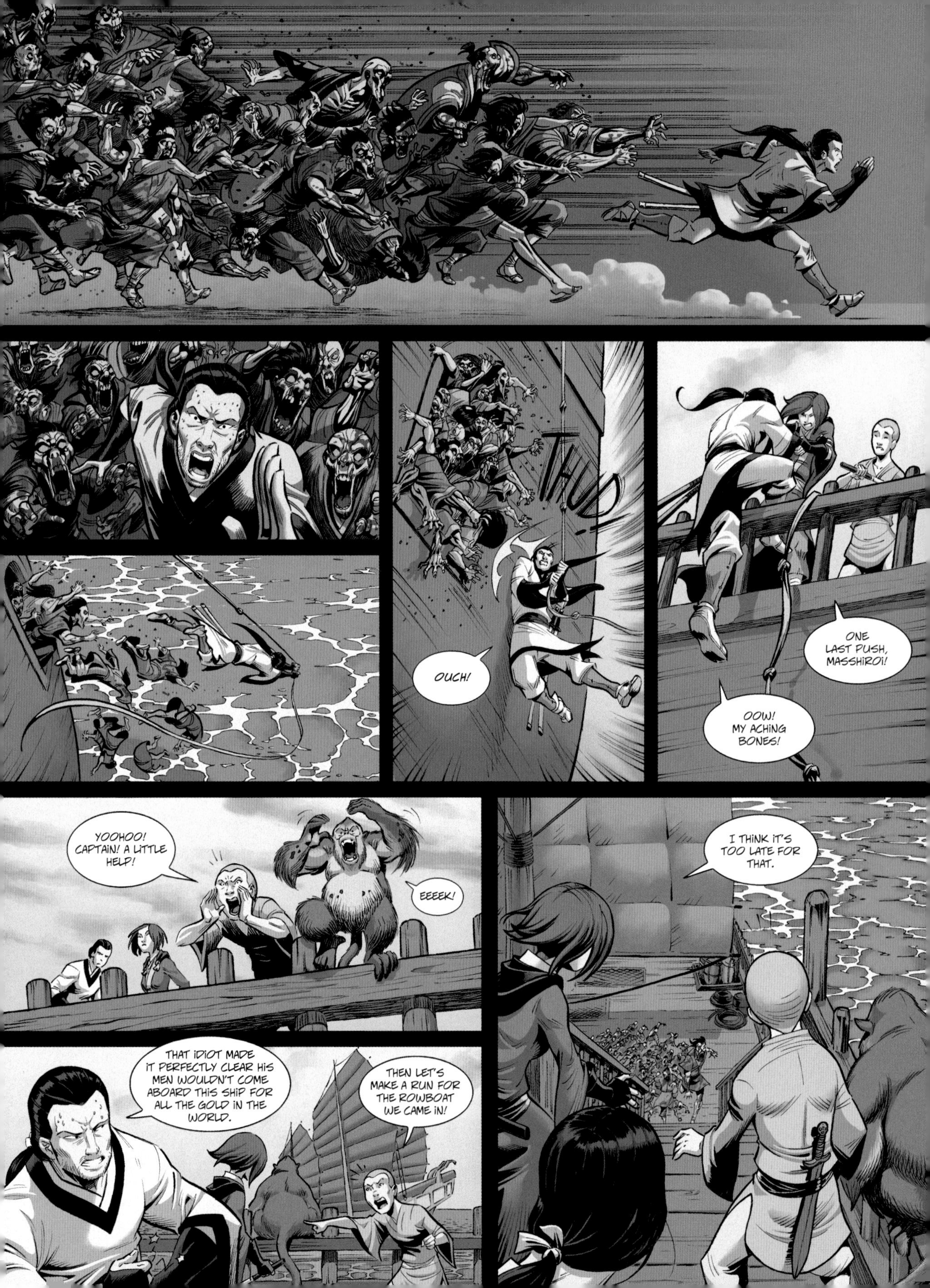
THUD
OUCH!
ONE LAST PUSH, MASSHIROI!
OOW! MY ACHING BONES!
YOOHOO! CAPTAIN! A LITTLE HELP!
EEEEK!
I THINK IT'S TOO LATE FOR THAT.
THAT IDIOT MADE IT PERFECTLY CLEAR HIS MEN WOULDN'T COME ABOARD THIS SHIP FOR ALL THE GOLD IN THE WORLD.
THEN LET'S MAKE A RUN FOR THE ROWBOAT WE CAME IN!

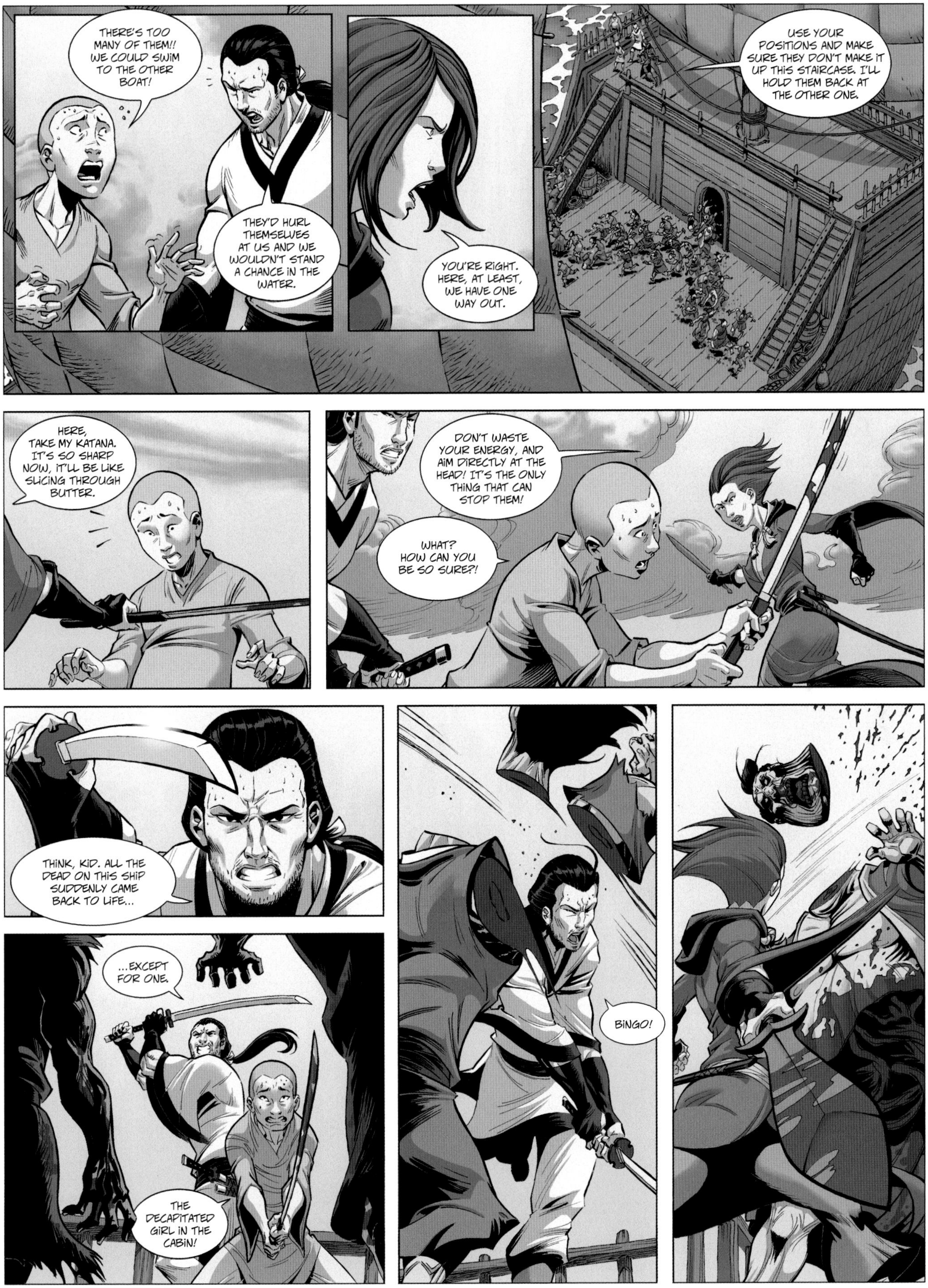
THERE'S TOO MANY OF THEM!! WE COULD SWIM TO THE OTHER BOAT!
THEY'D HURL THEMSELVES AT US AND WE WOULDN'T STAND A CHANCE IN THE WATER.
YOU'RE RIGHT. HERE, AT LEAST, WE HAVE ONE WAY OUT.
USE YOUR POSITIONS AND MAKE SURE THEY DON'T MAKE IT UP THIS STAIRCASE. I'LL HOLD THEM BACK AT THE OTHER ONE.
HERE, TAKE MY KATANA. IT'S SO SHARP NOW, IT'LL BE LIKE SLICING THROUGH BUTTER.
DON'T WASTE YOUR ENERGY, AND AIM DIRECTLY AT THE HEAD! IT'S THE ONLY THING THAT CAN STOP THEM!
WHAT? HOW CAN YOU BE SO SURE?!
THINK, KID. ALL THE DEAD ON THIS SHIP SUDDENLY CAME BACK TO LIFE...
...EXCEPT FOR ONE.
THE DECAPITATED GIRL IN THE CABIN!
BINGO!

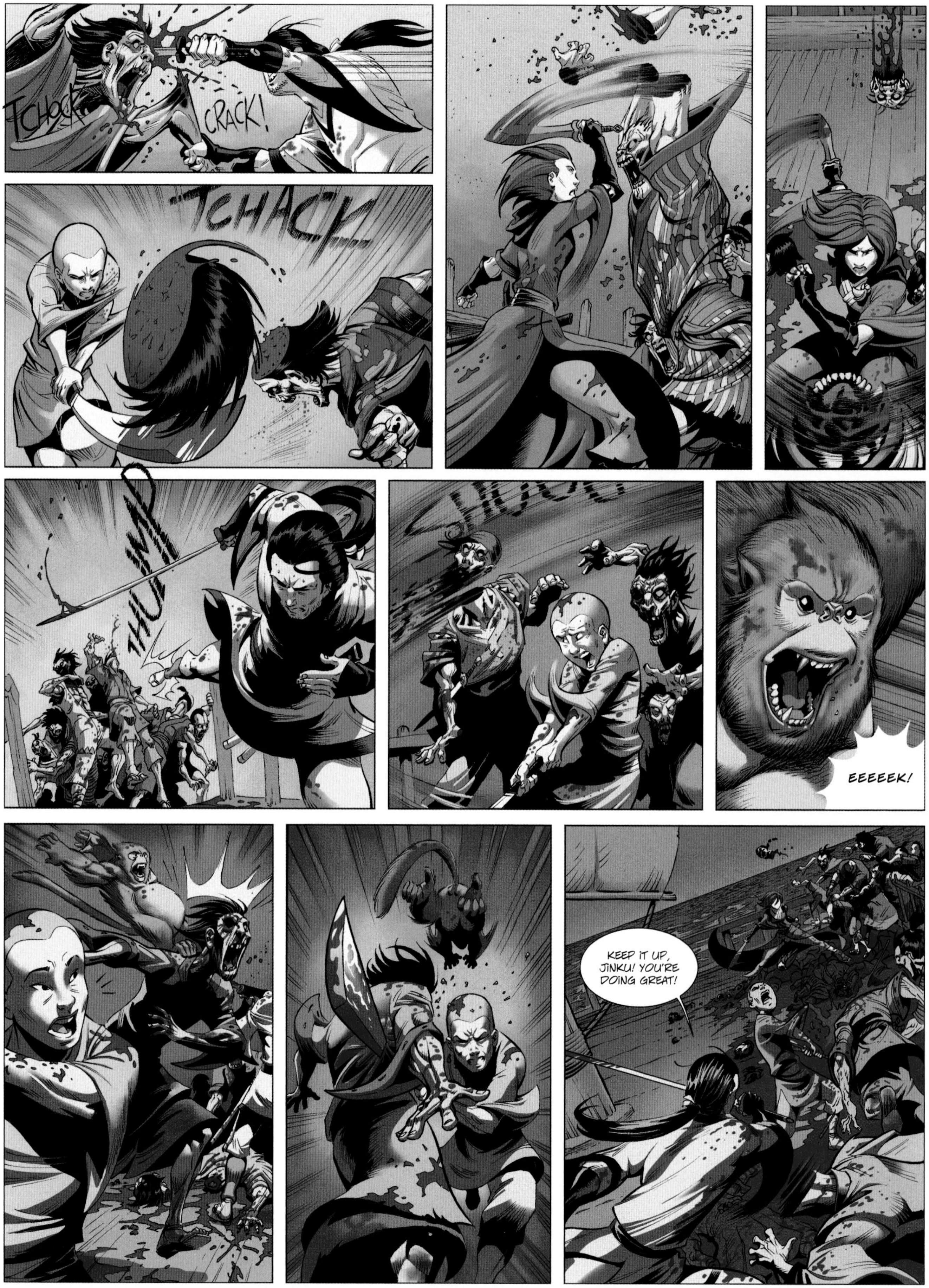
TCHOCK
CRACK!
TCHACK
THUMP
EEEEEK!
KEEP IT UP, JINKU! YOU'RE DOING GREAT!

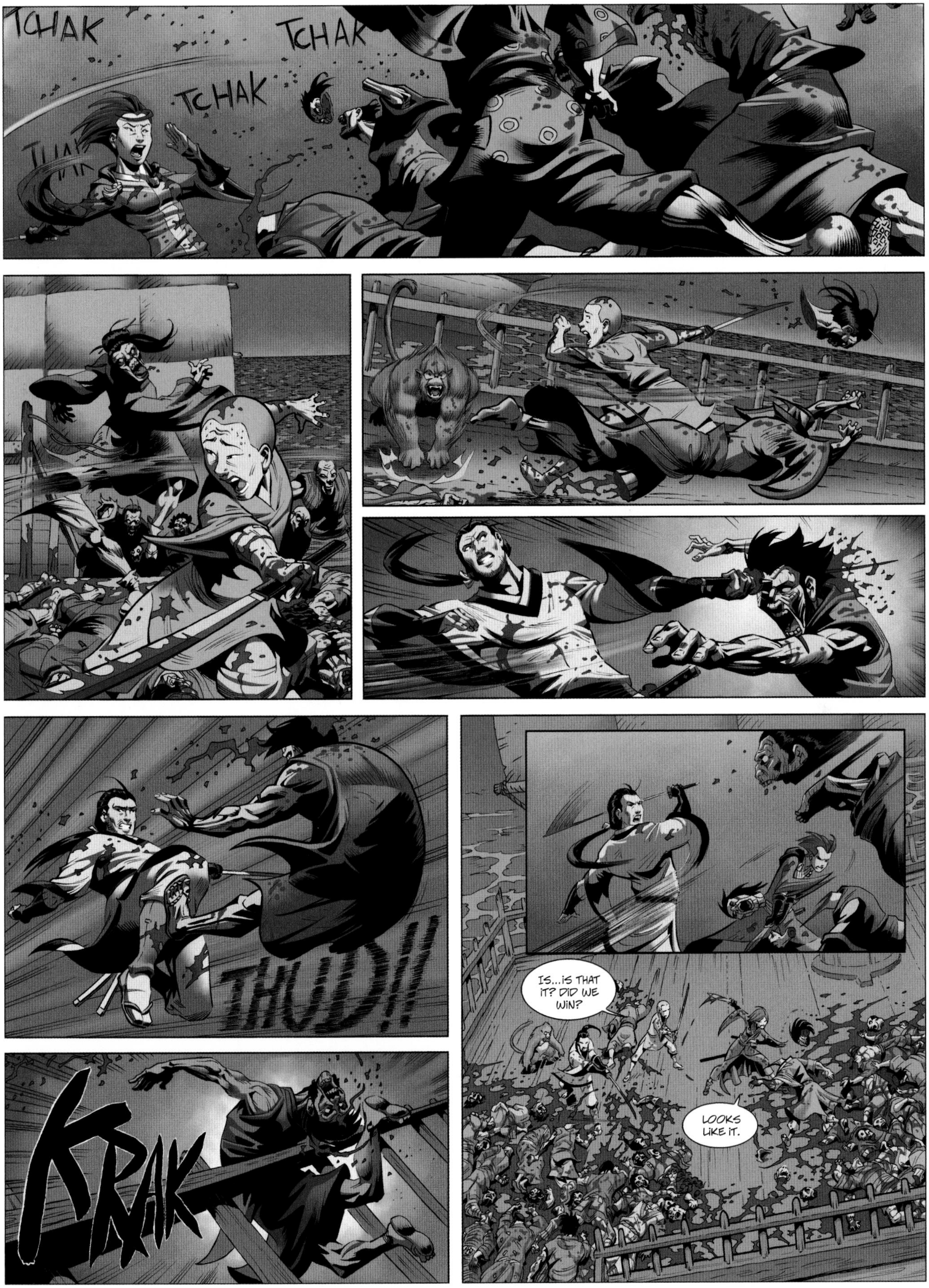
TCHAK
TCHAK
TCHAK
THUD!!
KRAK
IS...IS THAT IT? DID WE WIN?
LOOKS LIKE IT.

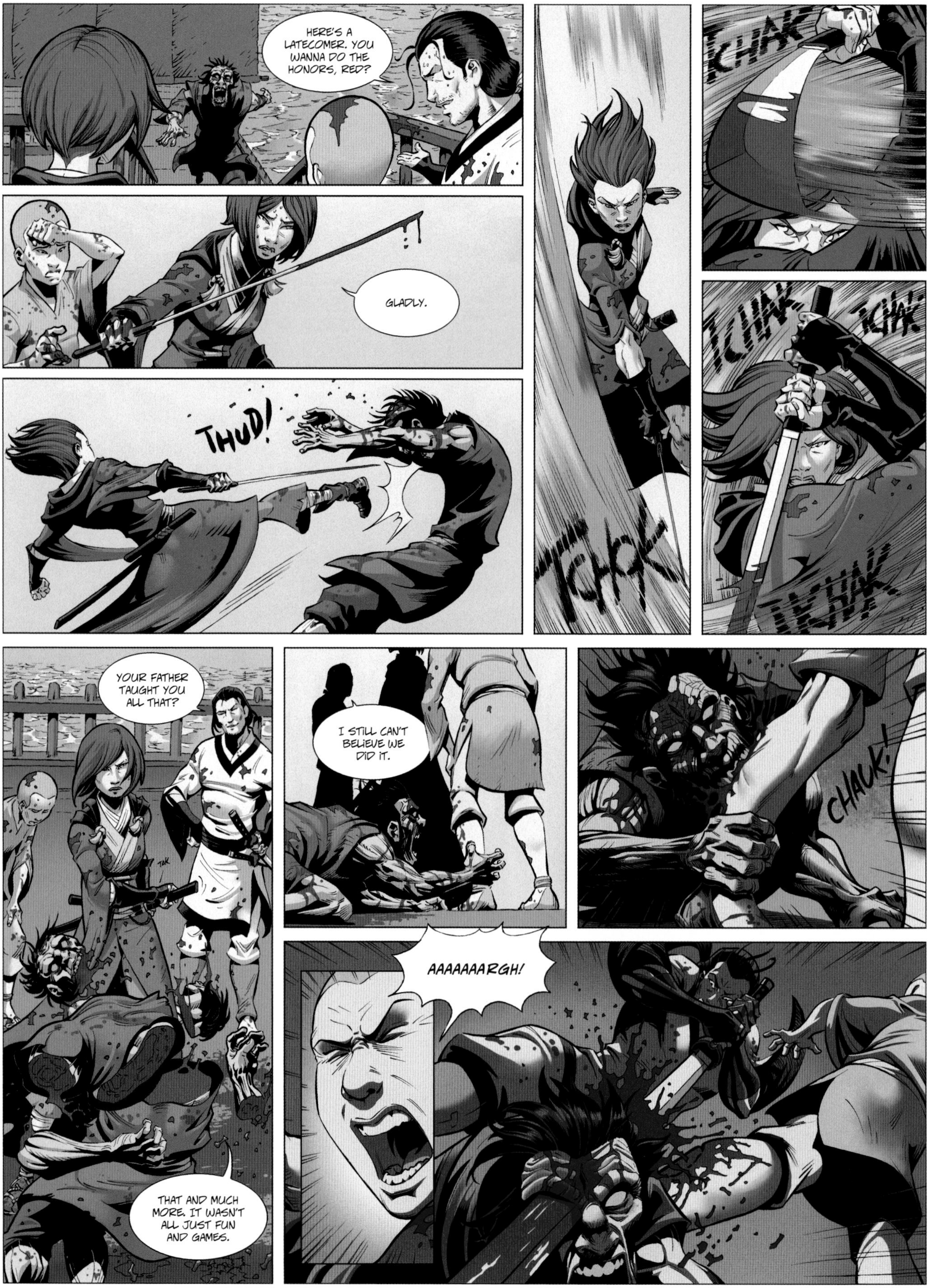
HERE'S A LATECOMER. YOU WANNA DO THE HONORS, RED?
GLADLY.
THUD!
TCHAK
TCHAK
TCHAK
TCHAK
TCHAK
YOUR FATHER TAUGHT YOU ALL THAT?
TAK
THAT AND MUCH MORE. IT WASN'T ALL JUST FUN AND GAMES.
I STILL CAN'T BELIEVE WE DID IT.
CHAUK!
AAAAAAARGH!

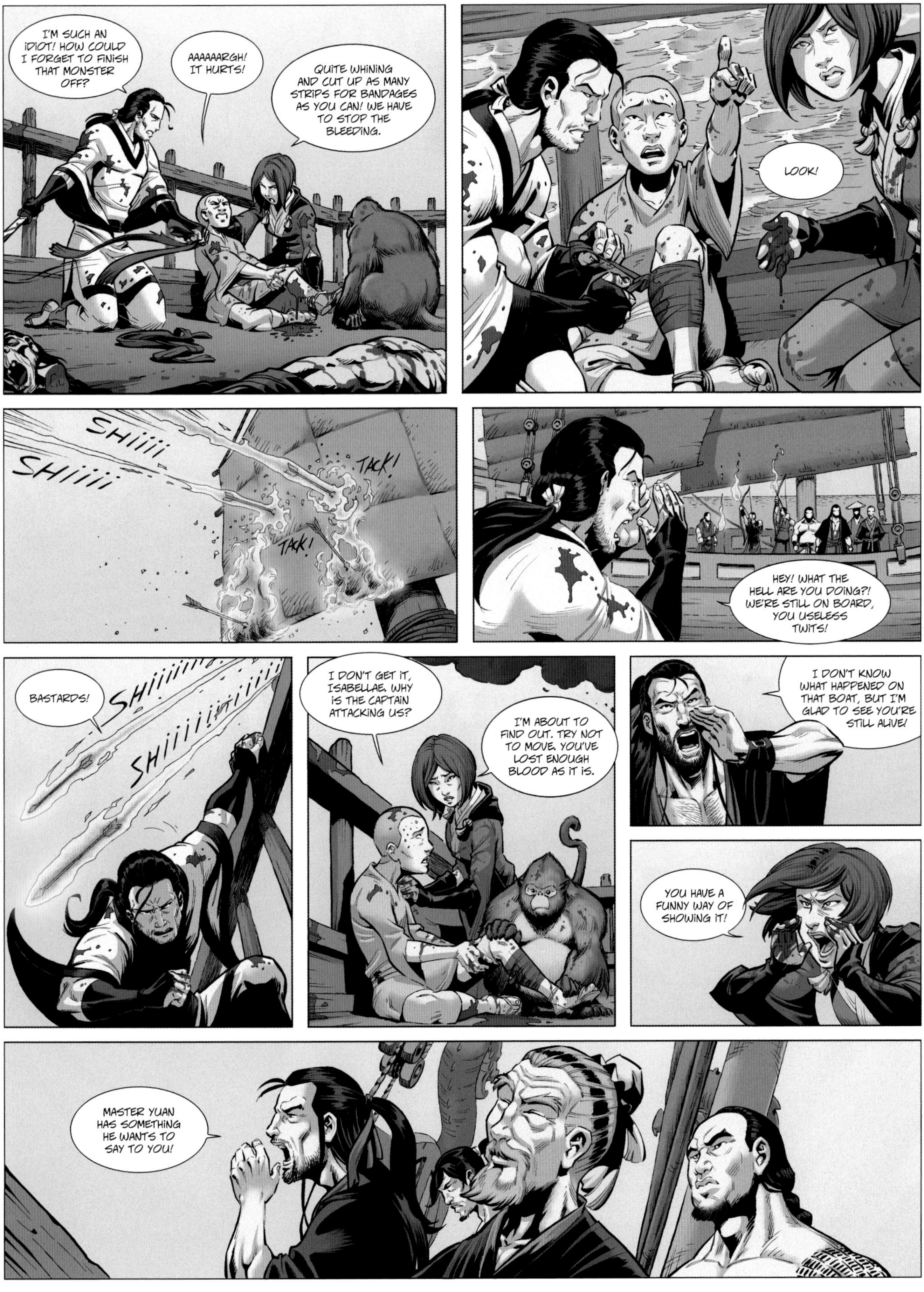
I'M SUCH AN iDIOT! HOW COULD I FORGET TO FINISH THAT MONSTER OFF?
AAAAAARGH! IT HURTS!
QUITE WHiNiNG AND CUT UP AS MANY STRiPS FOR BANDAGES AS YOU CAN! WE HAVE TO STOP THE BLEEDiNG.
LOOK!
SHiiiii
SHiiiii
TACK!
TACK!
HEY! WHAT THE HELL ARE YOU DOiNG?! WE'RE STiLL ON BOARD, YOU USELESS TWiTS!
BASTARDS!
SHiiiiiiii
SHiiiiiiii
I DON'T GET iT, ISABELLAE. WHY iS THE CAPTAiN ATTACKiNG US?
I'M ABOUT TO FiND OUT. TRY NOT TO MOVE. YOU'VE LOST ENOUGH BLOOD AS iT iS.
I DON'T KNOW WHAT HAPPENED ON THAT BOAT, BUT I'M GLAD TO SEE YOU'RE STiLL ALiVE!
YOU HAVE A FUNNY WAY OF SHOWiNG iT!
MASTER YUAN HAS SOMETHiNG HE WANTS TO SAY TO YOU!

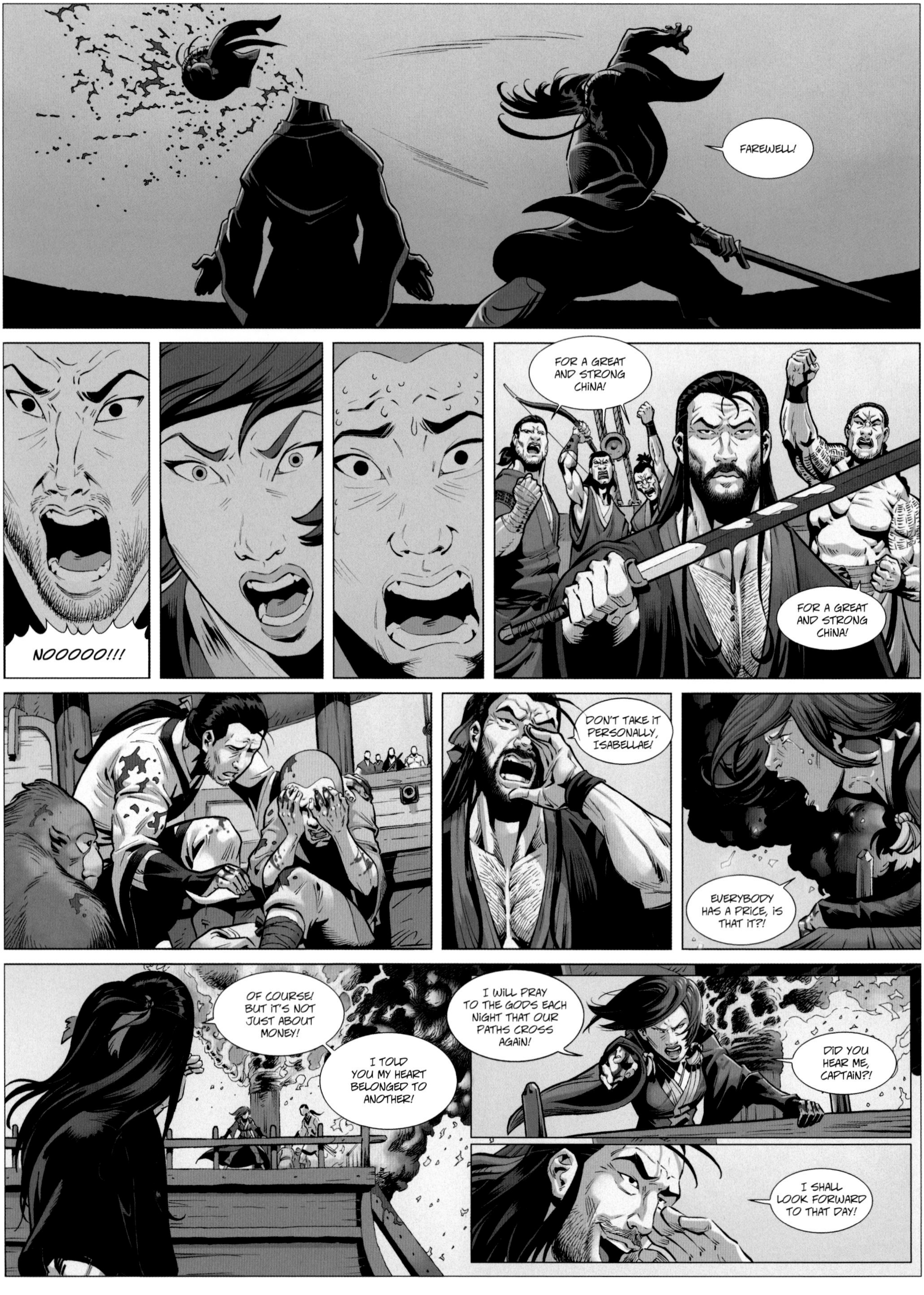
FAREWELL!
NOOOOO!!!
FOR A GREAT AND STRONG CHINA!
FOR A GREAT AND STRONG CHINA!
DON'T TAKE IT PERSONALLY, ISABELLAE!
EVERYBODY HAS A PRICE, IS THAT IT?!
OF COURSE! BUT IT'S NOT JUST ABOUT MONEY!
I TOLD YOU MY HEART BELONGED TO ANOTHER!
I WILL PRAY TO THE GODS EACH NIGHT THAT OUR PATHS CROSS AGAIN!
DID YOU HEAR ME, CAPTAIN?!
I SHALL LOOK FORWARD TO THAT DAY!

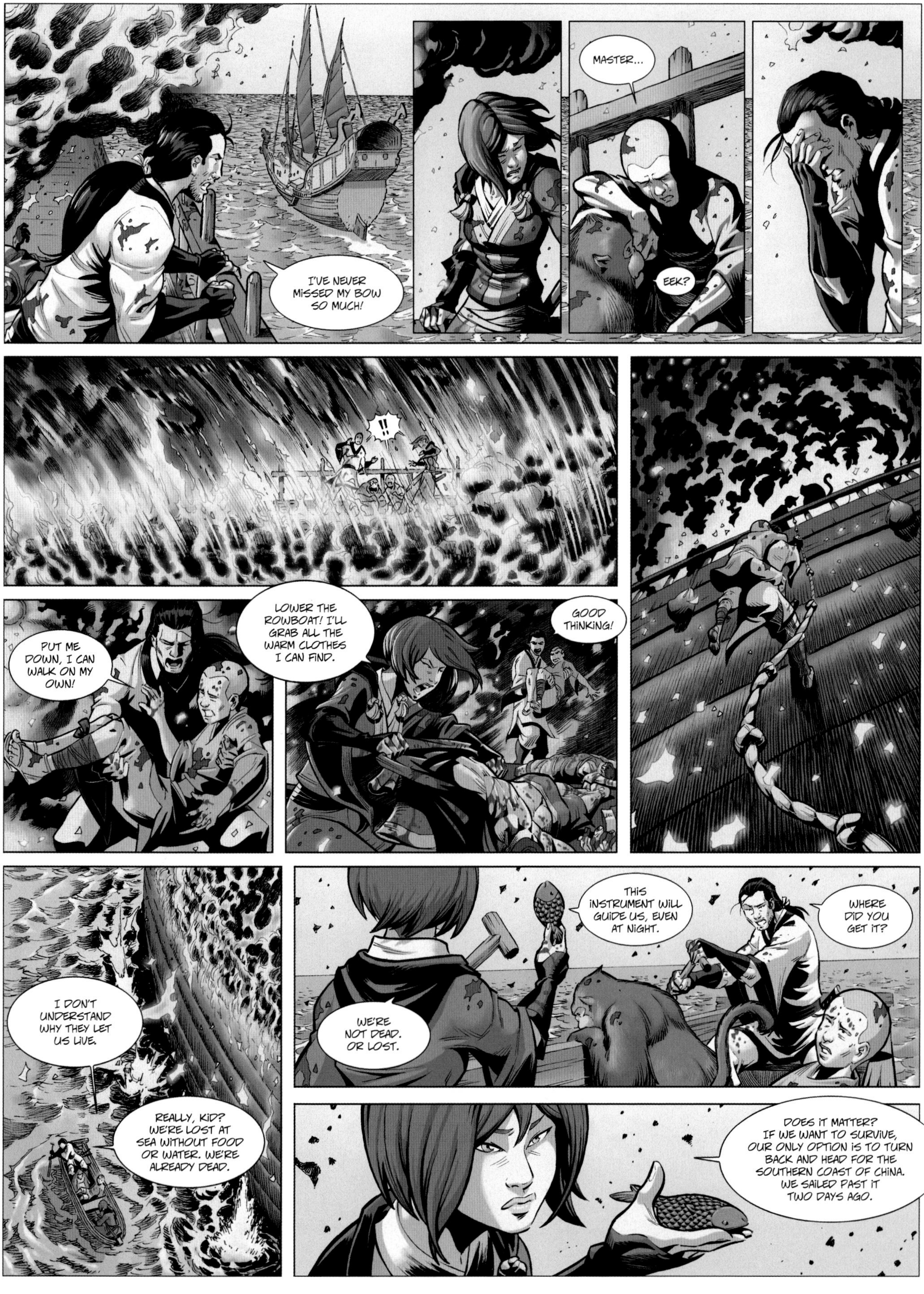
I'VE NEVER MISSED MY BOW SO MUCH!
MASTER...
EEK?
!!
PUT ME DOWN, I CAN WALK ON MY OWN!
LOWER THE ROWBOAT! I'LL GRAB ALL THE WARM CLOTHES I CAN FIND.
GOOD THINKING!
I DON'T UNDERSTAND WHY THEY LET US LIVE.
REALLY, KID? WE'RE LOST AT SEA WITHOUT FOOD OR WATER. WE'RE ALREADY DEAD.
WE'RE NOT DEAD. OR LOST.
THIS INSTRUMENT WILL GUIDE US, EVEN AT NIGHT.
WHERE DID YOU GET IT?
DOES IT MATTER? IF WE WANT TO SURVIVE, OUR ONLY OPTION IS TO TURN BACK AND HEAD FOR THE SOUTHERN COAST OF CHINA. WE SAILED PAST IT TWO DAYS AGO.

THAT WAS TWO DAYS ON A SHIP. LOOK AT THIS FLIMSY LITTLE TUB! AND NOT A SINGLE DROP OF WATER!

WE'LL NEVER REACH THE CHINESE COAST, RED, AND YOU KNOW IT.

I ALWAYS IMAGINED I WOULD DIE FIGHTING, OR EXECUTED, BUT NOT LIKE THIS.

WHY DON'T YOU JUST SHUT UP AND ROW?

ISABELLAE... YOUR FATHER...

MY FATHER?

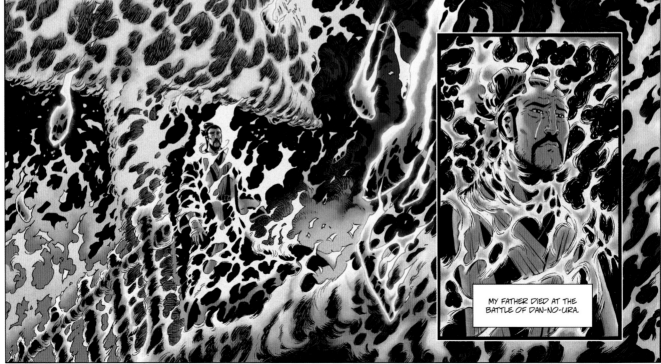

MY FATHER DIED AT THE BATTLE OF DAN-NO-URA.

END OF BOOK 2

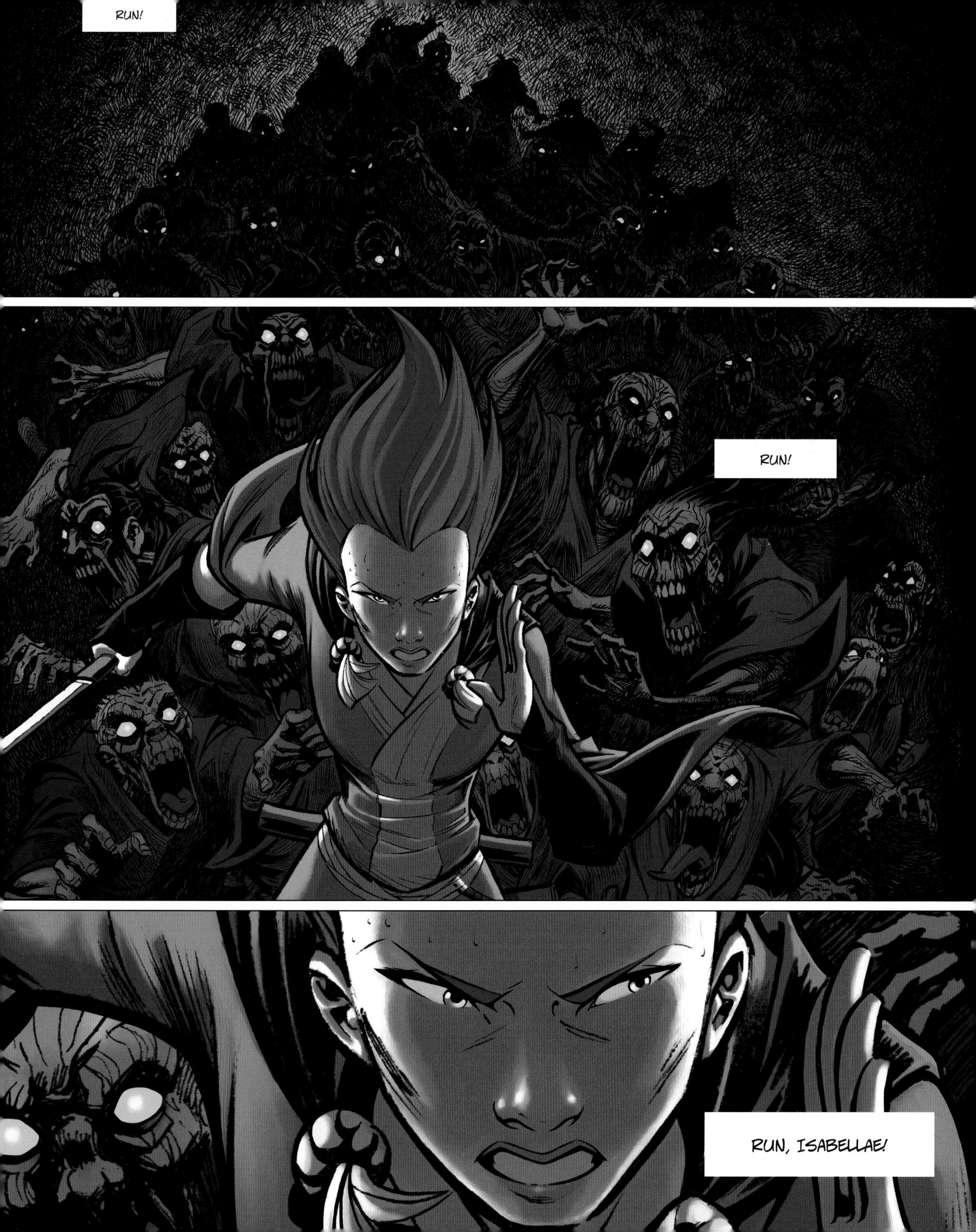
RUN!
RUN!
RUN, ISABELLAE!

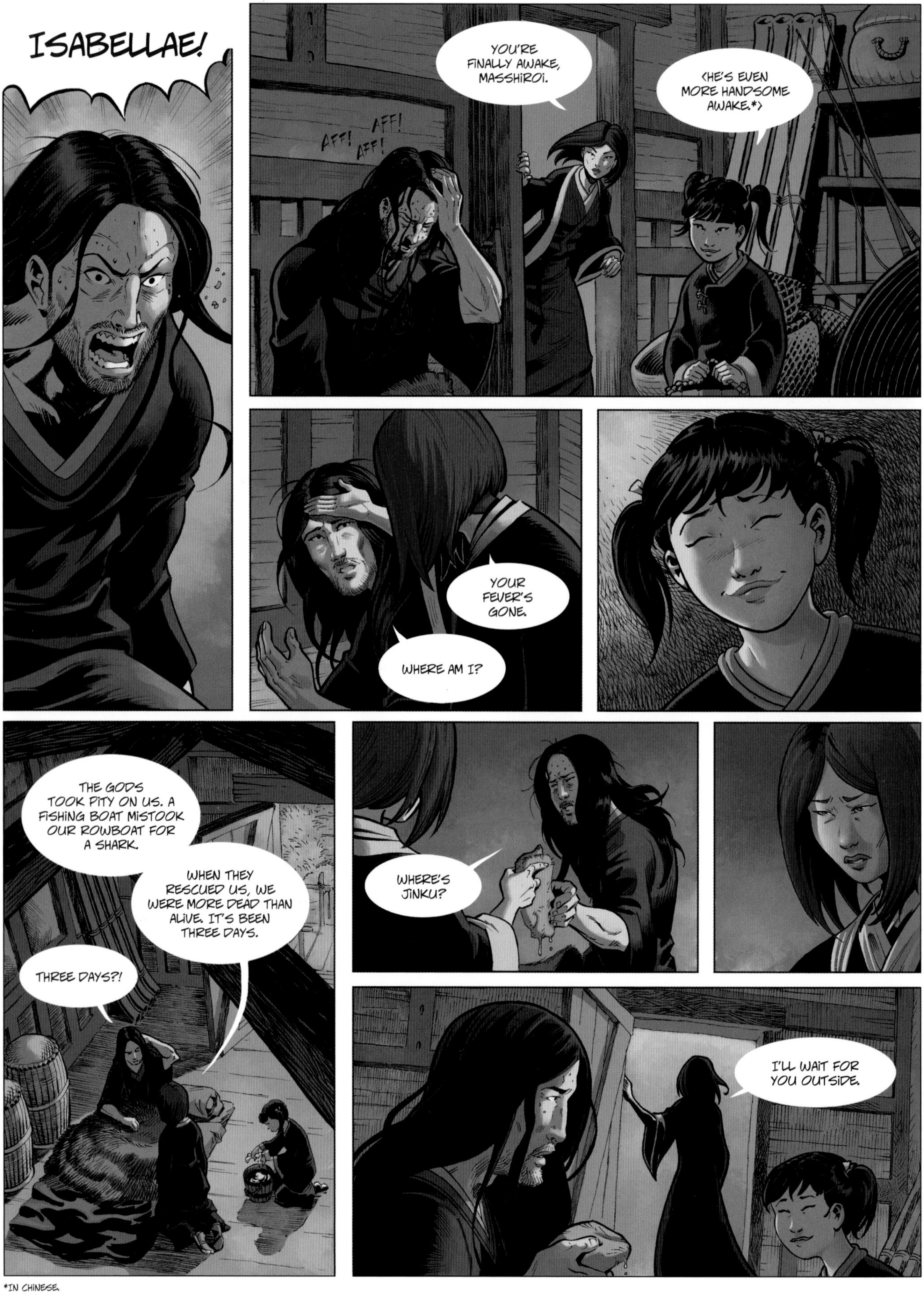
ISABELLAE!
AFF! AFF! AFF!
YOU'RE FINALLY AWAKE, MASSHIROI.
<HE'S EVEN MORE HANDSOME AWAKE.*>
YOUR FEVER'S GONE.
WHERE AM I?
THE GODS TOOK PITY ON US. A FISHING BOAT MISTOOK OUR ROWBOAT FOR A SHARK.
WHEN THEY RESCUED US, WE WERE MORE DEAD THAN ALIVE. IT'S BEEN THREE DAYS.
THREE DAYS?!
WHERE'S JINKU?
I'LL WAIT FOR YOU OUTSIDE.

*IN CHINESE.

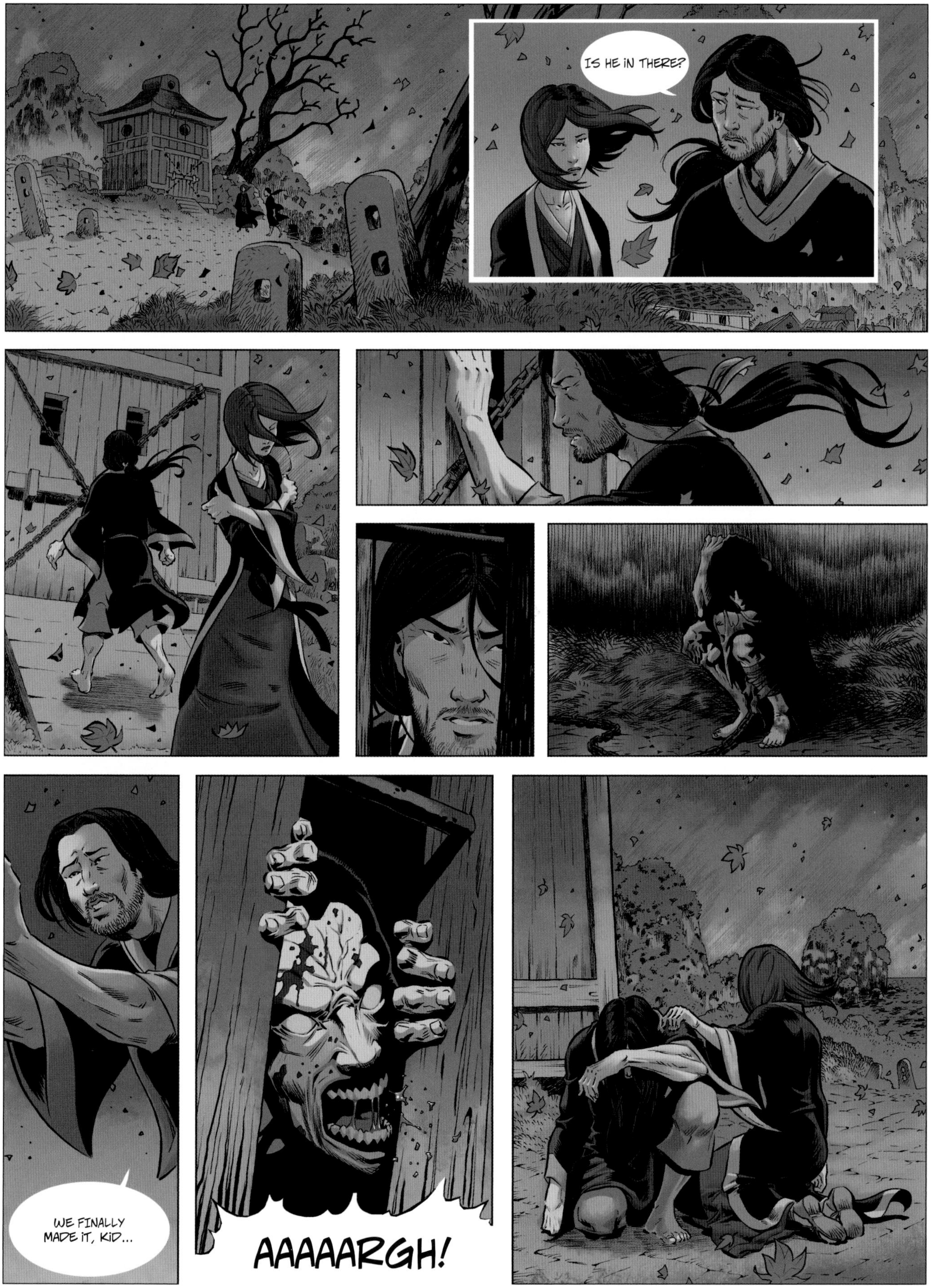
IS HE IN THERE?
WE FINALLY MADE IT, KID...
AAAAARGH!

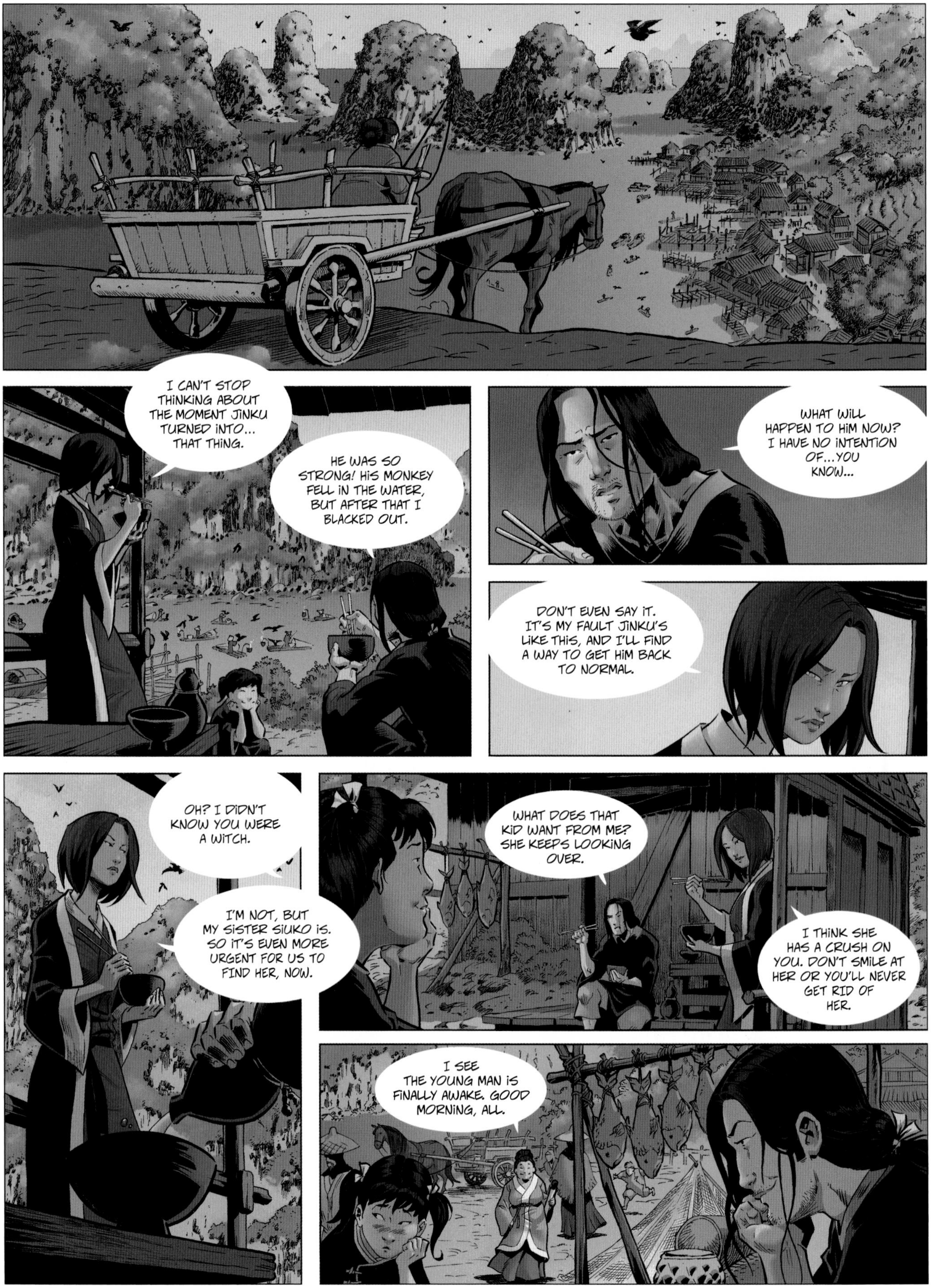
I CAN'T STOP THINKING ABOUT THE MOMENT JINKU TURNED INTO... THAT THING.
HE WAS SO STRONG! HIS MONKEY FELL IN THE WATER, BUT AFTER THAT I BLACKED OUT.
WHAT WILL HAPPEN TO HIM NOW? I HAVE NO INTENTION OF...YOU KNOW...
DON'T EVEN SAY IT. IT'S MY FAULT JINKU'S LIKE THIS, AND I'LL FIND A WAY TO GET HIM BACK TO NORMAL.
OH? I DIDN'T KNOW YOU WERE A WITCH.
I'M NOT, BUT MY SISTER SIUKO IS. SO IT'S EVEN MORE URGENT FOR US TO FIND HER, NOW.
WHAT DOES THAT KID WANT FROM ME? SHE KEEPS LOOKING OVER.
I THINK SHE HAS A CRUSH ON YOU. DON'T SMILE AT HER OR YOU'LL NEVER GET RID OF HER.
I SEE THE YOUNG MAN IS FINALLY AWAKE. GOOD MORNING, ALL.

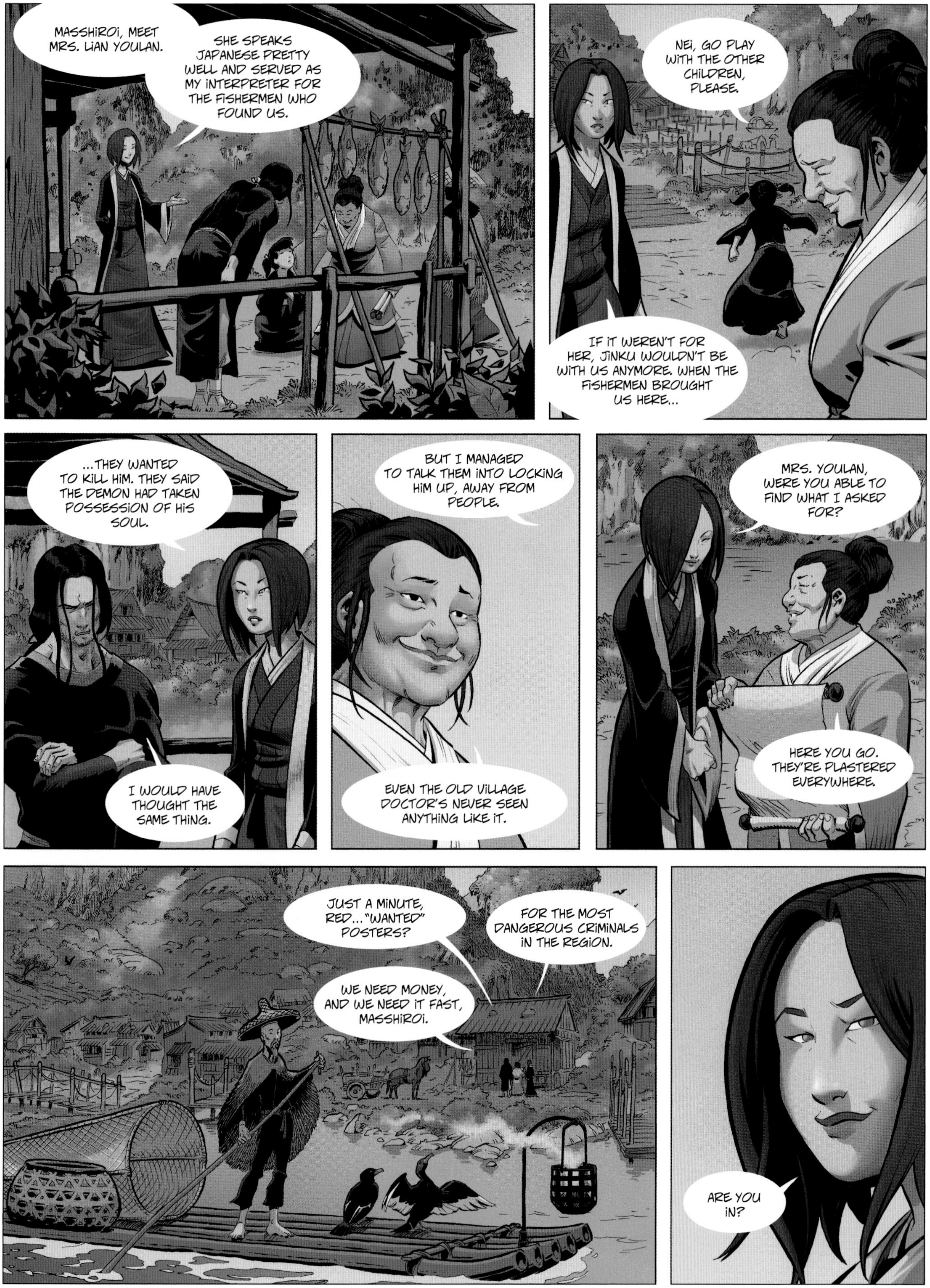
MASSHIROI, MEET MRS. LIAN YOULAN.
SHE SPEAKS JAPANESE PRETTY WELL AND SERVED AS MY INTERPRETER FOR THE FISHERMEN WHO FOUND US.
NEI, GO PLAY WITH THE OTHER CHILDREN, PLEASE.
IF IT WEREN'T FOR HER, JINKU WOULDN'T BE WITH US ANYMORE. WHEN THE FISHERMEN BROUGHT US HERE...
...THEY WANTED TO KILL HIM. THEY SAID THE DEMON HAD TAKEN POSSESSION OF HIS SOUL.
I WOULD HAVE THOUGHT THE SAME THING.
BUT I MANAGED TO TALK THEM INTO LOCKING HIM UP, AWAY FROM PEOPLE.
EVEN THE OLD VILLAGE DOCTOR'S NEVER SEEN ANYTHING LIKE IT.
MRS. YOULAN, WERE YOU ABLE TO FIND WHAT I ASKED FOR?
HERE YOU GO. THEY'RE PLASTERED EVERYWHERE.
JUST A MINUTE, RED... "WANTED" POSTERS?
FOR THE MOST DANGEROUS CRIMINALS IN THE REGION.
WE NEED MONEY, AND WE NEED IT FAST, MASSHIROI.
ARE YOU IN?

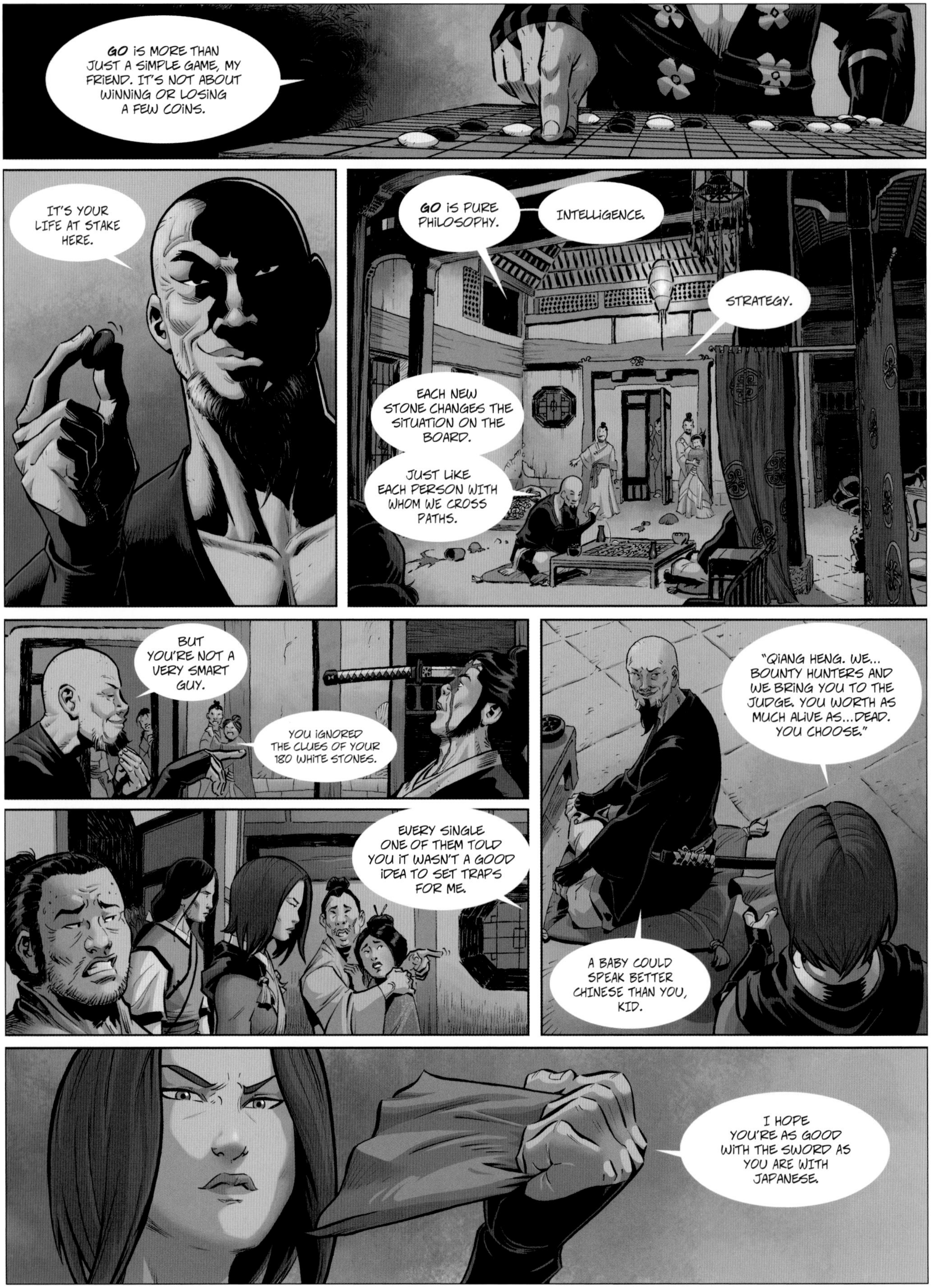
GO IS MORE THAN JUST A SIMPLE GAME, MY FRIEND. IT'S NOT ABOUT WINNING OR LOSING A FEW COINS.
IT'S YOUR LIFE AT STAKE HERE.
GO IS PURE PHILOSOPHY.
INTELLIGENCE.
STRATEGY.
EACH NEW STONE CHANGES THE SITUATION ON THE BOARD.
JUST LIKE EACH PERSON WITH WHOM WE CROSS PATHS.
BUT YOU'RE NOT A VERY SMART GUY.
YOU IGNORED THE CLUES OF YOUR 180 WHITE STONES.
EVERY SINGLE ONE OF THEM TOLD YOU IT WASN'T A GOOD IDEA TO SET TRAPS FOR ME.
"QIANG HENG. WE... BOUNTY HUNTERS AND WE BRING YOU TO THE JUDGE. YOU WORTH AS MUCH ALIVE AS...DEAD. YOU CHOOSE."
A BABY COULD SPEAK BETTER CHINESE THAN YOU, KID.
I HOPE YOU'RE AS GOOD WITH THE SWORD AS YOU ARE WITH JAPANESE.

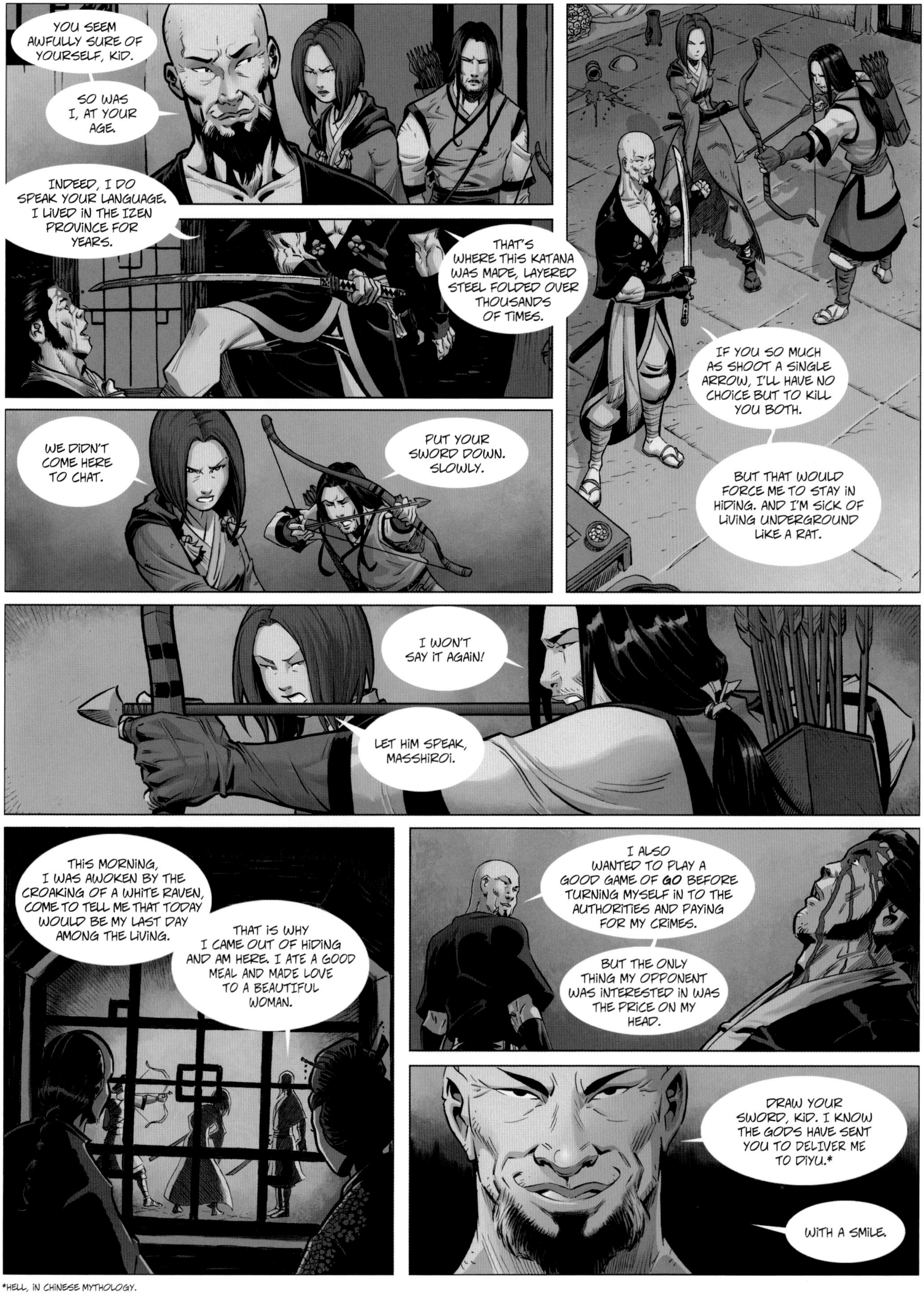
YOU SEEM AWFULLY SURE OF YOURSELF, KID.
SO WAS I, AT YOUR AGE.
INDEED, I DO SPEAK YOUR LANGUAGE. I LIVED IN THE IZEN PROVINCE FOR YEARS.
THAT'S WHERE THIS KATANA WAS MADE, LAYERED STEEL FOLDED OVER THOUSANDS OF TIMES.
WE DIDN'T COME HERE TO CHAT.
PUT YOUR SWORD DOWN. SLOWLY.
IF YOU SO MUCH AS SHOOT A SINGLE ARROW, I'LL HAVE NO CHOICE BUT TO KILL YOU BOTH.
BUT THAT WOULD FORCE ME TO STAY IN HIDING. AND I'M SICK OF LIVING UNDERGROUND LIKE A RAT.
I WON'T SAY IT AGAIN!
LET HIM SPEAK, MASSHIROI.
THIS MORNING, I WAS AWOKEN BY THE CROAKING OF A WHITE RAVEN, COME TO TELL ME THAT TODAY WOULD BE MY LAST DAY AMONG THE LIVING.
THAT IS WHY I CAME OUT OF HIDING AND AM HERE. I ATE A GOOD MEAL AND MADE LOVE TO A BEAUTIFUL WOMAN.
I ALSO WANTED TO PLAY A GOOD GAME OF **GO** BEFORE TURNING MYSELF IN TO THE AUTHORITIES AND PAYING FOR MY CRIMES.
BUT THE ONLY THING MY OPPONENT WAS INTERESTED IN WAS THE PRICE ON MY HEAD.
DRAW YOUR SWORD, KID. I KNOW THE GODS HAVE SENT YOU TO DELIVER ME TO DIYU.*
WITH A SMILE.

*HELL, IN CHINESE MYTHOLOGY.

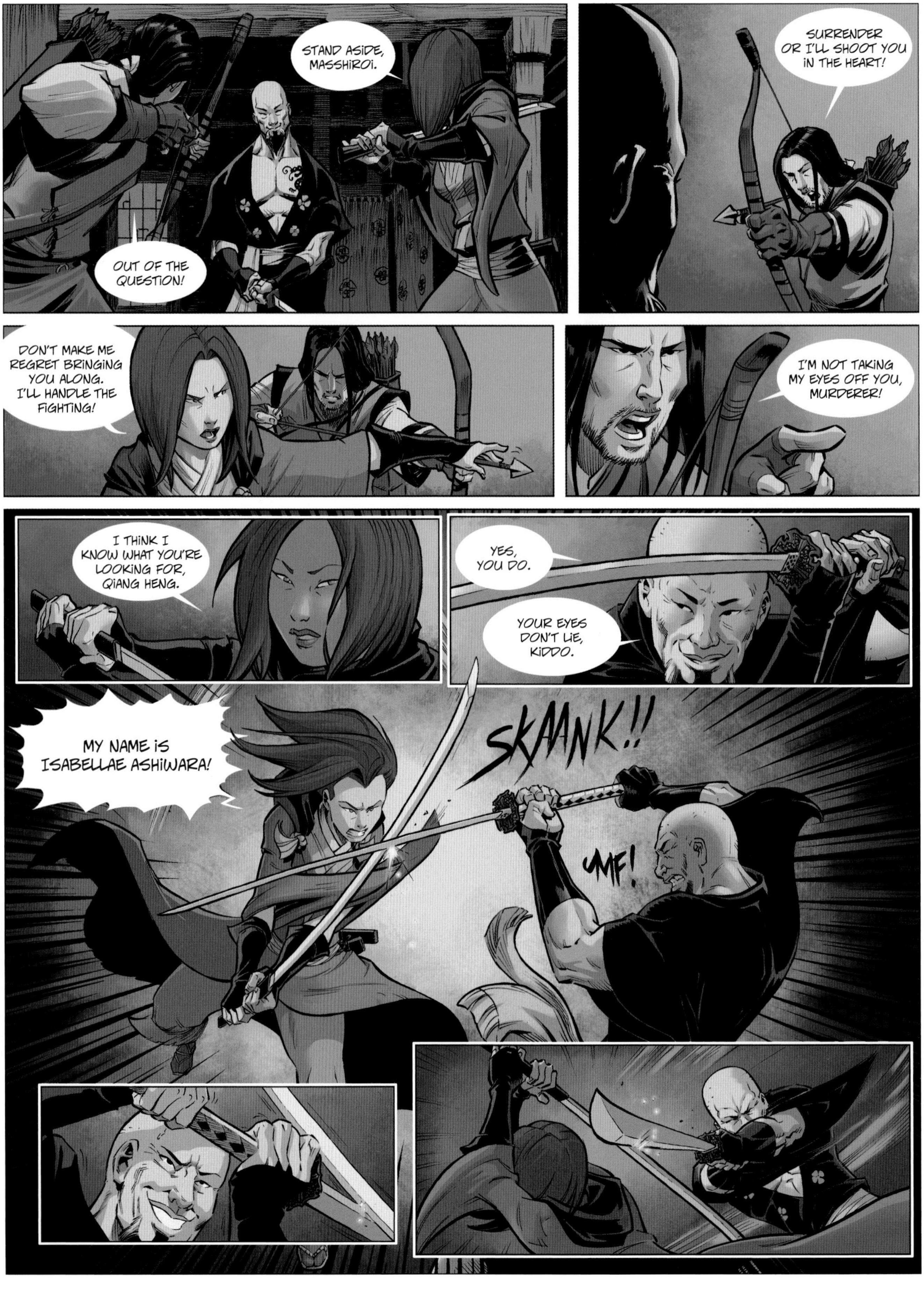
STAND ASIDE, MASSHIROI.
OUT OF THE QUESTION!
SURRENDER OR I'LL SHOOT YOU IN THE HEART!
DON'T MAKE ME REGRET BRINGING YOU ALONG. I'LL HANDLE THE FIGHTING!
I'M NOT TAKING MY EYES OFF YOU, MURDERER!
I THINK I KNOW WHAT YOU'RE LOOKING FOR, QIANG HENG.
YES, YOU DO.
YOUR EYES DON'T LIE, KIDDO.
MY NAME IS ISABELLAE ASHIWARA!
SKAANK!!
UMF!

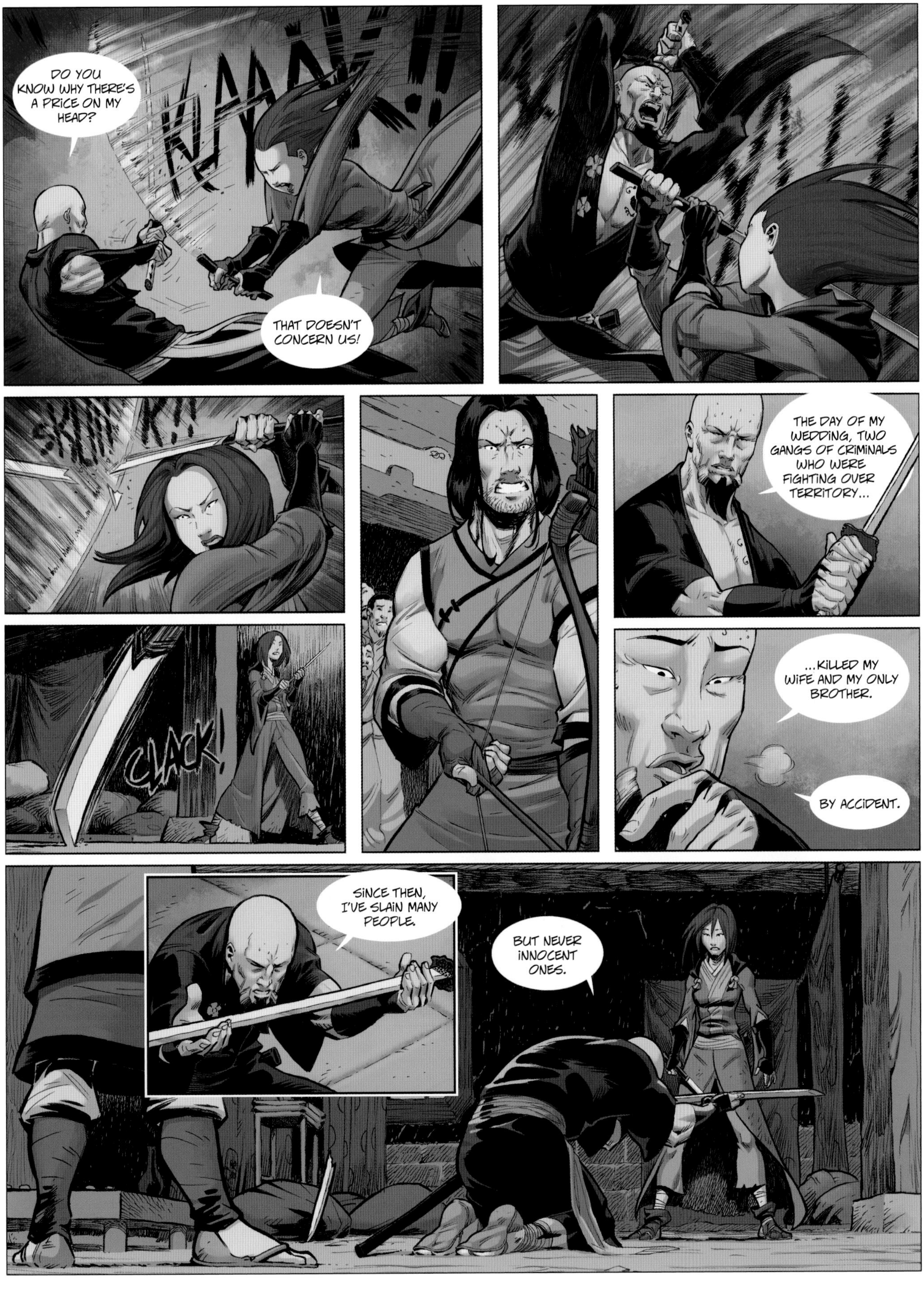
DO YOU KNOW WHY THERE'S A PRICE ON MY HEAD?
THAT DOESN'T CONCERN US!
THE DAY OF MY WEDDING, TWO GANGS OF CRIMINALS WHO WERE FIGHTING OVER TERRITORY...
CLACK!
...KILLED MY WIFE AND MY ONLY BROTHER.
BY ACCIDENT.
SINCE THEN, I'VE SLAIN MANY PEOPLE.
BUT NEVER INNOCENT ONES.

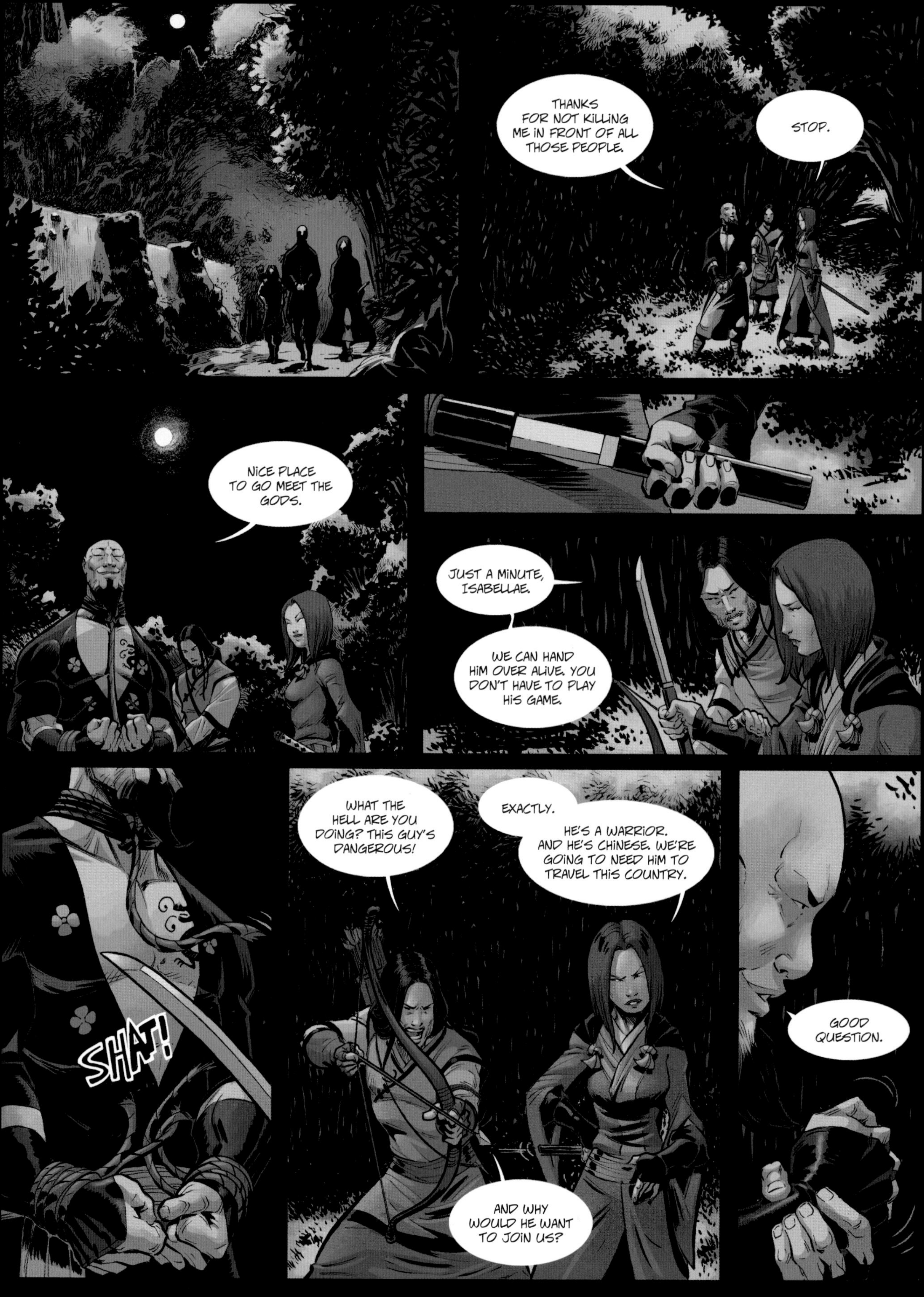
THANKS FOR NOT KILLING ME IN FRONT OF ALL THOSE PEOPLE.
STOP.
NICE PLACE TO GO MEET THE GODS.
JUST A MINUTE, ISABELLAE.
WE CAN HAND HIM OVER ALIVE. YOU DON'T HAVE TO PLAY HIS GAME.
SHAT!
WHAT THE HELL ARE YOU DOING? THIS GUY'S DANGEROUS!
EXACTLY.
HE'S A WARRIOR. AND HE'S CHINESE. WE'RE GOING TO NEED HIM TO TRAVEL THIS COUNTRY.
AND WHY WOULD HE WANT TO JOIN US?
GOOD QUESTION.

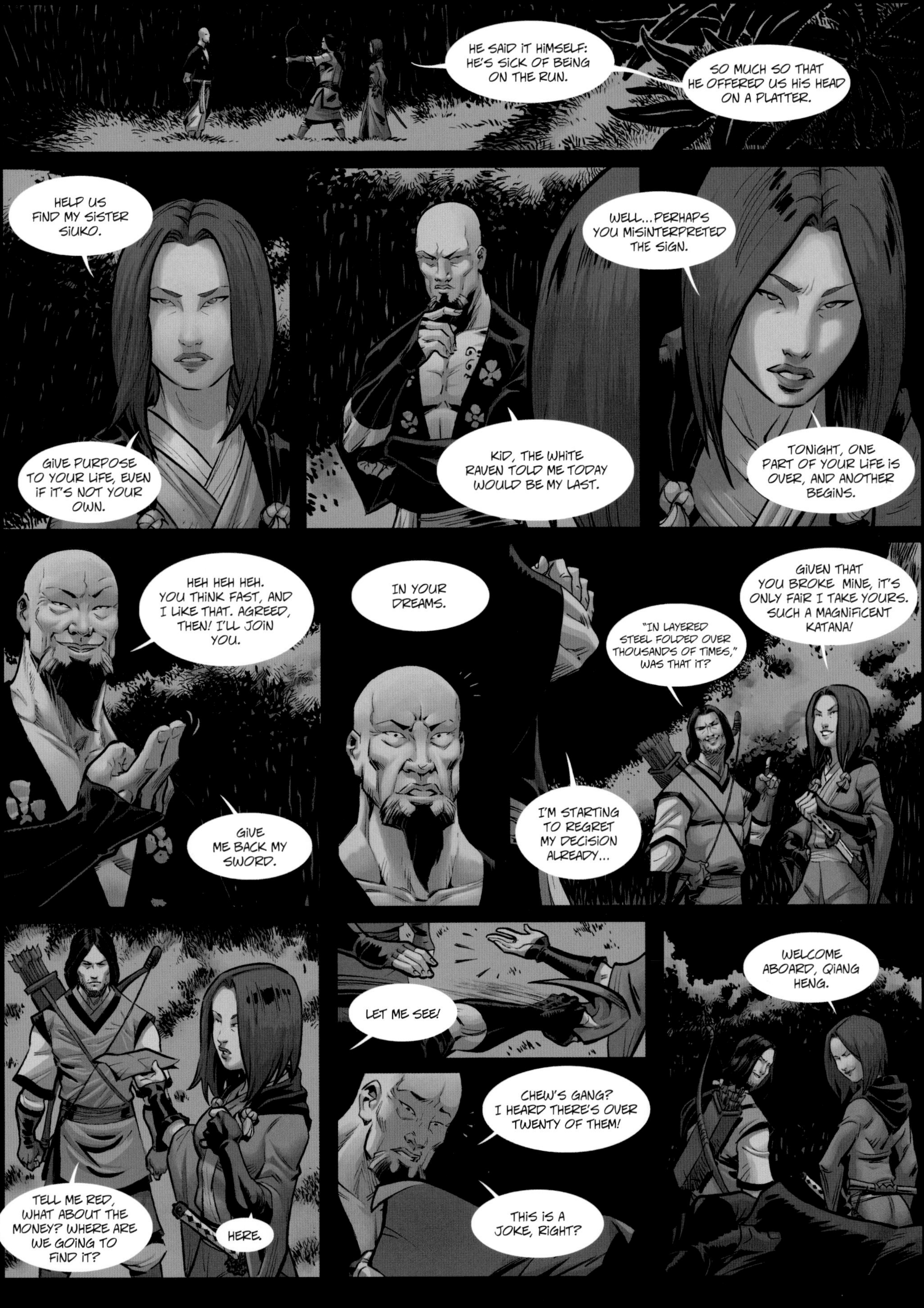
HE SAID IT HIMSELF: HE'S SICK OF BEING ON THE RUN.
SO MUCH SO THAT HE OFFERED US HIS HEAD ON A PLATTER.
HELP US FIND MY SISTER SIUKO.
GIVE PURPOSE TO YOUR LIFE, EVEN IF IT'S NOT YOUR OWN.
KID, THE WHITE RAVEN TOLD ME TODAY WOULD BE MY LAST.
WELL...PERHAPS YOU MISINTERPRETED THE SIGN.
TONIGHT, ONE PART OF YOUR LIFE IS OVER, AND ANOTHER BEGINS.
HEH HEH HEH. YOU THINK FAST, AND I LIKE THAT. AGREED, THEN! I'LL JOIN YOU.
GIVE ME BACK MY SWORD.
IN YOUR DREAMS.
"IN LAYERED STEEL FOLDED OVER THOUSANDS OF TIMES," WAS THAT IT?
GIVEN THAT YOU BROKE MINE, IT'S ONLY FAIR I TAKE YOURS. SUCH A MAGNIFICENT KATANA!
I'M STARTING TO REGRET MY DECISION ALREADY...
TELL ME RED, WHAT ABOUT THE MONEY? WHERE ARE WE GOING TO FIND IT?
HERE.
LET ME SEE!
CHEW'S GANG? I HEARD THERE'S OVER TWENTY OF THEM!
THIS IS A JOKE, RIGHT?
WELCOME ABOARD, QIANG HENG.

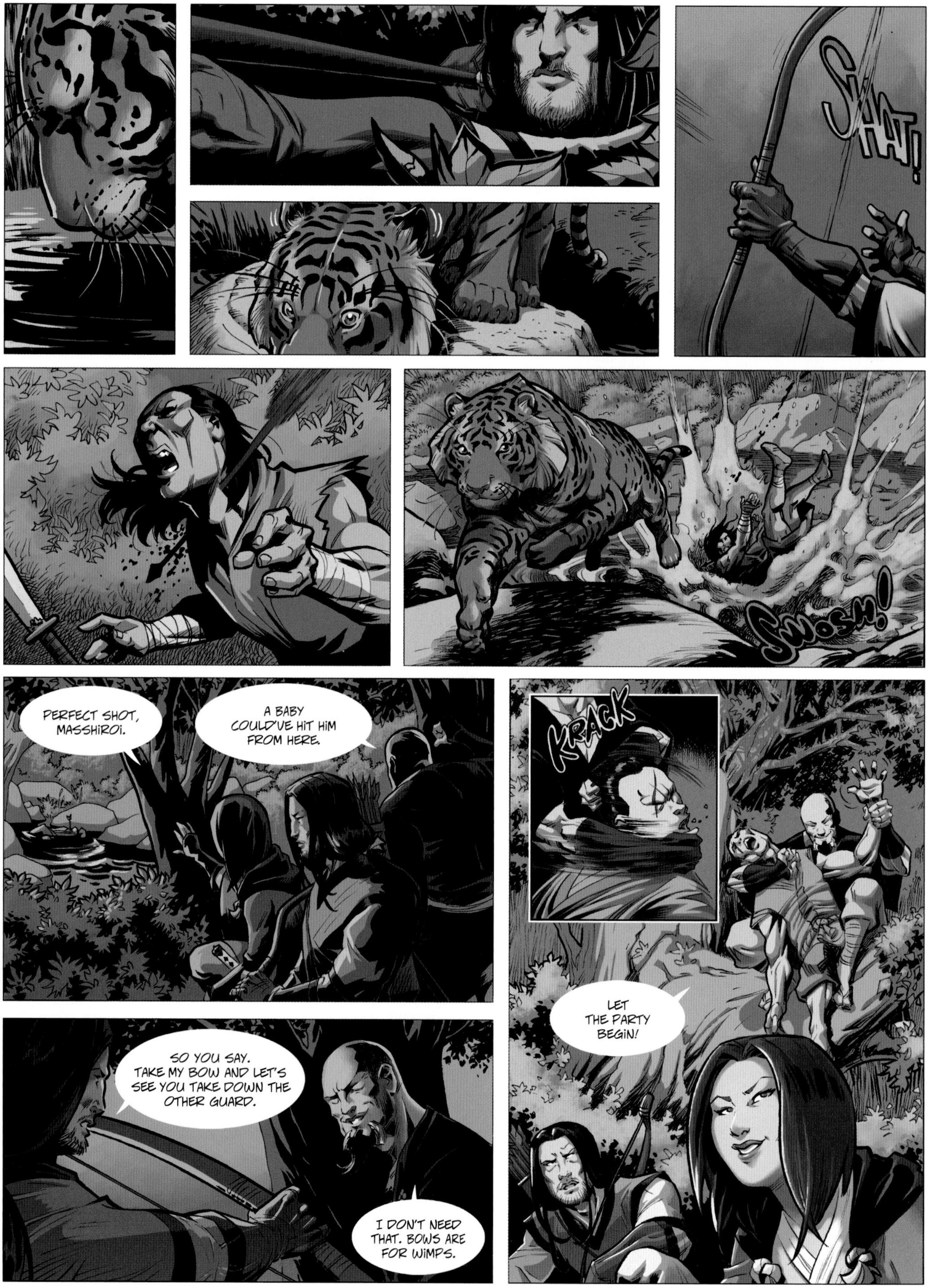
SHHAT!
SWOSH!
PERFECT SHOT, MASSHIROI.
A BABY COULD'VE HIT HIM FROM HERE.
KRACK
SO YOU SAY. TAKE MY BOW AND LET'S SEE YOU TAKE DOWN THE OTHER GUARD.
I DON'T NEED THAT. BOWS ARE FOR WIMPS.
LET THE PARTY BEGIN!

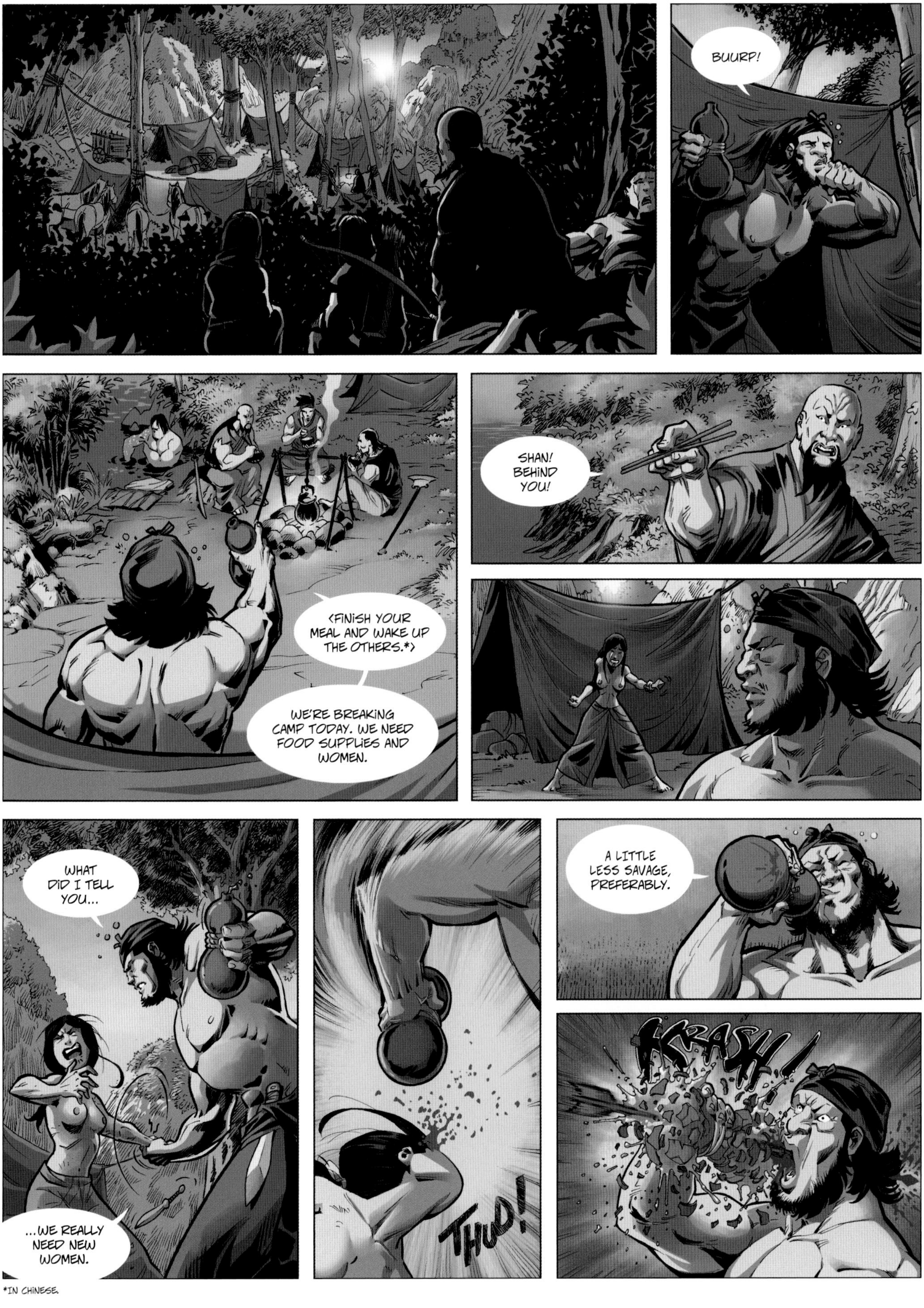
BUURP!
SHAN! BEHIND YOU!
<FINISH YOUR MEAL AND WAKE UP THE OTHERS.*>
WE'RE BREAKING CAMP TODAY. WE NEED FOOD SUPPLIES AND WOMEN.
WHAT DID I TELL YOU...
...WE REALLY NEED NEW WOMEN.
THUD!
A LITTLE LESS SAVAGE, PREFERABLY.
KRASH!

*IN CHINESE.

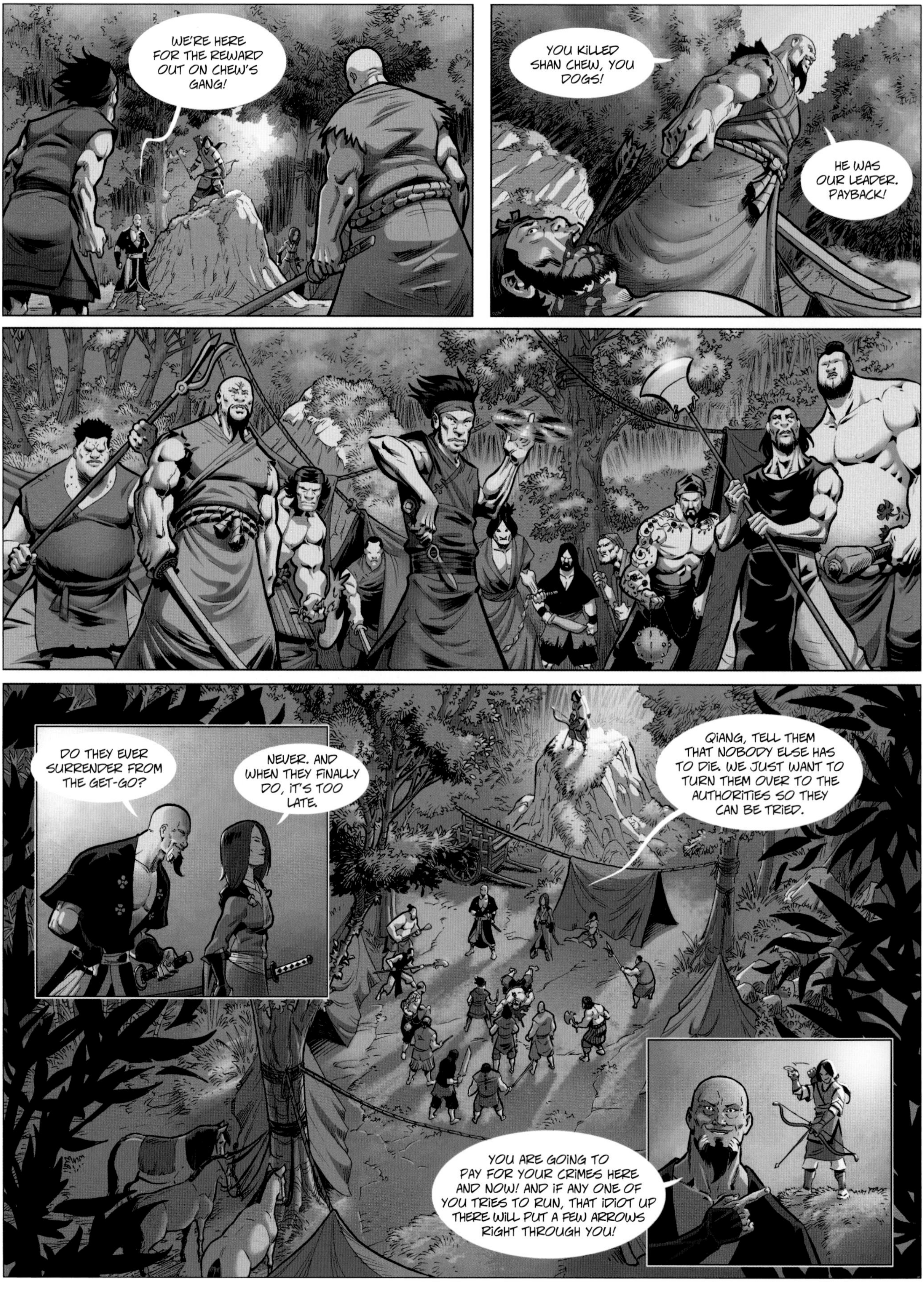
WE'RE HERE FOR THE REWARD OUT ON CHEW'S GANG!
YOU KILLED SHAN CHEW, YOU DOGS!
HE WAS OUR LEADER. PAYBACK!
DO THEY EVER SURRENDER FROM THE GET-GO?
NEVER. AND WHEN THEY FINALLY DO, IT'S TOO LATE.
QIANG, TELL THEM THAT NOBODY ELSE HAS TO DIE. WE JUST WANT TO TURN THEM OVER TO THE AUTHORITIES SO THEY CAN BE TRIED.
YOU ARE GOING TO PAY FOR YOUR CRIMES HERE AND NOW! AND IF ANY ONE OF YOU TRIES TO RUN, THAT IDIOT UP THERE WILL PUT A FEW ARROWS RIGHT THROUGH YOU!

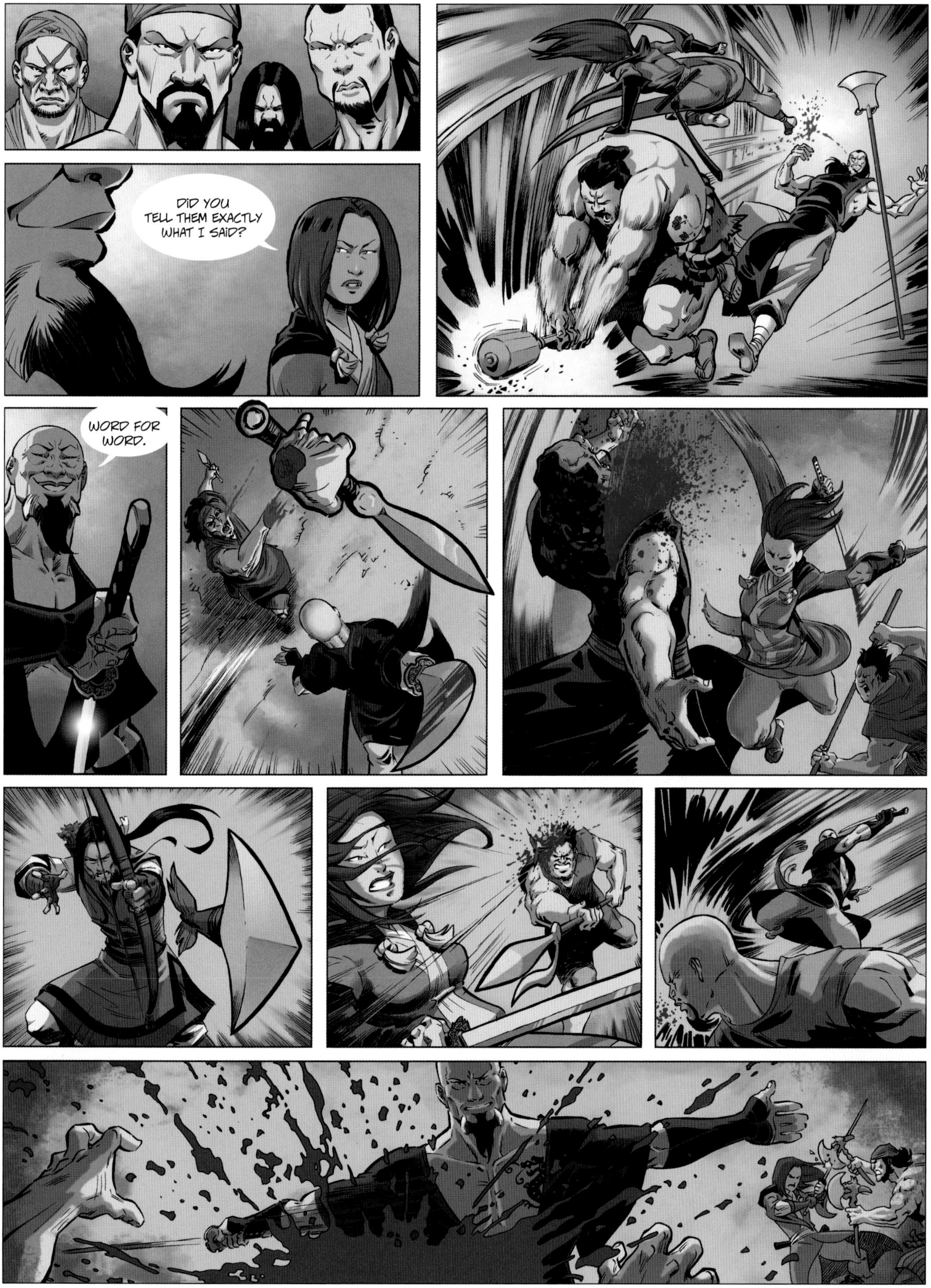
DID YOU TELL THEM EXACTLY WHAT I SAID?
WORD FOR WORD.

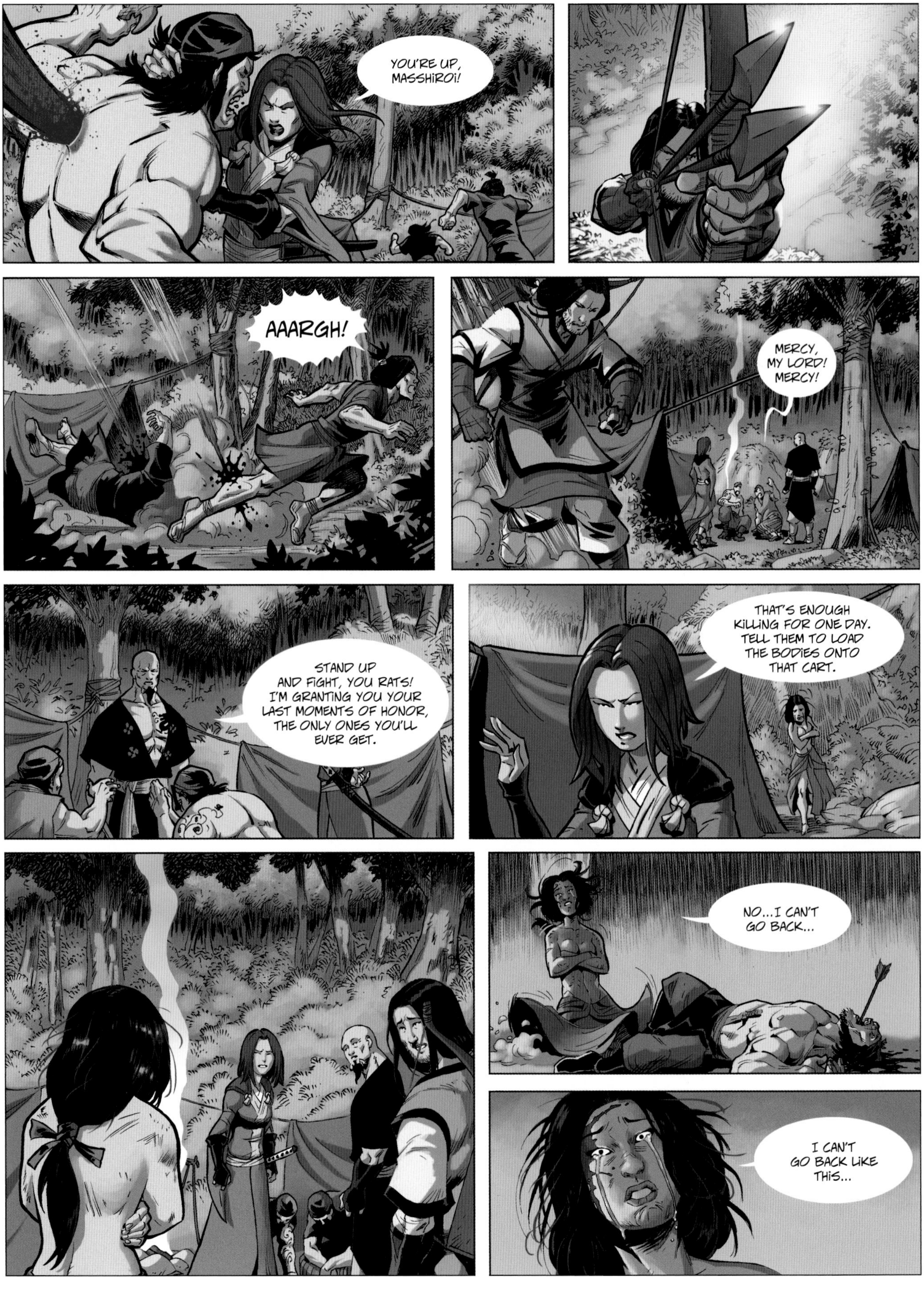
YOU'RE UP, MASSHIROI!
AAARGH!
MERCY, MY LORD! MERCY!
STAND UP AND FIGHT, YOU RATS! I'M GRANTING YOU YOUR LAST MOMENTS OF HONOR, THE ONLY ONES YOU'LL EVER GET.
THAT'S ENOUGH KILLING FOR ONE DAY. TELL THEM TO LOAD THE BODIES ONTO THAT CART.
NO... I CAN'T GO BACK...
I CAN'T GO BACK LIKE THIS...

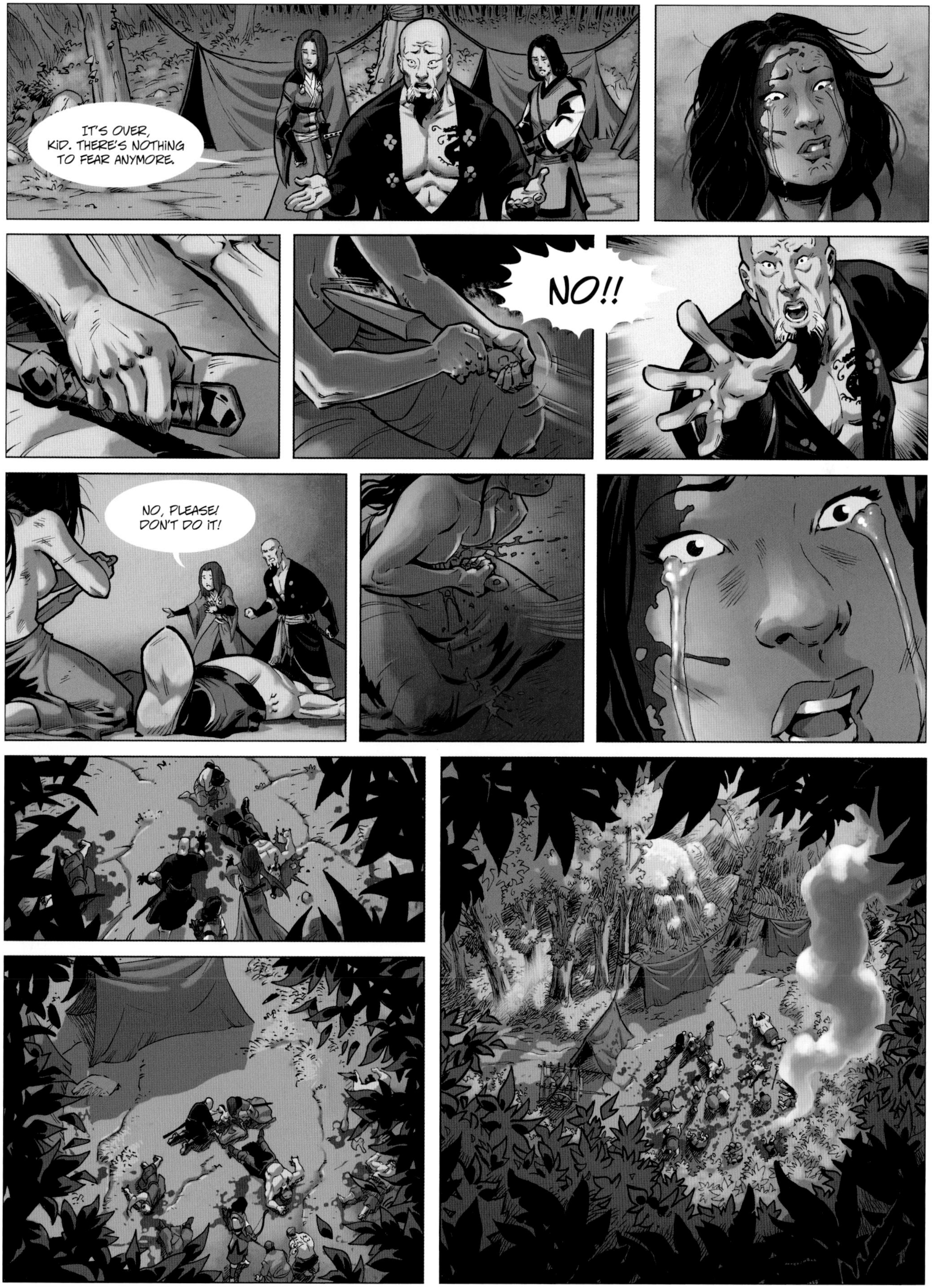
IT'S OVER, KID. THERE'S NOTHING TO FEAR ANYMORE.
NO!!
NO, PLEASE! DON'T DO IT!

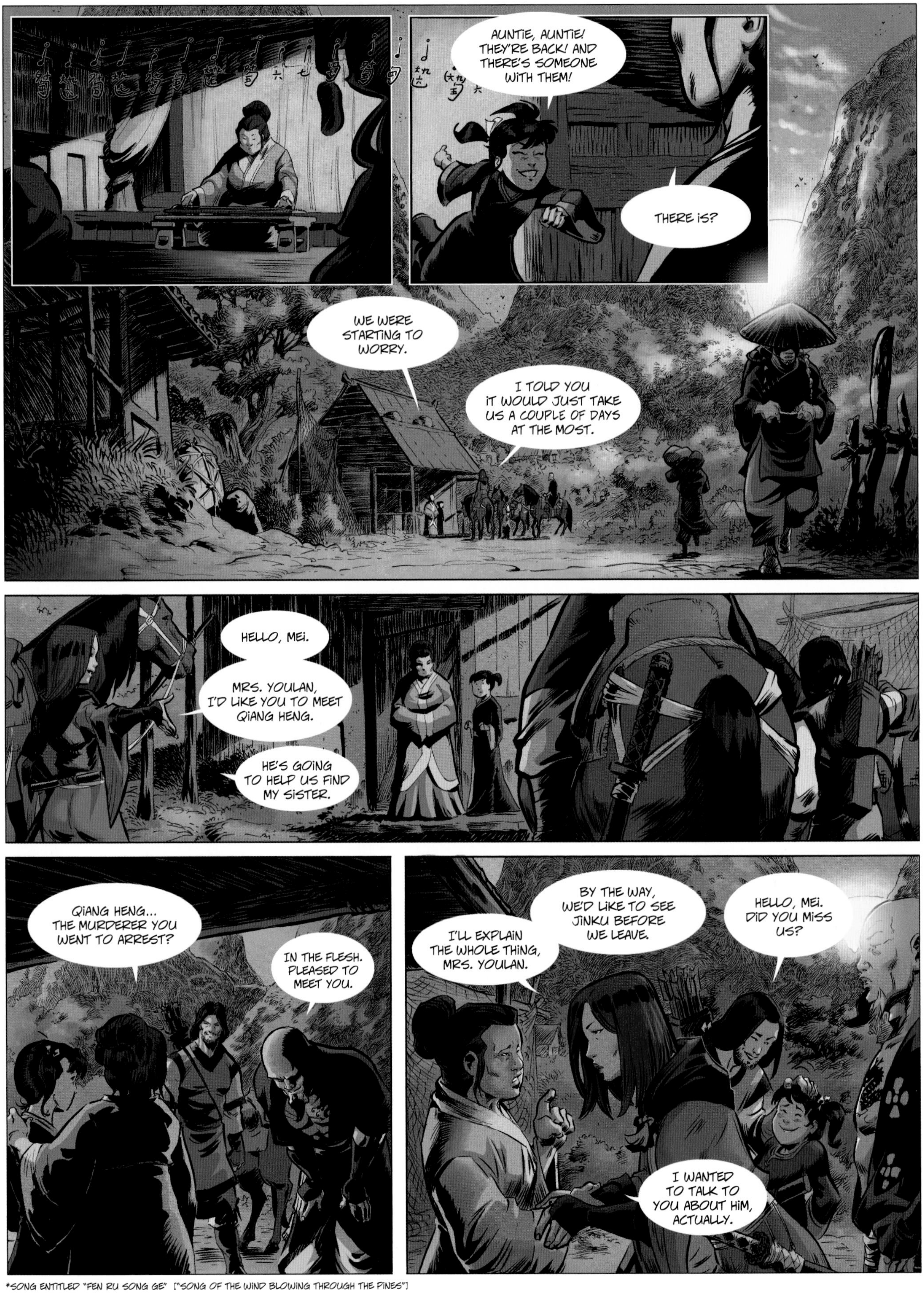
AUNTIE, AUNTIE! THEY'RE BACK! AND THERE'S SOMEONE WITH THEM!
THERE IS?
WE WERE STARTING TO WORRY.
I TOLD YOU IT WOULD JUST TAKE US A COUPLE OF DAYS AT THE MOST.
HELLO, MEI.
MRS. YOULAN, I'D LIKE YOU TO MEET QIANG HENG.
HE'S GOING TO HELP US FIND MY SISTER.
QIANG HENG... THE MURDERER YOU WENT TO ARREST?
IN THE FLESH. PLEASED TO MEET YOU.
I'LL EXPLAIN THE WHOLE THING, MRS. YOULAN.
BY THE WAY, WE'D LIKE TO SEE JINKU BEFORE WE LEAVE.
HELLO, MEI. DID YOU MISS US?
I WANTED TO TALK TO YOU ABOUT HIM, ACTUALLY.

*SONG ENTITLED "FEN RU SONG GE" ["SONG OF THE WIND BLOWING THROUGH THE PINES"]

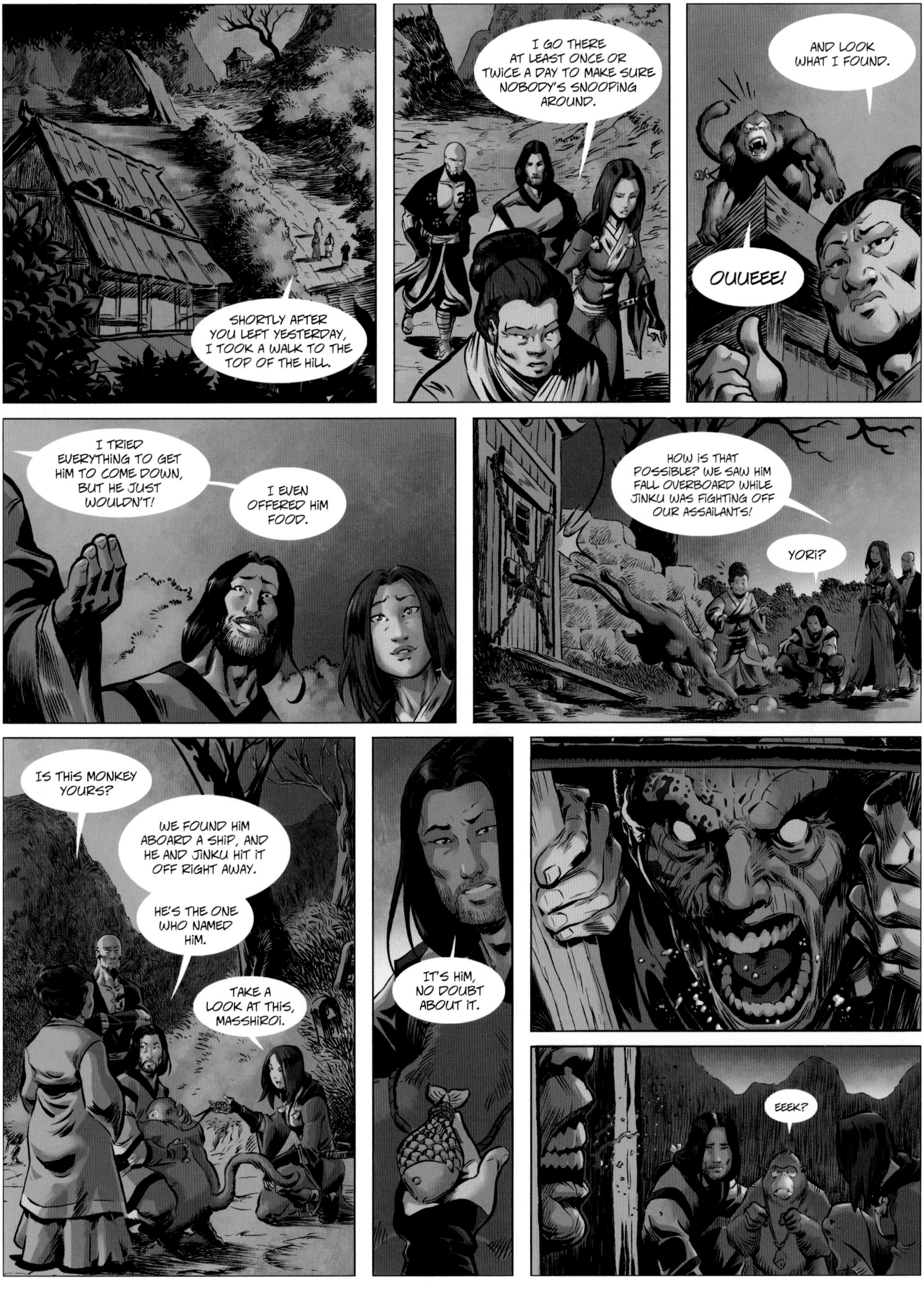
SHORTLY AFTER YOU LEFT YESTERDAY, I TOOK A WALK TO THE TOP OF THE HILL.
I GO THERE AT LEAST ONCE OR TWICE A DAY TO MAKE SURE NOBODY'S SNOOPING AROUND.
AND LOOK WHAT I FOUND.
OUUEEE!
I TRIED EVERYTHING TO GET HIM TO COME DOWN, BUT HE JUST WOULDN'T!
I EVEN OFFERED HIM FOOD.
HOW IS THAT POSSIBLE? WE SAW HIM FALL OVERBOARD WHILE JINKU WAS FIGHTING OFF OUR ASSAILANTS!
YORI?
IS THIS MONKEY YOURS?
WE FOUND HIM ABOARD A SHIP, AND HE AND JINKU HIT IT OFF RIGHT AWAY.
HE'S THE ONE WHO NAMED HIM.
TAKE A LOOK AT THIS, MASSHIROI.
IT'S HIM, NO DOUBT ABOUT IT.
EEEK?

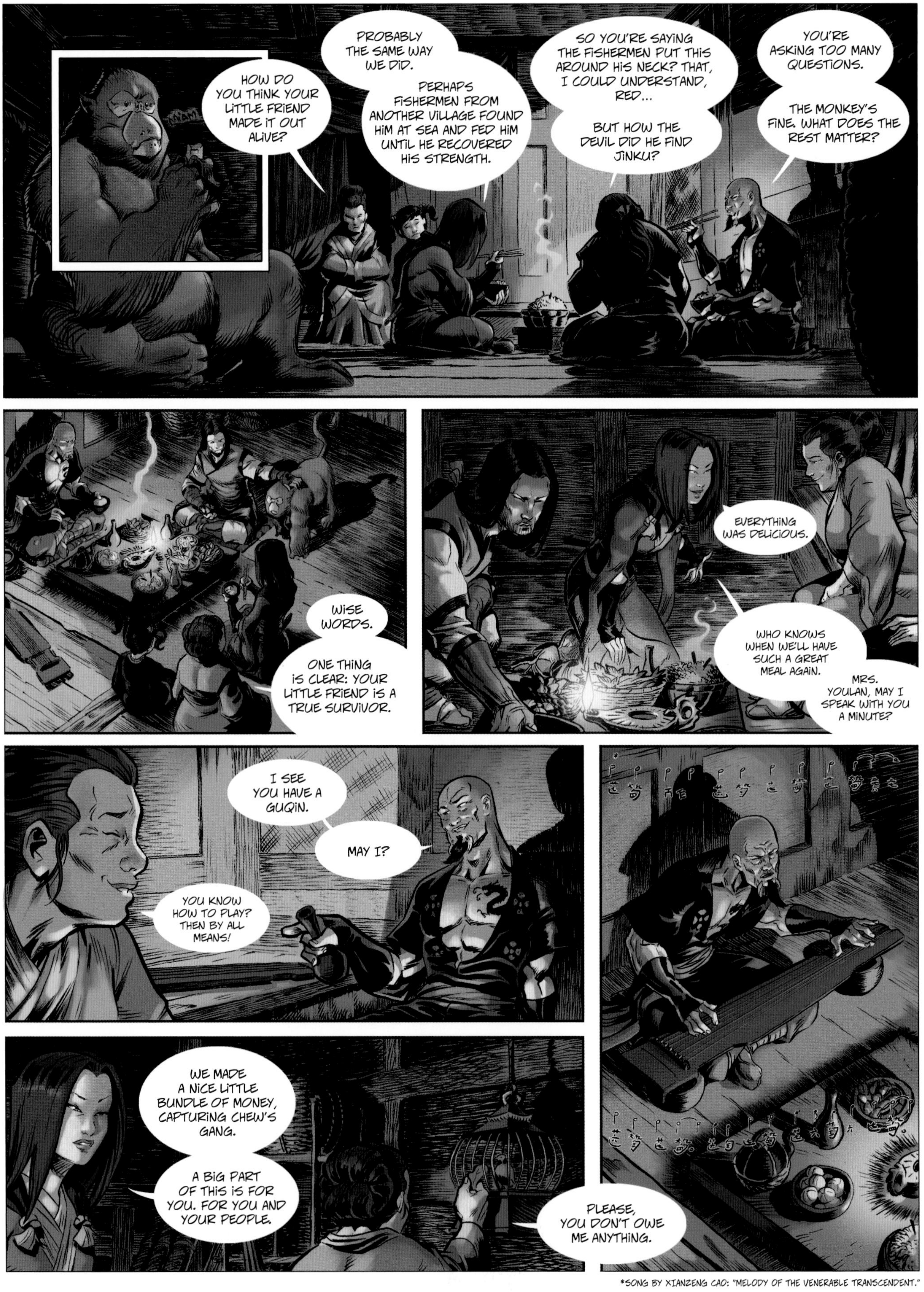
HOW DO YOU THINK YOUR LITTLE FRIEND MADE IT OUT ALIVE?
PROBABLY THE SAME WAY WE DID.
PERHAPS FISHERMEN FROM ANOTHER VILLAGE FOUND HIM AT SEA AND FED HIM UNTIL HE RECOVERED HIS STRENGTH.
SO YOU'RE SAYING THE FISHERMEN PUT THIS AROUND HIS NECK? THAT, I COULD UNDERSTAND, RED...
BUT HOW THE DEVIL DID HE FIND JINKU?
YOU'RE ASKING TOO MANY QUESTIONS.
THE MONKEY'S FINE. WHAT DOES THE REST MATTER?
WISE WORDS.
ONE THING IS CLEAR: YOUR LITTLE FRIEND IS A TRUE SURVIVOR.
EVERYTHING WAS DELICIOUS.
WHO KNOWS WHEN WE'LL HAVE SUCH A GREAT MEAL AGAIN.
MRS. YOULAN, MAY I SPEAK WITH YOU A MINUTE?
I SEE YOU HAVE A GUQIN.
MAY I?
YOU KNOW HOW TO PLAY? THEN BY ALL MEANS!
WE MADE A NICE LITTLE BUNDLE OF MONEY, CAPTURING CHEW'S GANG.
A BIG PART OF THIS IS FOR YOU. FOR YOU AND YOUR PEOPLE.
PLEASE, YOU DON'T OWE ME ANYTHING.

*SONG BY XIANZENG CAO: "MELODY OF THE VENERABLE TRANSCENDENT."

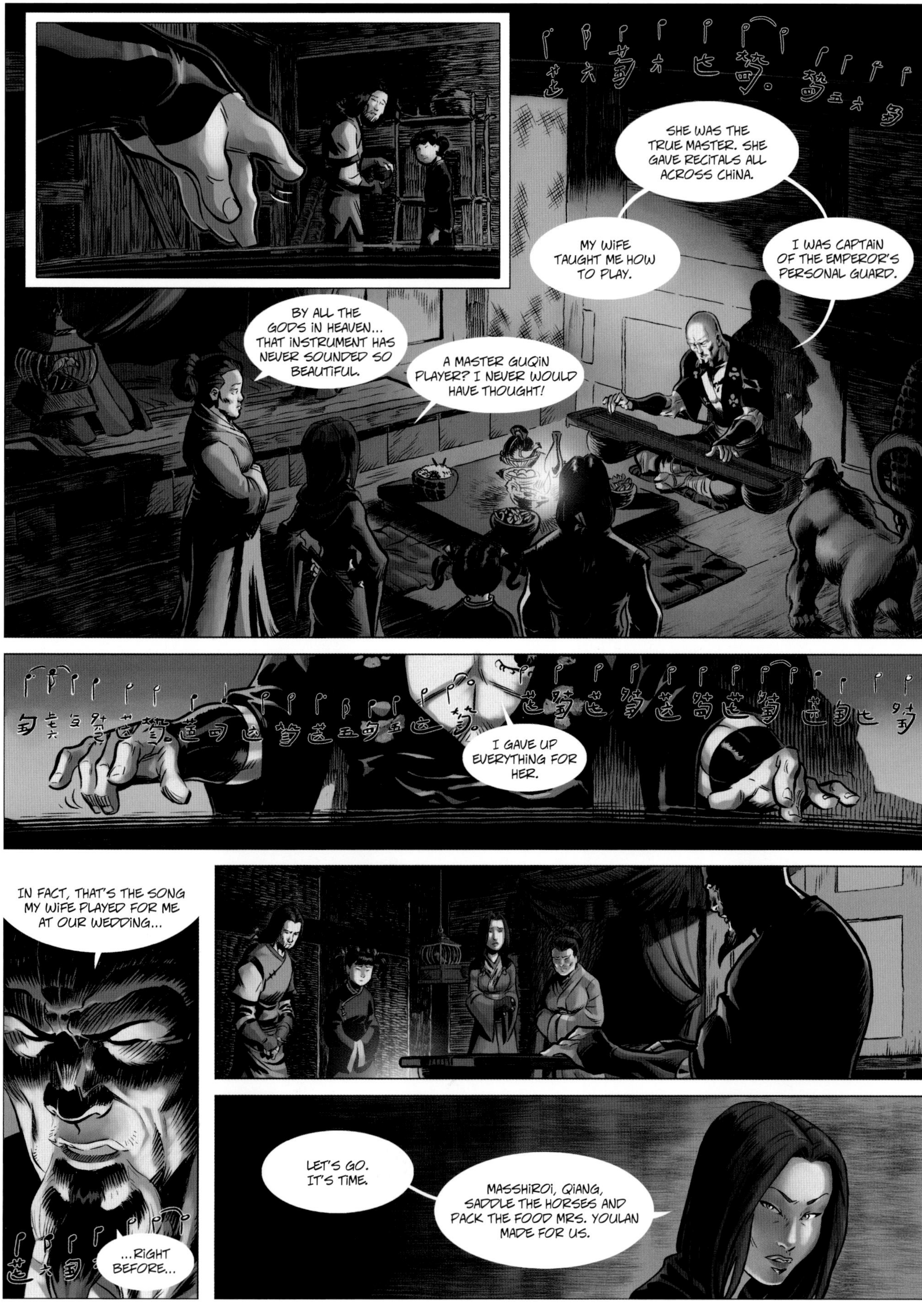
SHE WAS THE TRUE MASTER. SHE GAVE RECITALS ALL ACROSS CHINA.
MY WIFE TAUGHT ME HOW TO PLAY.
I WAS CAPTAIN OF THE EMPEROR'S PERSONAL GUARD.
BY ALL THE GODS IN HEAVEN... THAT INSTRUMENT HAS NEVER SOUNDED SO BEAUTIFUL.
A MASTER GUQIN PLAYER? I NEVER WOULD HAVE THOUGHT!
I GAVE UP EVERYTHING FOR HER.
IN FACT, THAT'S THE SONG MY WIFE PLAYED FOR ME AT OUR WEDDING...
...RIGHT BEFORE...
LET'S GO. IT'S TIME.
MASSHIROI, QIANG, SADDLE THE HORSES AND PACK THE FOOD MRS. YOULAN MADE FOR US.

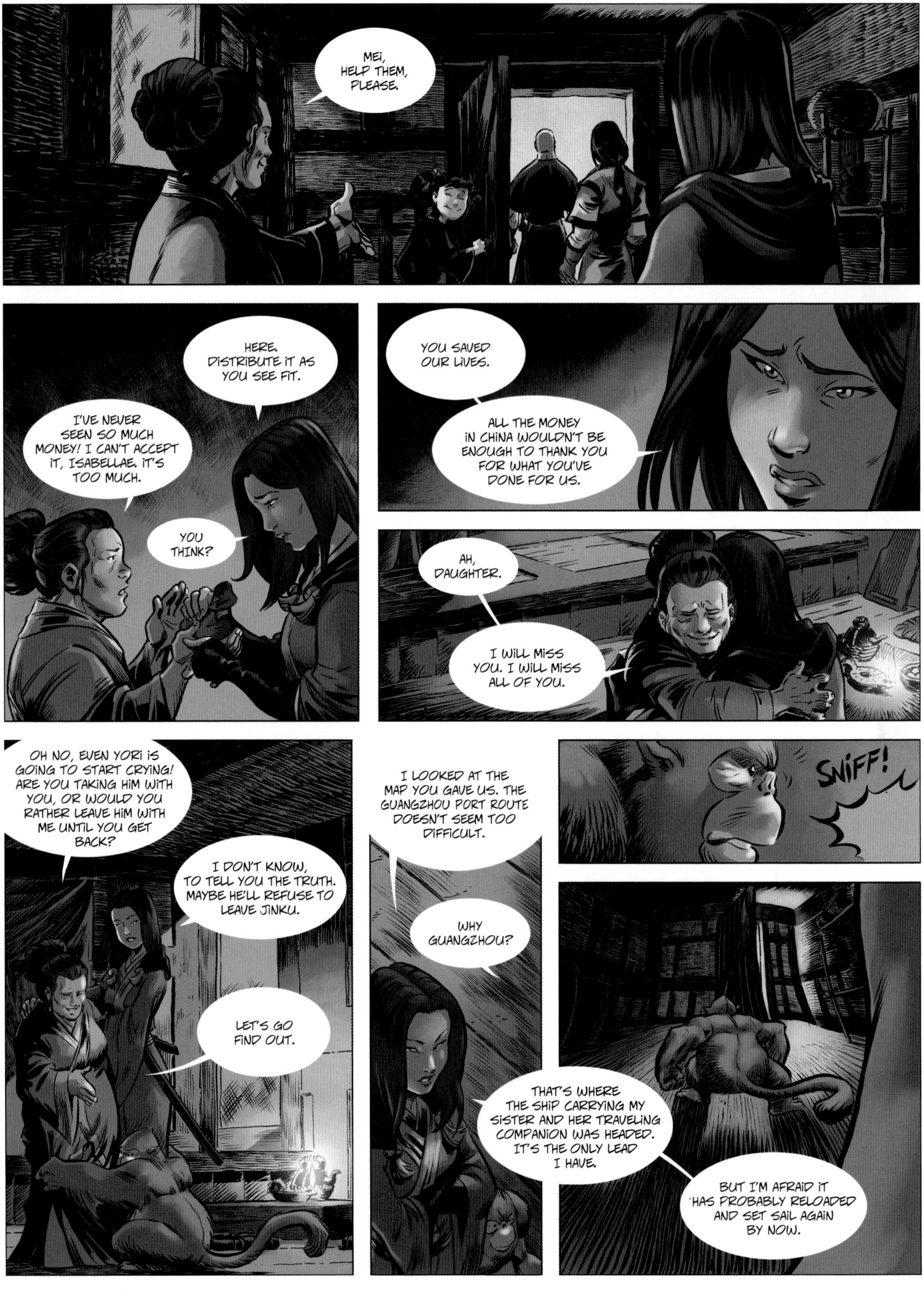
MEi, HELP THEM, PLEASE.
HERE. DiSTRiBUTE iT AS YOU SEE FiT.
I'VE NEVER SEEN SO MUCH MONEY! I CAN'T ACCEPT iT, ISABELLAE. iT'S TOO MUCH.
YOU THINK?
YOU SAVED OUR LiVES.
ALL THE MONEY iN CHINA WOULDN'T BE ENOUGH TO THANK YOU FOR WHAT YOU'VE DONE FOR US.
AH, DAUGHTER.
I WiLL MiSS YOU. I WiLL MiSS ALL OF YOU.
OH NO, EVEN YORi iS GOiNG TO START CRYiNG! ARE YOU TAKiNG HiM WiTH YOU, OR WOULD YOU RATHER LEAVE HiM WiTH ME UNTiL YOU GET BACK?
I DON'T KNOW, TO TELL YOU THE TRUTH. MAYBE HE'LL REFUSE TO LEAVE JiNKU.
LET'S GO FiND OUT.
I LOOKED AT THE MAP YOU GAVE US. THE GUANGZHOU PORT ROUTE DOESN'T SEEM TOO DiFFiCULT.
WHY GUANGZHOU?
THAT'S WHERE THE SHiP CARRYiNG MY SiSTER AND HER TRAVELiNG COMPANiON WAS HEADED. iT'S THE ONLY LEAD I HAVE.
SNiFF!
BUT I'M AFRAiD iT HAS PROBABLY RELOADED AND SET SAiL AGAiN BY NOW.

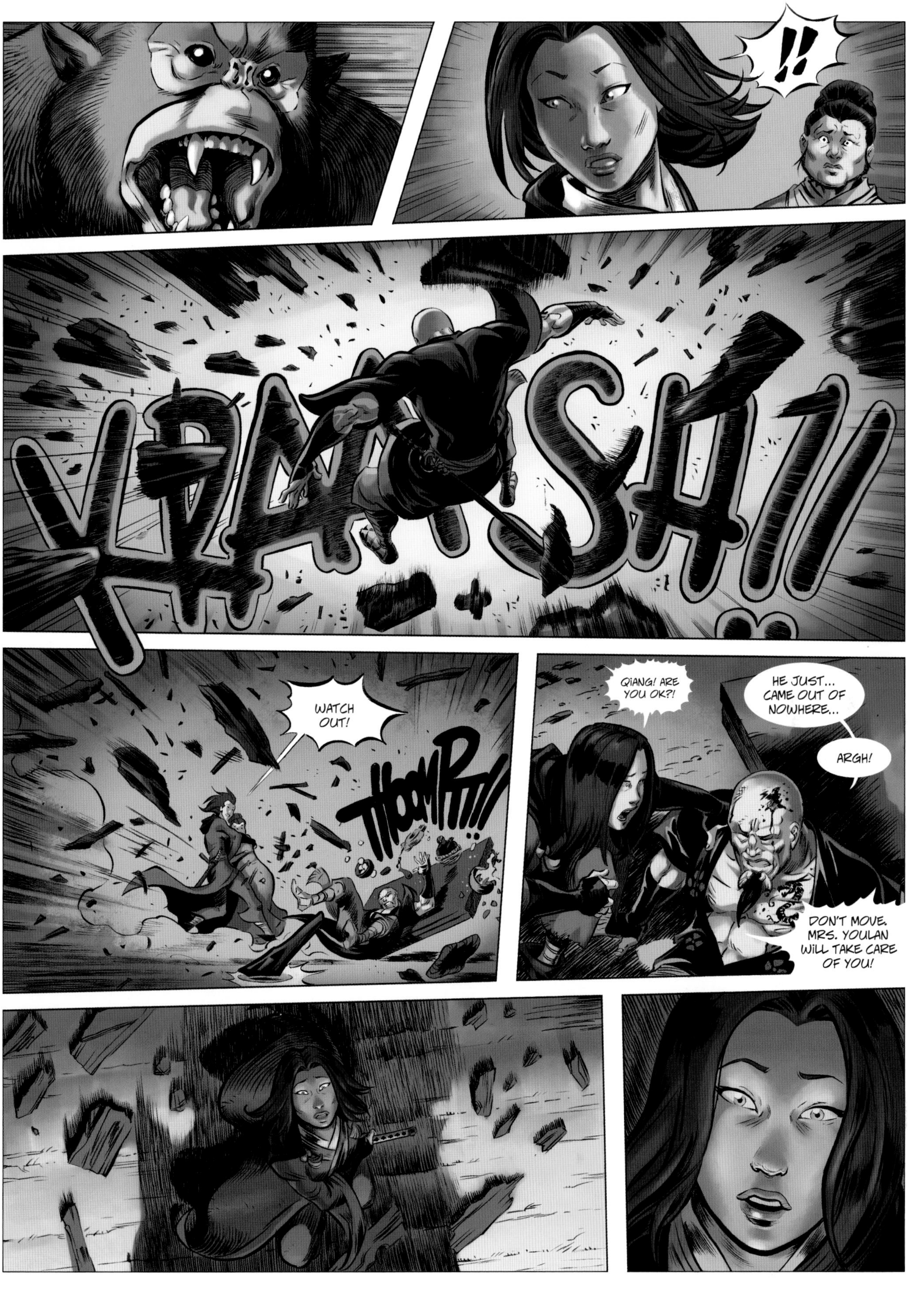
!!
WATCH OUT!
THOOMP!!!
QIANG! ARE YOU OK?!
HE JUST... CAME OUT OF NOWHERE...
ARGH!
DON'T MOVE. MRS. YOULAN WILL TAKE CARE OF YOU!

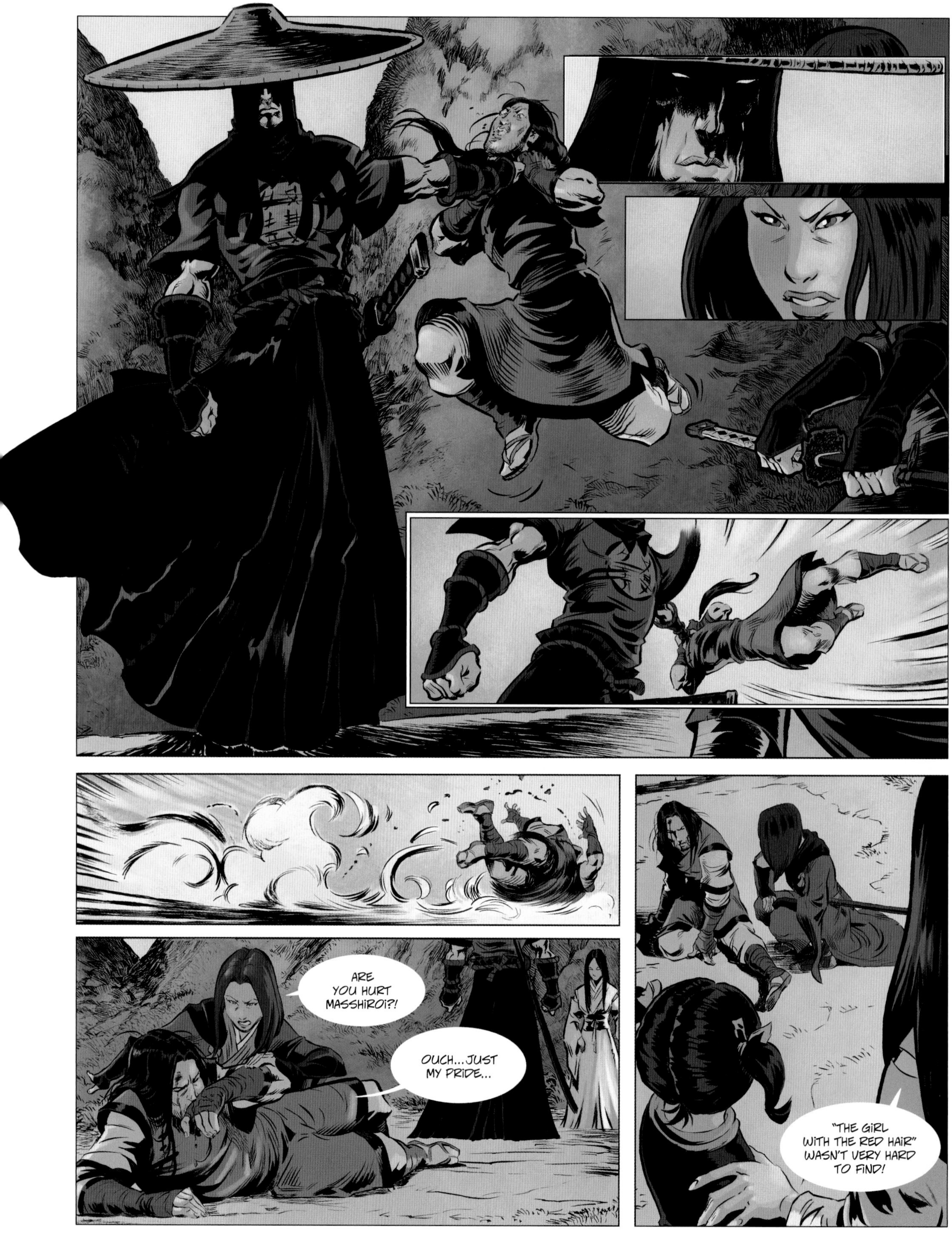
ARE YOU HURT MASSHIROI?!
OUCH... JUST MY PRIDE...
"THE GIRL WITH THE RED HAIR" WASN'T VERY HARD TO FIND!

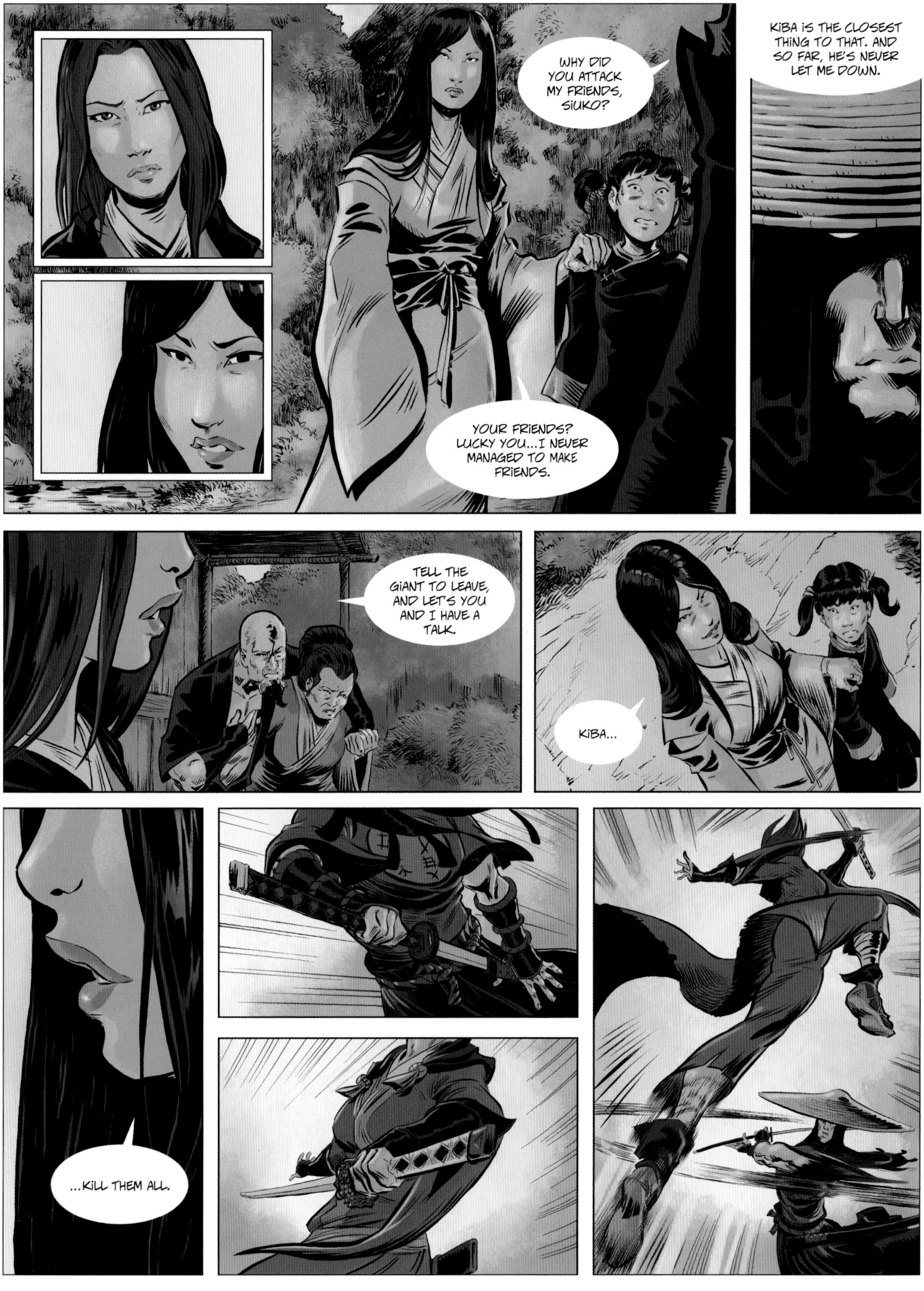
WHY DID YOU ATTACK MY FRIENDS, SIUKO?
YOUR FRIENDS? LUCKY YOU...I NEVER MANAGED TO MAKE FRIENDS.
KIBA IS THE CLOSEST THING TO THAT. AND SO FAR, HE'S NEVER LET ME DOWN.
TELL THE GIANT TO LEAVE, AND LET'S YOU AND I HAVE A TALK.
KIBA...
...KILL THEM ALL.

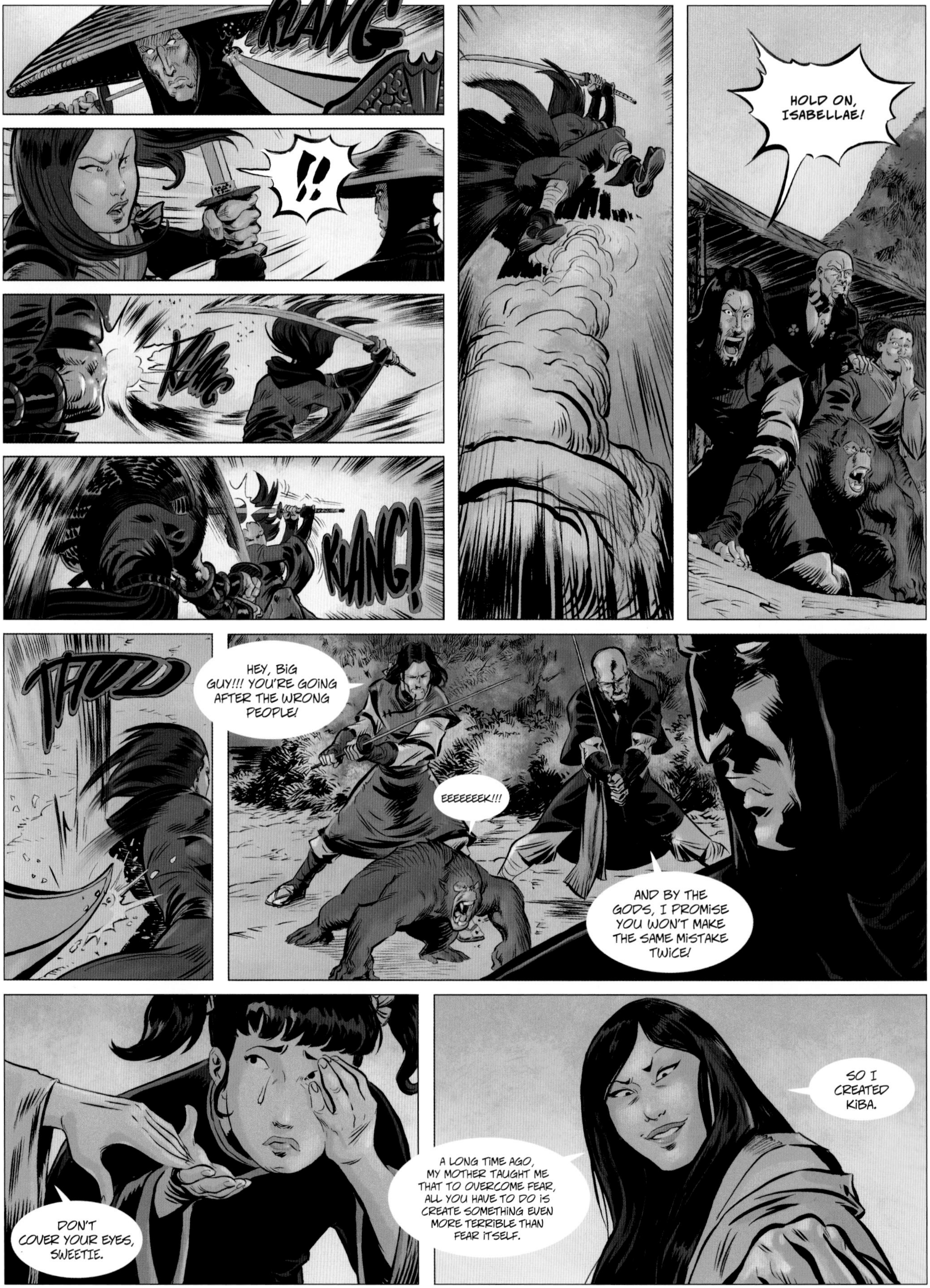
KLANG
!!
KLANG
KLANG!
HOLD ON, ISABELLAE!
THUD
HEY, BIG GUY!!! YOU'RE GOING AFTER THE WRONG PEOPLE!
EEEEEEEK!!!
AND BY THE GODS, I PROMISE YOU WON'T MAKE THE SAME MISTAKE TWICE!
DON'T COVER YOUR EYES, SWEETIE.
A LONG TIME AGO, MY MOTHER TAUGHT ME THAT TO OVERCOME FEAR, ALL YOU HAVE TO DO IS CREATE SOMETHING EVEN MORE TERRIBLE THAN FEAR ITSELF.
SO I CREATED KIBA.

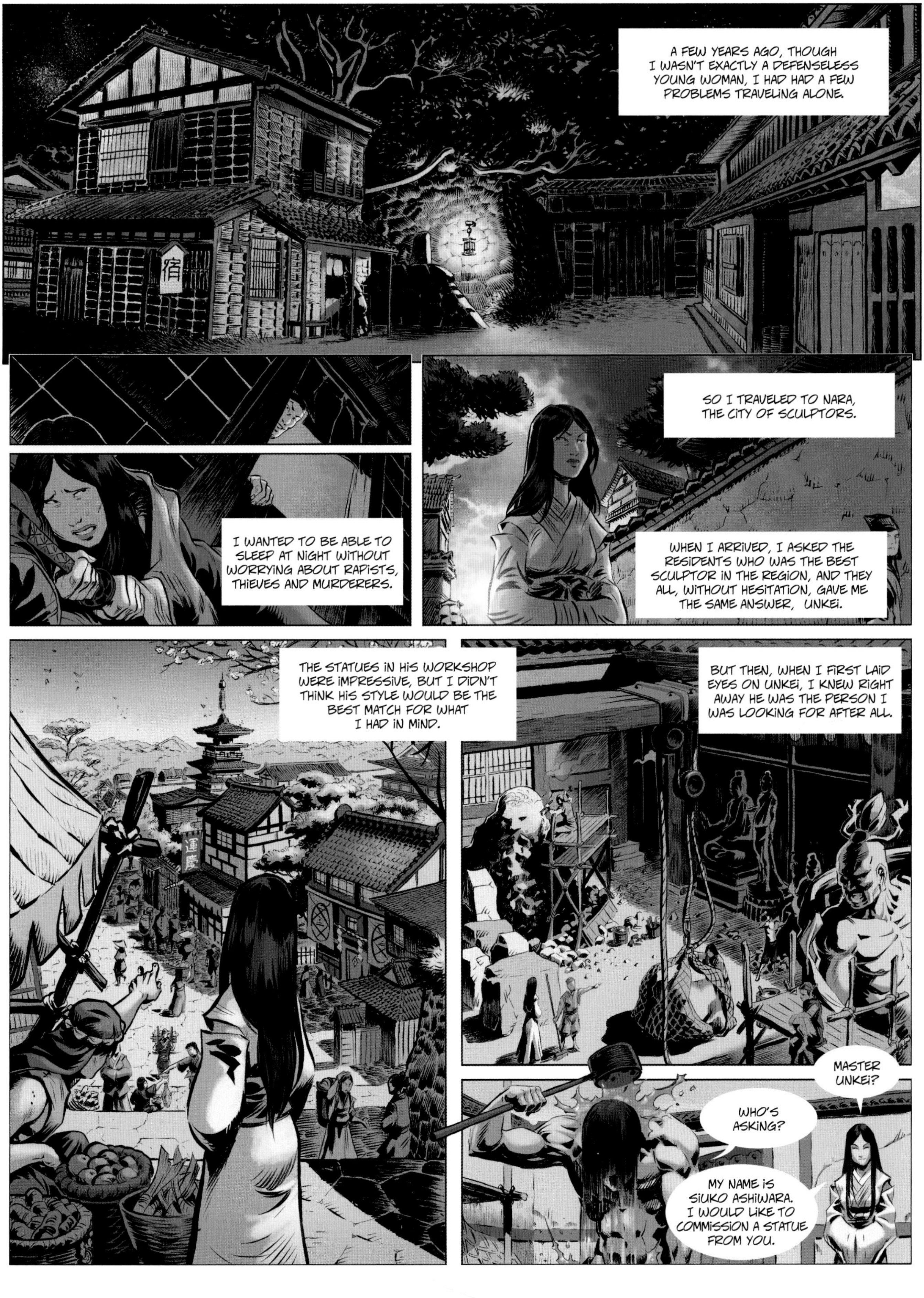
A FEW YEARS AGO, THOUGH I WASN'T EXACTLY A DEFENSELESS YOUNG WOMAN, I HAD HAD A FEW PROBLEMS TRAVELING ALONE.
宿
I WANTED TO BE ABLE TO SLEEP AT NIGHT WITHOUT WORRYING ABOUT RAPISTS, THIEVES AND MURDERERS.
SO I TRAVELED TO NARA, THE CITY OF SCULPTORS.
WHEN I ARRIVED, I ASKED THE RESIDENTS WHO WAS THE BEST SCULPTOR IN THE REGION, AND THEY ALL, WITHOUT HESITATION, GAVE ME THE SAME ANSWER, UNKEI.
THE STATUES IN HIS WORKSHOP WERE IMPRESSIVE, BUT I DIDN'T THINK HIS STYLE WOULD BE THE BEST MATCH FOR WHAT I HAD IN MIND.
BUT THEN, WHEN I FIRST LAID EYES ON UNKEI, I KNEW RIGHT AWAY HE WAS THE PERSON I WAS LOOKING FOR AFTER ALL.
MASTER UNKEI?
WHO'S ASKING?
MY NAME IS SIUKO ASHIWARA. I WOULD LIKE TO COMMISSION A STATUE FROM YOU.

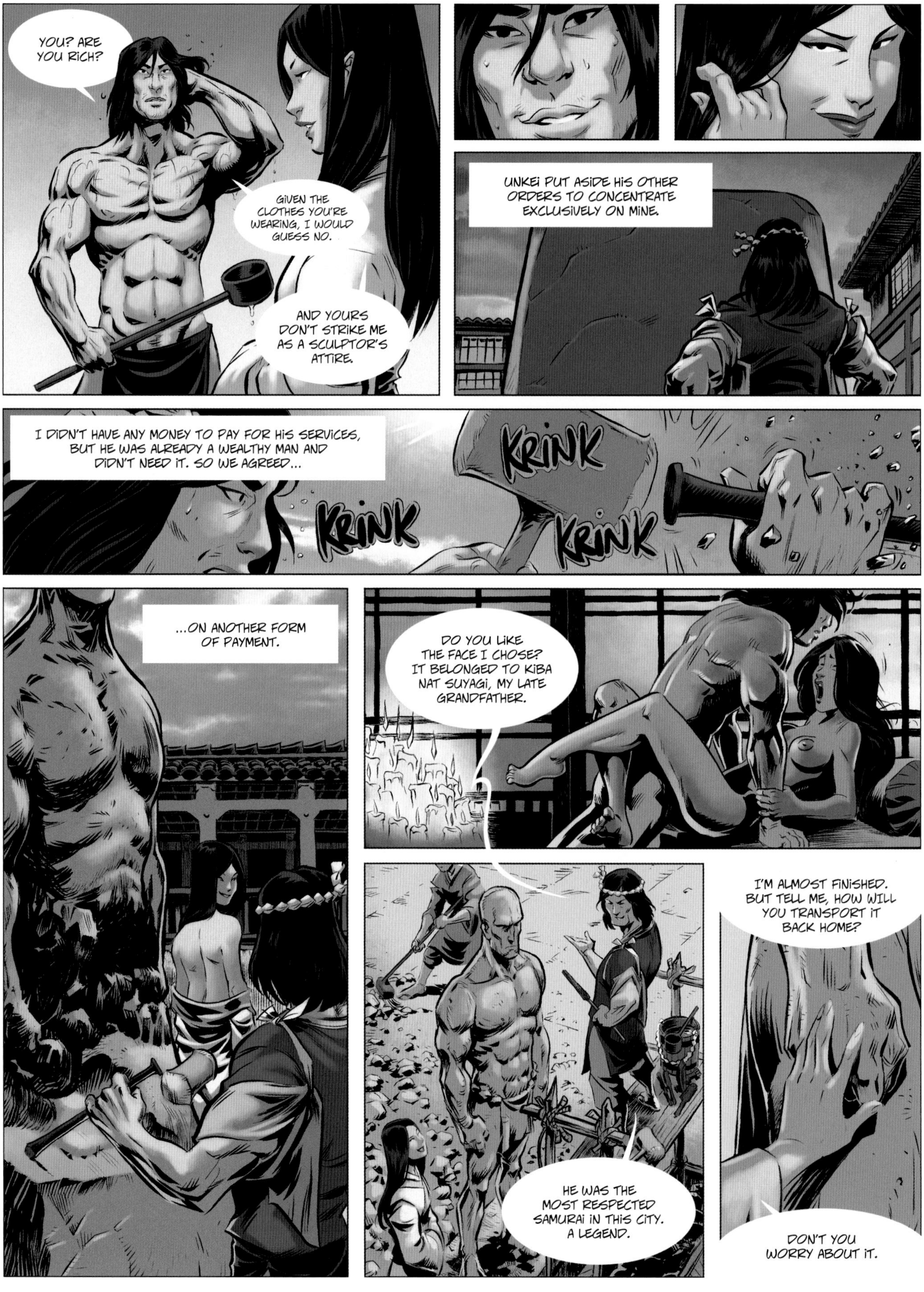
YOU? ARE YOU RICH?
GIVEN THE CLOTHES YOU'RE WEARING, I WOULD GUESS NO.
AND YOURS DON'T STRIKE ME AS A SCULPTOR'S ATTIRE.
UNKEI PUT ASIDE HIS OTHER ORDERS TO CONCENTRATE EXCLUSIVELY ON MINE.
I DIDN'T HAVE ANY MONEY TO PAY FOR HIS SERVICES, BUT HE WAS ALREADY A WEALTHY MAN AND DIDN'T NEED IT. SO WE AGREED...
KRINK
KRINK
KRINK
...ON ANOTHER FORM OF PAYMENT.
DO YOU LIKE THE FACE I CHOSE? IT BELONGED TO KIBA NAT SUYAGI, MY LATE GRANDFATHER.
HE WAS THE MOST RESPECTED SAMURAI IN THIS CITY. A LEGEND.
I'M ALMOST FINISHED. BUT TELL ME, HOW WILL YOU TRANSPORT IT BACK HOME?
DON'T YOU WORRY ABOUT IT.

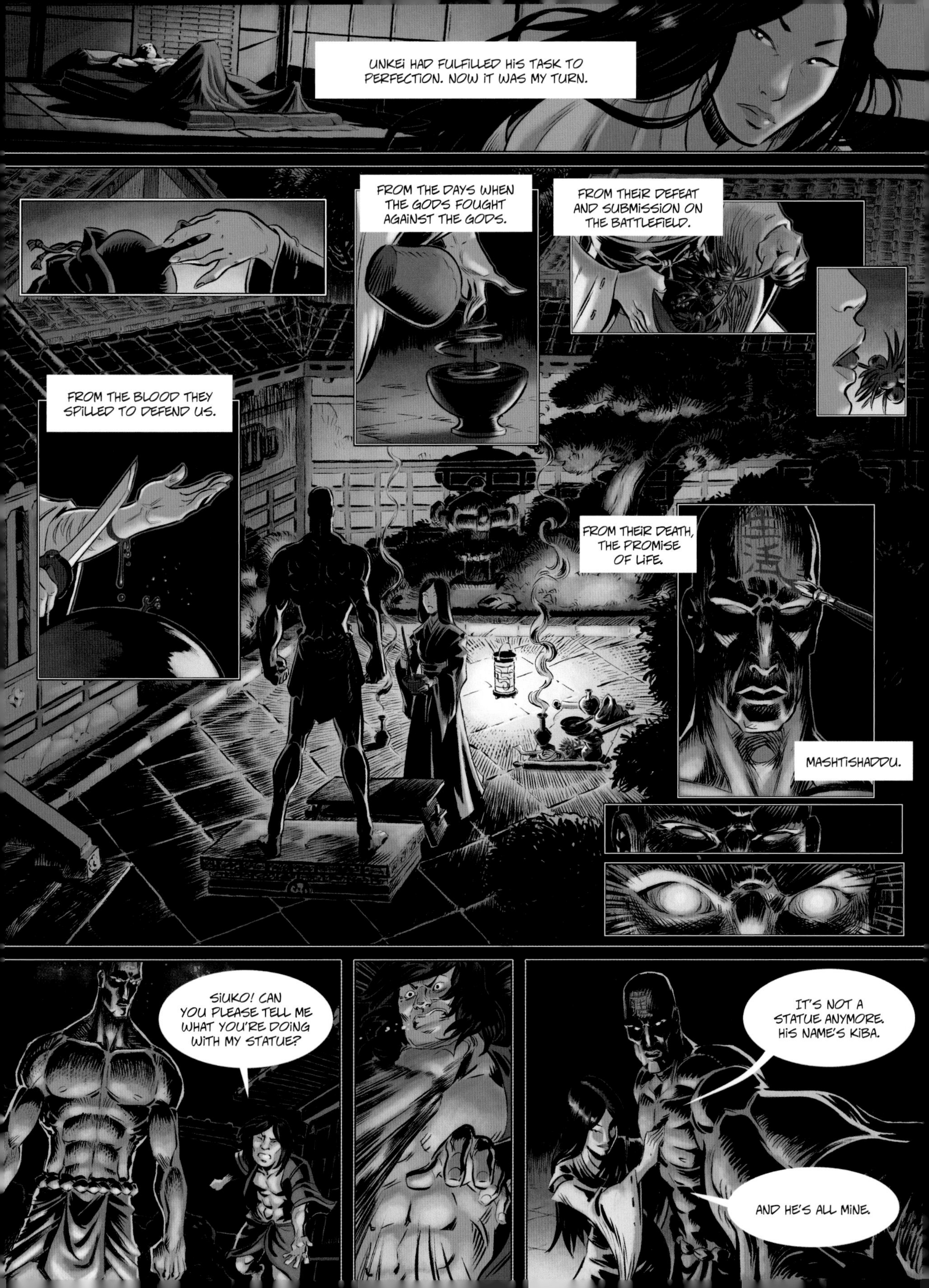
UNKEI HAD FULFILLED HIS TASK TO PERFECTION. NOW IT WAS MY TURN.
FROM THE DAYS WHEN THE GODS FOUGHT AGAINST THE GODS.
FROM THEIR DEFEAT AND SUBMISSION ON THE BATTLEFIELD.
FROM THE BLOOD THEY SPILLED TO DEFEND US.
FROM THEIR DEATH, THE PROMISE OF LIFE.
MASHTISHADDU.
SIUKO! CAN YOU PLEASE TELL ME WHAT YOU'RE DOING WITH MY STATUE?
IT'S NOT A STATUE ANYMORE. HIS NAME'S KIBA.
AND HE'S ALL MINE.

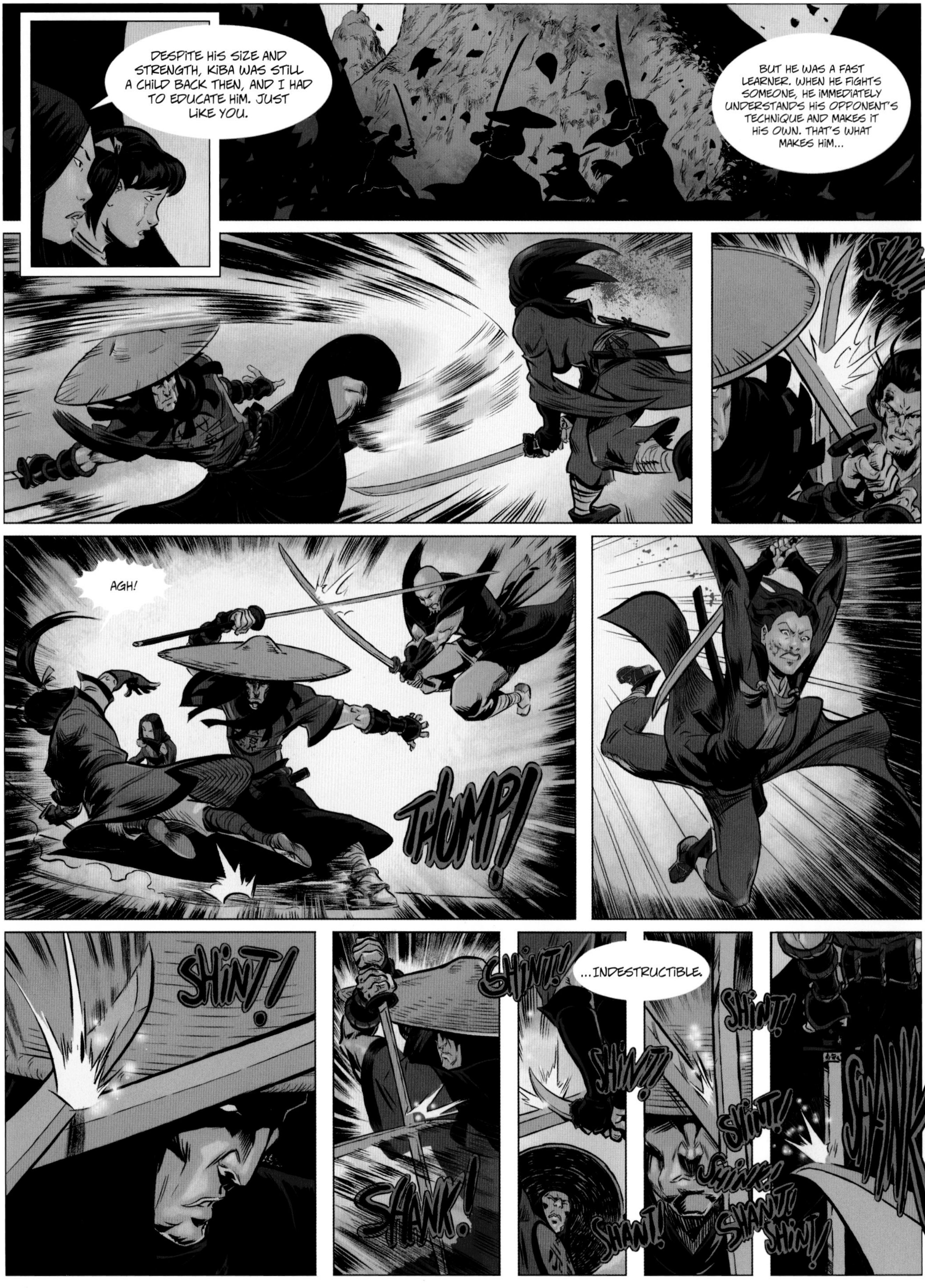
DESPITE HIS SIZE AND STRENGTH, KIBA WAS STILL A CHILD BACK THEN, AND I HAD TO EDUCATE HIM. JUST LIKE YOU.
BUT HE WAS A FAST LEARNER. WHEN HE FIGHTS SOMEONE, HE IMMEDIATELY UNDERSTANDS HIS OPPONENT'S TECHNIQUE AND MAKES IT HIS OWN. THAT'S WHAT MAKES HIM...
SHIN!
AGH!
THUMP!
SHINT!
SHINT!
SHANK!
...INDESTRUCTIBLE.
SHINT!
SHINT!
SHINT!
SHINK!
SHANT!
SHANT!
SHINT!
SHANK!

THUNH!

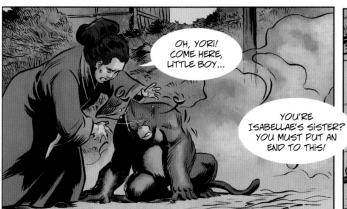

OH, YORI!
COME HERE,
LITTLE BOY...

YOU'RE
ISABELLAE'S SISTER?
YOU MUST PUT AN
END TO THIS!

THERE'S ONLY
ONE WAY TO
STOP KIBA.

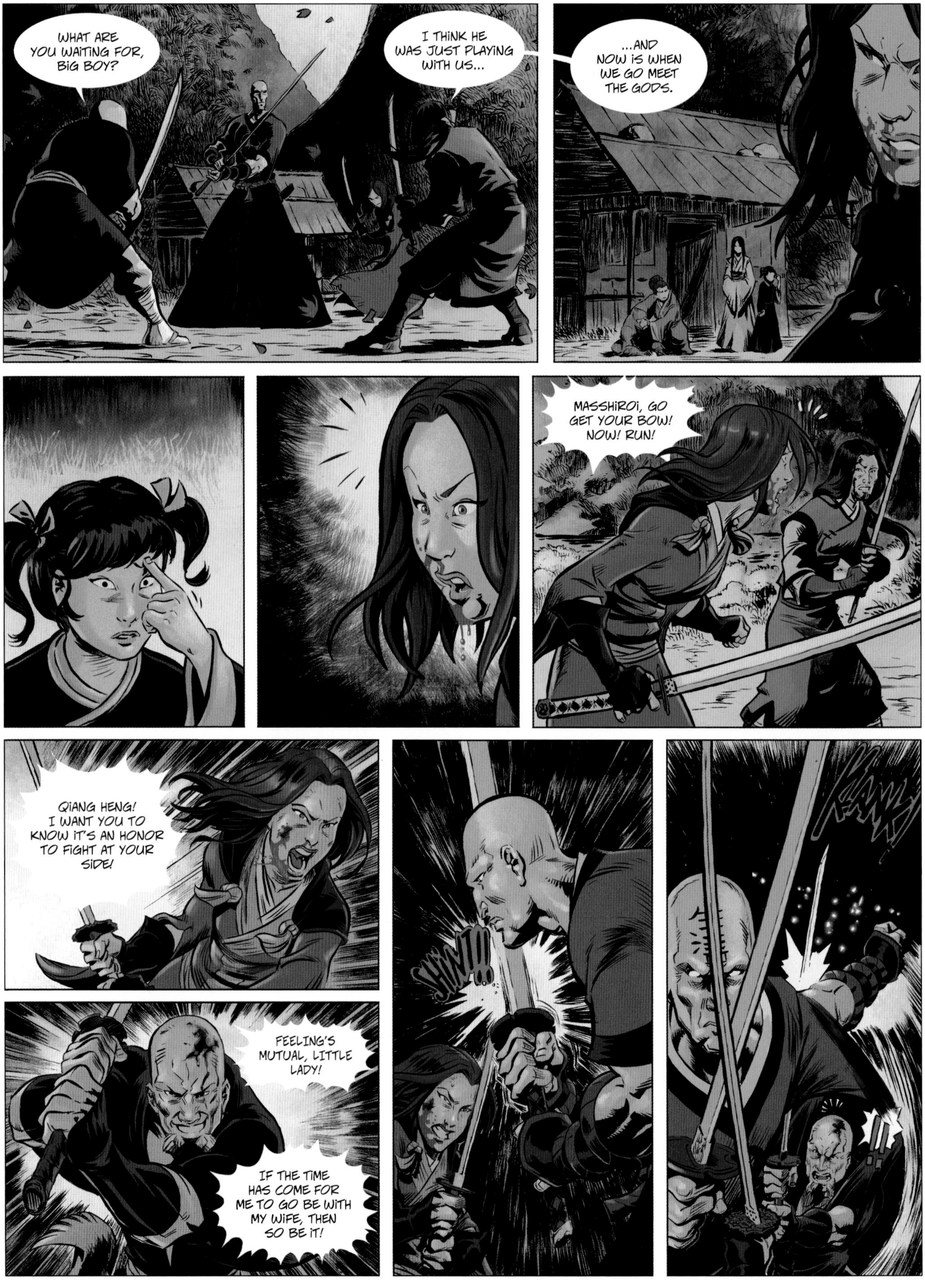
WHAT ARE YOU WAITING FOR, BIG BOY?
I THINK HE WAS JUST PLAYING WITH US...
...AND NOW IS WHEN WE GO MEET THE GODS.
MASSHIROI, GO GET YOUR BOW! NOW! RUN!
QIANG HENG! I WANT YOU TO KNOW IT'S AN HONOR TO FIGHT AT YOUR SIDE!
FEELING'S MUTUAL, LITTLE LADY!
IF THE TIME HAS COME FOR ME TO GO BE WITH MY WIFE, THEN SO BE IT!

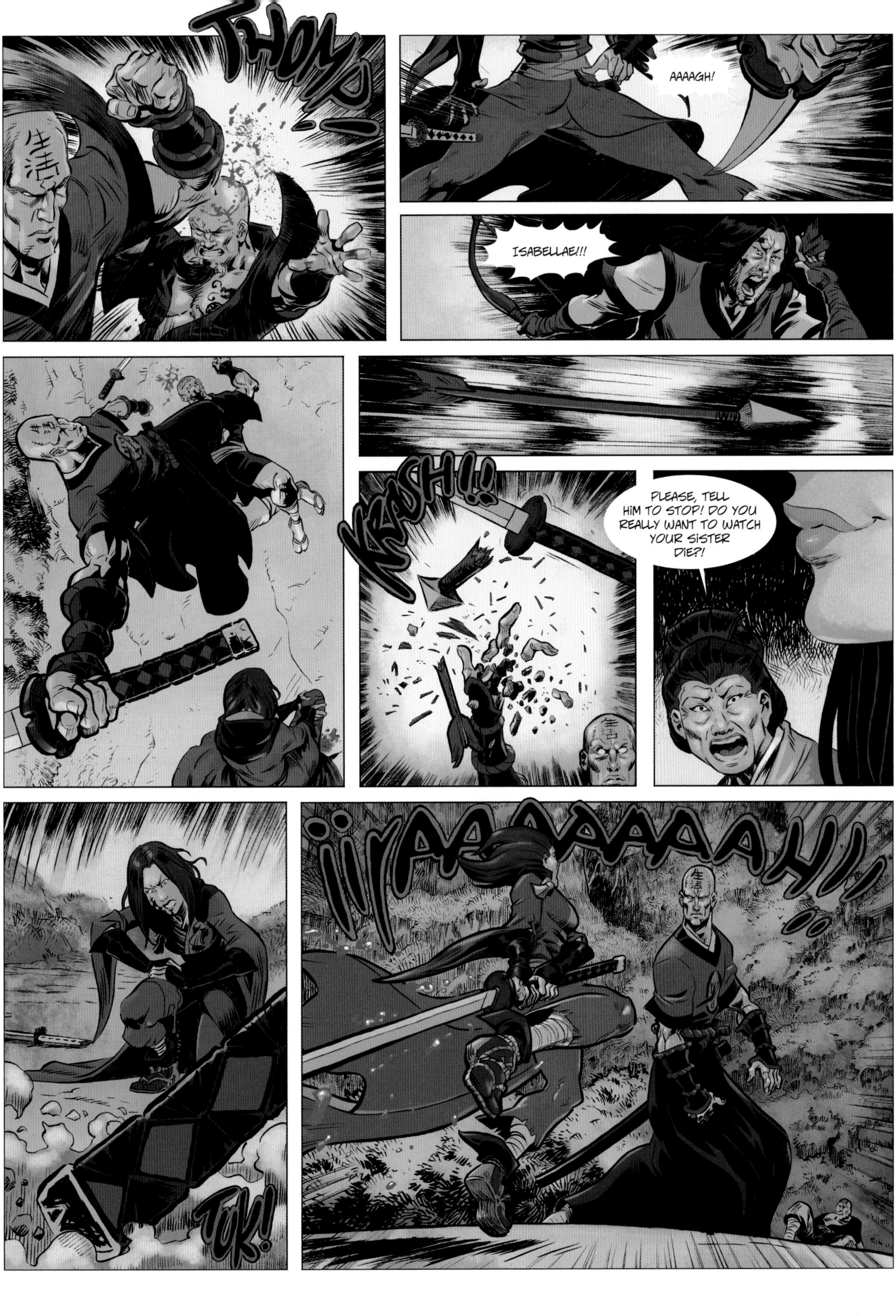
THOMP!!
AAAAGH!
ISABELLAE!!!
KRASH!!!
PLEASE, TELL HIM TO STOP! DO YOU REALLY WANT TO WATCH YOUR SISTER DIE?!
TUK!
¡¡YAAAAAAH!!

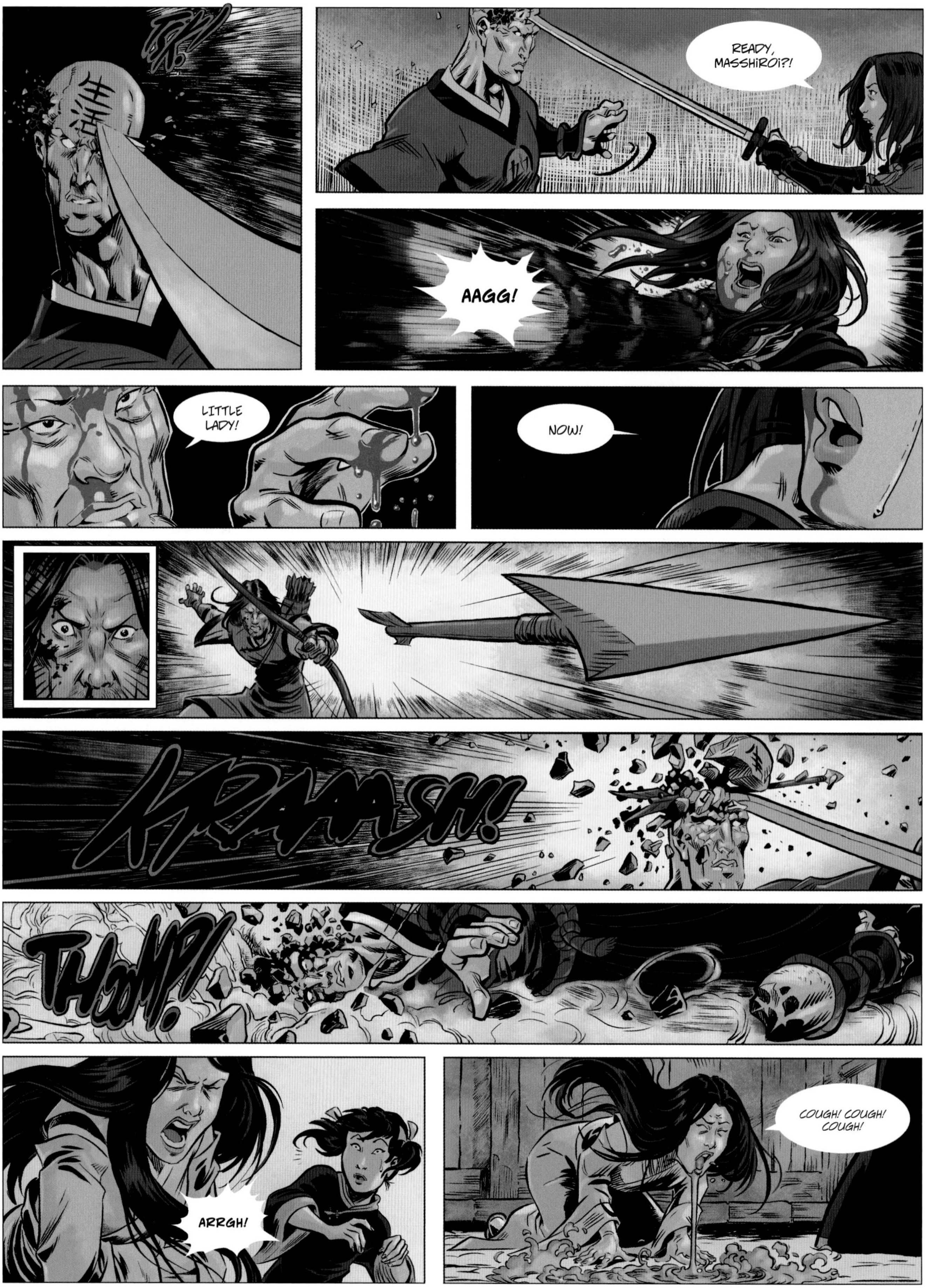

READY, MASSHIROI?!
AAGG!
LITTLE LADY!
NOW!
KRAAASH!
THOOMP!
ARRGH!
COUGH! COUGH! COUGH!

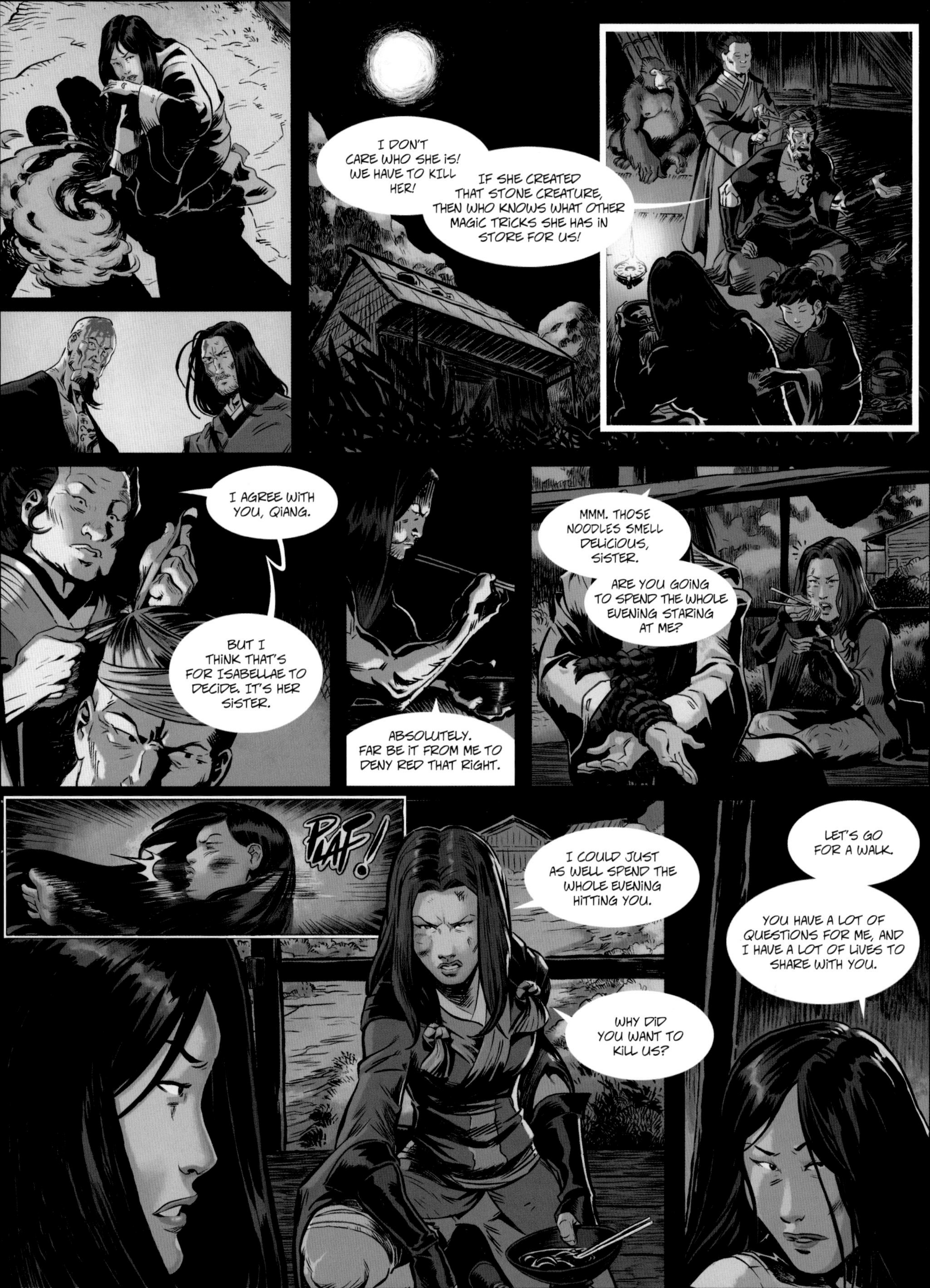
I DON'T CARE WHO SHE iS! WE HAVE TO KILL HER!
IF SHE CREATED THAT STONE CREATURE, THEN WHO KNOWS WHAT OTHER MAGIC TRICKS SHE HAS IN STORE FOR US!
I AGREE WITH YOU, QIANG.
BUT I THINK THAT'S FOR ISABELLAE TO DECIDE. IT'S HER SiSTER.
ABSOLUTELY. FAR BE iT FROM ME TO DENY RED THAT RIGHT.
MMM. THOSE NOODLES SMELL DELICIOUS, SiSTER.
ARE YOU GOiNG TO SPEND THE WHOLE EVENiNG STARING AT ME?
PLAF!
I COULD JUST AS WELL SPEND THE WHOLE EVENiNG HiTTING YOU.
WHY DID YOU WANT TO KiLL US?
LET'S GO FOR A WALK.
YOU HAVE A LOT OF QUESTIONS FOR ME, AND I HAVE A LOT OF LiVES TO SHARE WiTH YOU.

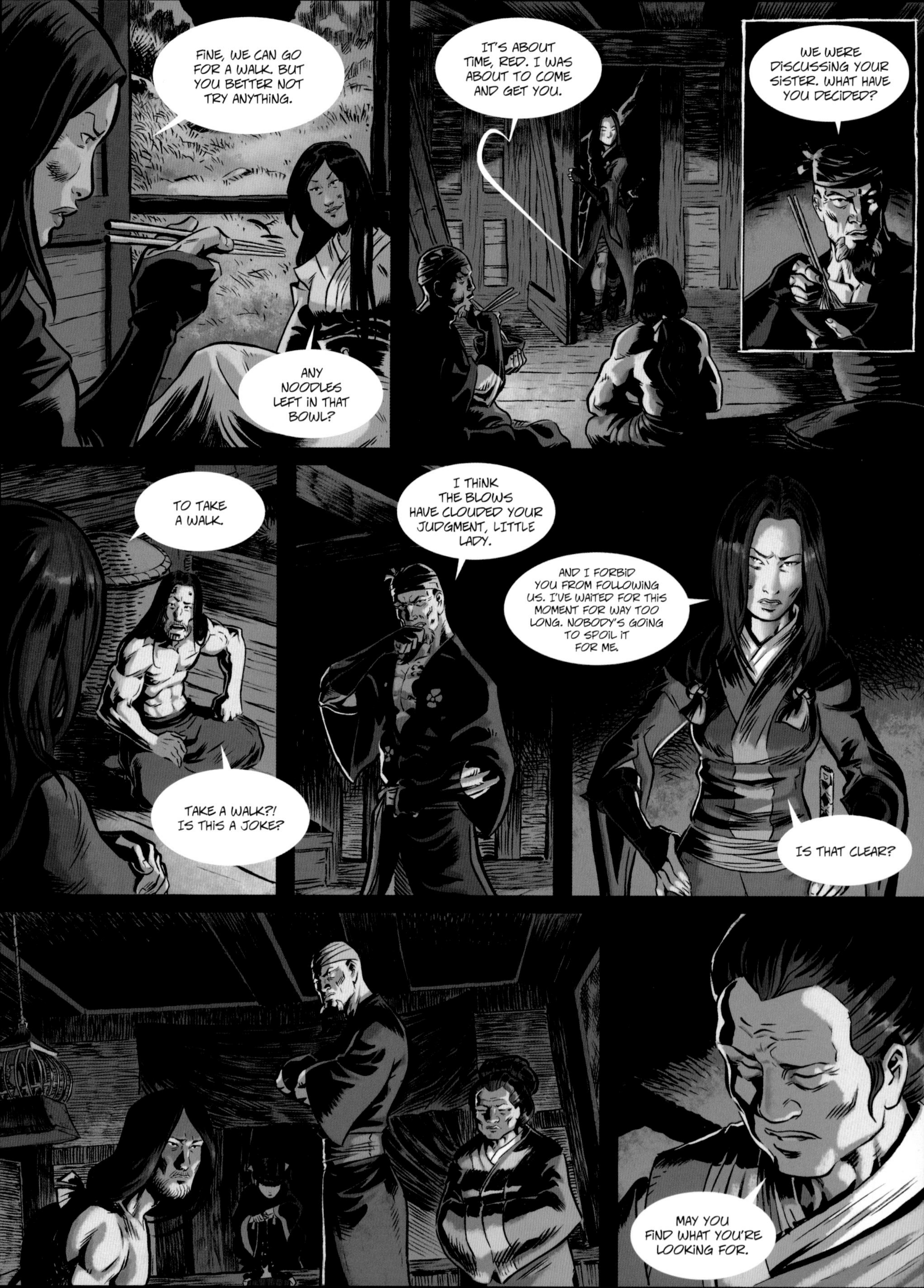
FINE, WE CAN GO FOR A WALK. BUT YOU BETTER NOT TRY ANYTHING.
ANY NOODLES LEFT IN THAT BOWL?
IT'S ABOUT TIME, RED. I WAS ABOUT TO COME AND GET YOU.
WE WERE DISCUSSING YOUR SISTER. WHAT HAVE YOU DECIDED?
TO TAKE A WALK.
TAKE A WALK?! IS THIS A JOKE?
I THINK THE BLOWS HAVE CLOUDED YOUR JUDGMENT, LITTLE LADY.
AND I FORBID YOU FROM FOLLOWING US. I'VE WAITED FOR THIS MOMENT FOR WAY TOO LONG. NOBODY'S GOING TO SPOIL IT FOR ME.
IS THAT CLEAR?
MAY YOU FIND WHAT YOU'RE LOOKING FOR.

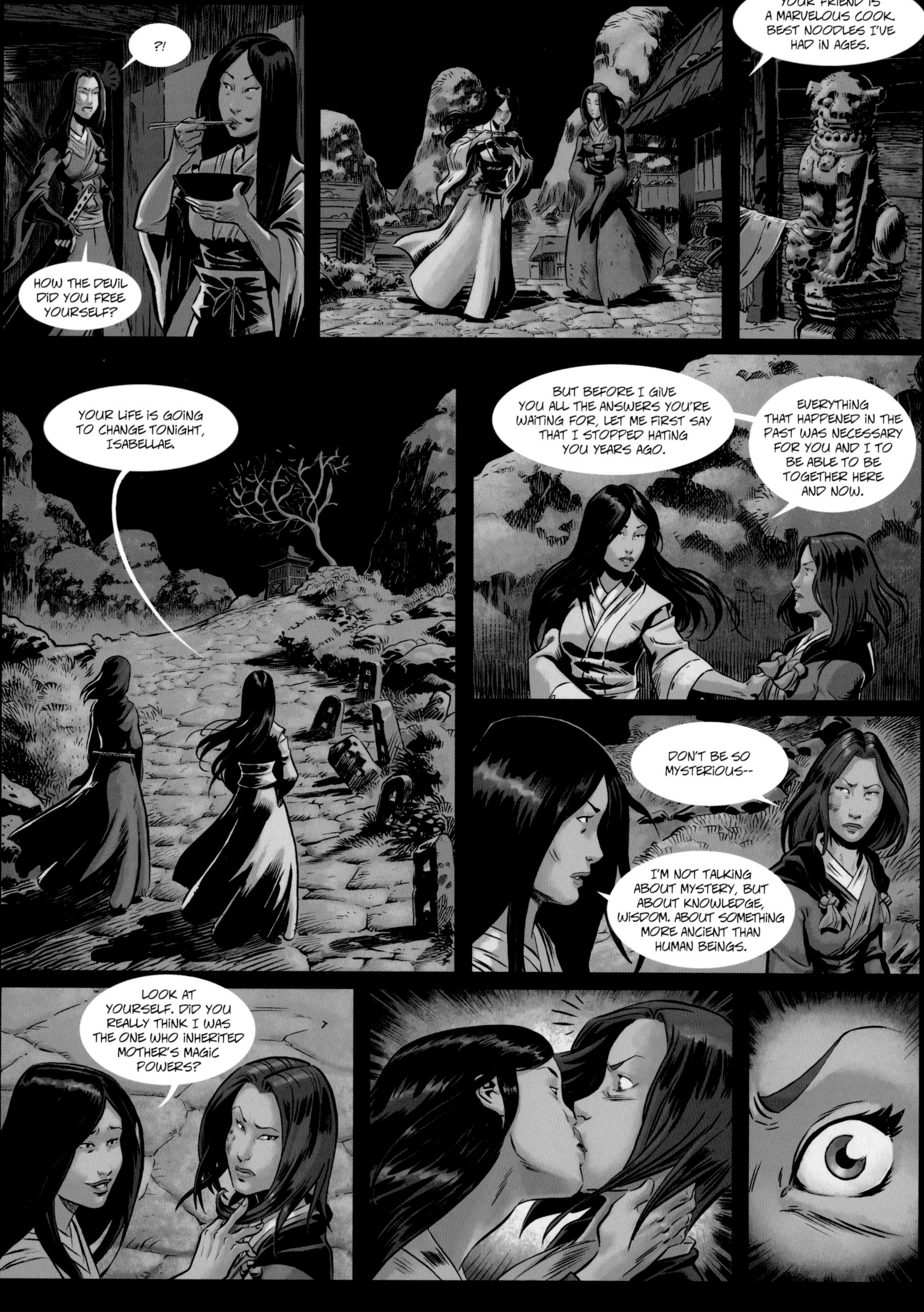

?!
HOW THE DEVIL DID YOU FREE YOURSELF?
YOUR FRIEND IS A MARVELOUS COOK. BEST NOODLES I'VE HAD IN AGES.
YOUR LIFE IS GOING TO CHANGE TONIGHT, ISABELLAE.
BUT BEFORE I GIVE YOU ALL THE ANSWERS YOU'RE WAITING FOR, LET ME FIRST SAY THAT I STOPPED HATING YOU YEARS AGO.
EVERYTHING THAT HAPPENED IN THE PAST WAS NECESSARY FOR YOU AND I TO BE ABLE TO BE TOGETHER HERE AND NOW.
DON'T BE SO MYSTERIOUS--
I'M NOT TALKING ABOUT MYSTERY, BUT ABOUT KNOWLEDGE, WISDOM. ABOUT SOMETHING MORE ANCIENT THAN HUMAN BEINGS.
LOOK AT YOURSELF. DID YOU REALLY THINK I WAS THE ONE WHO INHERITED MOTHER'S MAGIC POWERS?

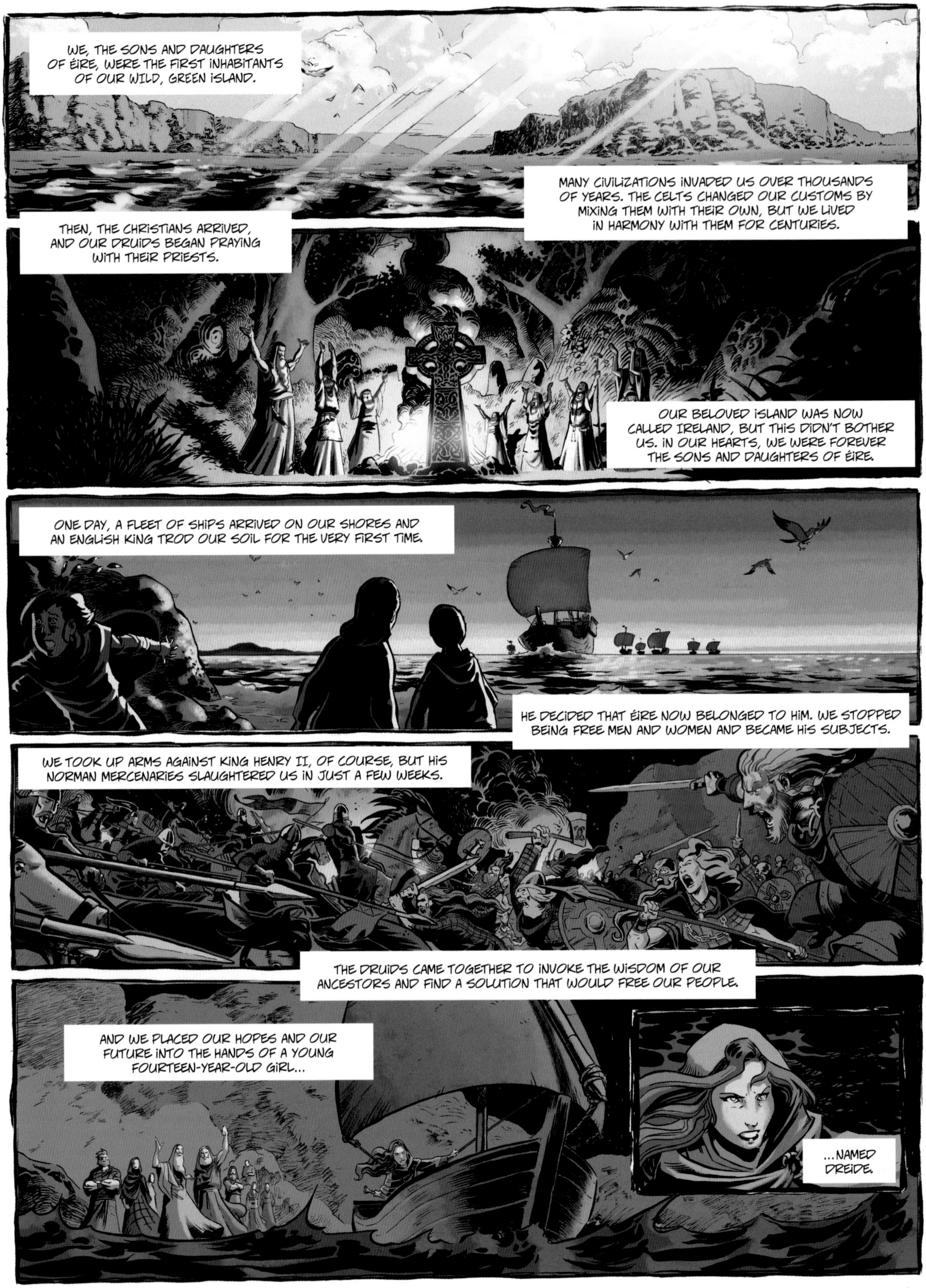
WE, THE SONS AND DAUGHTERS OF ÉIRE, WERE THE FIRST INHABITANTS OF OUR WILD, GREEN ISLAND.
MANY CIVILIZATIONS INVADED US OVER THOUSANDS OF YEARS. THE CELTS CHANGED OUR CUSTOMS BY MIXING THEM WITH THEIR OWN, BUT WE LIVED IN HARMONY WITH THEM FOR CENTURIES.
THEN, THE CHRISTIANS ARRIVED, AND OUR DRUIDS BEGAN PRAYING WITH THEIR PRIESTS.
OUR BELOVED ISLAND WAS NOW CALLED IRELAND, BUT THIS DIDN'T BOTHER US. IN OUR HEARTS, WE WERE FOREVER THE SONS AND DAUGHTERS OF ÉIRE.
ONE DAY, A FLEET OF SHIPS ARRIVED ON OUR SHORES AND AN ENGLISH KING TROD OUR SOIL FOR THE VERY FIRST TIME.
HE DECIDED THAT ÉIRE NOW BELONGED TO HIM. WE STOPPED BEING FREE MEN AND WOMEN AND BECAME HIS SUBJECTS.
WE TOOK UP ARMS AGAINST KING HENRY II, OF COURSE, BUT HIS NORMAN MERCENARIES SLAUGHTERED US IN JUST A FEW WEEKS.
THE DRUIDS CAME TOGETHER TO INVOKE THE WISDOM OF OUR ANCESTORS AND FIND A SOLUTION THAT WOULD FREE OUR PEOPLE.
AND WE PLACED OUR HOPES AND OUR FUTURE INTO THE HANDS OF A YOUNG FOURTEEN-YEAR-OLD GIRL...
...NAMED DREIDE.

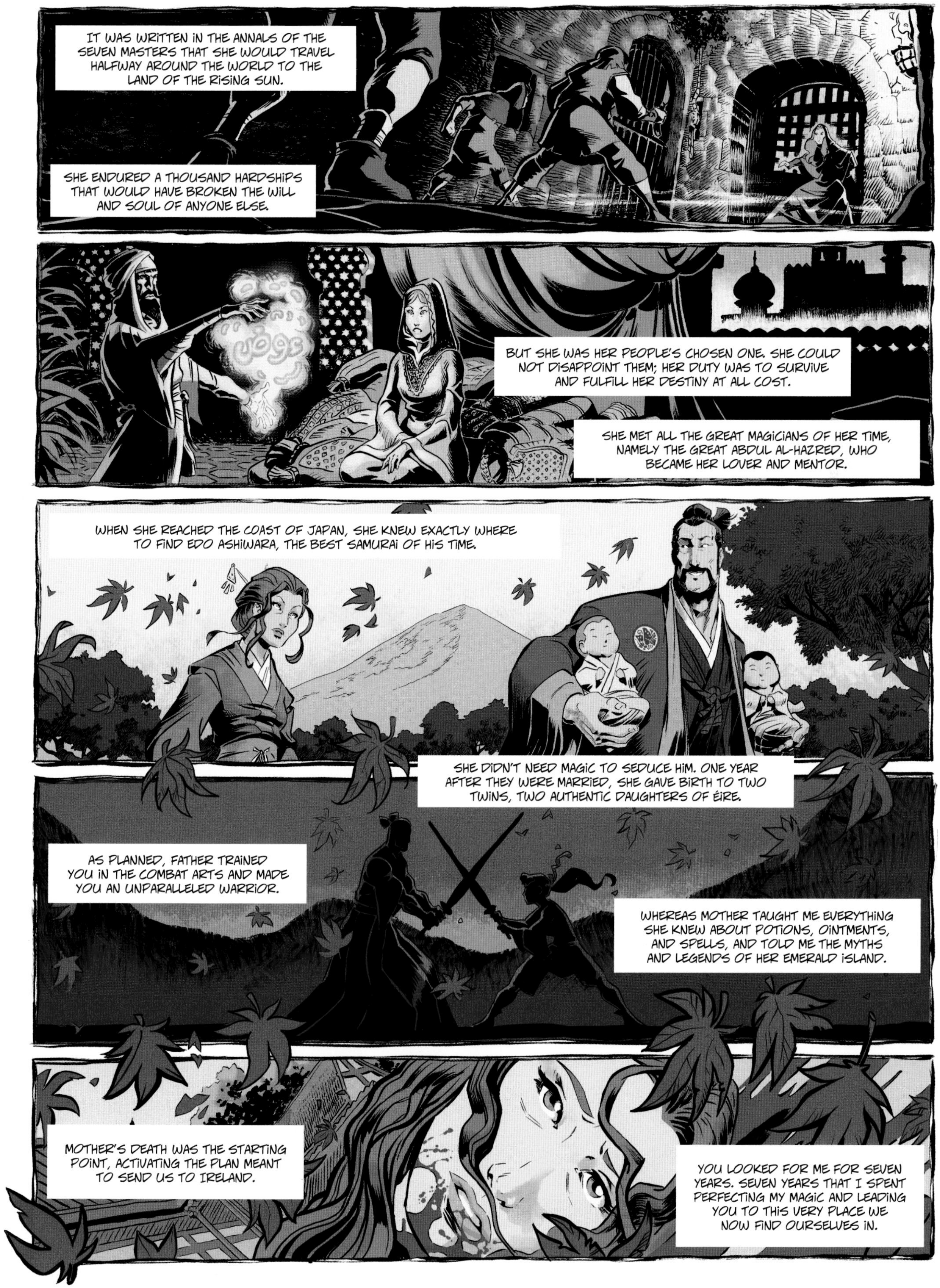
IT WAS WRITTEN IN THE ANNALS OF THE SEVEN MASTERS THAT SHE WOULD TRAVEL HALFWAY AROUND THE WORLD TO THE LAND OF THE RISING SUN.
SHE ENDURED A THOUSAND HARDSHIPS THAT WOULD HAVE BROKEN THE WILL AND SOUL OF ANYONE ELSE.
BUT SHE WAS HER PEOPLE'S CHOSEN ONE. SHE COULD NOT DISAPPOINT THEM; HER DUTY WAS TO SURVIVE AND FULFILL HER DESTINY AT ALL COST.
SHE MET ALL THE GREAT MAGICIANS OF HER TIME, NAMELY THE GREAT ABDUL AL-HAZRED, WHO BECAME HER LOVER AND MENTOR.
WHEN SHE REACHED THE COAST OF JAPAN, SHE KNEW EXACTLY WHERE TO FIND EDO ASHIWARA, THE BEST SAMURAI OF HIS TIME.
SHE DIDN'T NEED MAGIC TO SEDUCE HIM. ONE YEAR AFTER THEY WERE MARRIED, SHE GAVE BIRTH TO TWO TWINS, TWO AUTHENTIC DAUGHTERS OF ÉIRE.
AS PLANNED, FATHER TRAINED YOU IN THE COMBAT ARTS AND MADE YOU AN UNPARALLELED WARRIOR.
WHEREAS MOTHER TAUGHT ME EVERYTHING SHE KNEW ABOUT POTIONS, OINTMENTS, AND SPELLS, AND TOLD ME THE MYTHS AND LEGENDS OF HER EMERALD ISLAND.
MOTHER'S DEATH WAS THE STARTING POINT, ACTIVATING THE PLAN MEANT TO SEND US TO IRELAND.
YOU LOOKED FOR ME FOR SEVEN YEARS. SEVEN YEARS THAT I SPENT PERFECTING MY MAGIC AND LEADING YOU TO THIS VERY PLACE WE NOW FIND OURSELVES IN.

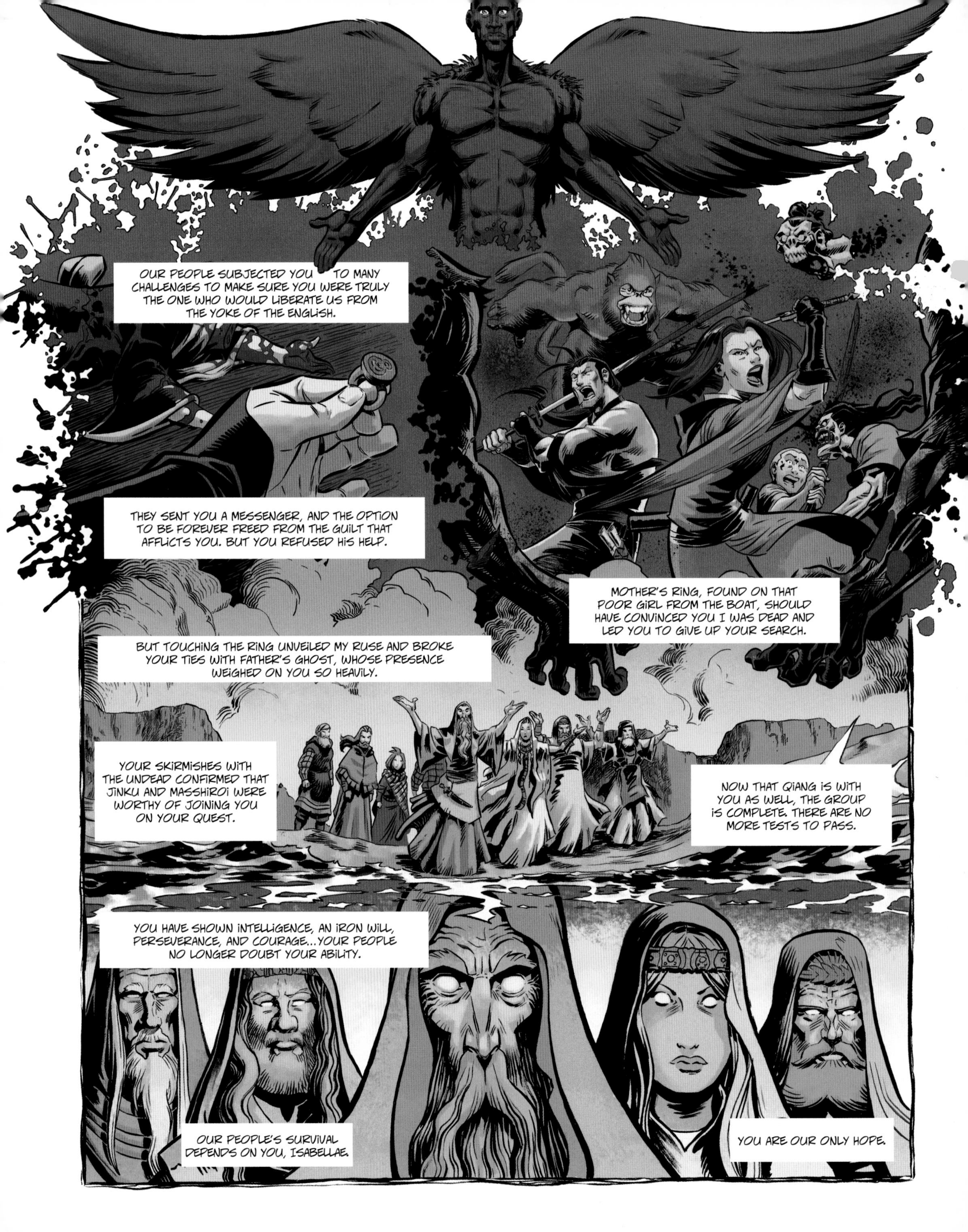
OUR PEOPLE SUBJECTED YOU TO MANY CHALLENGES TO MAKE SURE YOU WERE TRULY THE ONE WHO WOULD LIBERATE US FROM THE YOKE OF THE ENGLISH.
THEY SENT YOU A MESSENGER, AND THE OPTION TO BE FOREVER FREED FROM THE GUILT THAT AFFLICTS YOU. BUT YOU REFUSED HIS HELP.
MOTHER'S RING, FOUND ON THAT POOR GIRL FROM THE BOAT, SHOULD HAVE CONVINCED YOU I WAS DEAD AND LED YOU TO GIVE UP YOUR SEARCH.
BUT TOUCHING THE RING UNVEILED MY RUSE AND BROKE YOUR TIES WITH FATHER'S GHOST, WHOSE PRESENCE WEIGHED ON YOU SO HEAVILY.
YOUR SKIRMISHES WITH THE UNDEAD CONFIRMED THAT JINKU AND MASSHIROI WERE WORTHY OF JOINING YOU ON YOUR QUEST.
NOW THAT QIANG IS WITH YOU AS WELL, THE GROUP IS COMPLETE. THERE ARE NO MORE TESTS TO PASS.
YOU HAVE SHOWN INTELLIGENCE, AN IRON WILL, PERSEVERANCE, AND COURAGE...YOUR PEOPLE NO LONGER DOUBT YOUR ABILITY.
OUR PEOPLE'S SURVIVAL DEPENDS ON YOU, ISABELLAE.
YOU ARE OUR ONLY HOPE.

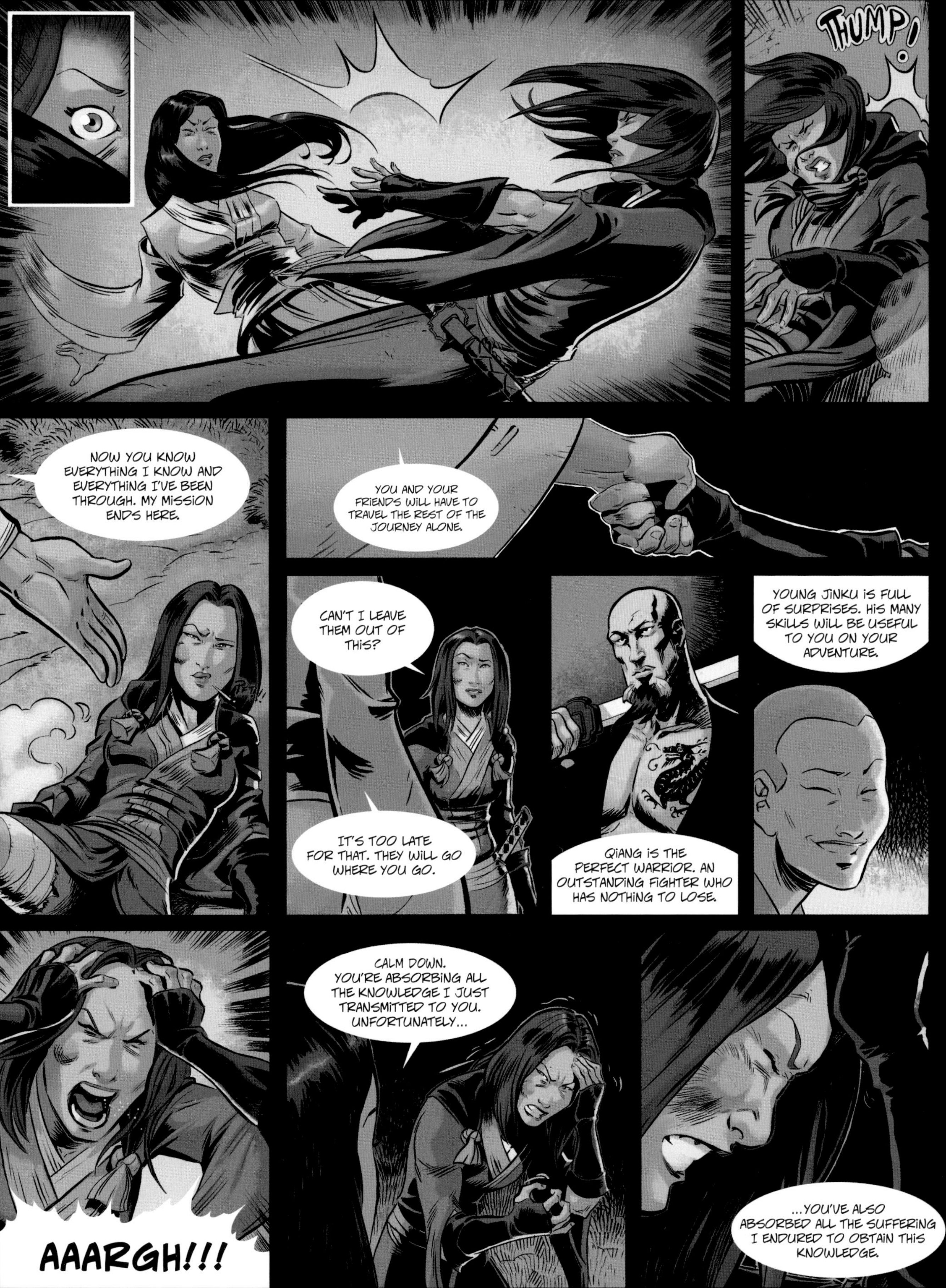
THUMP!
NOW YOU KNOW EVERYTHING I KNOW AND EVERYTHING I'VE BEEN THROUGH. MY MISSION ENDS HERE.
YOU AND YOUR FRIENDS WILL HAVE TO TRAVEL THE REST OF THE JOURNEY ALONE.
CAN'T I LEAVE THEM OUT OF THIS?
IT'S TOO LATE FOR THAT. THEY WILL GO WHERE YOU GO.
QIANG IS THE PERFECT WARRIOR. AN OUTSTANDING FIGHTER WHO HAS NOTHING TO LOSE.
YOUNG JINKU IS FULL OF SURPRISES. HIS MANY SKILLS WILL BE USEFUL TO YOU ON YOUR ADVENTURE.
AAARGH!!!
CALM DOWN. YOU'RE ABSORBING ALL THE KNOWLEDGE I JUST TRANSMITTED TO YOU. UNFORTUNATELY...
...YOU'VE ALSO ABSORBED ALL THE SUFFERING I ENDURED TO OBTAIN THIS KNOWLEDGE.

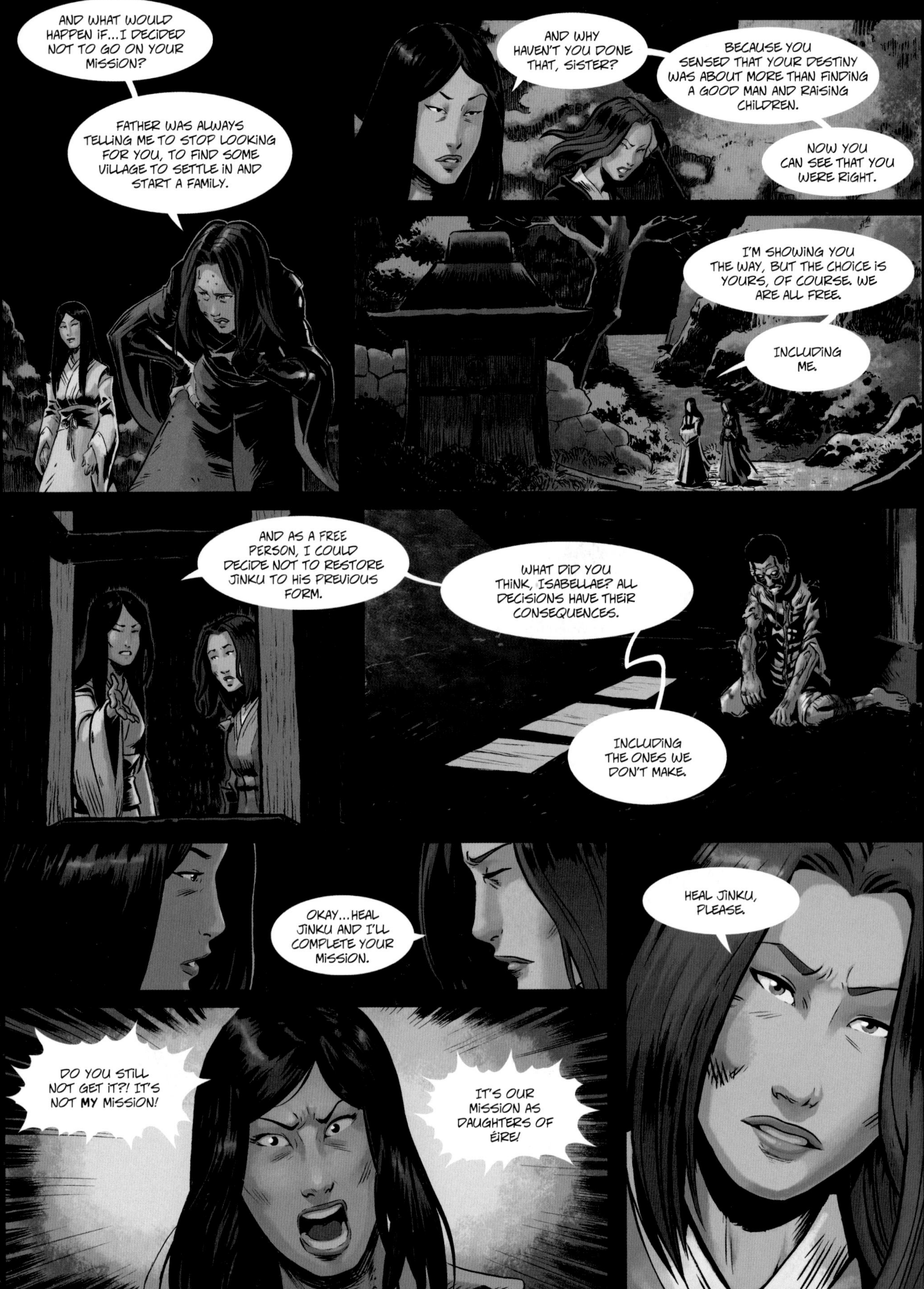

AND WHAT WOULD HAPPEN IF...I DECIDED NOT TO GO ON YOUR MISSION?
FATHER WAS ALWAYS TELLING ME TO STOP LOOKING FOR YOU, TO FIND SOME VILLAGE TO SETTLE IN AND START A FAMILY.
AND WHY HAVEN'T YOU DONE THAT, SISTER?
BECAUSE YOU SENSED THAT YOUR DESTINY WAS ABOUT MORE THAN FINDING A GOOD MAN AND RAISING CHILDREN.
NOW YOU CAN SEE THAT YOU WERE RIGHT.
I'M SHOWING YOU THE WAY, BUT THE CHOICE IS YOURS, OF COURSE. WE ARE ALL FREE.
INCLUDING ME.
AND AS A FREE PERSON, I COULD DECIDE NOT TO RESTORE JINKU TO HIS PREVIOUS FORM.
WHAT DID YOU THINK, ISABELLAE? ALL DECISIONS HAVE THEIR CONSEQUENCES.
INCLUDING THE ONES WE DON'T MAKE.
OKAY...HEAL JINKU AND I'LL COMPLETE YOUR MISSION.
HEAL JINKU, PLEASE.
DO YOU STILL NOT GET IT?! IT'S NOT **MY** MISSION!
IT'S OUR MISSION AS DAUGHTERS OF ÉIRE!

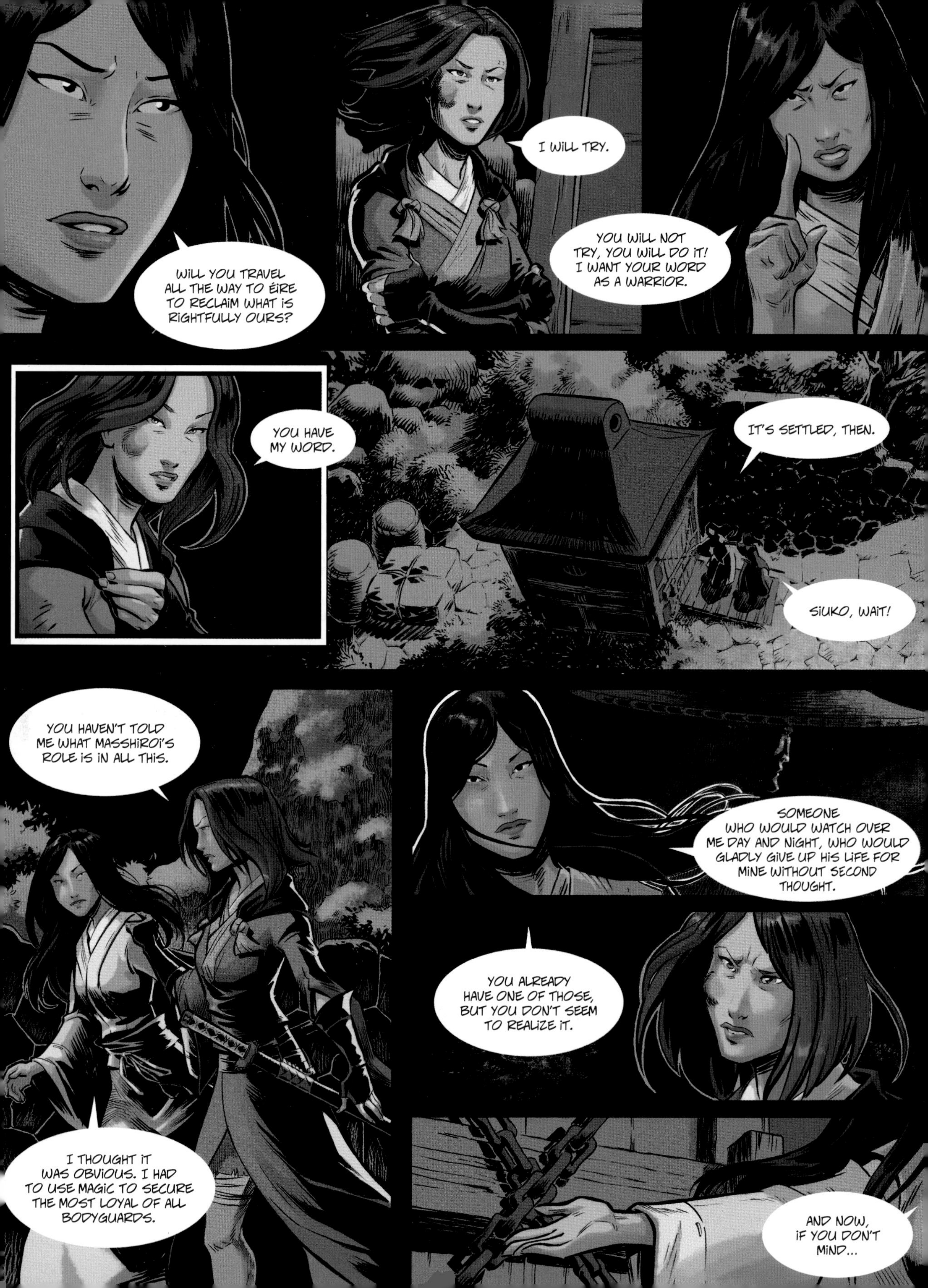
WILL YOU TRAVEL ALL THE WAY TO ÉIRE TO RECLAIM WHAT IS RIGHTFULLY OURS?
I WILL TRY.
YOU WILL NOT TRY, YOU WILL DO IT! I WANT YOUR WORD AS A WARRIOR.
YOU HAVE MY WORD.
IT'S SETTLED, THEN.
SIUKO, WAIT!
YOU HAVEN'T TOLD ME WHAT MASSHIROI'S ROLE IS IN ALL THIS.
I THOUGHT IT WAS OBVIOUS. I HAD TO USE MAGIC TO SECURE THE MOST LOYAL OF ALL BODYGUARDS.
SOMEONE WHO WOULD WATCH OVER ME DAY AND NIGHT, WHO WOULD GLADLY GIVE UP HIS LIFE FOR MINE WITHOUT SECOND THOUGHT.
YOU ALREADY HAVE ONE OF THOSE, BUT YOU DON'T SEEM TO REALIZE IT.
AND NOW, IF YOU DON'T MIND...

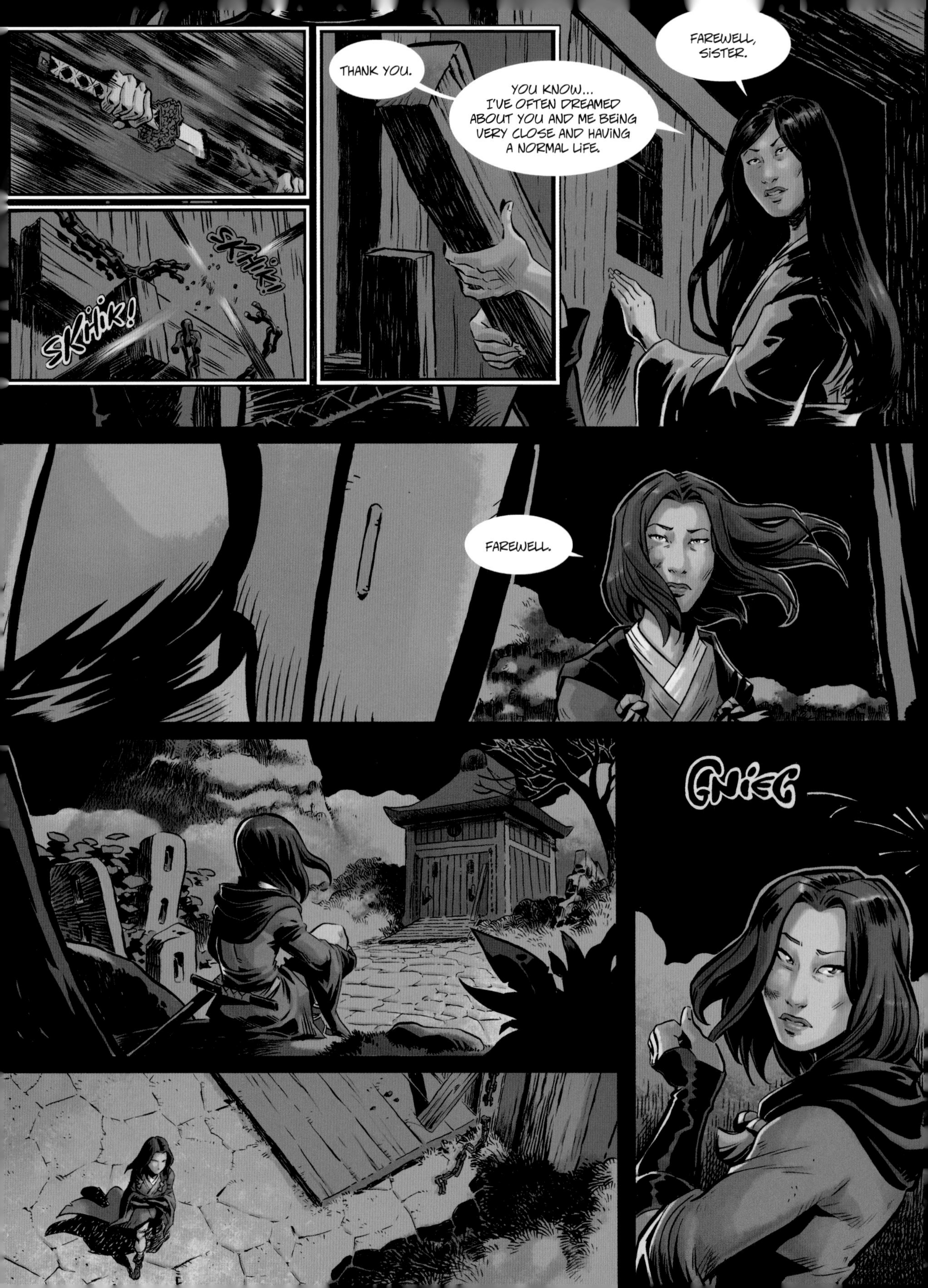
SKHIK!
SKHIK!
THANK YOU.
YOU KNOW... I'VE OFTEN DREAMED ABOUT YOU AND ME BEING VERY CLOSE AND HAVING A NORMAL LIFE.
FAREWELL, SISTER.
FAREWELL.
GNIEG

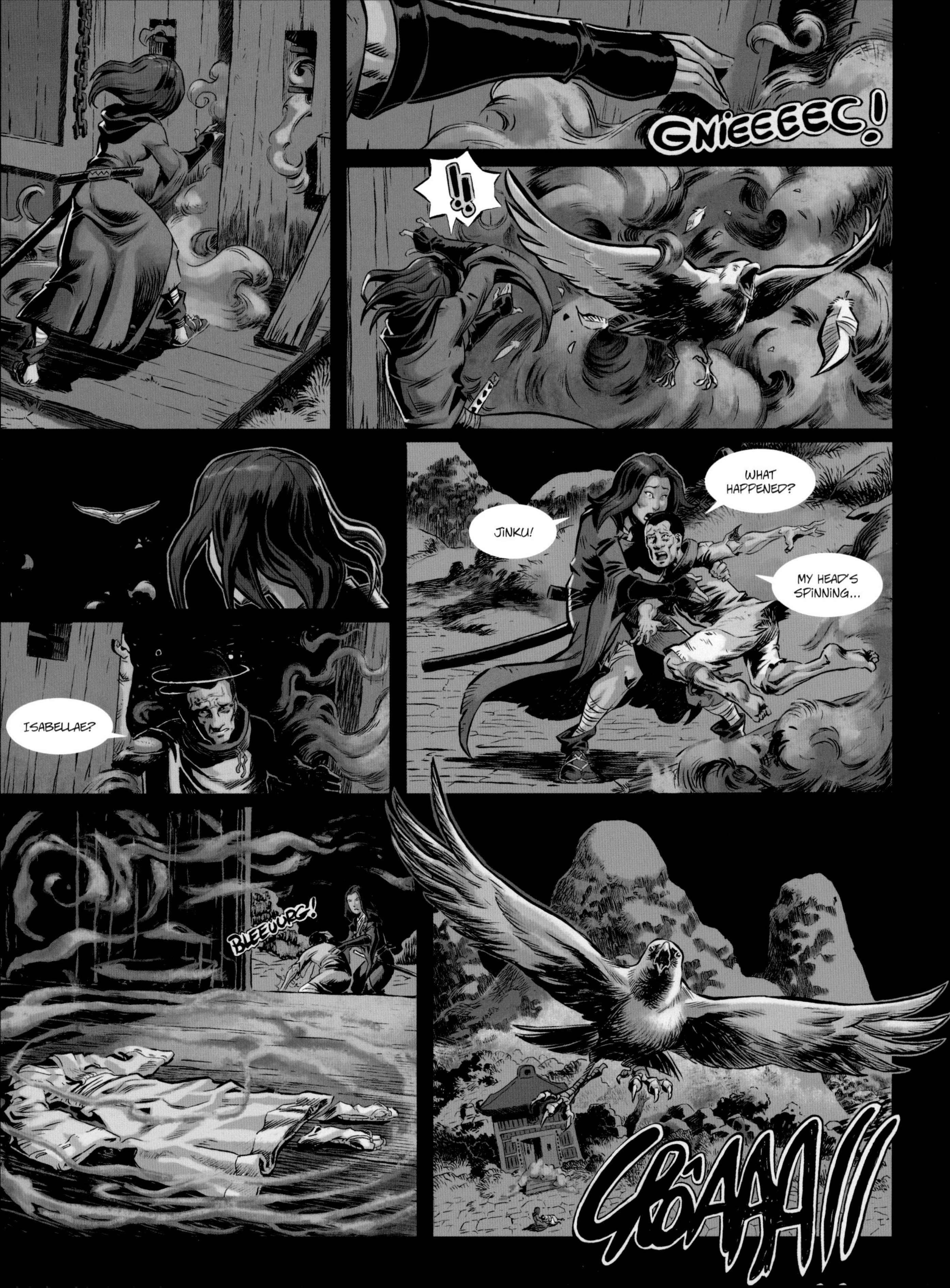
GNIEEEEC!
!!
WHAT HAPPENED?
JINKU!
MY HEAD'S SPINNING...
ISABELLAE?
BLEEUURG!
GRAAAA!!

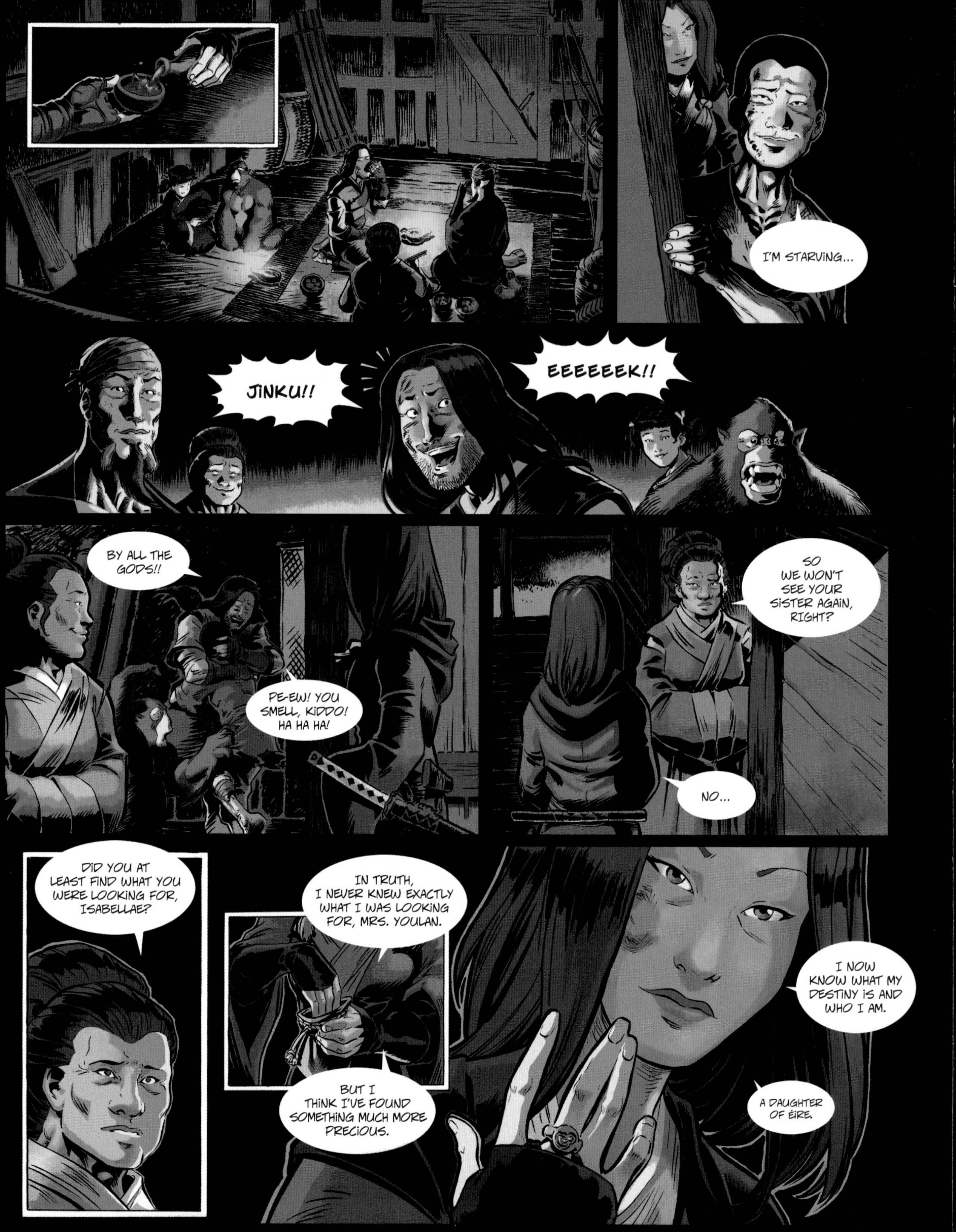

I'M STARVING...
JINKU!!
EEEEEEK!!
BY ALL THE GODS!!
PE-EW! YOU SMELL, KIDDO! HA HA HA!
SO WE WON'T SEE YOUR SISTER AGAIN, RIGHT?
NO...
DID YOU AT LEAST FIND WHAT YOU WERE LOOKING FOR, ISABELLAE?
IN TRUTH, I NEVER KNEW EXACTLY WHAT I WAS LOOKING FOR, MRS. YOULAN.
BUT I THINK I'VE FOUND SOMETHING MUCH MORE PRECIOUS.
I NOW KNOW WHAT MY DESTINY IS AND WHO I AM.
A DAUGHTER OF ÉIRE.

END OF BOOK 3. RAULE + GABOR '14

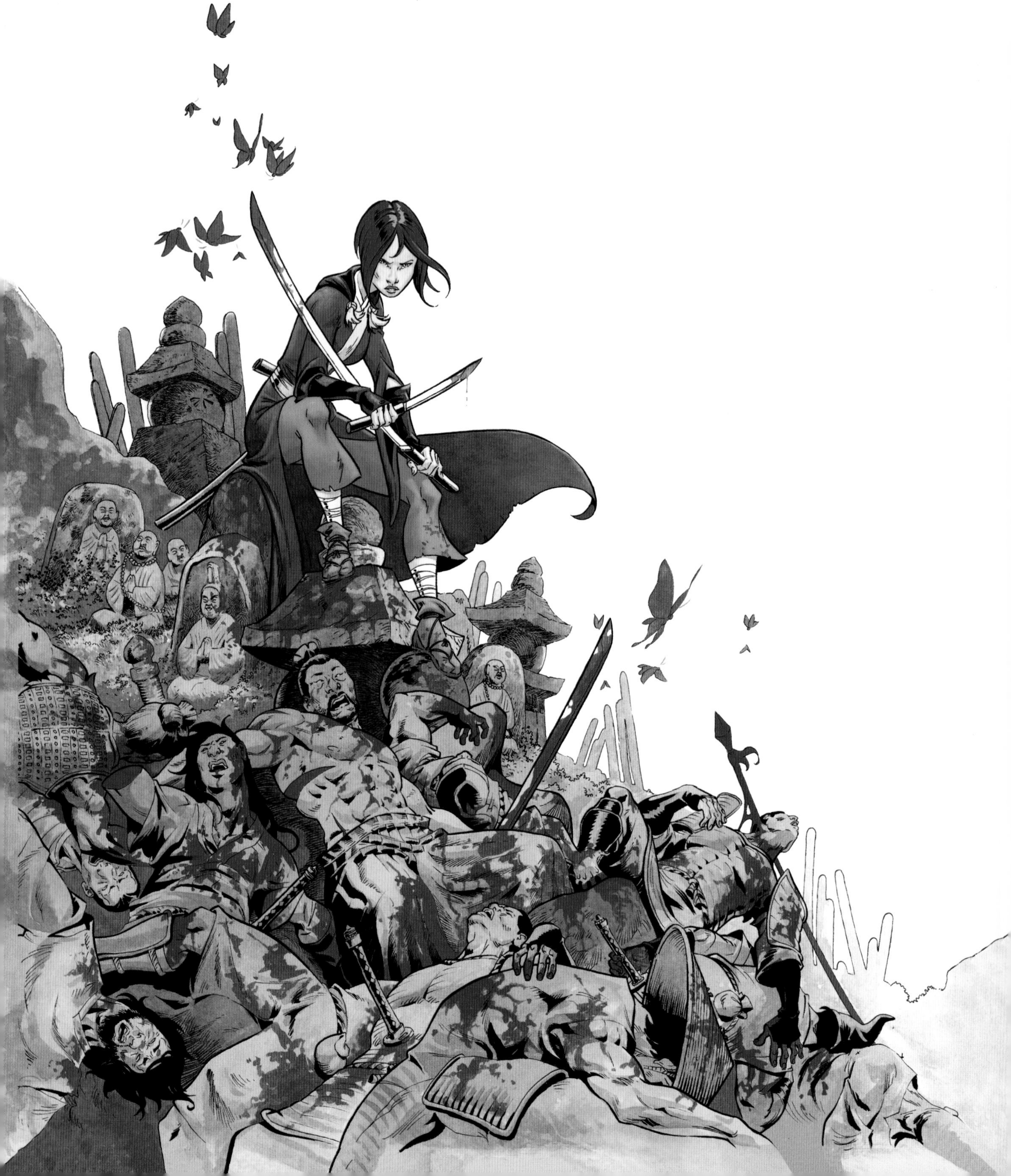

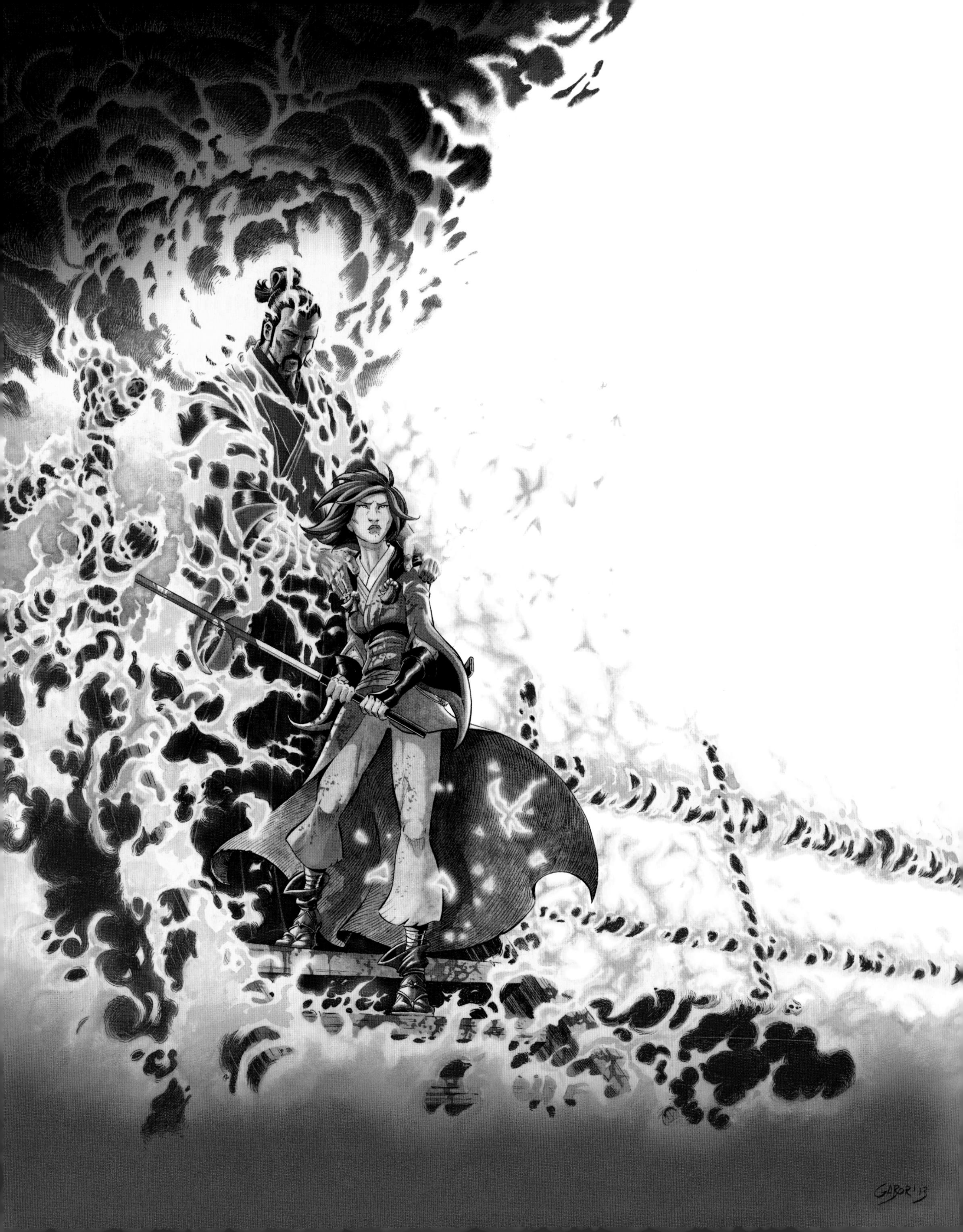
GABOR '13

ALSO FROM DARK HORSE BOOKS

AFRIKA

AFRIKA
Hermann
The masterpiece by Belgian comics creator Hermann, available in English for the first time! A misanthropic European expatriate acts as guardian of a Tanzanian wildlife preserve. Accompanied by a naive journalist, the expat discovers a village under fire from mysterious agents of the foreign-backed government. Now they must fight not only to protect the preserve, but to expose government corruption—and survive to see another day.

978-1-59582-844-6 | $15.99

MANARA
INDIAN SUMMER and OTHER STORIES
MILO MANARA
with HUGO PRATT

THE MANARA LIBRARY
Milo Manara with Hugo Pratt, Federico Fellini, and Silverio Pisu
The only comprehensive English collection of Manara's work! A master of storytelling and of the human form, Manara's unmatched draftsmanship and versatility are on full display in these newly-translated volumes.

VOLUME 1: INDIAN SUMMER AND OTHER STORIES
978-1-50670-262-9 | $29.99

VOLUME 2: EL GAUCHO AND OTHER STORIES
978-1-50670-263-6 | $29.99

VOLUME 3: TRIP TO TULUM AND OTHER STORIES
978-1-50670-907-9 | $29.99

THE RED VIRGIN
AND THE VISION OF UTOPIA
MARY M TALBOT · BRYAN TALBOT

THE RED VIRGIN AND THE VISION OF UTOPIA
Mary M. Talbot and Bryan Talbot
A portrait of revolutionary feminist Louise Michel, who took up arms against a French regime that executed thousands. Deported to a penal colony, Michel joined the cause of the indigenous population against colonial oppression.

ISBN 978-1-50670-089-2 | $19.99

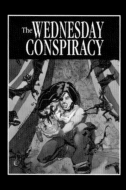

The WEDNESDAY CONSPIRACY

THE WEDNESDAY CONSPIRACY
Sergio Bleda
Think you've got problems? Meet the patients in Dr. Burton's Wednesday afternoon support group: Violet carries a jar of demons. Roger can read minds. Akiko talks with her dead parents through the bathroom mirror. Joe is an exorcist. Brian is pyrokinetic. And then, of course, there's Charles. They've been thrown together by the luck of the draw, stuck with supernatural powers they don't want and can't control. But when something begins to pick them off one by one, the surviving members of the Wednesday Conspiracy find themselves the last, reluctant line of defense between the reincarnation of an ancient evil and the fate of the world.

978-1-59582-563-6 | $19.99

MORE EUROPEAN INTRIGUE FROM

DARK HORSE BOOKS

BLACKSAD
"As good as it gets!"

BLACKSAD

Juan Díaz Canales and Juanjo Guarnido

The *Blacksad* books first took Europe by storm in 2000 and sold over 200,000 copies in France alone. Now Dark Horse Comics presents the beautifully painted stories of private investigator John Blacksad, up to his feline ears in mystery, digging into the backstories behind murders, child abductions, and nuclear secrets.

Volume 1
978-1-59582-393-9 | $29.99
Volume 2: A Silent Hell
978-1-59582-931-3 | $19.99

VAMPIRE BOY
CARLOS TRILLO
EDUARDO RISSO

VAMPIRE BOY

Carlos Trillo and Eduardo Risso

Left nameless by his father and sentenced to eternal life by a trick of fate and fortune, the protagonist of Carlos Trillo and Eduardo Risso's *Vampire Boy* has spent fifty centuries in a body that never ages, locked in an eternal struggle with a rival as immortal as he. Acclaimed writer Carlos Trillo teams with legendary artist Eduardo Risso (*100 Bullets*) to produce a poignantly engrossing twist on the classic vampire mythos, now presented in English for the first time!

978-1-59582-562-9 | $24.99

STATION 16
HERMANN
YVES H

STATION 16

Hermann and Yves H.

May 1997, Russia, north of the Arctic Circle: A border patrol rookie receives a distress call from the long-abandoned Station 16, uninhabited since the heyday of massive nuclear testing more than thirty years ago. When he and his squad fly out to investigate the call, they find an injured man who claims that the rookie was his attacker—and suddenly a nuclear explosion blasts the sky!

978-1-61655-481-1 | $19.99

ENTER A WORLD OF MAGIC AND FANTASY!
DRAGONERO
Luca Enoch • Stefano Vietti • Giuseppe Matteoni

DRAGONERO

Luca Enoch, Stefano Vietti, and Giuseppe Matteoni

Beyond the civilized lands of Erondàr, the Stone Towers are crumbling. The great monoliths are falling one after another under the wild thrusts of an evil force. The Ancient Prohibition that binds the Abominables inside their dark world is soon to be broken. Alben the Wizard will send for Myrva, a young follower of the powerful Technocrats; he will choose Ecuba, the fighting nun, to protect him; and he will call back Ian Aranill, a former Empire officer—followed by Gmor the Orc, his loyal friend—to use his scouting experience. Together they will face the Painers, the evil beings who still live in the barren Dragonlands. Can Ian prevail against the last, horrible threat they will be facing?

978-1-59582-291-8 | $19.99

AVAILABLE AT YOUR LOCAL COMICS SHOP OR BOOKSTORE! • To find a comics shop near you, visit comicshoplocator.com.
For more information or to order direct visit DarkHorse.com or call 1-800-862-0052 Mon.–Fri. 9 a.m. to 5 p.m. Pacific Time. Prices and availability subject to change without notice.

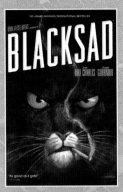

Hiroaki Samura's Eisner Award–winning manga epic

BLADE
OF THE IMMORTAL
OMNIBUS

Volume 1
ISBN 978-1-50670-124-0
$21.99

Volume 2
ISBN 978-1-50670-132-5
$21.99

Volume 3
ISBN 978-1-50670-172-1
$21.99

Volume 4
ISBN 978-1-50670-569-9
$21.99

Volume 5
ISBN 978-1-50670-567-5
$21.99

Volume 6
ISBN 978-1-50670-568-2
$21.99

Volume 7
ISBN 978-1-50670-655-9
$21.99

Volume 8
ISBN 978-1-50670-817-1
$21.99

Volume 9
ISBN 978-1-50670-818-8
$21.99

Also by Hiroaki Samura:

**Hiroaki Samura's Emerald
and Other Stories**
ISBN 978-1-61655-065-3
$12.99

Ohikkoshi
ISBN 978-1-59307-622-1
$12.95

**The Art of
Blade of the Immortal**
ISBN 978-1-59582-512-4
$29.99

AVAILABLE AT YOUR LOCAL COMICS SHOP OR BOOKSTORE • To find a comics shop in your area visit comicshoplocator.com.
For more information or to order direct visit DarkHorse.com or call 1-800-862-0052 Mon.–Fri. 9 a.m. to 5 p.m. Pacific Time.
*Prices and availability subject to change without notice.

子連れ狼 LONE WOLF & CUB

OMNIBUS

THE BRILLIANT STORYTELLING OF SERIES CREATOR KAZUO KOIKE AND THE GROUNDBREAKING CINEMATIC VISUALS OF GOSEKI KOJIMA CREATE A GRAPHIC-FICTION MASTERPIECE OF BEAUTY, FURY, AND THEMATIC POWER. NOW AVAILABLE IN NEW, LARGER, VALUE-PRICED EDITIONS OF OVER 700 PAGES, FEATURING COVER ART BY *SIN CITY*'S FRANK MILLER!

Volume 1:   ISBN 978-1-61655-134-6   Volume 7:   ISBN 978-1-61655-569-6
Volume 2:   ISBN 978-1-61655-135-3   Volume 8:   ISBN 978-1-61655-584-9
Volume 3:   ISBN 978-1-61655-200-8   Volume 9:   ISBN 978-1-61655-585-6
Volume 4:   ISBN 978-1-61655-392-0   Volume 10:   ISBN 978-1-61655-806-2
Volume 5:   ISBN 978-1-61655-393-7   Volume 11:   ISBN 978-1-61655-807-9
Volume 6:   ISBN 978-1-61655-394-4   Volume 12:   ISBN 978-1-61655-808-6

$19.99 each

AVAILABLE AT YOUR LOCAL COMICS SHOP OR BOOKSTORE. To find a comics shop near you, visit comicshoplocator.com. For more information or to order direct: • On the web: DarkHorse.com • E-mail: mailorder@darkhorse.com • Phone: 1-800-862-0052 Mon.–Fri. 9 a.m. to 5 p.m. Pacific Time.

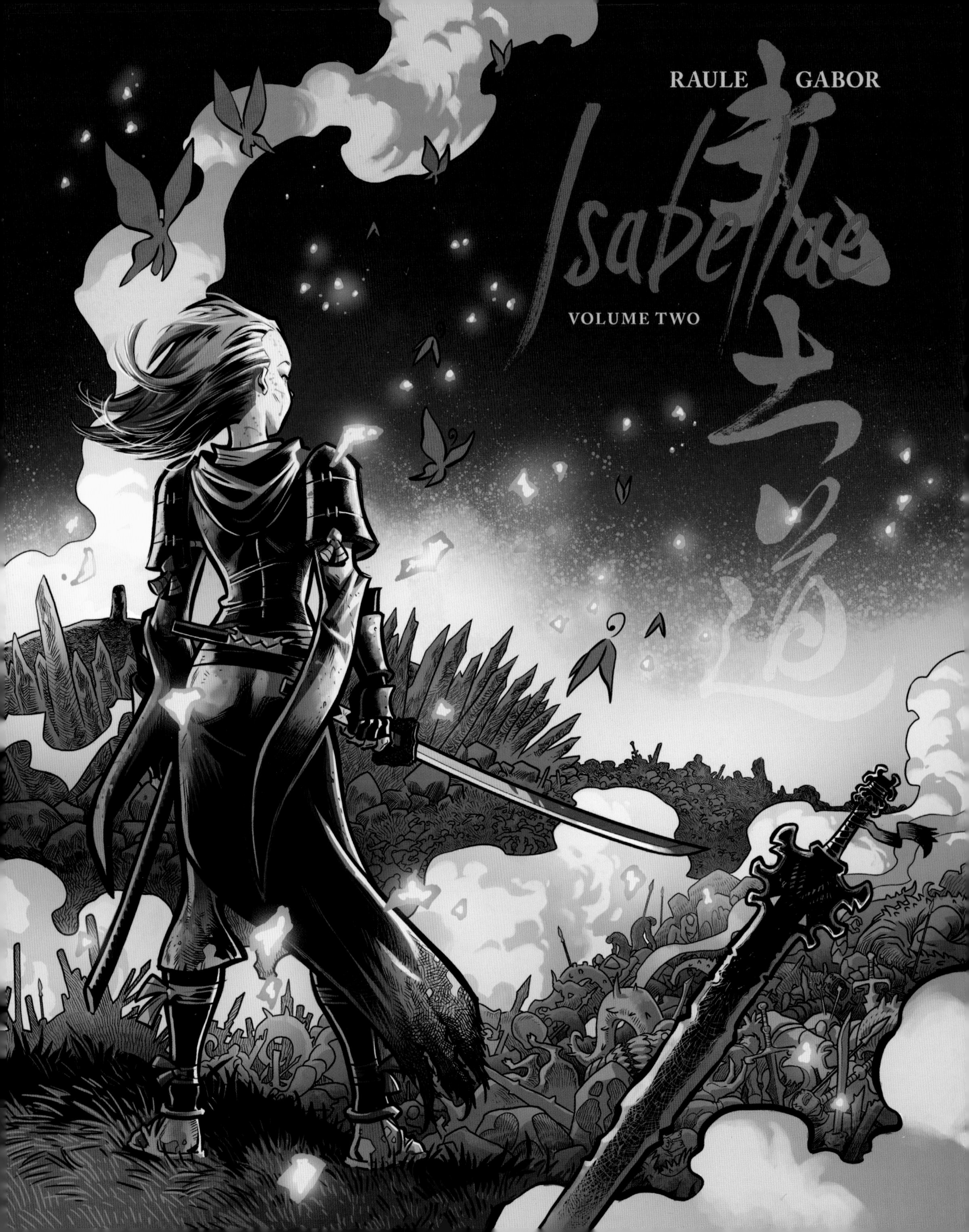
RAULE
GABOR
Isabellae
VOLUME TWO

COMING SOON—*ISABELLAE VOLUME 2*!

Curious about her origins and in search of long-lost Celtic relatives, Isabellae travels to Ireland. But when the ancient druids of the Emerald Isle make a deal with the monstrous Formorian gods, Isabellae finds herself battling in a war for control with her English and Irish allies! In this epic conclusion to the series, Isabellae battles against ancient Celtic beasts and deities that threaten the destruction of humanity.

From the innovative minds of Spanish creators Raule and Gabor, Dark Horse Books is excited to present *Isabellae Volume 2*, closing out this epic tale with the final three volumes of the original French series, available in English for the first time.

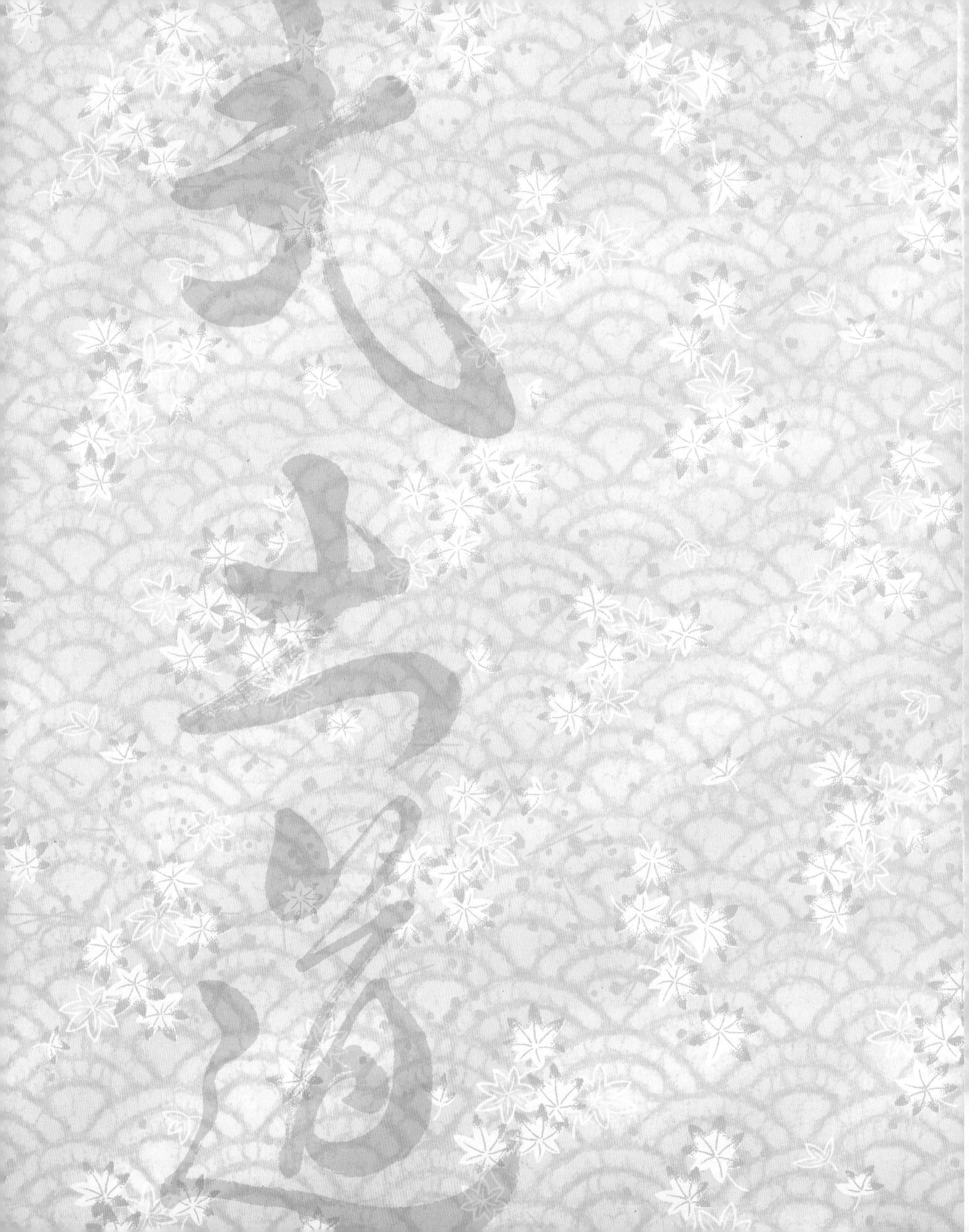